# SHRUBS

# THE RANDOM HOUSE BOOK OF
# SHRUBS

## ROGER PHILLIPS & MARTYN RIX

Assisted by Alison Rix    Layout by Jill Bryan

Random House New York

# Acknowledgements

We would like to thank Peter Barnes and Jacqui Hurst for their contributions and help, especially with the Hebes and other southern hemisphere and late-flowering shrubs.

Most of the specimens photographed in the studio came from the following gardens and we should like to acknowledge the help we had from them, and from their staff:

The Crown Estate Commissioners at the Savill and Valley gardens; Windsor Great Park; The Royal Botanic Gardens, Kew and Wakehurst Place, Sussex; The Royal Horticultural Society's Garden, Wisley; The Hillier Arboretum, Hampshire; University Botanic Garden, Cambridge; The Chelsea Physic Garden; Treasures Nurseries of Tenbury, Worcestershire and Cannington College, Somerset.

We would also like to thank the following for their help, encouragement or for providing shrubs to photograph:

Susyn Andrews, Peter Addington, Inge Baker, Oliver Baxter, Igor Belolipov, John Bond, Edward and Ann Boscawen, Christopher Brickell, James Compton, Duncan Donald, Pamela Egremont, Jack Elliott, Raymond Evison, Hans Fliegner, Jim Gardiner, Kathleen and Geoffrey Goatcher, Francois Goffinet, Tony Hall, Brian Halliwell, Carolyn and Alan Hardy, Diana Hewitt, Nigel Holman, Tinge Horsfall, Kasha Jenkinson, Jim Keesing, Shaun Killand, Roy Lancaster, Christopher Lloyd, Roger Macfarlane, Walter Magor, Peter Maudsley, Rosemary Meade, Bob Mitchell, Mike Nelhams, Mikinori Ogisu, Charles Quest-Ritson, Norman Robson, Peter Rose, Tony Schilling, James Smart, Philippa Staniland, Martin Stanniforth, John Treasure, David Trehane, Isabelle Vaughan, Dotty Wedderburn, Peter Wolkonsky, Peter Yeo.

We would also like to thank Martin Gardiner for the photographs taken in the wild in Chile, and Brent Elliott and the staff of the Lindley Library for their boundless patience.

Published in the United States by Random House, Inc, New York.
Originally published in Great Britain by Pan Books Ltd.

Library of Congress Cataloging-in-Publication Data.
88-43363 (p.l.)
Phillips, Roger, 1932 –
    The Random House book of shrubs/Roger Phillips and Martyn Rix, assisted by Alison Rix, layout by Jill Bryan.
    p.ca.
    Includes index
    ISBN 0-679-72345-5

Photoset by Parker Typesetting Service, Leicester
Printed by Toppan Printing Co. (Singapore) Limited

987654

# Contents

# Introduction

In this book we have tried to share some of the pleasure and excitement we experienced while searching for shrubs to photograph; usually in gardens, but also in hills and mountains from the Rockies to the Likiang mountains and the Caucasus. With the exception of six photographed in the wild in Chile, we have ourselves seen all the shrubs shown in this book. The diversity of shrubs is immense; evergreen ones are decorative all year round, and few plants can compete with the show of flowers or scents of azaleas, lilacs or philadelphus. Many are also beautiful in autumn with their yellow, red or purple leaves.

Many of the shrubs are shown twice; once in a close-up picture, taken in the studio, so that the details are clear, and again growing either in the wild or in a garden so that their habit of growth can be seen. Both are useful for identification and a knowledge of their habit and native habitat helps the gardener to put them in the right place in the garden.

We have tried to cover the shrubs which will grow in temperate climates. Everything shown grows outside somewhere in the British Isles, though many are more reliable in warmer climates such as California or the Mediterranean area. Most will also grow in the eastern states of the USA or in northwestern Europe. Roses are described in a separate volume, already published; trees were covered in Roger Phillips' *Trees* in 1978. Dwarf and alpine shrubs have been omitted, as they associate naturally with rock garden and alpine plants which will be the subject of a later volume.

There is no clear distinction between a tree and a shrub. A shrub is usually considered to be either low-growing on one stem, or taller-growing with many stems, and freely sprouting from the base. However, trees such as oak or beech naturally grow as scrub in areas where the climate is too harsh for trees to grow into large specimens, or where trees are coppiced for firewood or other uses. Regular burning or grazing also preserves shrubby growth, especially in the Mediterranean regions, by periodically reducing all the woody plants to ground level.

# How to use this book

The shrubs are arranged roughly by flowering seasons, beginning with late winter and spring, and ending with the autumn fruits and autumn colour. Within this scheme the major genera, such as *Rhododendron* and *Camellia*, are grouped together. The dates on which the laid-out pictures were taken are noted to give an extra guide for identification and to help plan a planting scheme in the garden. Many were photographed in an exceptionally late spring in southern England, and they may sometimes flower 2–3 weeks earlier than the dates shown.

Measurements are given in metres and centimetres. 1 metre equals about 3 feet, and 2½ centimetres equals about 1 inch.

# The Names

The text gives the Latin name of the plant and its English name where this is commonly used without ambiguity. The Latin name, in italics, is followed by that of the botanist (usually abbreviated) who first named the plant, and where an alternative Latin name has been commonly used, that is also given. Next the family name is given in brackets; it usually ends in *-ceae* or *-ae* and is based on the name of a common genus e.g. *Ericaceae* (heather family from *Erica* = heather). The Latin name is made up of two words, the generic name, such as *Rhododendron*, and the specific name, such as *luteum* which describes the species. It is either descriptive (*luteum* = yellow), or is named after a place (*ponticum* = from the Pontus, the Black Sea) or a botanist or collector (*augustinii* after Augustine Henry, a collector in China) who was associated with the species. A multiplication sign before the specific name indicates the plant is a hybrid; this is often followed by a fancy English name, of a selected clone; e.g. *Mahonia* × *media* 'Charity'.

# The Place

The text gives the place from which a plant originated, i.e. where it is native. Other areas, where it is commonly found wild, but escaped from gardens or was otherwise introduced by man are also given. The kind of place in which the shrub grows is also mentioned, whether it is in forest, on open hillsides or by water. A knowledge of this is a great help in making the plant grow and flower happily in a garden. In addition, the months of flowering in the wild are given, as it is hoped this book will be of use not only to the gardener, but also to travellers who may wish to see and identify shrubs flowering in their native habitat.

For hybrids and garden cultivars, the parentage of the shrub and its raiser, where known, are given.

# The shrub in the garden

The second part of the text gives the ultimate likely height of the shrub in the garden; its habit, if unusual; whether it is evergreen or loses its leaves in winter; any points by which it can be recognized and, where space permits, the dimensions of the leaves and flowers. If there are any special requirements of soil or aspect, these are also indicated, especially if they are not obvious from the rest of the text. Where no guide is given it may be assumed that the plant will grow on either alkaline or acid soil, and tolerate sun or light shade. Hardiness is also given, by an indication of the lowest temperature a shrub is likely to stand without being killed. Hardiness is a complex and inexact subject and is discussed more fully on pages 10–11.

Finally the usual flowering time in gardens is given, especially where this is not obvious from the flowering time in the wild.

# Associations in the Garden, using Shrubs

**Shrubs on wood edges**   This is one of the most natural habitats for shrubs, on the edges of forest, forming a transition zone between woodland and lawn or grassland. Many shrubs benefit from the shelter of the trees, and can tolerate the partial shade. Where a clearing has been made in an existing forest, the trees will have bare trunks without side branches, and shrubs will soften the unnatural edges of the woodland and keep cold wind out of the woods. Suitable genera for this association are: *Ilex, Magnolia, Cornus, Rhododendron, Philadelphus, Prunus, Viburnum.*

**Shrubs as an understory beneath large trees**   Many shrubs, particularly evergreen, grow naturally in open deciduous or mixed forest, beneath a tall canopy of trees. Rhododendrons, Camellias and Magnolias naturally live in this type of habitat, and this combination forms the basis of many of the famous woodland gardens in the British Isles and North America. Some deciduous shrubs also grow and flower well in this partially shaded habitat, provided that the canopy is not too dense. Many, such as *Hamamelis*, flower early before the leaves have developed on the large trees; in warmer climates most deciduous shrubs, e.g. deciduous azaleas, benefit from partial shade. Most shade-tolerant shrubs are suitable for this association, but especially *Rhododendron, Camellia, Magnolia, Mahonia, Hamamelis, Corylopsis, Enkianthus, Hydrangea,* Bamboos .

**Shrubs in a shrub border**   In shrub borders the shrubs should be planted close enough that their branches touch, but not so close that they interfere with one another's growth. The taller and more robust growers are planted at the back, the smaller or more delicate near the front. Careful planning is needed for optimum effect, and it is inevitable that the border will be planted rather too closely and require thinning after a few years. Sun-loving shrubs will mostly be planted in this type of border, and it will suit

Deciduous azaleas at Sandling Park, Kent

particularly those such as lilacs or *Philadelphus* which do best in full exposure on rich soils. Weeding by herbicides is possible because no herbaceous plants are grown, though early flowering bulbs which die down by mid-summer will do well beneath deciduous shrubs. Suitable genera for this association are: *Syringa, Deutzia, Hibiscus, Philadelphus, Weigela, Ribes*. Suitable bulbs are snowdrops, aconites, scillas and daffodils.

In borders of shrubs which do not require regular feeding or mulching, moss can be encouraged as ground-cover by the use of paraquat as a herbicide, and when well established the effect can be most beautiful.

**Shrubs in a mixed border**  The mixed border, in which trees, shrubs, herbaceous plants and bulbs grow together in harmony, is the most difficult, labour-intensive, but at the same time, the most rewarding of garden associations.

Here shrubs may be the dominant feature and the other plantings kept simple, or only a few shrubs may be planted to give height and substance to the border, as well as some interest in winter and early spring. In both cases the shrubs should be planted so as to create the effect of small glades or clearings, with herbaceous plants enclosed in semi-circles of shrubs.

Where shrubs are the major feature of the border, evergreen weed-smothering perennials, collectively called 'ground-cover', may be used, but tough, single perennials are more suitable as they are more easily weeded and manured. Hellebores, Primroses, Pulmonarias or Dicentras for the spring; Cranesbills, Hostas, Day-lilies or Ferns for summer; Lilies and Japanese anemones for autumn.

Any shrubs may be grown in this association, but in practice they will usually be smaller or more refined ones, which have some special feature such as scent, rarity or elegant growth habit.

**Shrubs as hedges**  All hedges are composed of shrubs, with the exception of a few such as the 26 m-high, half-mile-long hedge at Mickleour in Perthshire which is composed of fully grown beech trees; it is now about 240 years old.

Other trees often used are *Cupressus* × *Cupressocyparis Taxus* and *Carpinus*, but in most hedges, they are kept to shrub size. A hedge may be made from lower deciduous or flowering shrubs, as well as from the tree species commonly used. The larger species of *Philadelphus* make a good hedge, quick-growing, spectacular and scenting the whole garden in mid-summer. Nothing is more impenetrable than a hedge of *Ponciris trifoliata*, and it is also beautiful when in flower. Other suitable garden species are: *Ilex, Prunus lusitanica, Buxus, Salix*.

**Climbers and other shrubs on walls**  In the wild most climbing shrubs grow on forest trees, struggling up into the canopy to get the light they need to flower and fruit. In gardens most climbers are grown on walls, though some of the most spectacular effects are to be had by *Wisteria*, climbing hydrangeas or huge vines grown up trees.

Walls also provide a protected environment for shrubs which need more heat than they would receive in the open air, either in winter for those that are tender, or in summer to produce flowers or ripen their summer growth. Numerous shrubs will grow in areas otherwise too cold when protected by a wall. Climbers: *Clematis*; *Wisteria*; Roses. Tender shrubs: *Ceanothus*.

**Shrubs as ground cover**  Creeping shrubs or creeping mutants of otherwise upright shrubs can be used as ground cover in place of the more usual herbaceous ground-cover. Many Cotoneasters are naturally creeping and are used for this purpose, low-growing evergreen azaleas are also very suitable. Possible genera include: *Hedera, Hebe, Euonymus fortunei, Cotoneaster, Ceanothus*, Evergreen azalea.

*Trachycarpus fortunei*, a hardy Chinese Palm, and tree ferns, at Trebah, Cornwall

Rhododendrons in early spring

**Shrubs as specimens in lawns**  Any shrub can, of course, be grown as a specimen in a lawn, but some are more suitable than others. The important features required are a good rather upright habit of growth, and interesting leaf shape, colour or bark, and at least reasonable appearance when not in flower. Some suggestions are: *Cornus*, *Magnolia*, Hardy Hybrid Rhododendron, Acer, Bamboo, *Davidia*, *Euonymus* (deciduous).

**Shrubs in pots**  Shrubs may be grown in pots either by those who have only a paved garden, or where the garden soil is unsuitable for shrubs, such as Rhododendrons or Camellias, which do not tolerate chalky or alkaline soil. All shrubs can be grown in pots, in fact nowadays most are container grown by nurseries, but the most suitable subjects for permanent pot culture are those which naturally grow slowly and flower well without making long, strong shoots; they should also be able to tolerate drying out for a day or two without dying, as even the most careful gardeners may omit to water often enough in dry weather. They can also be brought inside in winter. The most suitable shrubs are: Camellias, Rhododendrons, *Ceanothus*, *Fuchsia* and Oleanders.

**Shrubs in the conservatory**  All the shrubs shown in this book are hardy enough to be grown outside all the year round somewhere in the British Isles. Many however will be killed in hard winters in southeast England, or in normal winters in northeast USA or northern Europe, but can be easily grown outside in summer with their pots plunged and brought into a greenhouse or conservatory to flower in winter. Little artificial heat will be needed to protect them from more than −5°C or so on the coldest of winter nights.

Suitable subjects for growing outside in summer and bringing indoors to flower in winter include: *Buddleia officinalis*, *Jasminum polyanthum*, *Correa* species, *Erica canaliculata*, *Sutherlandia frutescens*, Camellias, Tender Rhododendrons (p. 19).

**Shrubs for difficult places**  Most shrubs grow easily in well-drained soil, particularly if it is acid or neutral, in sun or part shade. Fewer are happy in dry shady places, especially under overhanging trees or in waterlogged soil. Very chalky soil also restricts the number of species which can be grown, although many normally considered lime-haters grow happily on limestone in the wild or in high rainfall areas.

**Shrubs for dry shade**  *Camellia japonica*, *Daphne laureola*, *Lonicera nitida*, *Mahonia*, *Euonymous* (evergreen), *Aucuba*, Ivy, *Phillyrea decora*, *Pieris*, *Sarcococca*, *Viburnum davidii*, *Skimmia*, *Fatsia*.

**Shrubs suitable for waterlogged soil**  *Cornus stolonifera*, *Cornus alba*, *Salix* species, *Amelanchier*, *Aronia*, *Lindera*, *Sambucus*, *Viburnum opulus*, Bamboos, *Aralia*.

**Shrubs for chalk soil**  *Liliacs*, *Colutea*, *Potentilla fruticosa*, *Philadelphus*, *Forsythia*, *Phillyrea*, *Deutzia*, *Fuchsia*, *Spartium junceum*, *Cistus*, *Hypericum*, *Cornus sanguinea*, *Ceanothus*, *Sarcococca*, *Aesculus californica*, *Paeonia*.

# Shrubs in the wild

The shrubs shown in this book come from all temperate areas of the world, with a few from mountains in the subtropics. Some areas have comparatively few garden-worthy shrubs, some very many. The main areas from which garden shrubs originated, their climates and the major collectors of shrubs in each area, are given below.

**Europe and North Africa**  The earliest shrubs to be grown in gardens were fruits and medicinal or aromatic plants, such as Myrtle, Pomegranate, Box, Elderberry or *Cornus mas*. Many were native of southern Europe or western Asia, and grown by the Romans and Arabs in the Middle Ages. Clusius was one of the first botanist-gardeners to go on a plant collecting expedition, to Spain in 1564.

Shrubs native to northern and western Europe experience both wet and cold in winter, and require water in summer. Those from the Mediterranean region tolerate a little frost, but will stand heat and drought in summer.

**The Canary Islands**  The Canary Islands and Madeira have an unusual shrub flora which contains many ancient species which grew in Europe before the Ice Ages but are now extinct, as well as many species of African affinity or shrubby members of normally herbaceous genera. Sadly most will tolerate little frost, though they grow well in Mediterranean climates and in areas with mild winters: down to about −5°C. The Canary climate is cool and wet in winter, hot and dry in summer, though in some areas in the mountains where there is mist forest, it can be moist all year round. Because the Canaries and Madeira were used as stopping-off points for sailing ships going round the Cape to the East Indies, many Canary plants have been grown in Europe since the seventeenth and eighteenth centuries.

**Central and Western Asia**  Shrubs from central and western Asia are mostly very hardy, but require warm summers to grow and flower well. The steppe areas of Turkey, Iran and Afghanistan and Soviet Central Asia contain many good shrubs, especially Almonds, Cherries, Plums and other members of the Rose family, and numerous brooms. Most would do well in the drier inland parts of North America. They normally get wet spring and

*Camellia* 'Donation' in Eccleston Square

Moupine, today Baoxing, in Sichuan, China; the seminary in which Père
David lived in 1869

autumn weather, and hot summers with only the occasional
shower. More moisture-loving species, which do well in northern
Europe, are found along the Black Sea and Caspian Sea coasts and
in the Caucasus, where summers are warm and wet.

Shrubs from this area have been coming into cultivation since
the sixteenth century.

**The Himalayas** Rhododendrons are the glory of the Himalayas,
and played a very important part in the development of the
woodland gardens of Victorian Britain. J. D. Hooker, son of W. J.
Hooker, the first director of Kew, visited the eastern Himalayas
around the borders of Nepal and Sikkim in 1848 and remained until
1851. He collected seeds and numerous plants, including twenty-
four species of *Rhododendron* in a single day. This great range of
mountains, which extends from Pakistan into western China, has
proved a fertile hunting ground for beautiful hardy shrubs and has
been visited repeatedly since Hooker's day by numerous famous
botanists and gardeners who have introduced new plants; famous
names such as Frank Ludlow, George Sherriff, Frank Kingdon-
Ward, Oleg Polunin and Tony Schilling are especially associated
with the Himalayas of Nepal, Tibet, Bhutan and N. Burma.

The Himalayan climate is characterized by cold, dry winters
and warm, very wet summers. The cold-tolerance of the shrubs is
closely connected with the altitude from which they come. Most of
the slightly tender forest species are particularly susceptible to
cold dry winds in winter and do best in very sheltered gardens.
Most Himalayan species also require wet summers to grow well,
and are less tolerant of adverse conditions than similar species
from China. Most of the rain comes from the monsoons, which
begin in June and last until the end of September in the east.
Spring and autumn are warm, dry and sunny. In the west the
monsoon rains last only from July to mid-September, and more
rain falls at others times of year.

**China** Western China is without doubt the richest area for hardy
flowering shrubs in the whole world. All flat surfaces have long
been cleared and cultivated, but the mountainous areas which
escaped the last glaciation have marvellously rich flora.

The early Chinese civilizations were the first to breed garden
flowers purely for their beauty, and developed such familiar
shrubs as roses, tree paeonies, *Prunus mume*, peaches, azaleas and

camellias, as early as the eighteenth century. Chinese gardeners
tended to concentrate on a few chosen plants, and ignored the
great wealth of wild species found in the western mountains.

Before the eighteenth century China was almost unknown to
Europeans, and the writings of Marco Polo were probably the best
travel information available. A few plants then reached European
gardens from the southern coast of China, but the first
professional plant collector to visit China was William Kerr, sent
out in 1803 by Sir Joseph Banks. He is remembered in *Kerria
japonica*. Later Robert Fortune, sent by The Horticultural Society
in 1842, made several visits, and by 1861 thought that he had
covered the country well. It was only in 1869 that the French
naturalist and missionary Père Armand David spent a year at
Moupine (today Baoxing), then on the borders of Tibet and
China, and revealed the astonishing richness of the woody flora of
the western Chinese mountains. Numerous species, and the genus
*Davidia* are named after him. A fellow Frenchman, Père Jean
Delavay, spent several years in N. Yunnan, and explored the
mountains around Dali Lake. Later these areas were covered in
greater detail by Ernest Wilson, collecting for Messrs Veitch and
the Arnold Arboretum, and George Forrest, sent out on several
expeditions by a group of English gardeners. Wilson concentrated
on hardy shrubs of all kinds; Forrest on Rhododendrons,
Camellias and Primulas. After the communist victory in 1947
botanical travel in China became impossible until the 1970s. Since
then numerous botanists and gardeners have visited China in
search of new garden plants. Roy Lancaster has made several
visits and introduced many new or little-known plants. I visited
Lijiang, Forrest's favourite hunting ground, and Baoxing in May
1984, and it was then that most of the plants shown here in China
were photographed.

The climate of western China is similar to that of the rest of the
Himalayas, but with a drier, colder winter; a warm dry spring is
followed from June to September by heavy rain, cloud and
humidity; autumn is again dry and sunny. Most of the shrubs
flower in May before the rain starts. Soils vary from acid to
alkaline, and limestone is commoner in China than in the central
Himalayas. Many Rhododendrons grow on pure limestone, and it
is still not clear why these do not tolerate more alkaline soils in
cultivation.

# INTRODUCTION

**Japan** The Japanese flora is very similar to that of China. Korea forms an extension of the continent towards the southeast, and its plants have affinities both with the northern Chinese provinces of Jilin and Heilongjiang (formerly called Manchuria), and with southern Japan. Hokkaido, the northernmost island of Japan, has a flora closer to that of eastern Siberia. Only a few genera such as *Ilex*, *Hydrangea* and *Prunus* are as well represented in Japan as in China.

The Japanese have long been keen gardeners and developed further many of the plants grown first by the Chinese. European trade with Japan was very restricted throughout the seventeenth and eighteenth centuries, foreigners being confined to Deshima island near Nagasaki. Englebert Kaempfer spent about two years here around 1691 and noted down and drew some plants, but Carl Thunberg who reached Japan in 1775 was the first to introduce large numbers of Japanese plants to Europe, and further plants were sent back by Philip von Siebold (*c*.1850), Charles Maries (*c*.1879) and E. H. Wilson (in 1920).

The climate in Japan is less extreme than that of China; summers are wet, warm in the south, temperate in the north and the mountains; winters are drier, but mostly less cold than those in China. Yakushima in the far south has rain all year round, and frequent high, wet winds and hurricanes. Soils are mostly acid, but well drained. Japanese plants do well in the warmer parts of the eastern USA.

**South Africa** The southernmost part of Africa extends even less far south than South America or New Zealand, and contains few frost-tolerant shrubs. On a recent visit to the coldest part of the Drakensberg mountains in Natal and the northern Cape Province, shrubs were almost absent above 2000 m, an altitude at which −15°C is regularly reached. Low-growing *Euryops* and other *Compositae* and *Leguminosae* such as *Lotononis* and *Sutherlandia* were the main genera. We hope that *Sutherlandia montana* (shown here) may prove hardy in southern England, as, in its native habitat, it should experience a dry, cold wind from the high plateau of Lesotho. The glorious shrubs of the Cape flora are adapted to a Mediterranean climate and do well in California or southern Europe, but few tolerate much frost. Some heathers, Leucodendrons, and one or two Proteas may be grown outside on Tresco, or make fine subjects for conservatories in colder areas.

*Sutherlandia montana* in northern Cape Province

**Eastern North America** The earliest plants to come to Europe from the Americas were brought by the Spanish from Mexico and the West Indies, and included such tender plants as Dahlias, Agave and *Mirabilis*, the Marvel of Peru. The first plants from Virginia and the colder parts of the eastern states did not arrive in Europe until the seventeenth century. One of the first collecting expeditions to look for garden plants was made by John Tradescant the younger in 1638. He visited Virginia and even acquired some land in York County. Such shrubs as *Lonicera sempervirens* were grown by the Tradescants, and listed in *Museum Tradescantianum*, published in 1654.

Another well-known collector was Mark Catesby who was born in Suffolk around 1682 and arrived in Williamsburg, Virginia in 1712. He sent back many boxes of plants and seeds to Europe, and published, in 1763, *Hortus Brittanico-Americanus* or *A Curious Collection of Trees and Shrubs. The Produce of the British Colonies in North America; adapted to the soil and Climate of England etc.* Sixty-two trees and shrubs are illustrated including *Magnolia grandiflora*, *Cornus florida* and *Kalmia angustifolia*.

John Bartram (1699–1777), born in Pennsylvania, lived and had a garden near Philadelphia. He is noted for the discovery of *Gordonia altamaha*, a tree related to *Stewartia*, now extinct in the wild, but preserved in his garden and now grown in many other gardens both in America and Europe.

The climate in eastern North America is more extreme than that of western Europe. Summers are hotter and often wetter; autumn is fine and sunny; winters are often much colder; soils are generally poor and acid. Many shrubs, such as American azaleas, grow very well in Europe; others such as Flowering Dogwood, *Cornus florida*, which are so beautiful in their native habitat, do not grow or flower nearly so freely.

**Western North America** The earliest plants from northwestern North America were seen by Georg Steller, who accompanied Bering's expedition to Alaska in 1739. Later some were collected by Archibald Menzies in 1792, who accompanied Captain Vancouver's voyage of exploration. In 1805 Captain Merriweather Lewis and Captain William Clark crossed the Rockies and collected both scientific specimens and seeds, which included *Mahonia aquifolium*, but it was another eighteen years before more than a small sample of the great richness of the northwestern flora was sent back east. In 1823 The Horticultural Society sent David Douglas to collect seed of trees and shrubs in California and Oregon, and he spent the next eleven years scouring the area for new plants. Among his introductions were *Gaultheria shallon*, *Ribes sanguineum*, and *Garrya elliptica*.

The climate of western North America varies greatly, even over small distances, because of its proximity to the sea and high mountains. In most of coastal California the climate is similar to that of the European Mediterranean, wet in winter, with some frosty spells; dry and hot in summer. Many of these plants thrive in coastal climates in Europe, but few can tolerate the very cold winters and wet summers of the eastern United States. In northern coastal California, Oregon and northwards, summers are cooler and moister, and the chances of extreme cold are greater, especially inland and along the Columbia river valley. Most plants from this area grow very well in northwest Europe, and will grow also in the coastal states of the northeast.

**South America** Because it has more sea, and fewer large land masses, the southern hemisphere is warmer in winter and cooler in summer than are similar at latitudes in the north. The southern tip of South America extends further south than any other land mass outside Antarctica (which is everywhere too cold for the growth of shrubs). It is here, in southern Chile and Argentina, that the frost is sufficiently heavy for some species to survive outdoors in Britain. Valdivia, at 40°S, is roughly on the same latitude as New York, Madrid or Beijing, but has much milder winters. The hardiest species come either from the Andes or from the southernmost coastal areas such as Chile or Tierra del Fuego, and even there the cold air is moist and snow-laden, coming across the sea from the Antarctic, not dry as it is in most of the northern hemisphere. Most Chilean shrubs can therefore tolerate cold only when very sheltered, and the most beautiful such as *Desfontainea*, *Eucryphia* or *Embothrium* (p. 216) survive only in moist sheltered gardens on the western coasts of Europe or North America. *Fuchsia magellanica* survives as a shrub near these western coasts, but behaves as a herbaceous plant, sprouting each year from below ground, in colder areas.

The Chilean flora was introduced to Europe mainly through the efforts of the great nursery firm of Veitch. They sent William Lobb to Chile in 1840 and again in 1845. Later collectors in this area were H. J. Elwes and Harold Comber, son of the head gardener at Nymans, Sussex, who visited southern Argentina and Chile in 1925 and 1927. Many of Comber's plants can still be seen growing at Nymans.

**Australia, Tasmania and New Zealand** Shrubs from this area are generally less hardy than those from Chile, and are also intolerant of cold, dry wind.

Many Australian shrubs do well in California and the Mediterranean region, so well that they even become pests. *Acacia dealbata* is widely naturalized in most temperate parts of the world where it can survive the winters. The commonest New Zealand shrubs in Europe are probably the hebes, but only smaller alpine ones are reliably hardy even in southern England. Other genera commonly grown in warm gardens are *Olearia*, *Eucryphia*, *Leptospermum*, *Correa*, and *Sophora*.

No horticultural collectors were pre-eminent in introducing Australian or New Zealand plants in the nineteenth century. In recent years Lord Talbot de Malahide introduced many Tasmanian plants to his garden near Dublin, and Graham Hutchins of County Park Nursery continues to introduce many New Zealand species.

# Planting

Nowadays shrubs are usually bought growing in pots. Try to choose a plant that is growing strongly, not necessarily one which has plenty of flowers, and avoid those that are obviously starved or have been a long time in a small pot.

Before planting a new shrub into the garden it is essential to soak it in water; for an hour or so if it is growing in loam, all day or overnight if in a peat or soil-less compost. If it is winter and the plant is dormant, tease most of the soil from the roots before planting. Add plenty of peat and some fertilizer to the planting hole. A good gardener I know always uses half a bale of peat with every tree or shrub planted, and this on a good neutral soil in northwestern France. If the plant is a *Rhododendron*, a *Camellia*, or has a similar compact root system, only the outer inch or so of compost need be worked off, and the soil round the planting hole should be made exceptionally peaty. If it is summer and the plant is in full growth, it may be planted into the garden without disturbing the roots, but then it is absolutely vital to exhume the plant again in autumn, winter or early spring, while it is dormant, and tease out the roots; in the case of non-peat lovers remove all the peat compost from among the roots and spread the roots out properly before replanting. Shrubs received from the nurseryman bare-rooted, i.e. dug from the open ground, are moved only when dormant and planted in the usual way, spreading out the roots around the planting hole and shortening any which are damaged or over-long. In dry areas or very well-drained soils, plant the new shrub in a shallow saucer-shaped depression to make watering easier and more effective.

**Mulching** All shrubs, and especially those newly planted, benefit from a surface mulch which retains moisture, provides extra humus for the surface roots, and keeps down competition from weeds. Leafmould and leaves, bracken, coarse peat or bark chippings are all suitable. Old newspapers may be used too, and can be hidden with a layer of soil.

**Planting in grass** When planting new shrubs in grass, or in an already established shrub border, clear an area at least two feet

*Coronilla valentina subsp. glauca* in Eccleston Square

wide, or for a large shrub, three feet wide, digging the ground and removing weeds and roots and, of course, the turf. This area should be kept clear and mulched for the first couple of years or until the shrub is well established.

**Fertilizing** Established shrubs do not need extra fertilizer unless the soil is very poor and light. The mulch will provide a source of nutrients to the surface-feeding roots, and if growth is still poor some slow-acting fertilizers can be applied. Osmacote is now available to amateurs and different formulations are recommended for varying soil types.

# Soil types

As far as gardeners are concerned, soils vary in three main ways: they are either heavy with much clay, or light with much sand or fine gravel in their composition; they are either humus-rich, as in peat or most dark soils, or humus-poor, as are most pale sandy, chalky or clay soils that have been derived from sub-soil. They also differ chemically, being either acid, neutral or alkaline. Most shrubs grow best in a soil which is neutral or slightly acid; others such as most *Ericaceae*, e.g. Rhododendrons, need a definitely acid soil; others tolerate chalky or alkaline soils.

From the gardener's point of view, an average or rather light soil is best as its acidity is more easily varied by the application of different chemicals. Most soils also benefit by having extra humus added. Neutral or slightly alkaline soils may be made acid by the addition of sulphur. On strongly chalky soils, it is better not to attempt to grow plants which prefer acid soil, as chemicals never seem to get the soil acid enough for lime-haters to thrive. In the text we have tried to give an indication of the habitats of the plants so that their preferred soil type may be inferred, and we have also noted those which require an acid soil.

# Pruning

More shrubs are probably prevented from flowering by being pruned wrongly, than are helped by being pruned correctly. 'If in doubt, leave it', should be the novice pruner's motto. Wild shrubs are never pruned by gardeners, and are often covered with flowers as can be seen here in many of the photographs of shrubs taken in the wild.

The purpose of pruning should be to either improve the shape

Autumn colour in the mountains in Hokkaido, Japan

of a shrub or to encourage it to flower better. Minor shaping is best done in spring, after flowering for spring-flowering shrubs; before growth begins for summer-flowering ones. Really drastic pruning of deciduous shrubs is best done in autumn after the leaves have fallen, while the plant is dormant, or of evergreens in early spring.

When pruning for better flower production it is important to know whether the flowers are produced on the stems made the previous year or on the new wood formed during the current year. Further, some shrubs flower best on vigorous shoots, others on slow-growing ones.

Shrubs which flower well on slow-growing wood formed the previous summer include Rhododendrons, Magnolias, *Ribes*, Lilacs, and most evergreens. Every healthy growing shoot ends in a bud or buds, if conditions for bud setting have been suitable at the end of the previous summer. No pruning is needed and if flowering is not prolific, the shrub is either not growing happily, or not getting the right temperatures in summer. Many shrubs of this type do however benefit greatly from the removal of the dead flower heads as soon as they have faded, and especially if flowering has been prolific. If they bear a heavy crop of seed they may flower well only every other year.

Shrubs which flower best on vigorous stems produced the previous summer include *Forsythia*, *Philadelphus*, *Deutzia*, winter and spring-flowering Buddleias, *Cestrum elegans* and some *Clematis*. They respond to pruning immediately after flowering, taking out stems that have flowered to encourage strong, new growth from below, and removing also some of the weakly ones that may be developing.

Shrubs which flower on new wood formed during the current year are mostly late summer- or autumn-flowering and include Fuchsias, some Hydrangeas, deciduous *Ceanothus*, late-flowering Buddleias, *Cestrum parqui* and some late-flowering *Clematis*. They are best pruned in early spring and can mostly be cut back quite hard to encourage strong shoots that will flower well. Cuts are usually made just above a healthy bud, towards the base of the previous season's growth.

Some shrubs do need special pruning: Wisterias should have the long twining shoots shortened to about six buds, usually about four inches from the old wood, in July or about two months after flowering. They may then have a second flowering, less good than the first; these flowered shoots, and any later twining shoots, should be cut back to two or three buds in early autumn, to encourage bud production for the following spring (if sparrows do not take the buds during winter). *Clematis* need pruning in different ways according to their flowering habit; instructions for each variety are given in the text. Pruning of *Clematis* is usually done in early spring.

# Hardiness

We have tried in the text to give an indication of the lowest temperatures a shrub can tolerate without damage, but there are so many variables in assessing the hardiness of a particular species, that the figures given are a mere guideline, based on various published sources and on our own observations, mainly in southern England. The most important variables are:

**Soil type** On well-drained sandy soils, especially those that are rather dry in late summer, plants are generally hardier than those grown in rich, heavy, poorly-drained soil. On these soils autumn colour is usually good on deciduous trees.

**Summer ripening of wood** In climates with a sunny late summer and autumn, warm days and cool nights, shrubs tolerate colder winter temperatures than in climates, such as England, with cloudy, wet autumns. The better-ripened wood is hardier.

**Shelter** Evergreens in particular are killed by dry, freezing winds which dessicate the leaves. Shelter from the north and east in Europe, from the west and north in eastern North America, is essential for the survival of many evergreens, especially those from New Zealand and Chile.

**Shade** In China, and in many other Continental and northern areas, spring comes late and then is soon followed by summer. In England and in maritime areas of Europe, warm spells in March or April may be followed by frosts in May and even early June. These can kill the flowers and young leaves of many shrubs, especially if the early morning sun strikes the still-frozen flowers and young shoots causing them to thaw quickly. Early-flowering shrubs are therefore best grown in a west-facing position or even a cold north-facing one, so that the new growth comes later in spring, and the flowers and new shoots are not exposed to the early morning sun. Similarly an overhead canopy of trees, either deciduous, or evergreens such as conifers, can protect slightly tender shrubs on still, frosty nights. Quick freezing is as damaging as quick thawing, so in very cold sunny areas any protection from sun is beneficial to evergreens of borderline hardiness.

**Provenance** The provenance of a plant is the place from which it was originally collected, and is generally mentioned in connection with its likely hardiness.

# Propagation

Numerous books have been written on the propagation of trees and shrubs. For the amateur, who only wants a few plants of each type, the following methods are the most suitable.

**Seed** Where seed has been collected in the wild, a species will normally come true, but will show something of the variation of that wild population. The gardener may be able to select an especially good form from his seedlings. Where seed has been collected in a garden, the seedlings are likely to be hybrids, unless the flowers were hand-pollinated. Seeds of hardy shrubs are best sown in autumn, as many require a cold period to induce germination. Many, notably some *Rosaceae* or *Viburnum*, do not all germinate in the first or even the second year after planting. More tender shrubs, from climates in which there is little frost, or growth is mainly in winter, germinate immediately they are sown, and so are best planted under cover in early spring. Most very small seeds come into this group. Large nut-like seeds generally need sowing as soon as possible, as most of them, e.g. Buckeyes or oaks, germinate as soon as they fall, and quickly die if they dry out. They should be stored cool and moist. Seedlings are best potted as soon as possible, so they have made good growth before their first winter: the larger they are, the more likely they are to survive.

Self-strangling roots on a container-grown shrub

**Seedlings**   Seedlings are a good way of bringing back trees and shrubs from the wild, if seed is not available. The smaller the seedlings, the better they will travel; they can be kept for several weeks potted in a polythene bag held with a rubber band, either in soil or in moss. Be careful not to let them dry out, keep them cool, and give them as much light as possible. Self-sown seedlings may also be collected from the garden and potted up or put into a nursery.

**Cuttings and Layering**   These have the advantage that the new shrub is genetically identical to the parent bush, so a good form or named clone may be propagated. Cuttings are taken either in summer, 'softwood cuttings', or in autumn or winter after leaf fall, 'hardwood cuttings'.

Hardwood cuttings should be about 30 cm long, and be wounded at the base or have a heel of the old wood. They are put in sandy soil or compost, outdoors or in a shady frame, in autumn and begin to grow both shoots and roots in spring.

Softwood cuttings are taken as soon as the wood has begun to harden; too soon and the shoot will collapse; too late and the shoot is woody and will not form roots easily. Mist propagation has proved the greatest help in rooting softwood cuttings, and mist combined with bottom heat and the right degree of shading will induce many of the most difficult subjects, such as deciduous azaleas, to root. They should be then kept growing as long as possible into autumn, so that they survive the winter. An ideal compost for rooting most cuttings consists of perlite and sphagnum peat in about equal proportions; the size of the perlite used depends on the thickness of the roots, the thicker-rooted plants needing a coarser compost.

Layering was formerly used commercially for propagation of difficult subjects such as Japanese maples, deciduous azaleas etc., but has now been replaced by mist propagation or grafting. Layering can still however be very useful for amateurs, especially for rejuvenating old plants of Rhododendrons or for difficult plants such as Magnolias. The layer can remain attached for several years after it has rooted and so be larger by the time it has to rely on its own roots.

**The production of new species by Colchicine treatment**
Several new plants, e.g. *Forsythia*, 'Beatrice Farrand', have been produced by treating a hybrid between two wild species with Colchicine. Colchicine, an alkaloid derived from the bulb *Colchicum*, has the effect of preventing the formation of cell walls between dividing cells, so that polyploid cells are formed. A sterile hybrid between two species may become fertile, with double its original number of chromosomes, if a growing point is treated with lanoline containing colchicine, or if a seedling is treated. The new fertile plant is a new species, able to breed true from seed. Several wild plants have evolved in this way, but, of course, without Colchicine.

# Pests and diseases

Shrubs are probably less beset by pests and diseases than most other garden plants, but they have their share of enemies, which differ from place to place. I remember seeing a garden in France after a herd of wild boar had passed through in the night. Even large rhododendrons had been uprooted and smashed. Fortunately not many gardens have to contend with them, but deer are a common problem and can nibble almost any shrub, or rub the bark off when trying to clean their new antlers of velvet. Bullfinches are another terrible animal pest, and can clear a shrub of buds in a very short time. *Forsythia*, *Prunus*, *Ribes*, *Amelanchier* and even *Deutzia* are regularly attacked. Netting the susceptible shrubs is the only answer, as however many birds are shot, more will come. A pet sparrowhawk would act as an excellent deterrent. The worst disease of shrubs is certainly the Honey Fungus *Armillariella mellea*, which can attack and kill almost any genus, though Magnolias are said to be less affected than many others; work is now being done at Wisley on a remedy. Formulations are on the market, such as Armillaritox, which have been known to kill it in some places. Mixing a handful of copper carbonate at planting time into the surrounding soil has been said to keep it at bay. Honey Fungus attacks weakened plants, especially in wet, poorly drained soil; the black rhizomorphs, like thin leather bootlaces grow through the soil, and can infect the base of the shrub, leaving a flat, white mass of fungal mycelium under the dead bark as a sign of what has caused the sudden or lingering death of your favourite shrub. Both remedies are worth trying until a scientifically proven treatment becomes available.

# The Photographs

When shooting shrubs in the garden or the field, it is preferable to work from a tripod so that you can take advantage of the opportunity to use a slow shutter speed and thus a smaller aperture, giving a greater depth of field. In practice the best speed is normally 1/15 sec. although if there is a strong wind you may have to go up to 1/30 or in extremes 1/60.

The studio shots are taken on a Bronica 120, with a normal lens, with two Bowens quad units as a light source. The field shots are taken with a Nikon FM. The film in both cases is Ektachrome 64, that used for the field shots being pushed one stop in development.

Infected roots and the dreaded black bootlaces of honey fungus

13

'Feuerzauber'

Hamamelis
japonica 'Rubra'

'Jelena'

'Pallida'

'Diane'

'Orange Beauty'

H. japonica

'Sulfurea'

'Brevipetala'

Hamamelis
mollis

H. japonica var. arborea

H. vernalis
'Red Imp'

'Arnold Promise'

'Zucchariniana'

'Sunburst'

Life size. Specimens from Wisley, 22nd February

*Hamamelis mollis* at the Valley Gardens, Windsor

**Hamamelis japonica** Sieb. & Zucc.
(*Hamamelidaceae*) Japanese Witch Hazel
Native of Japan, in S. Hokkaido, Honshu,
Shikoku and Kyushu, where it flowers in
March–April. A deciduous large shrub or small
tree, variable in leaf shape, hairiness and flower
colour. Var. *bitchuensis* (Makino) Ohwi from the
Chugoku district has persistently stellate-
pubescent leaves, while var. *obtusa* has very
blunt leaves, with deciduous hairs, and is found
in eastern and northern Honshu. Easily
cultivated, preferring rather moist, acid soil, in
semi-shade. Hardy to −20°C. Late winter.

**H. japonica** f. *flavopurpurascens* (Mak.)
Rehder This is a form of var. *obtusa* in which
the crinkled petals are reddish at the base. It is
known both in the wild and in cultivation.

**H. japonica 'Sulfurea'** A pale yellow-flowered
variety of *H. japonica* raised by Russell's of
Windlesham in around 1958. Spreading habit.

**H. japonica 'Zuccariniana'** This variety is
characterized by pale flowers with a green calyx
and by flowering later than other varieties.

**H. japonica** var. *arborea* (Mast.) Gumbleton
(syn. *H. arborea* Ottol. ex Mast.) Described
from cultivated plants, introduced from Japan
by Siebold in 1832, and not recognized by
Japanese floras. As commonly cultivated it has
deep red calyces and very crinkled petals on a
tall-growing, twiggy shrub.

**H. × intermedia 'Feuerzauber'** (Magic Fire)
Raised in Weener, in 1958, by Messrs Hesse.
The old form, 'Ruby Glow', is said to be
similar.

**H. × intermedia 'Pallida'** Raised at Wisley
shortly before 1932 from seeds sent from 'a
neglected nursery in Holland', but probably
Kalmthout in Belgium, close to the Dutch
border. Often listed under *H. mollis* but
probably a hybrid.

**H. × intermedia 'Diane'** Raised at Kalmthout
Arboretum by Robert and Jelena de Belder, and
named after their daughter, Diane. The finest of
the red-flowered witch hazels.

**H. × intermedia 'Jelena'** Raised at Kalmthout
by Kost and named by M. Robert de Belder for
his wife, Jelena. A very vigorous variety, with
orange-pink petals, darker at the base. The
origin of *H. × intermedia* Rehder is not recorded
but it is almost certainly *H. japonica × H. mollis*.
The red-flowered forms of *H. × intermedia* are
thought to be derived from *H. japonica* f.
*flavopurpurascens*. Hardy to −25°C.

**H. × intermedia 'Orange Beauty'** (syn. 'Orange
Bruns') Raised by Heinrich Bruns in Germany
and introduced in 1955. Upright, vigorous habit.

**H. × intermedia 'Arnold Promise'** A selection
of *H. × intermedia* made at the Arnold
Arboretum, USA, in 1963. Notable for its
reddish autumn colour.

**H. × intermedia 'Sunburst'** A variety with
good, bright yellow flowers but little scent, and
with the unpleasant habit of retaining its dead
leaves into winter.

**H. vernalis** Sarg. **'Red Imp'** Native of eastern
North America, from Missouri to Louisiana and
Oklahoma, growing on the banks of streams and
on shingle banks, flowering in December–
March. A suckering, rather quick-growing
shrub up to 2 m high. Red-flowered forms, var.
*carnea* Rehd., are frequent in the wild and 'Red
Imp' is an especially dark-flowered selection.
'Sandra', selected by Roy Lancaster from a
batch of seedlings at Hillier's nursery, is distinct
in its purplish young leaves and fine red to
orange autumn colour. Hardy to −25°C. Late
winter.

**H. mollis** Oliver Native of W. Hubei and
Kiangsi, in scrub and woods at 1300–2500 m,
flowering in April. First collected in 1879 by

*Loropetalum chinense*

Charles Maries near Kinkiang in northern
Kiangsi province, and later by Henry and
Wilson. It differs from *H. japonica* in its hairier
leaves and wider, not crinkled, petals. Easily
cultivated and said to be more lime-tolerant
than *H. japonica*, but best in semi-shade and
leafy soil. Hardy to −20°C.

**H. mollis 'Brevipetala'** A strong-growing
upright clone, probably of *H. mollis*, with well-
scented, deep yellow but rather short petals.
One of the easiest to grow, but least attractive of
the witch hazels. Introduced by Chenault of
Orleans in around 1935. Branches often
produce deformed leaves, possibly the result of
virus infection.

**Loropetalum chinense** (R. Br.) Oliver
(*Hamamelidaceae*) Native of Assam, China
and Japan (Ise province west of Osaka only), on
rocky hills and in dry open woods, flowering in
February–April; not scented. Hardy only in the
warmest gardens in the British Isles, but good in
the south of France, e.g. at the Villa Noailles,
and as a conservatory plant. Any non-chalky
soil. Hardy to −5°C. Late spring.

*Mahonia 'Charity'* The original plant at the Savill Garden, Windsor

*Mahonia japonica*

**Mahonia japonica** (Thunb.) DC
(*Berberidaceae*)   Native distribution uncertain,
but probably native of Taiwan, and possibly
also of mainland China. Commonly cultivated in
gardens in Japan, and from there introduced to
Europe in the late 19 C. A very hardy shrub
with lax drooping inflorescences throughout the
winter. Very sweetly scented. Easy to grow and
exceptionally shade tolerant. Hardy to −20°C.

**Mahonia bealei** (Fort.) Carr. (*Berberidaceae*)
Native of China, in Hupeh, Hubei, Sichuan and
Taiwan, growing in woods at around 2000 m.
Introduced to Europe by Robert Fortune in
around 1850. This is much rarer in cultivation
than *M. japonica*, from which it differs in its
shorter, more or less erect inflorescences, and
very small bracts. The two were often confused
in the past. Hardy to −20°C. Spring.

**Mahonia leschenaultiana** (Wall.) Takeda
Native of S. India, in the Nilgiri, Anamalai and
Pulney hills, growing in scrub and open forest at
1500–2000 m, flowering in September–
February. A large shrub up to 4 m high, with
rich orange-yellow flowers, and large leaflets.
Hardy to −5°C, perhaps. Photographed at
Kodaikanal in October. The rather similar *M.
siamensis* Takeda from N. Thailand and Yunnan
was introduced to Menton under the same
collection as *M. lomariifolia*, and has been
grown in the temperate house at Cambridge
Botanic Garden. It has stout orange-yellow
spikes in February.

**Mahonia × media** Brickell **'Charity'**   *Mahonia
× media* is a name for the hybrid between *M.
lomariifolia* and *M. japonica*; the first hybrids
were chance seedlings of *M. lomariifolia* from
the Slieve Donard Nurseries, Co. Down, and
one was selected from a line of *M. lomariifolia*
growing at Russell's at Windlesham, by Sir Eric
Savill in 1952, who named it 'Charity'. It is
easily grown, and now one of the finest and most
popular winter-flowering shrubs. Height up to

3 m and in time as much across. Shade tolerant.
Hardy to −15°C. Late autumn–winter.

**Mahonia × media** Brickell **'Buckland'**   This
was the result of a cross between *M. lomariifolia*
and *M. japonica*, made by Lionel Fortescue of
Buckland Monachorum, Devon. Out of around
200 seedlings he raised, he chose the best,
naming it 'Buckland'. It has some scent. Hardy
to −15°C. Winter.

**Mahonia nepaulensis** DC. (Syn. *M.
acanthifolia* G. Don)   Native of N.E. India,
Bhutan, Sikkim, Nepal and Uttar Pradesh,
growing in evergreen forest at 1525–3000 m,
flowering in October–April; it can make a large
shrub up to 7 m, but usually around 4 m, with
6–13 pairs of leaflets. The characters used to
distinguish *M. acanthifolia* and *M. nepaulensis* in
cultivation do not hold good for the species in
the wild, but the cultivated *M. acanthifolia* has
leaflets with a dull surface, flowers in autumn
and is hardier than some spring-flowering
introductions of *M. nepaulensis*. Hardy to
−10°C.

**Mahonia lomariifolia** Takeda   Native of
Burma and Yunnan, growing in forest at around
2000 m. A large shrub up to 10 m in the wild,
flowering in autumn or sometimes in spring,
with 9–18 pairs of leaflets. Damaged especially
by cold, dry winds. Hardy to −10°C.
Introduced from Tengchong (Tengyueh) in
1931 by Major Johnston to his garden at
Menton.

*Mahonia leschenaultiana* at Kodaikanal

*Mahonia lomariifolia* at Washington, Sussex

*Mahonia bealei*

*Mahonia × media 'Buckland'*

*Mahonia nepaulensis* at the Savill Garden, Windsor

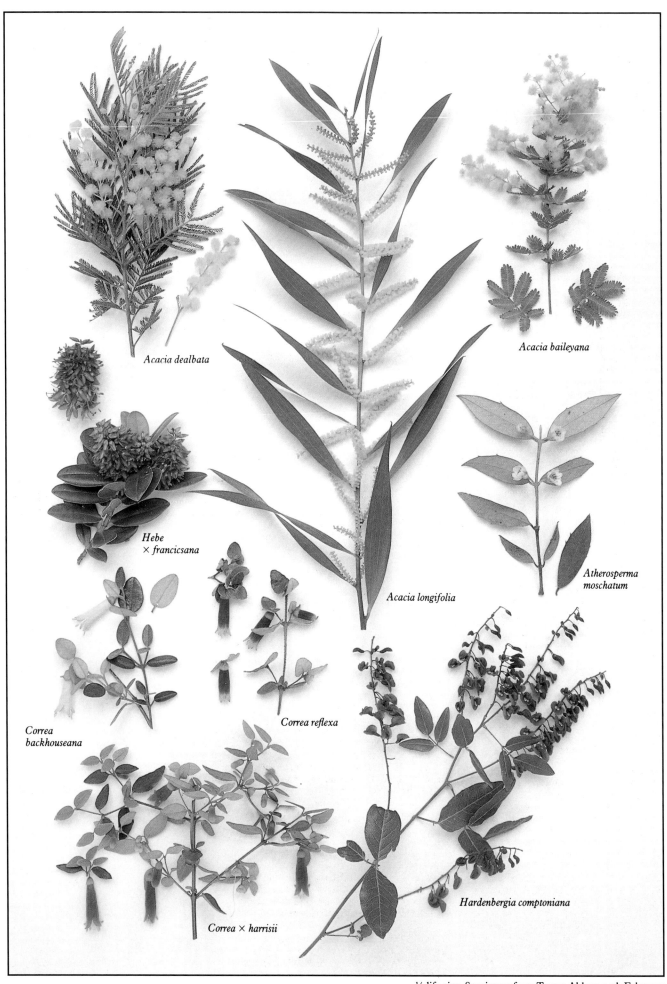

Acacia dealbata

Acacia baileyana

Hebe
× francicsana

Atherosperma
moschatum

Acacia longifolia

Correa
backhouseana

Correa reflexa

Hardenbergia comptoniana

Correa × harrisii

½ life-size. Specimens from Tresco Abbey, 14th February

*Acacia cyanophylla* in Spain

*Correa schlectendahlii*

**Acacia dealbata** A. Cunn. (*Leguminosae*)
Mimosa   Native of New South Wales,
Victoria, and Tasmania, in many habitats by
streams, in gullies or on mountains, flowering in
July–October. In mild climates it makes a tree
up to 30 m, but in colder climates seldom
reaches more than 10 m before being cut back
by a cold winter. Hardy to −10°C.

**Acacia longifolia** (Andrews) Willd.
(*Leguminosae*) Sydney Golden Wattle   Native
of New South Wales, Victoria, Tasmania and
South Australia, growing especially on
sandstone. An evergreen shrub or small tree to
8 m. Leaves (strictly phyllodes) 7–15 cm long;
flower spikes 25–50 mm. Tolerant of poor soil
and dry sites, where it can make a large shrub.
Hardy to −10°C, for short periods.

**Acacia baileyana** F. Mueller (*Leguminosae*)
Cootamundra Wattle, Bailey Acacia   Native of
New South Wales, in the area around
Cootamundra, but widely cultivated, flowering
in July–September. Evergreen shrub or small
tree to 10 m, flowering from January to
February, in the northern hemisphere. There
are also golden- and purple-leaved forms. Said
in the *Western Garden Book* to be as hardy as *A.
dealbata*. Well-drained soil; but intolerant of
drought; full sun. Hardy to −10°C.

**Hebe × franciscana** (Eastw.) Souster
(*Scrophulariaceae*)   A hybrid between *H.
elliptica* and *H. speciosa*. Much cultivated and
appears wild in the Scilly Isles; a bush about
2.5 m high, wind- and salt-tolerant. Hardy to
−10°C.

**Atherosperma moschatum** Lab.
(*Atherospermataceae*)   See also p. 35.

**Correa backhousiana** Hook. (*Rutaceae*) Native
of Tasmania and Victoria growing near the
coast. A tall shrub up to 2 m high, flowering in
May–November. It is one of the hardiest of the
correas, surviving and making hedges on
Tresco. Well-drained soil; full sun or part
shade. Hardy to −8°C(?). Winter.

**Correa reflexa** Vent. (*Rutaceae*) Common
Correa   Native of E., S. & W. Australia and
Tasmania, in open forest or on heathland and
sandy places near the coast, flowering March–
September. Evergreen shrub to 3 m, sometimes
prostrate. Very variable. Flowers 2–4 cm long,
green to red or bicoloured, with a pair of leaf-
like bracts just above the flower. Well-drained
soil, lime-tolerant; full sun. Hardy to −5°C
perhaps. Autumn–spring.

**Correa × harrisii** Paxton (*Rutaceae*)   A hybrid
of *C. reflexa* and *C. pulchella* made by Mr D.
Beaton and first flowered in the garden of his
employer, T. Harris, Esq., in the 1840s. An
easily grown shrub, either in sunny places
outdoors in Mediterranean climates (hardy
down to about −5°C) or brought indoors in
winter. *C. × mannii* is very similar or identical.

**Hardenbergia comptoniana** (*Leguminosae*)
Wild Sasaparilla   Native of western Australia,
in jarrah (*Eucalyptus marginata*) forest, and
coastal scrub, climbing into the trees, flowering
in June–November. Evergreen climber to 10 m.
Leaves with 3–5 leaflets, ovate to lanceolate, to
75 cm or more long. Racemes to 12 cm, rarely
even to 25 cm long. Flowers about 1 cm across.
Any sandy soil; dry in summer; sun or part
shade. Hardy to −5°C. January–April.

**Acacia cyanophylla** Lindl. (*Leguminosae*)
Orange Wattle   Native of western Australia, in
scrub on sandy soils, flowering in June–
November. Commonly planted in southern
Europe, especially near the coast. Evergreen
shrub or small tree to 6 m, and almost as much
across. Hardy to −5°C, and tolerant of heat, and
drought in summer. Spring.

**Acacia verticillata** (L'. Her.) Willd.
(*Leguminosae*) Prickly Moses   Native of
Victoria, New South Wales, South Australia
and Tasmania, flowering in June–September.
Evergreen spreading bush up to 5 m with
conifer-like needles. It is resistant to salt-laden
wind, and may be clipped to form a hedge.
Well-drained soil; full sun. Hardy to −5°C.
Tolerant of lime and damp. Spring.

**Correa schlectendahlii** Behr. (*Rutaceae*) Native
of South Australia, in the area west of Adelaide,
in scrub inland. Leaves smooth and shining
above, almost glabrous below, cuneate at the
base. Stamens much longer than the bells. An
evergreen shrub up to 50 cm. Sandy, well-
drained soil; sun. Hardy to −5°C.

**Correa calycina** Black (*Rutaceae*)   Native of
South Australia, in valleys near Adelaide,
flowering in May–November. Leaves ovate or
oblong, hairy below. Calyx 4-lobed; stamens
longer than bell. Sandy, moist, well-drained
soil; sun. Hardy to −5°C(?). Autumn to spring.

**Correa 'Dusky Bells'**   Probably a hybrid
between *C. pulchella* and *C. reflexa*, with good
pinkish-red flowers in autumn to spring. Height
to 1 m. Flowers 4 cm long.

*Acacia verticillata*

*Correa 'Dusky Bells'*

*Correa calycina*

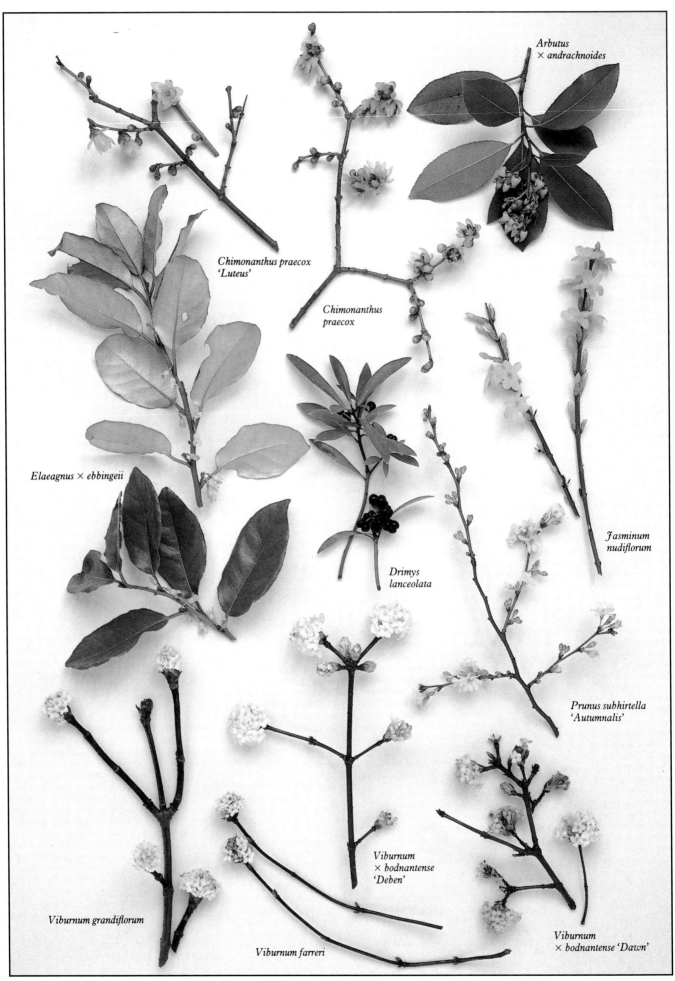

*Arbutus*
× *andrachnoides*

*Chimonanthus praecox*
'*Luteus*'

*Chimonanthus*
*praecox*

*Elaeagnus* × *ebbingeii*

*Drimys*
*lanceolata*

*Jasminum*
*nudiflorum*

*Prunus subhirtella*
'*Autumnalis*'

*Viburnum*
× *bodnantense*
'*Deben*'

*Viburnum grandiflorum*

*Viburnum farreri*

*Viburnum*
× *bodnantense* '*Dawn*'

⅖ life size. Specimens from Kew, 26th January

*Arbutus* × *andrachnoides* at Kew

*Arbutus andrachne* near Tokat, Turkey

**Chimonanthus praecox** Link (syn. *C. fragrans* Lindl.) (*Calycanthaceae*) Winter Sweet   Native of China, in mountains up to 3000 m, from Sichuan and Hubei to Chekiang, but also long cultivated in gardens for its very fragrant flowers. A deciduous shrub up to 3 m high and across, with rough, ovate-lanceolate, opposite leaves. It may be sparse-flowering after cool summers and is usually planted against a wall, so that with extra heat it sets better buds in the leaf axils of the current year's growth. It should be pruned immediately after flowering. Hardy to −25°C. Late winter.

**Chimonanthus praecox** 'Luteus' (syn. 'Concolor')   Inner petals are yellow and flowers somewhat larger than those of the ordinary form. 'Grandiflorus' has even larger flowers with red-stained inner petals.

**Elaeagnus × ebbingii** hort. (*Elaeagnaceae*)   A hybrid of *E. macrophylla* probably with *E. pungens* (see p. 31). Flowers sweetly fragrant, in early spring. Hardy to −10°C.

**Drimys lanceolata** (Poir.) Baillon (syn. *D. aromatica* Muell., *Tasmannia lanceolata* (Poir.) A. C. Smith) (*Winteraceae*)   Native of S. Australia, in Victoria, New South Wales and Tasmania, growing in moist places in the mountains up to 1500 m. It is an evergreen and can reach 10 m in height but is usually less. Bark and leaves aromatic, like cinnamon. Flowers greenish-yellow or white, male, female and bisexual, in terminal umbels; petals 2–8. In cultivation usually a low shrub of dense habit, liable to damage in cold winters. Hardy to −15°C. Spring.

**Jasminum nudiflorum** Lindl. (*Oleaceae*) Winter Jasmine   Native of China where it has been cultivated since ancient times. Known in the wild only as var. *pulvinatum* W. W. Smith, collected by Forrest in Yunnan; a dwarf, possibly grazed form. A spreading, sprawling shrub up to 3 m when trained on a wall but naturally making a mound of straight green angular twigs with glossy deciduous leaves, and unscented flowers at each node. Hardy to −15°C. Winter and early spring.

**Prunus subhirtella** Miq. 'Autumnalis' (*Rosaceae*)   This winter-flowering cherry has been grown in Japanese gardens since 1500; it makes a shrub or small tree up to 5 m and may flower at any time from autumn (before leaf fall) to spring, when the flowers of the white form have a pink flush. In the wild *P. subhirtella* is native of central Japan. Hardy to −25°C.

**Arbutus × andrachnoides** Link (*Ericaceae*)   A hybrid between *A. unedo* (p. 257) and *A. andrachne*, found in the wild in Greece, W. Turkey and the Black Sea coast where the parents grow together. It is variable in many characters but often has the beautiful bark of *A. andrachne*. It flowers from autumn to spring and produces fruit. Many beautiful old specimens are found in gardens, such as that shown here at Kew. Like *A. andrachne* it is tolerant of chalk or serpentine soils. Full sun. Hardy to −15°C.

**Arbutus andrachne** L. (*Ericaceae*)   Native of the E. Mediterranean from S. Albania and Greece to Turkey and the Crimea on the Black Sea, south to Lebanon, and east to N. Iraq, up to 800 m, flowering in March to May with fruit ripening in autumn. It grows on limestone, serpentine and igneous rocks in areas which are very dry in summer. The leaves are toothed only on young plants; the mature bark is smooth, red or purplish, peeling off in patches. It is usually an evergreen shrub, but can make a small tree up to 6 m. Rare in cultivation, though it should be as hardy as *A. unedo*; fresh seed germinates freely but I have found young plants liable to damp off, and very slow-growing. Hardy to −15°C, perhaps.

**Viburnum × bodnantense** Aberconway 'Dawn'   A hybrid between *V. farreri* (female) and *V. grandiflorum* raised at Bodnant, North Wales, in about 1935. It makes a deciduous many-stemmed shrub up to 3 m high, with flowers from October to April; the autumn flowers are usually white, flushed pink, the spring flowers deep pink on a more expanded inflorescence, all well-scented and frost resistant. Any soil in sun or shade. Hardy to −20°C.
**'Deben'** (*Caprifoliaceae*)   Of similar parentage

*Arbutus andrachne* fruit in October

to 'Dawn', raised by Nottcutt's Nursery. It is slightly paler in colour and more graceful in form than 'Dawn', with a longer corolla tube.

**Viburnum grandiflorum** Wallich ex DC. (incl. *V. foetens* Deene) (*Caprifoliaceae*)   Native of the Himalayas from Kashmir to S. E. Mizang, in open forest often forming dense scrub, at 2700–3600 m, flowering mainly in April–May. Deciduous shrub to 2 m, or taller in the east. Flowers white or pink. Any soil; sun or part shade. Hardy to −10°C. The western form, formerly called *V. foetens*, has shorter stems and white flowers.

**Viburnum farreri** Stearn (syn. *V. fragrans* Bunge) (*Caprifoliaceae*)   Native of Gansu, where it is wild and cultivated in gardens, flowering in April. Leaves opposite, obovate or oval, 6–10 cm long. It makes a deciduous shrub up to 2.5 m high, with many upright stems from the base. Flowers scented, usually white, flushed pink, but a pure white form, var. *candidissimum* Lancaster, is cultivated. There is also a dwarf cv. 'Nanum' up to 1 m high which seldom has more than a few flowers. Introduced to Europe by Purdom in 1910 and later by Farrer. Any soil; sun or part shade. Hardy to −20°C. Winter and early spring.

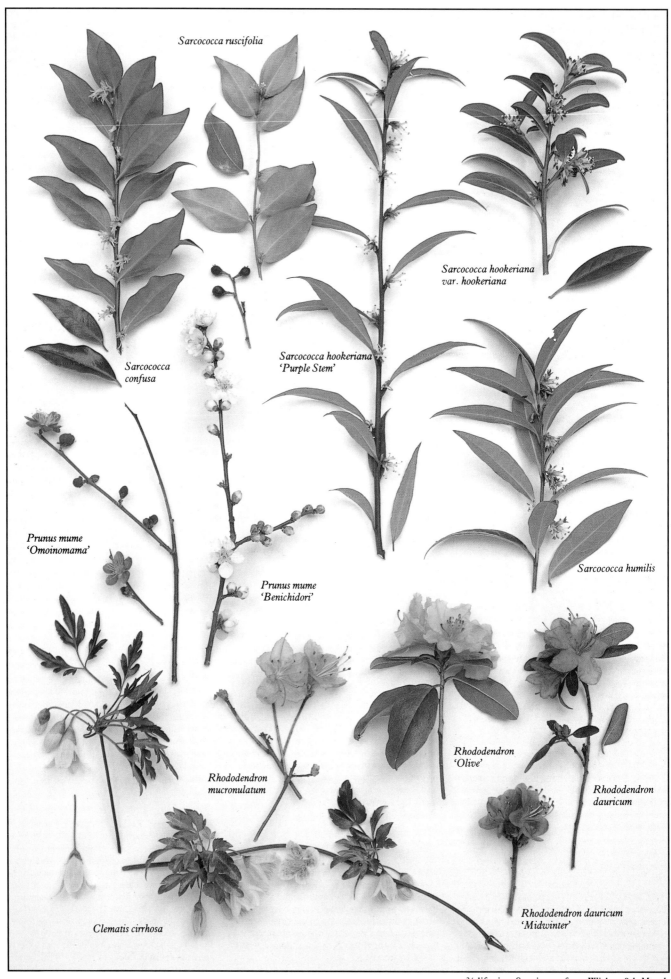

Sarcococca ruscifolia

Sarcococca hookeriana
var. hookeriana

Sarcococca
confusa

Sarcococca hookeriana
'Purple Stem'

Prunus mume
'Omoinomama'

Prunus mume
'Benichidori'

Sarcococca humilis

Rhododendron
mucronulatum

Rhododendron
'Olive'

Rhododendron
dauricum

Clematis cirrhosa

Rhododendron dauricum
'Midwinter'

⅔ life size. Specimens from Wisley, 8th March

*Sarcococca ruscifolia* Stapf (*Buxaceae*)  Native of W. Hubei, Sichuan and Yunnan, growing in forest and on cliffs, especially on limestone, at 600–1600 m, flowering in March–April. Evergreen bush up to 2 m; flowers sweetly scented; stigmas 3; fruits dark reddish. Leaves shining green, shorter and broader than most other species. Easily cultivated and good for dry shade. Hardy to −10°C. Early spring. Var. *chinensis* (Franch.) has narrower leaves.

*Sarcococca confusa* Sealy (*Buxaceae*)  Known only in cultivation; similar to *S. ruscifolia* var. *chinensis*, but with black berries and 2 or 3 stigmas. It makes a much-branched evergreen shrub up to 2 m high, not forming a thicket. Hardy to −10°C.

*Sarcococca hookeriana* Baillon var. *hookeriana* (*Buxaceae*)  Native of the Himalayas from W. Nepal eastwards, growing in forests at 2100–3600 m, flowering in February–April. It makes a thicket of stems up to 1 m, with lanceolate leaves, and scented flowers. Styles 3. Easily grown on acid soils, but less beautiful than var. *digyna*. Hardy to −15°C. Early spring.

*Sarcococca hookeriana* var. **digyna** Franch. **'Purple Stem'** (*Buxaceae*)  Var. *digyna* replaces var. *hookeriana* in S. China, being found in Sichuan and Yunnan. It has only two styles and rather narrower leaves than var. *hookeriana*, and is somewhat hardier. 'Purple Stem' shown here is particularly attractive in its blackish-purple stems. Easily grown and best in shade or half-shade. Any soil. Hardy to −15°C.

*Sarcococca humilis* (Rehd. & Wils.) Stapf (*Buxaceae*)  Native of W. Hubei, Sichuan and Yunnan, growing in scrub at around 2000 m. An evergreen up to 1.5 m high, but usually around 0.6 m, forming suckering thickets. Leaves shining, elliptic; berries black. Any soil; tolerant of dry shade. Hardy to −15°C. Early spring.

*Prunus mume* Sieb. & Zucc. (*Rosaceae*) Japanese Apricot  Native of China, found wild in scrub in W. Sichuan and W. Hubei at 300–2500 m, with light pink or white flowers in March–April. Long cultivated both in China and Japan for its flowers and fruit, which are round, like large cherries, and often eaten pickled. A beautiful deciduous shrub or small tree, with black bark and long slender green twigs; the leaves, which emerge after the flowers, are broadly ovate, with an acuminate apex. Many varieties are grown in Japan with scented flowers red to white, and single to semi-double. 'Benichidori' is a single rich, deep pink. 'Omoinomama' is semi-double, usually white-flowered, but with some pink-flowered branches. *Prunus mume* is of great and refined beauty, but rare in cultivation. It is often grown on a wall, but makes a beautiful specimen in sheltered woodland. Hardy to −15°C. Early spring.

*Clematis cirrhosa* L. (syn. *C. balearica* Pers.) (*Ranunculaceae*)  Native of the Mediterranean region, from Spain and Portugal, eastwards to Syria, growing in scrub and on rocks and cliffs at up to 400 m, flowering in February–April. The silky tassels of the fruiting heads, produced in May, are more conspicuous than the flowers,

(p. 193). *C. balearica* was described as having more finely divided leaves; the amount of red spotting on the flowers is also variable. An evergreen climber up to 4 m, the leaves often tinged purple in winter. Flowers scented. Easily grown on a warm wall or in a sunny sheltered position up a tree. Any soil, preferably dry. Hardy to −15°C. Early spring.

*Rhododendrom mucronulatum* Turcz. (*Ericaceae*)  Native of Japan in Honshu and N. Kyushu, Korea, N. & N.E. China and E. Siberia, growing in scrub in the hills, flowering in April–May. A deciduous shrub up to 2.5 m. Leaves 3–10 × 0.8–3 cm, elliptic-lanceolate or lanceolate. Flowers varying from reddish-purple to pink. Acid soil. Sun or part shade. Hardy to −25°C. Early spring.

*Rhododendron* **'Olive'**  A hybrid between *R. dauricum* and *R. moupinense*, raised by Stirling Maxwell before 1942. Evergreen shrub to 1.5 m. Acid soil; sun or part shade. Hardy to −25°C.

*Rhododendron dauricum* L.  Native of N. Japan (Hokkaido), Korea, N. China and E. Siberia, on high, dry mountains or in subalpine forest, flowering in April–May. An evergreen or semi-evergreen shrub up to 2.5 m, with flowers 2–5 cm across, in warm spells from late winter to spring. Acid soil, some shade. 'Midwinter' is a semi-evergreen clone with richer-coloured flowers. There are also beautiful white forms. Hardy to −30°C.

*Rhododendron moupinense* Franch.  Native of C. Sichuan and Guizhou, growing usually as an epiphyte in the forest at 2000–4000 m, flowering in March–April. An evergreen shrub up to 1.5 m. Leaves 3–4 cm long. Flowers white or pink-flushed, spotted, 6 cm across. Moist, acid soil; part shade. Hardy to −10° to −15°C. Early spring.

*Corylus avellana* L. **'Contorta'** (*Corylaceae*) Corkscrew Hazel  The common hazel is native of all Europe and W. Asia to Turkey, the Caucasus and N.W. Iran, in scrub and forest; it forms a deciduous multi-stemmed large shrub or small tree. The purple-leaved hazel is a variety 'Purpurea' of the Filbert *C. maxima* Miller, a native of S.E. Europe to the Caucasus, which differs in its larger nuts completely concealed by the elongated husk. *C. avellana* 'Contorta' makes a dense twiggy shrub up to 3 m high, slower-growing because it lacks the strong upright shoots of the normal variety. It was discovered in Gloucestershire in about 1863. Any soil; sun or part shade. Hardy to −30°C.

*Garrya elliptica* Lindl. (*Garryaceae*) Coast Silk Tassel  Native of W. North America, in the coast ranges, from S. California to Oregon, growing in chaparral and forest at up to 600 m, flowering from January to March. It makes an evergreen shrub or small tree up to 8 m high, the male and female catkins on different plants. Leaves woolly beneath. In the wild the male catkins are usually up to 15 cm, but they reach 35 cm in good specimens of the cv. 'James Roof' selected in California. *G. elliptica* is very hardy, but in cold climates the leaves are often scorched by cold winds, and the catkins usually killed by frost within a week of expanding. Full sun. Hardy to −15°C. Winter.

*Corylus avellana* 'Contorta'

*Garrya elliptica*

*Rhododendron moupinense*

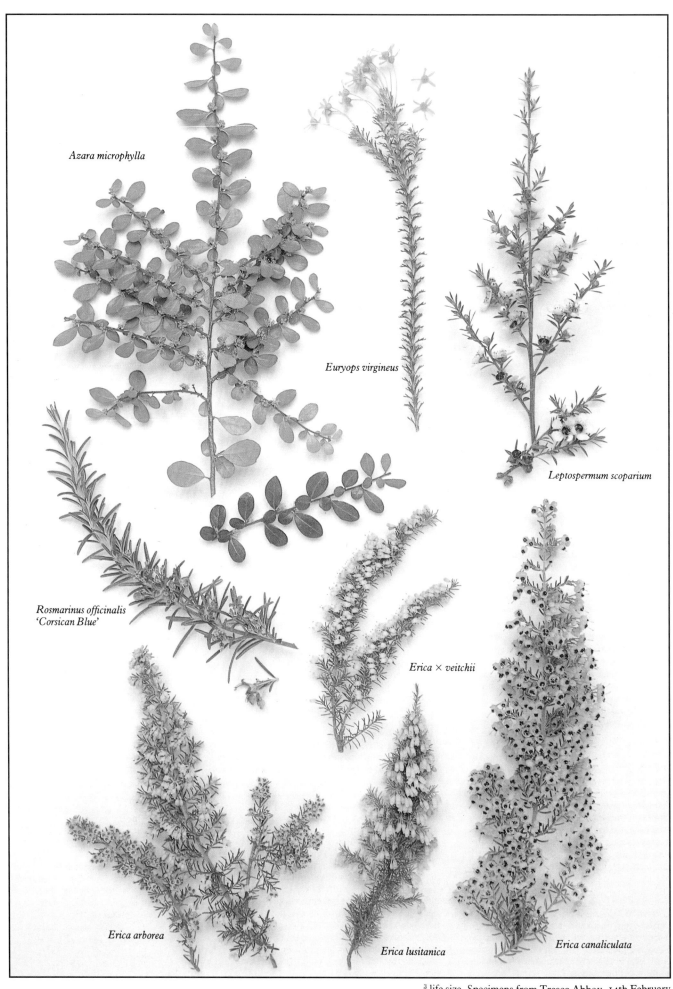

Azara microphylla

Euryops virgineus

Leptospermum scoparium

Rosmarinus officinalis
'Corsican Blue'

Erica × veitchii

Erica arborea

Erica lusitanica

Erica canaliculata

$\frac{3}{5}$ life size. Specimens from Tresco Abbey, 14th February

*Erica australis* near Ronda, Spain

**Azara microphylla** Hooker fil. (*Flacourtiaceae*)
Native of Chile and S. Argentina, growing in
forests with *Nothofagus obliqua*. The hardiest
species of *Azara*, but the least colourful; the tiny
flowers, produced in early spring, are vanilla-
scented. Any soil; sun. Hardy to −15°C.

**Euryops virgineus** (L. fil.) DC. (*Compositae*)
Native of South Africa, in the eastern Cape
between Bredasdorp and Port Elizabeth,
flowering throughout the year. A small upright
shrub up to 3 m high, but usually around 1.5 m.
Sun. Hardy to −5°C.

**Leptospermum scoparium** J. R. & G. Forst.
(*Myrtaceae*) Manuka   Native of Australia and
New Zealand, in both North and South Islands,
where it is common, from the coast where it
may be a small evergreen tree up to 8 m high, to
the mountains where it forms a prostrate mat or
cushion; it grows in both wet and dry ground,
and even tolerates warm soil in the vicinity of
geysers. In the wild the flowers are usually
white, and all parts of the plant are aromatic. In
cultivation in Europe, *L. scoparium* is rare,
having been superseded by more showy
cultivars. It is hardy only on the southwest and
west coasts, and is very common on Tresco in
the Scilly Isles. Sun. Hardy to −10°C. Autumn
to spring.

**L. scoparium 'Winter Cheer'**   *L. scoparium*
'Nichollsii', a single red, crossed with a double
pink form in California produced in the second
generation double red-flowered plants of which
one was named 'Red Damask' and another
'Ruby Glow': 'Winter Cheer', shown here,
seems to have the same parentage. These are
excellent garden plants in California or other
sunny climates with mild winters, where they
flower in winter or early spring, and sometimes
also in summer. Double pink 'Pompom' and
double white 'Snow White' are also in
cultivation. In England these cultivars will grow
only in the mildest gardens, though 'Red
Damask' survived for several years outdoors at
Wisley. Hardy to −10°C.

**Erica × veitchii** Bean (*Ericaceae*)   A hybrid
between *E. arborea* and *E. lusitanica* raised by
R. Veitch & Sons at Exeter, and introduced in
1905. The flowers and the hairs on the young
shoots are intermediate between those of the
parents. In cultivation *E. × veitchii* is said to be
a robust grower but is otherwise no
improvement on its parents. A clone 'Exeter' is
that usually cultivated.

**Erica arborea** L. (*Ericaceae*) Tree Heath Native
of the Mediterranean region from S.W. France
and Portugal eastwards to the Black Sea and
south to the Canaries and the mountains of East
Africa, such as Mt. Kenya and Mt. Kilimanjaro
at around 4000 m; it is also found in the Tibesti
and the Yemen growing in scrub and on
hillsides, flowering (in Europe) in March–May.
It makes a large shrub or small tree up to 7 m
high, in forest, with a single trunk, but usually
sprouting from the base. Flowers always white;
corolla 2.5–4 mm; style stout with a white
stigma; hairs on young shoots much branched.
Somewhat tender except in the southwest of
England and southern Europe. The variety
*alpina* Dieck introduced in 1899 from near
Cuenca, at around 1200 m, is possibly hardier
and later-flowering than the usual forms in
cultivation, and of a somewhat stiffer habit.
Acid soil. Hardy to −10°C.

*Erica australis*

*Leptospermum 'Winter Cheer'*

**Erica lusitanica** Rudolphi (*Ericaceae*)   Native
of S.W. France, Spain and Portugal, growing
on wet heaths and on the edges of woods,
flowering in March–May. It is naturalized in
Cornwall. It makes a large shrub up to 3.5 m
high, similar to *E. arborea*, but smaller, and
with larger flowers, the corolla 4–5 mm long,
pink-tinged, and the stigma red. The hairs on
the young shoots are not branched. In
cultivation it is a more beautiful plant than *E.
arborea*, but equally tender, surviving best near
the southwest and west coasts of Europe. Acid
soil. Hardy to −10°C.

**Erica canaliculata** Andrews (*Ericaceae*)   Native
of South Africa, in Cape Province, where it
grows in damp places and forest borders from
the George to Humansdorp districts, flowering
mainly in summer. It makes a bush or small tree
up to 2 m or more in favourable conditions. The
flowers are usually pale pink, but in cultivation
in Europe may be white, either because of the
poor light in the European winter when it
mostly flowers, or because a pale-flowered form
was the one introduced to Europe, in about
1802. It is one of the easiest of the South African
heathers to grow, doing well under glass or in
the open in mild gardens such as Tresco, where
it flowers from February to April. Hardy to
−5°C.

**Erica australis** L. (syn. *E. aragonensis* Willk.)
(*Ericaceae*)   Native of Portugal and W. Spain
growing in heathland on hills, flowering from
March to June. It makes a tall, somewhat lax
shrub up to 2 m high. A beautiful plant with the
largest flowers, 6–9 mm long, of the tall
European species, but rather tender and killed
in cold winters in Europe, except in
southwestern England and the Atlantic and
Mediterranean coasts. A white form, 'Master
Robert', is known in cultivation. Requires lime-
free soil. Hardy to −10°C.

**Rosmarinus officinalis** L. (*Labiatae*)
Rosemary   Native of the Mediterranean region
from Portugal and North Africa, east to Greece
and Turkey, growing in rocky places at low
altitudes, usually near the sea, flowering mainly
in autumn and spring. It is an evergreen shrub
up to 2 m high, very variable in flower colour
from almost white to pink, purple and blue, and
in leaf width from 1.2–3.5 mm. Prostrate
narrow-leaved forms with deep blue flowers, as
shown here, are common in Corsica but are
rather tender. 'Fastigiatus' or 'Miss Jessop's
Variety' is a hardier, upright, broad-leaved
plant with pale flowers. 'Benenden Blue' and
'Severn Sea' are prostrate narrow-leaved forms
with deep blue flowers, probably also from
Corsica. Hardy to −10° or −15°C.

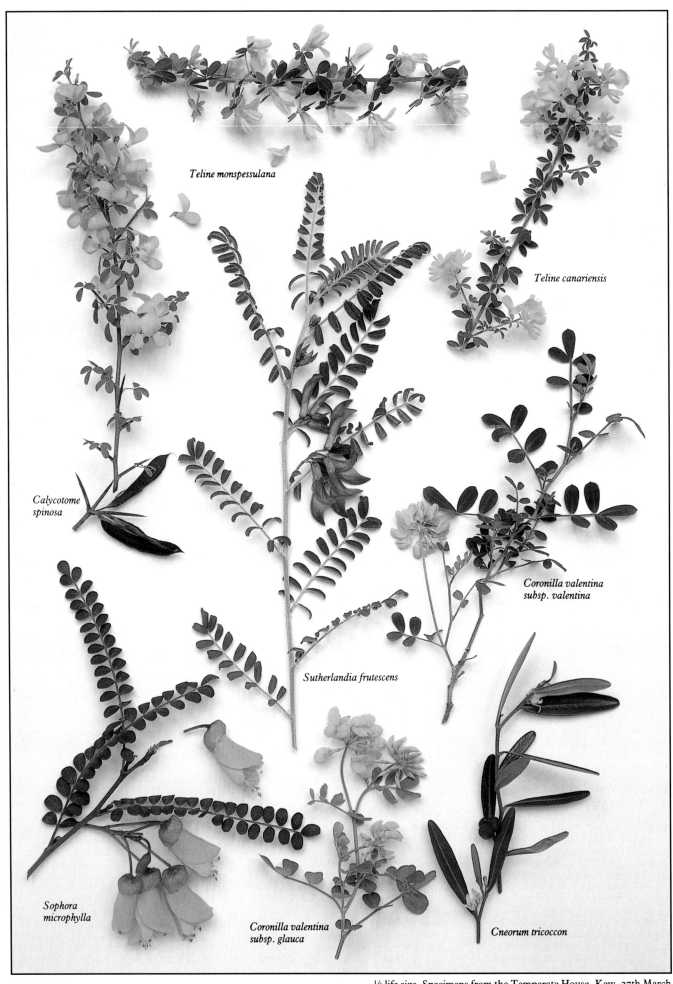

*Teline monspessulana*

*Teline canariensis*

*Calycotome spinosa*

*Coronilla valentina subsp. valentina*

*Sutherlandia frutescens*

*Sophora microphylla*

*Coronilla valentina subsp. glauca*

*Cneorum tricoccon*

½ life size. Specimens from the Temperate House, Kew, 27th March

*Banksia speciosa*

*Banksia occidentalis*

*Clianthus puniceus*

**Calicotome spinosa** (L.) Link (*Leguminosae*)
Native of the western Mediterranean region
from Sardinia and Italy to Morocco, growing in
maquis and on rocky hills, flowering in spring.
A much-branched shrub up to 3 m, with stout
spines. Any soil; full sun. Hardy to −10°C.
Spring.

**Teline monspessulana** (L.) C. Koch (syn.
*Cytisus monspessulanus* L.) (*Leguminosae*) Native
of the Mediterranean region, Portugal and the
Azores, growing in scrub and open forest,
flowering in spring. An erect much-branched
shrub up to 3 m high. Leaves hairy on both
surfaces. Any soil; full sun. Hardy to −10°C.
Spring.

**Teline canariensis** (L.) Webb & Berth. Native
of the Canary Islands, on Tenerife and Gran
Canaria, in forests and scrub on the north coasts
from 500–1500 m, flowering in summer. An
erect shrub up to 3 m, with twigs and underside
of leaves silky-hairy. Flowers in terminal
racemes. Hardy only in Mediterranean areas to
−5°C. Spring.

**Sutherlandia frutescens** (L.) R. Br.
(*Leguminosae*) Cancer Bush   Native of South
Africa, growing on hillsides, flowering in July–
December. A shrub to around 2 m high, usually
less, with silvery leaves, and inflated papery
pods, which help seed dispersal. Grown in
Europe since about 1680 in greenhouses, and
easily grown outside in the Mediterranean, and
coastal and desert California. Any dry soil; full
sun. Hardy to −5°C perhaps. Spring.

**Sophora microphylla** (*Leguminosae*) Ait.
Kowhai   Native of both islands of New
Zealand, in open forest, along rivers and in
damp and rocky places, flowering from July to
October. Deciduous shrub or small tree to 5 m.
Leaves usually with more than 30 pairs of
almost round leaflets. Full sun, with wall
protection in borderline areas. Hardy to −10°C.

**Coronilla valentina** L. subsp. **valentina**
(*Leguminosae*)   Native of the C. Mediterranean
region from eastern France to Albania, and
North Africa, growing in scrub and on cliffs,
flowering in February–May. A low evergreen
shrub up to 1.5 m high; flowers scented. Hardy
to −10°C. Spring.

**Coronilla valentina** subsp. **glauca** (L.) Batt.
(*Leguminosae*)   Native of the Mediterranean
region from Portugal and Spain to Greece and
North Africa, growing in similar places to
subsp. *valentina*, from which it differs in having

2–3, not 3–6 pairs of leaflets, and stipules
2–6 mm (not 5–10 mm), ovate or lanceolate,
membranous, and a pod with 1–4 (or rarely
more) segments. Intermediates between the two
subspecies are known both in the wild and in
cultivation. A variegated and a pale yellow-
flowered form are both cultivated. Flowering in
autumn and spring. Hardy to −10°C.

**Cneorum tricoccon** L. (*Cneoraceae*)   Native of
the western Mediterranean region, from Italy
and Sardinia west to Spain, growing on rocky,
usually limestone hills. An evergreen shrub up
to 1 m tall. Hardy to −15°C. Summer.

**Banksia occidentalis** R. Br. (*Proteaceae*) Red
Swamp Banksia   Native of S.W. Australia, in
wet peaty sand near the coast, flowering in
January–April. Erect bushy shrub to 7 m.
Leaves 5–15 cm long, linear. Flowers orange to
red, in spikes 10–15 cm tall. Full sun. Hardy to
−5°C perhaps. Summer–autumn.

**Banksia speciosa** R. Br. (*Proteaceae*)   Native
of W. Australia, between Hopetown and
Israelite Bay, on deep sandy soil near the coast,
flowering throughout the year. Evergreen
spreading shrub to 5 m. Leaves 30–40 cm long;
flower heads 10 cm across. Infertile soil; full
sun. Hardy to −5°C, perhaps. Any season.

**Clianthus puniceus** Banks & Solander
(*Leguminosae*) Kaka Beak   Native of New
Zealand, on North Island growing wild in the
inlets of the Bay of Islands, on the coast near
Thames and at Lake Waikaremoana, where
there are large, ancient specimens reputed to be
over 100 years old. In cultivation it makes a
small spreading shrub up to 3 m with support,
flowering in the northern hemisphere in spring.
The colour varies from bright red to pink and
creamy white; the individual flowers may be
8 cm long. Hardy to −10°C perhaps, with
shelter from cold dry wind. Spring.

**Pittosporum tobira** (Thunb.) Aiton
(*Pittosporaceae*) Tobira   Native of the coasts of
southern Japan, southern Korea, and China,
growing on rocky hillsides, flowering from
April–June. Widely planted in warm climates
around the world for its orange-scented flowers
and glossy, salt-resistant, evergreen foliage. It
makes a dense shrub up to 10 m high. but
usually around 2 m, and is hardier than
generally known, surviving well in London, on
the south coast of England, and as far north, on
the Pacific coast, as the Canadian border. The
bright orange, sticky seeds are also attractive.
Hardy to −10°C. Spring.

*Clianthus puniceus*

*Pittosporum tobira*

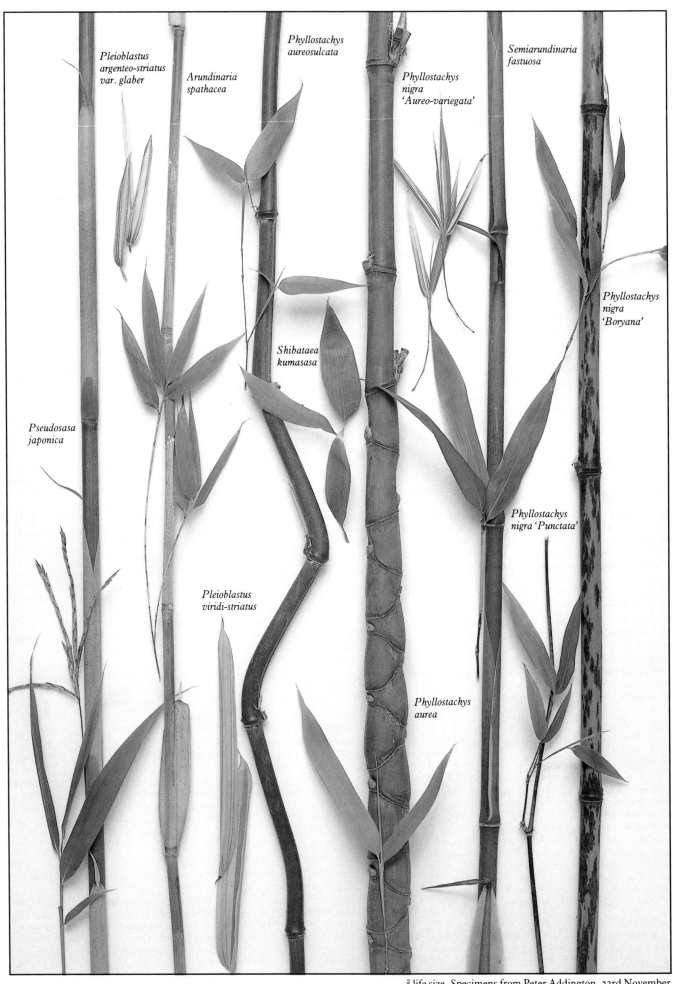

*Pleioblastus
argenteo-striatus
var. glaber*

*Arundinaria
spathacea*

*Phyllostachys
aureosulcata*

*Phyllostachys
nigra
'Aureo-variegata'*

*Semiarundinaria
fastuosa*

*Phyllostachys
nigra
'Boryana'*

*Shibataea
kumasasa*

*Pseudosasa
japonica*

*Pleioblastus
viridi-striatus*

*Phyllostachys
nigra 'Punctata'*

*Phyllostachys
aurea*

$\frac{2}{5}$ life size. Specimens from Peter Addington, 23rd November

*Arundinaria spathacea* with *Euonymus*

*Chusquea couleou* with *Gunnera*

**Chusquea couleou** E. Desv. (*Graminae*) Native of Chile and Argentina, in the Andes. Rhizomes shortly creeping, forming slow-growing, dense thickets. Stems 4–6 m tall (rarely to 10 m), 3.5–4 cm in diameter, with rather close, hairy nodes. Sheaths persistent, glabrous. Leaf-blades 5–10 × 1 cm. Moist soil; shelter. Hardy to −15°C. Recognized by its narrow, arching, leafy branches.

**Pseudosasa japonica** (Steud.) Mak. (syn. *Arundinaria japonica* (Sieb. & Zucc.) Makino) Native of Honshu, Shikoku, Kyushu and S. Korea, in woods and damp places. Rhizone shortly creeping forming dense clumps. Stems 2–5 m tall, 5–15 cm in diameter. Sheaths pale brown, persistent, rough. Leaf-blades narrowly lanceolate, 8–30 cm long, 1–4.5 cm wide, glabrous. Most clumps in gardens have recently flowered or are flowering and may be dying or regenerating feebly at the base. Moist, rich soil; shelter. Hardy to −15°C.

**Arundinaria spathacea** (Franch.) McClintock (syn. *Arundinaria murielae* (Gamble) Native of W. Hubei, forming dense thickets of golden stems at 2000–3000 m. A densely tufted clump of short rhizomes. Stems 2–4 m tall, at first green, later yellow, to 10 mm in diameter. Leaf-blades 6–11 cm long, 10–15 mm across, minutely bristly on the margins. Moist, rich soil; shelter. Hardy to −20°C.

**Pleioblastus argenteo-striatus** var. **glaber** Tsuboi   The wild unvariegated form is native of S.W. Honshu, Shikoku and Kyushu, in open woods and on hillsides.

**Pleioblastus viridi-striatus** (André) Makino Native of Japan. Rhizomes creeping, forming wide mats. Stems to 1.5 m, 6 mm in diameter. Sheaths downy when young, persistent. Leaves 18 × 2.8 cm, downy on both sides. Hardy to −15°C.

**Pleioblastus linearis** (Hack.) Nakai (syn. *Arundinaria linearis* Hack.)   Native of the Ryukyu islands in S. Japan (and cultivated in S. Kyushu) in forests. Rhizomes short, producing dense clumps. Stems 2–3 m tall, glabrous. Leaf-blades broadly linear, 4–15 cm long, 4–10 mm wide, with a long slender point. Moist rich soil; shelter and partial shade. Hardy to −10°C.

**Semiarundinaria fastuosa** (Mitf.) Makino Native of C. and W. Honshu, Shikoku and Kyushu, in forests and moist places. Rhizomes elongated, creeping, forming open thickets.

*Pleioblastus linearis*

*Sasa palmata*

Stems 5–10 m tall, 3–7 cm in diameter. Sheaths usually deciduous. Leaf-blades narrowly lanceolate, glabrous. Moist, rich soil; shelter, sun or shade. Hardy to −10°C, but regenerating when cut down by very cold winters.

**Phyllostachys aurea** (Carr.) Rivière   Native of S.E. China. Stems 4–8 m, 3–4 cm in diameter, smooth, greyish or brownish-yellow; lower nodes compressed. Sheaths soon falling. Leaf-blades 6–15 × 1–2 cm. Hardy to −15°C.'

**Phylllostachys nigra** (Lodd.) Munro '**Boryana**' Native of E. China. Stems 3–5 m, 2–2.5 cm in diameter. Sheaths deciduous. Leaf-blades 6–13 × 0.8–1.8 cm. Hardy to −15°C. In the typical variety, the mature canes are shining black. '**Punctata**' canes speckled with purplish-brown. '**Aureo-variegata**' has leaves striped with yellow.

**Phyllostachys aureosulcata** McClure   Native of N.E. China. Stems 3–6 m, 1–3 cm in diameter, sometimes zigzag at the base. Sheaths striped, deciduous. Leaf-blades 15 × 2 cm. Hardy to −15°C.

**Shibataea kumasasa** (Zoll.) Makino   Native of S.W. Japan, in woods, and widely cultivated. A graceful bamboo with shortly creeping rhizomes forming rather open patches of dark, crooked stems to 1.5 m high, *c*.5 mm in diameter. Leaf-blades 6–10 cm long, 15–25 mm wide, in apparent whorls of 3–4 at each node. Moist, leafy soil; shelter and shade. Hardy to −10°C.

**Sasa palmata** (Bean) Nakai   Native of Hokkaido, Honshu, Shikoku and Kyushu, and Sakhalin, growing in damp places and woods. Rhizomes creeping, producing wide-spreading clumps. Stems 1–1.5 m tall. Leaf-blades 10–35 cm long, 5–8 cm wide, glabrous on both sides or slightly hairy beneath. Moist, rich soil; shelter and partial shade. Hardy to −20°C. *S. veitchii* (Carr.) Rehder   Has shorter stems, and leaf-blades white-edged, hairy beneath.

Aucuba japonica 'Variegata' (female)

Aucuba japonica
(female)

Aucuba japonica
(male)

Aucuba japonica
'Variegata' (male)

Aucuba chinensis
subsp. *omeiensis*
*R.L. 614*

Aucuba japonica
f. longifolia

Elaeagnus pungens
'Dicksonii'

Elaeagnus
macrophylla

Elaeagnus
'Gilt Edge'

Skimmia
laureola

Skimmia japonica
'Rubella'

Skimmia japonica

⅝ life size. Specimens from Eccleston Square and Chelsea Physic Garden, 30th April

*Griselinia littoralis 'Variegata'*

*Pseudopanax ferox*

*Skimmia laureola*

*Buxus wallichiana* at Borde Hill

**Aucuba japonica** Thunb. (*Cornaceae*) Native of Japan, in S.W. Honshu, Shikoku and Kyushu, growing in woods, flowering in March–May. Evergreen shrub to 3 m high, dioecious, with red or more rarely yellow (f. *luteocarpa*) or white (f. *leucocarpa*) berries. Numerous forms, mostly with spotted leaves, were popular in Victorian shrubberies, and one of these, 'Variegata' – a female, was the first introduced by John Graeffer in 1873. Male plants have a more showy elongated inflorescence than the female, and both are required for a good set of berries. Very shade- and drought-tolerant; leggy plants may be cut to the ground in spring and will break from the base. Any soil. Hardy to −15°C. Spring.

**Aucuba japonica** var. **longifolia** (T. Moore) Schelle
Narrow-leaved forms of *Aucuba japonica* may conveniently be lumped under this name and have been in cultivation since the 19 C.

**Aucuba chinensis** Bentham subsp. *omeiensis* (Fang) Fang & Soong (*Cornaceae*) Native of W. China, notably Mount Omei in S.W. Sichuan, where it was collected by E. H. Wilson and Roy Lancaster. Similar plants are found in Hong Kong (*A. chinensis* Bentham). A large shrub to 6 m with leaves 20 cm long; fruits 2 cm long, in elongated panicles. As it is found at rather low altitudes, 800–1300 m, it is unlikely to be hardy to lower than −10°C. Shown here Lancaster 614.

**Elaeagnus macrophylla** Thunb. (*Elaeagnaceae*) Native of Japan, in S.W. Honshu, Shikoku and Kyushu, and Korea, in thickets near the sea, flowering in October–November. Flowers shortly tubular, sweetly-scented. Leaves with brown scales when young, later usually only with white scales, glossy above. This species makes a lax or scrambling evergreen shrub up to 2 m high. Fruits, when produced, pinkish with white scales. Hardy to −15°C

**Elaeagnus pungens** Thunb. (*Elaeagnaceae*) Native of Japan, in S.W. Honshu, Shikoku and Kyushu, in thickets near the sea. It forms a tall, evergreen shrub, often sending out long, trailing branches, with long-tubed flowers in October–November. Leaves rounded at both ends,

crinkly on the edges, with numerous brown scales beneath, and a rather dull upper surface. Fruits red, with brown scales. Shown here is 'Dicksonii'. Sun or partial shade. Hardy to −15°C.

**Elaeagnus × ebbingei** hort. (*Elaeagnaceae*) This hybrid was raised by S. G. A. Doorenbos from seed of *E. macrophylla* with, probably, *E. pungens* as the other parent. A similar hybrid has been named *E. × submacrophylla* Serv. Shown here the cultivar **'Gilt Edge'** raised by Waterer & Crisp in 1961. Hardy to −20°C.

**Skimmia japonica** Thunb. (*Rutaceae*) Native of Japan, E. Siberia (Sakhalin), Taiwan and possibly Luzon in the Philippines, where it grows in forests, sometimes as an epiphyte on old Cryptomerias (e.g. on Yakushima). Introduced from Japan by Robert Fortune in 1861. Many varieties are found in cultivation and are described in detail by P. D. Brown in *The Plantsman* vol. 1 pt. 4 (1980). Cultivation is easy and skimmias prefer rich, slightly acid soil; they are especially tolerant of shady sites in urban gardens. In order to get a good crop of berries, both male and female plants are needed and should be planted side by side. Hand pollination, by removing a male flower head which is releasing its pollen, and brushing it over the female flowers, usually results in a better set of berries. Hardy to −15°C.
**'Rubella'** A distinct male clone with red colour in the upper leaves, petioles, pedicels and sepals. Very attractive in bud, paler when the flowers are open. Cultivated since 1865 when it was introduced to France from China by Eugene Simon. Growth, bushy, up to 1.1 m; flowers scented. Hardy to −15°C.

**Skimmia laureola** (DC.) Sieb. & Zucc. (*Rutaceae*) Native of the Himalayas from E. Nepal to W. China, and in mountains to E. China, especially as an undershrub in rocky places in forest from 1600–3600 m, flowering from April to June. An evergreen shrub, usually less than 1 m tall, with aromatic leaves, sweetly-scented flowers and black berries.

**Buxus wallichiana** Baillon (*Buxaceae*) Native of the Himalayas from Afghanistan to central

Nepal, from 1800–2700 m, usually growing in steep, shady, rocky ravines, flowering in March–May. It makes an evergreen shrub or small tree up to 7 m high, distinct in its narrow, linear-lanceolate to elliptic leaves up to 6 cm long, and downy shoots. It is rare in cultivation, but hardy; the specimen photographed here was from a large specimen just below the walled garden at Borde Hill. Hardy to −10°C.

**Pseudopanax ferox** (Kirk) Kirk (*Araliaceae*) Native of New Zealand, in lowland forests, flowering in February. Shown here is the juvenile stage, with a straight stem and downward-pointing leaves. The adult trees are rounded, up to 15 m, with lanceolate, toothed leaves to 15 cm long. Any soil; sun or part shade. Hardy to −10°C.

**Griselinia littoralis** Raoul **'Variegata'** (*Cornaceae*) Broadleaf Native of New Zealand, in forest in lowlands and mountains, flowering in November–January. Evergreen rounded shrub to 15 m. Leaves leathery, 5–10 cm long. Flowers *c*.5 mm across, male and female on separate bushes. Berries small, black. Any moist soil; sun or part shade. Hardy to −10°C with shelter from cold wind. Summer. The variegated form, shown here, can have leaves either white-edged or white-centred.

*Salix atrocinerea*

*Salix magnifica* at Baoxing, China

*Salix magnifica (female)*

*Salix magnifica (male)*

**Salix atrocinerea** Brot. (*Salicaceae*) Sallow, Pussy Willow   Native of W. Europe from Ireland and Scotland south Portugal, and North Africa, in marshes, by streams and roadside ditches and on the edges of woods, flowering in March–May. Deciduous shrub to 10 m; twigs glabrous in their second year. Leaves obovate or oblong, oblanceolate. Catkins 2.5 cm long, before the leaves. Any good soil; sun. Hardy to −20°C.

**Salix magnifica** Hemsl. (*Salicaceae*)   Native of W. Sichuan, in mountain scrub and by streams at 2000–3000m, flowering in May–June. Deciduous shrub to 7.5 m. Male catkins 10–18 cm long, female 18–30 cm. Moist soil; sun or part shade. Hardy to −15°C. Spring.

**Salix lanata** L. (*Salicaceae*) Woolly Willow Native of Scotland where it is very rare and Iceland eastwards to Arctic Russia and Siberia, growing on mountain rocks and cliffs, flowering in June. Deciduous shrub to 1.5 m. Moist well-drained soil, cool position in part shade. Hardy to −25°C and below.

**Salix discolor** Muhl. (*Salicaceae*) Pussy Willow Native of Labrador east to Alberta, south to Kentucky and S. Dakota, in swamps, by lakes and creeks and in damp scrub, flowering in

February–May in the north. Deciduous large shrub or tree to 6 m. Male catkins 2.5–6 cm long, female rather longer, showing silvery hairs on the naked shoots in late winter, before opening with yellow stamens or greenish styles in spring. Moist soil; sun. Hardy to −25°C and below. The common Pussy Willow in North America.

**Salix hastata** L. **'Wehrhahnii'** (*Salicaceae*) Native of Europe from Norway and Spain eastwards to Albania, Romania and Siberia, in wet places and in mountains in the south, flowering in April–June. 'Wehrhahnii', a male, was discovered in about 1930 by Garteninspektor Bonstedt of Geismar, in the Engadine. A shrub to 2 m with many stems. Young shoots purplish-brown in winter. Leaves elliptic to obovate. Catkins *c.* 5 cm long; bracts conspicuous with long white hairs. Any moist soil; sun. Hardy to −25°C. Spring.

**Prinsepia utilis** Royle (*Rosaceae*)   Native of the Himalayas from Pakistan to Yunnan, and in Taiwan, in forest, scrub and hedges at 1200–2700 m, flowering in October–November, and in April–May, with fruit often ripe in spring. Wide-spreading deciduous spiny shrub to 3 m. Stems green. Spines 2–4 cm. Flowers white, in few-flowered racemes. Fruit to 1.7 cm long. Any well-drained soil; sun. Hardy to −10°C.

**Lonicera microphylla** Roem. & Schult. (*Caprifoliaceae*)   Native of Central Asia from Uzbekistan and Afghanistan, east to Xizang and Mongolia, on dry rocky hillsides, flowering in April–June. Deciduous bushy shrub to 2 m. Flowers *c.* 1 cm on stalks to 15 mm long. Berries fused, red. Well-drained soil, good on chalk; sun. Hardy to −25°C. Spring.

**Xanthorrhiza simplicissima** Marsh (*Ranunculaceae*) Yellowroot   Native of New York and West Virginia south to Florida and Alabama, in damp woods, scrub and by streams, flowering in April–May. Suckering deciduous shrub to 1 m, forming wide patches. Bark and roots yellow. Leaves purplish when young, colouring in autumn. Flowers 4 mm across. Moist acid soil; sun or part shade. Hardy to −20°C. Spring.

**Maddenia hypoleuca** Koehne (*Rosaceae*) Native of W. Hubei at 1200–1500 m flowering in April and May. Open deciduous dioecious shrub, 2–6 m tall. Flowers appearing with the leaves, with no petals, but 25–40 stamens, 6 mm long, in the male flower, one style in the female. Plum-like fruit, black elliptical, 8 mm long. Any good soil; sun. Hardy to −15°C. Early spring.

Lonicera microphylla at Ferghana, C. Asia

Salix lanata

Xanthorrhiza simplicissima

Salix discolor near New York

Prinsepia utilis

Salix hastata 'Wehrhahnii'

Maddenia hypoleuca

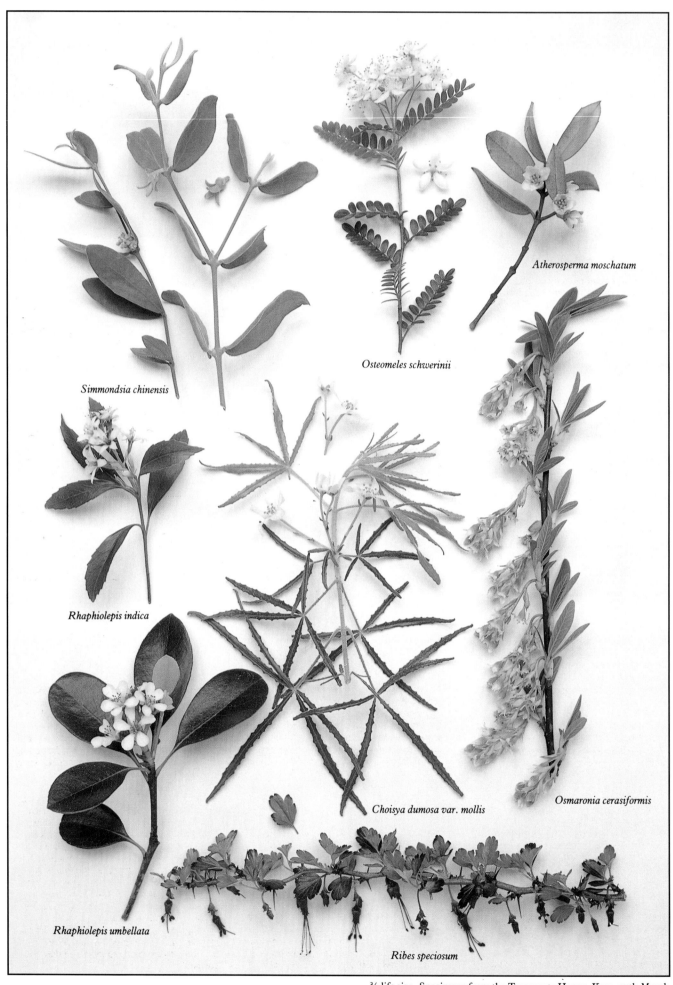

Atherosperma moschatum

Osteomeles schwerinii

Simmondsia chinensis

Rhaphiolepis indica

Choisya dumosa var. mollis

Osmaronia cerasiformis

Rhaphiolepis umbellata

Ribes speciosum

¾ life size. Specimens from the Temperate House, Kew, 27th March

*Rhaphiolepis indica 'Springtime'* in Texas

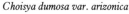

*Choisya dumosa var. arizonica*

*Choisya ternata*

**Choisya ternata** Kunth (*Rutaceae*) Mexican Orange   Native of Mexico. An evergreen shrub up to 3 m; leaves aromatic; flowers scented, some in autumn but mainly in spring. A common and valuable plant in cultivation especially in cities. Responds well to clipping. Tolerant of drought, but needs good drainage and shelter in cold climates; undamaged in −10°C, but defoliated by −15°C.

**Atherosperma moschatum** Labill. (*Atherospermataceae*) See also p. 19   Native of S.E. Australia and Tasmania, growing in forests. An evergreen tree up to 30 m high. The stems and leaves are aromatic; the male and female flowers borne on separate trees. Tender in cultivation, but surviving in mild gardens, where it makes an upright shrub up to 6 m, flowering when quite young. Acid or neutral soil. Hardy to −5°C.

**Choisya dumosa** (Torr.) Gray (*Rutaceae*) Native of W. Texas, New Mexico, Arizona and northern Mexico, in deserts and mountains at 1200–2000 m, often in Pinyon pine or oak forest, flowering in April–July. Three varieties are recognized; var. *dumosa* with 5–13 leaflets; var. *arizonica* (Standl.) Benson from Arizona with 3–5 leaflets and petals 10–13 mm long and var. *mollis* (Standl.) Benson also with 3–5 leaflets, and petals 8–10 mm long. Low evergreen shrubs to 1 m; leaflets to 5 cm long, scented of citrus when crushed. Well-drained dry soil; full sun. Hardy to −10°C. Spring.

**Ribes speciosum** Pursh (*Grossulariaceae*) Fuchsia-flowered Gooseberry   Native of California and Mexico from northern Baja California to Santa Clara Co., growing in shaded canyons near the coast, in sage scrub and chaparral below 500 m, flowering in January–May. A twiggy evergreen shrub up to 2 m high with spreading branches. Unlike many *Ribes* the plant is scentless. In cultivation in northern Europe *R. speciosum* is generally grown against a warm wall for protection against winter cold, but its flowers are not seen to advantage against red brick, and it will grow equally well self-supported in the open in a sunny sheltered position, in well-drained soil. Hardy to −15°C.

**Osmaronia cerasiformis** (Torr. & Gr.) Greene (syn. *Nuttallia cerasiformis*) (*Rosaceae*) Oso Berry   Native of western North America from Santa Barbara Co. in California northwards to British Columbia, growing in rocky valleys and canyons below 1700 m, flowering from February to April. A deciduous thicket of stems up to 2 m or a large shrub to 5 m tall, with fragrant, sometimes unisexual, flowers in drooping racemes, and bitter glaucous black fruit. Hardy to −20°C.

**Osteomeles schwerinii** G. Schneid. (*Rosaceae*) Native of western China in Yunnan and W. Sichuan, growing in hot, dry valleys at 350–2000 m, flowering in April–May. A low, twiggy, semi-deciduous bush up to 3 m tall, but usually c.1 m, easily recognized by its pinnate leaves. The fruits are small, black, and glabrous. *O. schwerinii* var. *microphylla* Rehder & Wilson with fewer, smaller leaflets, is said to be hardier. Any well-drained soil; full sun. Hardy to −5°C to −10°C.

**Simmondsia chinensis** (Link) C. K. Schneid. (*Buxaceae*) Jojoba Goatnut   In spite of its name, native to the deserts of southern California, Arizona and Mexico, below 1500 m, where it makes a much-branched evergreen shrub up to 2 m tall, with, from March to May, small green flowers, the male and female on different plants. Nuts edible and full of oil, so possibly of use as a crop in desert climates. In cultivation the plants will withstand some frost when established, and their main use is as a hedge in desert climates. Dry soil; full sun. Hardy to −10°C.

**Rhaphiolepis umbellata** (Thunb.) Makino (*Rosaceae*)   Native of Japan, except Hokkaido, and of Quelpaert Island, growing in scrub on the coast, flowering in April–June. An evergreen bushy shrub up to 4 m high; flowers scented; fruit about 1 cm across, black, shining. Easily grown, but intolerant of dry cold. Hardy to −10°C.

**Rhaphiolepis indica** Lindl. (*Rosaceae*) Indian Hawthorn   Native of southern China, from Yunnan eastwards at 150–1600 m, flowering both in autumn and spring. A low evergreen shrub; many different cultivars have been named, with white to deep pink flowers, and of varying height; 'Ballerina' is usually less than 0.6 m, while 'Majestic Beauty' can reach 5 m. Tolerant of full sun in all but the hottest desert climates, and hardier in winter than generally supposed. Hardy to −10°C.
'Springtime'   A strong-growing cultivar which can reach 2 m, but can be kept lower by pinching out the young shoots when they are still soft.

Rhus aromatica

Comptonia peregrina

Syringa pinnatifolia

Lindera umbellata

Daphne retusa

Daphne genkwa

Daphne pontica

Daphne collina

Daphne 'Manten'

Lonicera syringantha

Daphne 'Albert Burkwood'

Daphne × neapolitana

⅝ life size. Specimens from the Hillier Arboretum, 14th May

*Lindera benzoin* near New York

*Cornus mas*

*Daphne retusa*

**Rhus aromatica** Aiton (syn. *R. canadensis* Marsh) (*Anacardiaceae*) Fragrant Sumac Native of E. North America from Quebec to Florida and Indiana to Texas, growing in dry sandy and rocky places and open woods. A low shrub, often straggling, up to 2 m high. Leaves deciduous, trifoliate, the terminal leaflet often toothed; the whole plant aromatic. Flowers produced in April and May, usually before the leaves. A specially low-growing form, var. *arenaria*, is found on sand dunes in the mid-west. Hardy to −25°C.

**Comptonia peregrina** (L.) Coult. (*Myricaceae*) Sweet Fern Native of E. North America from Nova Scotia south to Georgia and east to Minnesota and Tennessee, growing in woods and pastures, flowering from April to June. A shrub up to 1.5 m high, suckering freely. Leaves linear-lanceolate, dark green, leathery, deeply lobed with oblique rounded segments, aromatic. Moist, lime-free soil. Hardy to −25°C.

**Syringa pinnatifolia** Hemsl. (*Oleaceae*) Native of Sichuan especially Baoxing, growing in scrub at 2200–3000 m, flowering in May. Flowers pink or white. It makes a shrub 2–3 m high, distinct for a lilac in its pinnate leaves and early flowering. Introduced by E. H. Wilson in 1904. Hardy to −25°C.

**Lindera umbellata** Thunb. (*Lauraceae*) Native of China, in Kiangsi and Hubei to W. Sichuan, and Japan in Honshu, Shikoku and Kyushu, in scrub at up to 3000 m, flowering in March–May. A deciduous shrub to 6 m with narrowly oblong to ovate-oblong leaves, 5–9 cm long, of ·thin texture, turning yellow in autumn. Acid soil; sun or part shade. Hardy to −15°C.

**Lindera benzoin** (L.) Blume (*Lauraceae*) Spice Bush Native of E. North America from Maine and Ontario to Kentucky, Missouri and S.E. Kansas, growing commonly in wet woods and by streams, flowering in March–May. It makes a shrub up to 4 m high, with oblong-obovate leaves, tapering at the base, and red or yellow fruit on female plants. The bark is aromatic; autumn colour yellow. Moist acid soil; sun or shade. Hardy to −25°C.

**Daphne retusa** Hems. (*Thymelaeaceae*) Native of Bhutan and S.E. Xizang, to Yunnan, Sichuan and Gansu. It grows on rocky mountainsides, among scrub and in open pine forest from 3000–4500 m, flowering in May–July. It makes a slow-growing bush, up to 1.2 m, with sweetly scented flowers. In

cultivation it slowly reaches 1 m, is tolerant of a wide range of soil, provided that it is humus-rich and well-drained, often flowering in autumn as well as in spring. Sun. Hardy to −20°C.

**Daphne genkwa** Sieb. & Zucc. (*Thymelaeaceae*) Native of N. and C. China, recorded in the provinces of Shantung, Cheking and Hubei, but especially common around Ichang growing on limestone cliffs, on boulders, on conglomerate and in piles of stones removed from cultivated fields, flowering in March and April. It is also recorded on grassy hills and plains, usually below 100 m. Flowers lilac-blue, fragrant; fruit reported to be white. Cultivated in Japan. In English gardens this beautiful species has proved difficult. It can make a shrub up to 1.5 m high, and 3 m in diameter as in one famous specimen in New York. Brickell & Matthew suggest that warmer summers than are usual in England are needed to ripen the wood, and the flowers are often spoiled by late frosts. Hardy to −20°C. There is also a white-flowered form.

**Daphne pontica** L. (*Thymelaeaceae*) Native of the Black Sea coast from Bulgaria to Turkey and Soviet Georgia, where it grows in woods, on shady cliffs or at high altitudes in the open, from 50–2200 m, flowering from February to October in the wild. It makes an evergreen bush up to 1.5 m high and as much across, with scented flowers. In cultivation easily grown in shade or semi-shade in humus-rich alkaline or acid soil, flowering in spring. Hardy to −20°C.

**Daphne collina** Dickson (*Thymelaeaceae*) Native of S. Italy, around Naples, but now considered a mere variety of *D. sericea* (p. 39). Cultivated *D. collina* is more compact than *D. sericea* with wider leaves, hairer beneath, and more flowers (up to 15) in each inflorescence. Hardy to −10°C.

**Daphne × mantensiana** 'Manten' A garden hybrid raised by Jack Manten, a nurseryman from White Rock BC, by crossing *D. retusa* (pollen) with *D.* × *burkwoodii* 'Somerset'. It makes an evergreen shrub up to 75 cm high, with well-scented flowers from spring onwards. Hardy to −15°C.

**Daphne × burkwoodii** Turrill '**Albert Burkwood**' A small, dense, rounded semi-evergreen shrub to 1 m tall; a garden hybrid raised in 1931 by Albert and Arthur Burkwood, by pollinating *D. cneorum* with *D. caucasica* pollen. Two clones are common in cultivation, 'Albert Burkwood' and 'Somerset', both raised

at the same time. They differ in many minor characters, but 'Somerset' is taller up to 1.5 m, and usually less spreading in growth with pinker but smaller flowers and broader leaves. Both flower in late spring and are easy to grow in a sunny position in well-drained soil. Hardy to −20°C.

**Daphne × neapolitana** Lodd. A hybrid of unknown origin, known since 1823, probably of *D. collina* crossed with *D. oleioides* or *D. cneorum*. It makes an evergreen shrub up to around 1 m high, with very fragrant flowers in early spring and sporadically through the summer. Hardy to −10°C.

**Lonicera syringantha** Maxim (*Caprifoliaceae*) Native of Xizang, W. Gansu and W. Sichuan, where it grows in mountain scrub at around 3600 m, flowering in June and July. A twiggy shrub to 2 m high, with scented flowers in late spring. Hardy to −25°C.

**Cornus mas** L. (*Cornaceae*) Cornelian Cherry Native of C. and S.E. Europe, from Belgium and France to Russia and Turkey and the Caucasus, growing in woods and scrub, flowering in March and April. Deciduous large shrub or small tree to 8 m, with opposite, ovate or elliptical leaves, 4–10 cm long, with 3–5 pairs of veins. Fruits oval, 12–15 mm long, red, juicy. Garden varieties (p. 180) such as 'Elegantissima' with yellow and pink variegated leaves, and 'Variegata' with white variegated leaves, are pretty but lack the elegant habit of growth of *C. alternifolia*. Hardy to −25°C.

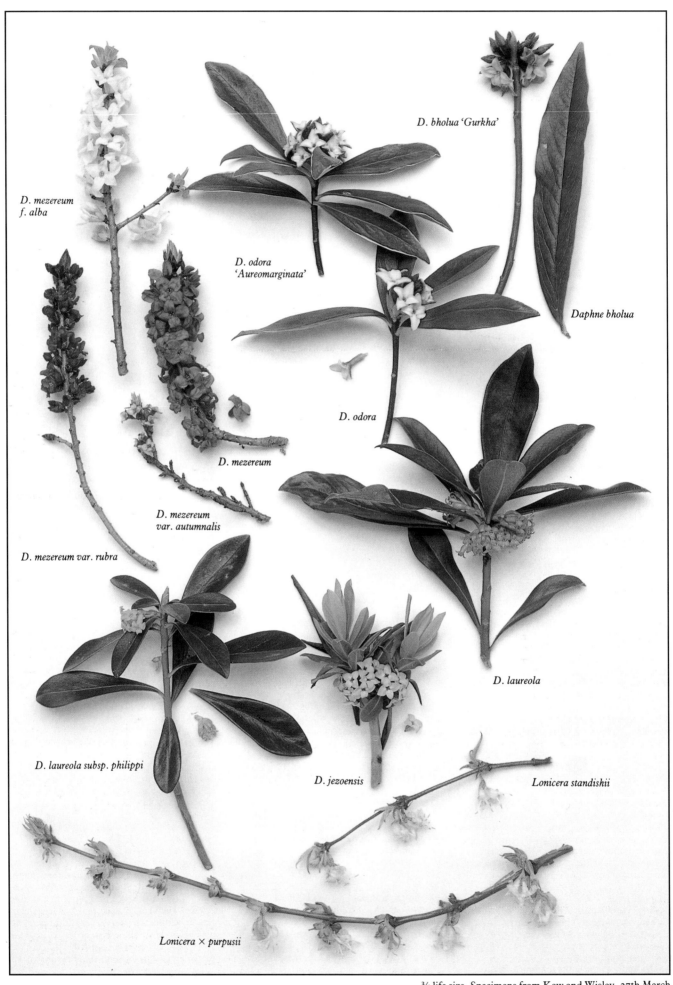

*D. mezereum
f. alba*

*D. bholua 'Gurkha'*

*D. odora
'Aureomarginata'*

*Daphne bholua*

*D. odora*

*D. mezereum*

*D. mezereum
var. autumnalis*

*D. mezereum var. rubra*

*D. laureola*

*D. laureola subsp. philippi*

*D. jezoensis*

*Lonicera standishii*

*Lonicera × purpusii*

¾ life size. Specimens from Kew and Wisley, 27th March

*Daphne sericea* near Mugla, Turkey

**Daphne mezereum** L. (*Thymelaeaceae*)
Mezereon   Native of Europe from Norway
and England to Spain and eastwards to Turkey,
Russia and Siberia, growing in woods, scrub
and on limestone screes at up to 2600 m,
flowering in early spring. A deciduous shrub up
to 1.5 m, with many upright stems. Easily
grown in sun or light shade. The beautiful red
berries are very poisonous. Hardy to −30°C.

**Daphne mezereum** f. *alba* (Weston) Schelle
White-flowered forms, with yellow or amber
fruit, occur wild and are frequently cultivated.
They apparently come true from seed.

**Daphne mezereum** var. *rubra* Aiton   Deep
red-purple flowered forms have been selected in
cultivation; a double red-purple form is
recorded.

**Daphne mezereum** var. *autumnalis* hort ex
Rehder   This variety begins flowering in late
autumn, continuing till spring. Its origin is not
recorded.

**Daphne odora** Thunb.   Native of China, and
long-cultivated so that its native range is
uncertain, but recorded wild in Chekiang,
Hupeh and Sichuan, at around 1000 m. An
evergreen shrub up to 1 m high and across, with
very sweetly scented flowers produced in
winter. The commonest form in cultivation
today is '**Aureomarginata**' (syn. 'Marginata') in
which the leaves are edged with a narrow yellow
line, and the flowers are pale inside, purplish-
pink outside. It is hardier than the plain-leaved
forms, doing well outdoors in London. There is
also a white form in cultivation. Hardy to
−10°C.

**Daphne bholua** Ham. ex D. Don   Native of
Uttar Pradesh eastwards to S.W. China
(Yunnan), growing in oak and rhododendron
forest and scrub from 1800–2600 m, flowering
from January to March. Evergreen or semi-
evergreen, and less hardy than var. *glacialis*,
growing and flowering well in dry shade, even in
central London. Common in the mountains
around Khatmandu, from where it was
introduced by Dr G. A. C. Herklots in 1962;
sometimes white flowered. Hardy to −5°C.
Var. *glacialis* (W. W. Smith & Cave)
Burtt   Native of western Nepal and Sikkim
growing in clearings in forest and in
Rhododendron scrub from 2000–3000 m,
flowering in February and March. Flowers
wonderfully scented. '**Gurkha**' is one
introduction of this variety, collected by Major
T. Spring-Smyth (T S-S 132 D) at 3000 m in E.
Nepal, illustrated here. Var. *glacialis* differs
from the type variety in being deciduous, with
white pink- to purple-backed flowers, mainly in
early spring. Tolerant of both acid and alkaline
soil. Hardy to −10°C or perhaps lower.

**Daphne laureola** L. Spurge Laurel   Native of
C. and S. England where it grows in woods and
hedges on chalk and limestone, and of Europe
from the Azores, France and Spain eastwards to
Greece and Turkey, and in North Africa, up to
2000 m, flowering in February and March, and
to June in the mountains. An evergreen shrub
up to 1.5 m high. Flowers scented towards
evening. Hardy to −20°C and shade tolerant.

**Daphne laureola** subsp. *philippi* (Gren.) Rouy
Native of the Pyrénées in France and Spain,
growing at high altitudes around 2000 m.
Differs from the type in its shorter often
decumbent stems and smaller flowers 3–5 mm
long.

**Daphne jezoensis** Maxim. ex Regel (syn. *D.
kamtschatica* var. *jezoensis* (Maxim.) Ohwi)
Native of Japan in Hokkaido and N.W.
Honshu, growing in woods usually under
deciduous trees, and in southern Sakkalin,
flowering in February–May. Flowers (usually
those of deeper colour) often scented. In
cultivation a small shrub up to 0.5 m, but up to
1 m in the wild. It requires woodland conditions
in leafy soil with good drainage. Often semi-
evergreen and late autumn or winter flowering
in cultivation in England. Hardy to −15°C.

**Daphne sericea** Vahl. (syn. *D. collina* Dickson)
Native of Italy, Sicily, Crete, W. and S.
Turkey, Syria and the Caucasus, growing in
open rocky scrub in maquis and in pine woods,
often on limestone, from sea level to 1800 m,
flowering in April and May and occasionally
again in autumn in cultivation. It makes a
rounded or upright shrub up to 1.1 m high,
suckers emerging at least 2 m from the parent
plant have been noted in Turkey. Flowers well-
scented. Hardiness very variable; the
horticultural form *D. collina* is reported to be
very hardy; more recent introductions very
tender. Hardy to −10°C or −15°C.

*Daphne sericea* f. *alba*

**Lonicera × purpusii** Rehder (*Caprifoliaceae*)
This is the hybrid between *L. standishii* and *L.
fragrantissima*, and is glabrous or slightly hairy,
with bristly-ciliate, ovate leaves. Known since
before 1920.

**Lonicera standishii** Jacques   Native of China
where it was long cultivated in gardens; found
wild in Ichang in W. Hubei (var. *lancifolia*
Rehder). A deciduous shrub up to 2.5 m, with
sweetly scented flowers produced in winter, and
oblong-lanceolate acuminate leaves in var.
*lancifolia*. The closely related *L. fragrantissima*
differs in its broadly obovate, evergreen leaves
and glabrous, not setose, branches and pedicels.
Native of eastern China. Both are easily grown,
but require a warm summer to set a good crop of
flower buds. Hardy to −15°C.

*F. suspensa*

*F. 'Arnold Dwarf'*

*Forsythia ovata
'Tetragold'*

*F. 'Arnold Giant'*

*F. 'Beatrix
Farrand'*

*R. odoratum*

*R. sanguineum
'Brocklebankii'*

*R. sanguineum
'Tydman's White'*

*Physocarpus opulifolius
'Dart's Gold'*

*R. sanguineum
'Lombartsii'*

*R. sanguineum
'Pulborough Scarlet'*

*R. sanguineum
'Atrorubens'*

*R. sanguineum
'King Edward VII'*

½ life size. Specimens from Wisley, 11th April

# FORSYTHIA AND RIBES

Ribes odoratum

Ribes × gordonianum

Ribes laurifolium

Ribes sanguineum

**Forsythia suspensa** (Thunb.) Vahl (*Oleaceae*) Native of China, found wild in W. Hubei, but cultivated in N. China. A lax and graceful shrub up to 3 m, distinguished by its hollow branches, with solid pith at the nodes. Leaves deciduous, ovate, cuneate, 6–10 cm long, toothed, often 3-foliate. The clone illustrated here is long-styled but other clones may be short-styled as is the case in primroses. Any soil; sun or part shade. Hardy to −25°C. Spring.

**Forsythia 'Arnold Giant'** *Forsythia × intermedia* 'Spectabilis' was treated with colchicine in order to produce a new fertile tetraploid species, and in 1939 the resulting seedling was named 'Arnold Giant'. It became the parent of several excellent hybrids such as 'Beatrix Farrand'.

**Forsythia ovata** Nakai **'Tetragold'** A tetraploid of *F. ovata*. produced artificially by colchicine, introduced in 1963. More robust than the type.

**Forsythia 'Arnold Dwarf'** A low shrub of spreading habit; a hybrid between *F. × intermedia* and *F. japonica* var. *saxatilis* raised at the Arnold Arboretum in 1941. Flowers greenish-yellow, long-styled. Leaves small.

**Forsythia 'Beatrix Farrand'** Raised by Professor Karl Sax at the Arnold Arboretum. This is said to be the result of backcrossing 'Arnold Giant', a tetraploid, to *F. × intermedia* 'Spectabilis'. Some tetraploid seedlings resulted and one was introduced to the trade both in America and later in Europe under the name 'Beatrix Farrand'. A very vigorous, erect shrub up to 3 m; leaves coarsely toothed; style pushing up between the stamens, so often self-fertilized and setting fruit. Hardy to −25°C.

**Ribes odoratum** Wendl. (*Grossulariaceae*) Native of C. North America, from Saskatchewan and Minnesota west to the Rockies, south to Texas, growing along streams, flowering in April–May. A spreading shrub up to 2.5 m high, with 3-lobed leaves, glabrous on both sides. Young stems downy. *R. aureum* Pursh. from south Dakota and New Mexico to Washington and California, at 800–

2600 m, is almost glabrous, with petals becoming orange as they age; flowers spicily scented. Both are attractive shrubs, flowering when young plants, suitable for sun or semi-shade. Hardy to −25°C.

**Physocarpus opulifolius** (L.) Maxim. **'Dart's Gold'** (*Rosaceae*) Nine Bark Native of E. North America from Quebec to Virginia, Tennessee and Michigan, growing in sandy and rocky places. The wild type makes a large shrub up to 3 m, with rounded corymbs of white or pinkish flowers in June, followed by swollen 3–5-lobed fruits which pop when squeezed. 'Dart's Gold' is a dwarf form with golden leaves, introduced in 1969. Hardy to −25°C.

**Ribes sanguineum** Pursh (*Grossulariaceae*) Native from N. California to British Columbia, in pine and *Thuja* forest from 600–1800 m, flowering from April to June. Var. *glutinosum* (Benth.) Loud. (syn. *R. albidum*) from chaparral and open woodland in California, below 600 m, has sometimes paler flowers and usually more flowers in a hanging raceme; many of the garden varieties belong to this. *R. indecorum* Eastw. from Santa Barbara southwards, has white flowers in October–March. *R. sanguineum* is an erect deciduous shrub 1–3 m high, with 3–5-lobed leaves, rounded in outline, dark green above, variably pubescent beneath; berries black with a grey bloom. Discovered by Archibald Menzies in 1793 and introduced by David Douglas in 1826. Any soil; sun or part shade. Hardy to −20°C. The following clones are those usually seen in cultivation:
**'Atrorubens'** An old variety, grown at the Horticultural Society's garden at Kensington in 1837. This probably originated from Douglas's introduction.
**'Tydman's White'** An improved pale form, later flowering than 'Albidum'.
**'Brocklebankii'** A golden-leaved variety, which makes a slow-growing shrub up to 1.5 m, with pale flowers. The leaves scorch in full sun, so planting in semi-shade is beneficial. Raised by Thomas Winkworth, head gardener to R. Brocklebank at Haughton Hall, Cheshire.
**'King Edward VII'** A lower and more spreading bush than 'Pulborough Scarlet', up to

2 m; slightly later flowering. Introduced by Cannell's nursery, before 1904.
**'Pulborough Scarlet'** An upright variety, to 3 m in height. Found in 1933 in Pulborough, Sussex.
**'Lombartsii'** A form with rather large, pink flowers, with a pale centre.

**Ribes × gordonianum** Beaton The hybrid between *R. sanguineum* and *R. odoratum* raised by Donald Beaton at Hatfield, Hertfordshire, and named after his employer, William Gordon. A robust shrub up to 2.5 m high, with orange-pink racemes, freely produced, and 3-lobed leaves smaller than *R. sanguineum*. Hardy to −20°C.

**Ribes laurifolium** Jancz. (*Grossulariaceae*) Native of W. Sichuan, where it was collected by Wilson at 2300 m on rocks on Wa-shan, and noted as rare. It makes a low, semi-prostrate evergreen shrub up to 1 m high, flowering in early spring. Male and female flowers are on different plants; the male are larger. Hardy to −15°C.

41

Forsythia ovata

Forsythia
koreana

Edgeworthia
chrysantha

Abeliophyllum
distichum

Forsythia
giraldiana

Forsythia suspensa

Forsythia
'Bronxensis'

Forsythia 'Spectabilis'

Forsythia 'Lynwood'

Forsythia
'Beatrix Farrand'

Forsythia 'Densiflora'

Shepherdia argentea

½ life size. Specimens from Kew, 28th March

*Forsythia 'Goldzauber'*

*Forsythia vitellina* in New York

*Forsythia 'Karl Sax'*

**Forsythia koreana** (Rehd.) Nakai (*F. viridissima* var. *koreana* Rehd.) (*Oleaceae*) Native of Korea. Introduced to the Arnold Arboretum from near Seoul by Wilson in 1917. Differs from *F. viridissima* in having lanceolate leaves to 12 cm long. An upright shrub to 3 m. Any soil. Sun or part shade. Hardy to −20°C.

**Forsythia ovata** Nakai (*Oleaceae*) Native of Korea. A small shrub up to 1.5 m; very early flowering in cultivation, easily recognized by its short-petalled flowers. Leaves ovate, rounded at base. Any soil; sun or part shade. Hardy to −20°C.

**Abeliophyllum distichum** Nakai (*Oleaceae*) Native of C. Korea. A spreading shrub to 2 m. Flowers scented, in April or May. In cultivation it is best on a wall, where it gets extra heat to ripen the wood. There is a pink-flowered form in cultivation in the USA. Hardy to −20°C.

**Forsythia giraldiana** Lingelsh. (*Oleaceae*) Native of N. China, in Gansu, Shensi and Hubei. Deciduous shrub to 3 m, graceful when old, often with black young shoots, with lamellate pith. The earliest of all forsythias. Any soil; sun or part shade. Hardy to −20°C.

**Forsythia 'Lynwood'** A sport of 'Spectabilis', from which it differs in having fewer toothed leaves, and stiffer, not curled petals.

**Forsythia 'Beatrix Farrand'** Raised by Professor Karl Sax at the Arnold Arboretum. This is said to be the result of backcrossing 'Arnold Giant', a tetraploid, to *F.* × *intermedia* 'Spectabilis'. A very vigorous erect shrub up to 3 m; style pushing up between the stamens, so often self-fertilized and setting fruit. Spring.

**Edgworthia chrysantha** Lindl. (syn. *E. papyrifera* Sieb. & Zucc.) (*Thymelaeaceae*) Native of China, especially Kiangsi, and commonly cultivated elsewhere, e.g. around Ichang, growing at 300–1600 m, especially by streams. A deciduous shrub to 1.6 m high, with narrowly ovate leaves to 12 cm long, silky beneath, flowering in April. The flowers are slightly scented, rarely reddish. It is cultivated also in Japan for making a special paper. Any soil; sun or part shade. Hardy to −15°C.

**Forsythia 'Bronxensis'** A seedling of *F. koreana* raised at the Bronx Botanic garden, New York, in about 1939.

**Forsythia suspensa** (Thunb.) Vahl (*Oleaceae*) Native of China, especially in W. Hubei, growing in scrub and on cliffs, at 300–1200 m, flowering in April. A lax and graceful shrub up to 3 m, distinguished from other species by having hollow branches, with solid pith at the nodes, not lamellate (interrupted) pith. Any soil; sun or part shade. Hardy to −25°C.

**Forsythia × intermedia** Zab. Most cultivated forsythias are clones of this hybrid between *F.suspensa* and *F.viridissima*, first raised in Germany in 1885. They have irregularly lamellate pith and often 3-lobed leaves on vigorous shoots.
**'Vitellina'** introduced in 1899, has rather deep yellow, long-styled flowers. Growth erect.
**'Densiflora'** has light yellow, long-styled flowers.
**'Spectabilis'** has bright yellow, short-styled flowers, sometimes with 5 or 6 corolla lobes. The commonest forsythia in cultivation both in Europe and North America.

**Shepherdia argentea** Nuttall (*Elaeagnaceae*) Buffaloberry. Native of the prairies from Manitoba to New Mexico, growing along streams, flowering in May. A rather thorny dioecious shrub up to 6 m high. Leaves opposite, narrowly oblong, silvery above and beneath. Fruits ovoid, scarlet, in autumn.

**Forsythia 'Goldzauber'** A hybrid between 'Beatrix Farrand' and 'Lynwood', introduced in Germany in 1974. Long-styled. An upright shrub up to *c*.2 m.

**Forsythia 'Karl Sax'** 'Arnold Giant' crossed with *F.* × *intermedia* 'Spectabilis' produced several seedlings. This one is named after its originator, Professor Sax. It is a tetraploid, similar to 'Beatrix Farrand' (q.v.) but bushier with slightly deeper yellow flowers.

**Forsythia 'Minigold'** A small-flowered but very free-flowering hybrid, probably of *F. ovata*. Deciduous shrub to 2 m.

*Forsythia 'Minigold'*

*Edgeworthia chrysantha* in Devon

43

Pieris formosa
var. forrestii F. 26518

Pieris 'Purity'

Pieris floribunda

Pieris taiwanensis

Pieris japonica 'Variegata'

P. japonica
from Yakushima

Pieris formosa

Pieris 'Grayswood'

Pieris japonica f. rosea

Pieris 'Flamingo'

Pieris 'Blush'

⅝ life size. Specimens from the Valley Gardens, Windsor, 11th April

**Pieris japonica** (Thunb.) D. Don (*Ericaceae*)
Native of Japan, where it grows in open forest in the mountains of Shikoku, Kyushu and Honshu, flowering during March and April. It requires a sheltered position as it is often damaged by frost but is easily grown in moist, peaty, acid soil. *P. japonica* makes an evergreen bush or small tree up to 4 m high and wide; the young leaves are copper red, turning green when mature. Hardy to −20°C. Spring.

**P. japonica 'Variegata'** This cultivar is slow-growing but will eventually make a shrub up to 4 m high.

**P. japonica 'Purity'** A native of Japan, this variety is thought to have come from Yakushima but its origins are uncertain. As the name suggests, the flowers are pure white and are larger than *P. japonica*.

**P. japonica** (from Yakushima) This form of *P. japonica* is found on the small island of Yakusima, off the south coast of mainland Japan, growing in low mountain forest with the dwarf *Rhododendron yakusimanum*, *Cornus kousa* and other shrubs. It is very compact in the wild and slow-growing but less compact in gardens.

**P. japonica 'Grayswood'** This cultivar is notable for its very long, more or less unbranched panicles of white flowers. It was raised as a seedling in the garden of Geoffrey Pilkington at Grayswood, near Haslemere, Surrey. Roy Lancaster suggests that *P. taiwanensis* (see below) was one parent.

**P. japonica** f. **rosea** This name can be given to any pink-flowered form of *P. japonica*. A plant collected on Mt. Daisen by K. Wada with deep pink flowers has been named *P. japonica* f. *rosea* 'Daisen'. Some seedlings from this have proved to be even deeper pink and one was named 'Christmas Cheer' by Mr Wada in around 1967.

**P. japonica 'Flamingo'** A variety with deep pink flowers introduced by Lambert Gardens, Portland, Oregon in 1961.

**P. japonica 'Blush'** A pale pink form introduced by Messrs Hillier in 1967.

**Pieris taiwanensis** Hayata (*Ericaceae*) Native of Formosa, where it is found in open, mountainous areas from 2000–3500 m. It was introduced to Britain by Wilson in 1918 and has proved to be hardy and generally undamaged by frost. It makes a compact, evergreen shrub up to 2 m high, producing flowers in Spring. It differs from *P. japonica* in its erect racemes of flowers, 8–15 cm long. Hardy to −15°C.

**Pieris floribunda** (Pursh) Benth. & Hook. (*Ericaceae*) Native of the S.E. United States where it grows on moist wooded hillsides in the Alleghanies from Virginia to Georgia, flowering in May. It makes a compact, evergreen shrub up to 2 m high; racemes erect, 5–10 cm long. Hardy to −25°C. Early spring.

**Pieris formosa** var. **forrestii** (Harrow) Airy Shaw (*Ericaceae*) Native of S.W. China, in Yunnan, both in the Dali mountains and at the southwestern end of the Likiang valley, as well as farther west on the Burma-Yunnan border, growing in *Rhododendron* scrub at 2000–3000 m, flowering in April–May. The collection shown here (**Forrest 26518**) comes from the latter locality and Forrest himself considered it the finest form of the variety, especially in its large

flowers, though the brown sepals are typical of var. *formosa*. Its young foliage is red, and in other clones of var. *forrestii* can be either bright pink, red, or green. 'Wakehurst' is a clone of var. *forrestii* of uncertain origin; its young leaves start brilliant red, before turning pink, then white to yellowish-green as they expand. Hardy to −15°C.

**Pieris formosa** (Wall.) D. Don (*Ericaceae*) Native of the E. Himalayas, Assam, Burma and parts of south-west and central China, this evergreen shrub will grow up to 8 m high. The leathery, rather stiff, broad leaves are a dull brownish-red when young, and the flowers are borne during May. The brown sepals are one character by which var. *formosa* can be distinguished from the white-sepalled var.

*forrestii*. The most tender of the species, usually with larger rounded flowers; hardy to −10°C.

**Pieris 'Firecrest'** This hybrid was introduced by Messrs Waterer, Sons and Crisp. It is similar to 'Forest Flame' (q.v.) and the parents are said to be *P. formosa* var. *forrestii* (F. 8945) × *P. japonica*.

**Pieris 'Forest Flame'** A very popular clone which occurred as a self-sown seedling; the parents are probably *P. japonica* × *P. formosa* or *P. formosa* var. *forrestii*. When young 'Forest Flame' makes a compact bush with well-coloured foliage; the flowers are produced in April–May. When mature it can grow up to 2.5 m. Hardy to −15°C.

Pieris 'Grayswood'

Pieris formosa var. forrestii

Pieris 'Forest Flame'

Pieris 'Firecrest'

Pieris formosa

*Stachyurus praecox*

*Corylopsis sinensis f. veitchiana*

*Corylopsis gotoana*

*Corylopsis spicata*

*Corylopsis sinensis f. veitchiana*

*Corylopsis pauciflora*

*Corylopsis sinensis var. willmottiae*

*Sycopsis sinensis*

½ life size. Specimens from the Savill Gardens, Windsor, 4th April

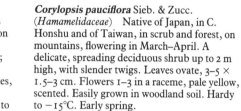

*Corylopsis sinensis* var. *sinensis* in Brooklyn Botanic Gardens

*Corylopsis 'Spring Purple'*

**Stachyurus praecox** Sieb. & Zucc.
(*Stachyuraceae*)   Native of Japan, where it is
common from S.W. Hokkaido southwards, on
the edges of forest and in scrub, flowering in
March and April. Deciduous shrub to to 5 m;
leaves nearly glabrous, 7–12 × 3–6 cm,
narrowly ovate, acuminate. Flowering racemes,
4–10 cm long. Fruit fleshy. Easily grown in
moist, woodland soil, and part shade. Hardy to
−20°C. Early spring.

**Corylopsis sinensis** Hemsley var. **sinensis**
(*Hamamelidaceae*)   Native of China, from
Jiangxi to Hubei and E. Sichuan, growing in
scrub and forest at 1300–2000 m, flowering in
April. Deciduous shrub to 4 m. Leaves obovate-
oblong to ovate, cordate at the base, apex
cuspidate, with curved elegant teeth, silky hairy
beneath and on the petiole. Raceme 3–7 cm
long. Flowers 12–18, yellow, semi-rotate,
scented; petals 7–8 mm; anthers shorter than
the petals, yellow or orange. See also p. 75. The
largest-flowered of the Chinese species, growing
especially well on the east coast of North
America. Moist, leafy soil; part shade. Hardy to
−15°C. Early spring.

**Corylopsis sinensis** f. **veitchiana** (Bean)
Morley & Chao (*Hamamelidaceae*)   Native of
China, in W. Hubei, fairly common (*fide*
Wilson) on forest edges and in scrub from 1300–
2000 m, flowering in April. A deciduous, bushy
shrub up to 2.5 m, with rather thick twigs.
Leaves oval or ovate, glabrous beneath when
mature. Flowers 6–10 in a raceme up to 4 cm
long, campanulate, scented. Anthers reddish
when fresh, equalling or longer than the petals.

**Corylopsis gotoana** Makino (*Hamamelidaceae*)
Native of Japan, in S. Honshu, Shikoku and
Kyushu, and Korea(?), flowering in April. A
large shrub or small tree up to 5 m in the wild,
but usually less than 2 m in cultivation, with
twigs between *C. spicata* and *C. pauciflora*.
Leaves obovate, bluish-green above, strongly
glaucous beneath. Flowers 5–10 in a raceme,
about 1 cm long. Stamens nearly as long as the
petals. Leafy soil; part shade. Hardy to −20°C.

**Corylopsis spicata** Sieb. & Zucc.
(*Hamamelidaceae*)   Native of Japan, in
Shikoku where it is rare in scrub in the
mountains, flowering in March and April. A
stiff spreading shrub, with zig-zag branches, up
to 2 m high, with thick twigs. Leaves ovate-
orbicular, glaucous beneath, 3–10 × 2–8 cm.
Flowers 7–10 in a narrow raceme, yellow-green;
anthers red, at first protruding. Needs acid,
woodland soil, and part shade. Hardy to −20°C.

**Corylopsis pauciflora** Sieb. & Zucc.
(*Hamamelidaceae*)   Native of Japan, in C.
Honshu and of Taiwan, in scrub and forest, on
mountains, flowering in March–April. A
delicate, spreading deciduous shrub up to 2 m
high, with slender twigs. Leaves ovate, 3–5 ×
1.5–3 cm. Flowers 1–3 in a raceme, pale yellow,
scented. Easily grown in woodland soil. Hardy
to −15°C. Early spring.

**Corylopsis sinensis** var. **willmottiae**. Stat nov.
(Basionym *C. willmottiae* Rehder & Wilson,
Plantae Wilsonianae 1:425 (1913)
(*Hamamelidaceae*)   Native of China, in W.
Sichuan, growing in dense scrub and forest, in
valleys from 1800–2500 m, flowering in April. A
deciduous shrub up to 4 m, with rather slender
twigs. Leaves oval to broadly ovate, apex
cuspidate, 4–10 × 2–8 cm, glabrous except on
the veins, or occasionally with a few stellate
hairs beneath. Raceme 5–7 cm long. Flowers
10–17, pale yellow, rotate, scented; petals
4–5 mm; anthers shorter than the petals, usually
yellow. A graceful species with rotate flowers in
long racemes, in size between var. *sinensis*
(p. 75) and var. *platypetala* (p. 75). Hardy to
−15°C. '**Spring Purple**' is an attractive selection
with purple young stems and reddish young
leaves.

**Corylopsis glabrescens** Franch. & Sav.
(*Hamamelidaceae*)   Native of Japan, in the
Kirishima mountains of Kyushu, flowering in
April. A large shrub, to 7 m in the wild, but to
2 m in cultivation, with rather slender twigs.
Leaves broadly cordate, acute, glaucous
beneath. Flowers 5–10 in a raceme, scented,
about 1.5 cm long (as large as *C. pauciflora*).
Stamens half as long as the usually notched
petals. Leafy soil; part shade. Hardy to −10°C.

**Sycopsis sinensis** Oliver (*Hamamelidaceae*)
Native of C. China, in W. Hubei and E.
Sichuan, in gorges and rocky places near
streams, at 600–1300 m, flowering in April. An
erect evergreen shrub up to 7 m. Leaves entire
or toothed. Flowers in short-stalked clusters,
male and female separate, surrounded by
characteristic brown hairy bracts. Easily grown
in sun or part shade on acid or chalky soils.
Hardy to −15°C.

× **Sycoparrotia semidecidua** Endress &
Anliker   A hybrid between *Parrotia persica* and
*Sycopsis sinensis*, which makes a spreading
shrub, with mostly evergreen leaves
intermediate in shape between its parents.
Raised in Switzerland and described in 1968.
Hardy to −20°C.

*Corylopsis sinensis* f. *veitchiana*

*Corylopsis glabrescens*

× *Sycoparrotia semidecidua*

Acer palmatum 'Senkaki'

Acer palmatum
f. dissectum

Acer triflorum

Acer palmatum
'Ozakozuki'

Acer maximowiczii

Acer japonicum
f. aconitifolium

Acer japonicum
'Aureum'

Acer monspessulanum

Acer circinatum

Acer pensylvanicum
'Erythrocladum'

Acer crataegifolium 'Veitchii'

⅖ life size. Specimens from the Hillier Arboretum, 14th May

Acer palmatum f. linearilobum

Acer palmatum 'Shindeshojo'

Acer glabrum

**Acer palmatum** Thunb. (*Aceraceae*) Momjii, Japanese Maple   Native of E. China, Korea and Japan, where it is common in woods in the hills and mountains, flowering in April and May. Deciduous shrub or small tree to 10 m in the wild; leaves in the wild 5–7 lobed, 4–7 cm wide, exceptionally variable; many garden forms have been selected, of which a sample is shown here. Any moist soil; part shade and shelter from drying wind. Hardy to −25°C. Spring, and good autumn colour.

**Acer palmatum 'Senkaki'** (Syn. 'Sango Kaku' (Coral Tower))   Noted for the brilliant red of its young twigs, which are especially bright in winter. Growth upright when young, finally to 7 m. Leaves rather small, light green, changing to orange-yellow in autumn.

**Acer palmatum 'Ozakazuki'**   This is one of the finest of the varieties of Japanese maple, with large green leaves, 12–14 cm wide, colouring bright scarlet in autumn. A robust cultivar forming a rounded tree up to 7 m in old age, known since the mid-19th C.

**Acer palmatum f. linearilobum**   In this form the leaves are divided almost to the base into 7 or sometimes 5 linear lobes with no or only shallow teeth. There are several named cultivars in this group, some purple or red as in 'Red Pygmy'. 'Scolopendrifolium' has 5-lobed leaves. 'Villa Taranto' is a low-growing cultivar with pinkish young leaves. In **f. dissectum** the lobes of the leaves are deeply toothed, narrow, and separate from the base.

**Acer palmatum 'Shindeshojo'**   A small cultivar with brilliant crimson-scarlet young foliage, turning to mottled green and red in summer, and red and orange in autumn. This plant reaches a height of about 2 m, with small leaves at most 6 cm long on young shoots.

**Acer triflorum** Komarov   Native of N. China and N. Korea, growing in coniferous and deciduous forests. Close to *A. nikoense*, but with dark brown, furrowed bark. A deciduous tree to 15 m; leaves glaucous beneath; nutlets hairy. Autumn colour very reliable, a brilliant crimson. Any soil; sun or part shade. Hardy to −25°C.

**Acer maximowiczii** Pax   Native of Gansu, of W. Hubei around Ichang, and N.W. Sichuan, in woods from 1200–2500 m, flowering in May. Deciduous small tree to 4 m. A member of the snakebark group. Leaves 3- or 5-lobed, with tufts of white hairs in the axils of the veins

beneath. Moist soil; sun or part shade. Hardy to −20°C.

**Acer japonicum** Thunb. **'Aureum'** Golden Full Moon Maple   *Acer japonicum* is native of Japan, on Hokkaido and Honshu, growing in forest in the mountains, flowering in May. The leaves are usually 9-lobed, less than halfway to the base of the leaf; the tree may reach 15 m. 'Aureum' is an excellent cultivar, with beautiful yellow-green leaves and contrasting red flowers and fruits. It has long been known in Japan, and has been in Europe since the mid-19th C. Specimens over 100 years old are 5–6 m high. Any good soil; sun or part shade, shelter from wind. Hardy to −25°C.
In f. **aconitifolium** the large leaves are divided to the base into usually 11 lobes and each lobe is further divided almost to the midrib. Autumn colour is usually a good red. Height around 5 m.

**Acer circinatum** Pursh. Vine Maple   Native of California to British Columbia, growing in forests along streams at up to 1500 m, flowering in April and May. An elegant shrub or small tree up to 10 m, more heat-tolerant than Japanese maples, turning yellow, orange and scarlet in autumn. A cut-leaved cultivar 'Munroe' is in cultivation, collected in the Cascades. Its leaves are rather similar to those of *A. japonicum* f. *aconitifolium*. Any good soil; part shade or shade. Hardy to −20°C.

**Acer monspessulanum** L.   Native of Germany, France and Portugal eastwards to Romania, Turkey and North Africa, growing in dry, rocky places, flowering from April to May. A small tree or shrub, to 12 m high, with 3-lobed, leathery leaves 3–8 cm long, glaucous beneath. A very hardy small tree, tolerant of winter cold and summer heat and drought. Any soil; full sun. Hardy to −25°C.

**Acer crataegifolium** Sieb. & Zuc. Hawthorn-leaved Maple   Native of Japan, in Honshu, Shikoku and Kyushu, where it is common in woods and scrub at low altitudes, flowering in May. **'Veitchii'** is a pink and white variegated cultivar with blotchy leaves, introduced in the late 19th C. A member of the snakebark group. A large deciduous shrub or small tree up to 6 m, of densely twiggy growth; leaves 5–8 cm long. Any soil; sun or part shade. Hardy to −25°C.

**Acer pensylvanicum** L. **'Erythrocladum'** Moosewood   Native of Quebec to Manitoba, south to Tennessee, growing in damp rich woods. The wild form makes a slender small deciduous shrub or tree, with beautiful striped

Acer forrestii in Yunnan

bark, and pendulous, scented flowers in May and June. Leaves yellow in autumn. 'Erythrocladum', introduced in Germany in 1904, was selected for its bright pink young twigs. It generally forms a rather weak growing shrub. *A. pensylvanicum* is the only American member of the snakebark maples, a common group in China and Japan. Acid or non-chalky soil; sun or part shade. Hardy to −35°C.

**Acer forrestii** Diels   Native of W. China, in S. Sichuan and on the eastern side of the Lijiang mountains in N. Yunnan, at *c.* 3000 m, on limestone. It makes a small deciduous tree up to 15 m, with reddish young twigs. Flowers green in an elongated hanging raceme appearing in May. Leaves 3-lobed, the middle lobe long acuminate, glaucous beneath, glabrous except in the vein axils. One of the hardier of the snake bark maples, of upright growth when young. Any soil; sun or part shade. Hardy to −20°C.

**Acer glabrum** Torr. Mountain Maple   Native of the mountains of W. North America, eastward to S. Dakota, on rocks and in coniferous woods, from 1300–2000 m, flowering in April and May. A small tree or shrub from 1–6 m high. Leaves usually 3-lobed, 1.5–5 cm long, 2–4 cm wide. In cultivation a rather upright tree, with leaves yellow in autumn. Any soil. Sun or part shade. Hardy to −25°C.

Magnolia stellata
'Norman Gould'

Magnolia × loebneri
'Merrill'

Magnolia sargentiana
var. robusta

Magnolia 'Eric Savill'

Magnolia × loebneri
'Leonard Messel'

Magnolia
'Neil McEchern'

Magnolia cylindrica

Magnolia denudata

Magnolia 'Wada's Memory'

Magnolia stellata

⅔ life size. Specimens from the Savill Garden, Windsor, 30th April

*Magnolia denudata*

*Magnolia dawsoniana* at Chyverton

*Magnolia campbellii var. mollicomata* in Cornwall

**Magnolia sargentiana** Rehd. & Wils. var. **robusta** Rehd. & Wils, (*Magnoliaceae*)   Native of W. Sichuan, on Wa-Shan, in woods and open country at 2300 m, flowering in April(?). Leaves 14–21 cm long, to 8.5 cm wide, narrowly oblong–obovate, cuneate at base. Acid or neutral rich soil; sun or part shade. Hardy to −15°C. Spring.

**M. × loebneri 'Merrill'**   Raised at the Arnold Arboretum around 1939; a cross between *M. kobus* and *M. stellata*. Shrub to 5 m.

**M. stellata** (Sieb. & Zucc.) Maxim.   Native of Japan, in E. C. Honshu, in woods in the mountains flowering in late March and April. Small tree or large shrub to 5 m. Flowers white, or pink in var. *keiskei*, the 12–18 narrow petals all equal, to 6 cm long. Acid or neutral soil; sun or part shade. Hardy to −15°C. *M. kobus* differs in having 3 narrow sepals and 6–9 broader petals. It makes a large tree to 18 m. Early spring.

**M. stellata** (Sieb. & Zucc.) Maxim. **'Norman Gould'**   A tetraploid form of *M. stellata* raised at Wisley by E. K. Janaki Ammal using colchicine. Heavier and more robust than normal *M. stellata*.

**M. cylindrica** Wilson   Native of Anhui, in shady ravines at 1000–1200 m on Wang Shan, and elsewhere in E. China, flowering in April. Flowers with small sepals which soon fall and 6 petals about 10 cm long. Acid or neutral leafy soil; sun or part shade. Hardy to −15°C.

**M. 'Eric Savill'**   A seedling of *M. sprengeri* var. *diva*, raised at the Savill Gardens, Windsor. It

has made a small tree about 7 m tall, with numerous ascending branches. Flowers 22 cm in diameter, before the leaves.

**M. × loebneri** Kache **'Leonard Messel'** Raised at Nymans, Sussex before 1950 and thought to be a cross between *M. kobus* and *M. stellata* var. *rosea*. Leaves to 12 cm, broadly oblanceolate, obtuse, hairy on the midrib beneath.

**M. 'Neil McEchern'**   A seedling of *M. stellata* raised at Windsor from seed collected at the Villa Taranto in N. Italy. Possibly a hybrid with *M. kobus*. A small tree, *c*.6m at present.

**M. denudata** Desrouss (*M. heptapeta*)   Native of China, but wild distribution uncertain, and long cultivated there and in Japan. Flowers with 9 similar petals, 7.5 cm long, pure white, scented. Acid or neutral leafy soil; sun or part shade. Hardy to −20°C. Spring.

**M. 'Wada's Memory'**   Named after the Japanese nurseryman. A small tree to 6 m, with characteristic nodding, floppy flowers.

**M. campbellii** Hook, fil. & Thoms. var. *mollicomata* (W. W. Sm.) F. K. Ward   Native of Yunnan, on either side of the Salween R. and of neighbouring Burma, in temperate rain forest, flowering in March and April. Deciduous large shrub or tree to 20 m. Leaves broadly elliptic, acute or acuminate, rounded or broadly cuneate at the base, 10–25 cm long. Flowers pink to purplish, crimson or white, on a downy peduncle. Acid or neutral, humus-rich soil; sun or part shade. Hardy to −10°C, but the flower buds often killed by late frosts. Subsp.

*Michelia doltsopa*

*campbellii* from C. Nepal to Bhutan, differs in its usually glabrous peduncle.

**M. dawsoniana** Rehd. & Wilson.   Native of W. Sichuan, to the southeast of Kangding at 2000–2300 m, flowering in May. Deciduous shrub or tree to 15 m, very rare in the wild. Leaves obovate, leathery, shining green above, 8–14 cm long. Flowers to 12 cm long. Moist, leafy soil; sun or part shade. Hardy to −10°C. Early spring.

**Michelia doltsopa** Buch-Ham. (*Magnoliaceae*) Native of S.W. Nepal, east to Burma and Yunnan, in evergreen oak forest at 1830–2500m, flowering in February–April. Evergreen tree to 25 m. Flowers in leaf axils, 10–15 cm across, very well-scented. Moist, acid soil; sun or part shade. Hardy to −5°C. Early summer.

*Magnolia × soulangiana*

*Magnolia 'Picture'*

*Magnolia 'Rustica Rubra'*

*Magnolia 'Manchu Fan'*

*Magnolia 'Lennei Alba'*

*Magnolia 'Heaven Sent'*

*Magnolia 'Ann'*

*Magnolia 'Rouged Alabaster'*

$\frac{2}{3}$ life size. Specimens from the Valley Gardens, Windsor, 13th May

**Magnolia × soulangiana** Soulange-Bodin
Raised in the garden of Mr Soulange-Bodin at
Fromont near Paris before 1825. A hybrid
between *M. denudata* and *M. liliiflora*. Many
different varieties have been raised and named
varying in colour from white to deep pinkish-
purple and in flower size and shape. All flower
in late spring, the first flowers opening before
the leaves, the later with the leaves. All need
rich, moist leafy soil, preferably acid or neutral,
and tolerate sun or light shade. They are hardy
to −20°C, but the opening flowers are often
damaged by late frosts.

**M. × soulangiana 'Picture'** Originated in
Japan by Wada's Nurseries and introduced to
England before 1968.

**M. × soulangiana 'Rustica Rubra'**
Originated in Boskoop before 1893. A fine deep
pink variety with large, very rounded flowers.

**M. 'Manchu Fan'** Raised by D. T. Gresham
in Santa Cruz, California, in 1955; a hybrid
between *M.* 'Lennei Alba' and *M. × veitchii*.
Flowers upright taller and narrower than
'Lennei Alba'. Growth strong, tree-like.

**M. × soulangiana 'Lennei Alba'** Raised in
Switzerland around 1900, possibly a seedling of
*M. soulangiana* 'Lennei'. A pure white of heavy
substance.

**M. 'Heaven Sent'** Raised by D. Todd
Gresham of Santa Cruz, California, in 1955, by
crossing *M. × veitchii* with *M. liliiflora*.

**M. 'Ann'** A hybrid between *M. liliiflora* and
*M. stellata*, raised at the National Arboretum in
Washington D.C. in 1955.

**M. 'Rouged Alabaster'** Raised by D. Todd
Gresham in 1955, by crossing *M. × veitchii* with
*M.* 'Lennei Alba'. The exterior of the sepals is
often more marked with purplish-pink than in
the flower shown here.

**M. × soulangiana 'Norbertii'** Raised in
France before 1935. Of erect habit.

**M. liliiflora** Desrouss (*M. pentapeta*)
(*Magnoliaceae*) Native of China, but so long
cultivated that its native habitat is obscure. A
deciduous shrub to 3 m. Leaves 10–18 cm long,
obovate or elliptic ovate. Flowers either before
or with the leaves, and usually flowering
intermittently through the summer, from April
onwards; petals 6, 8–10 cm long, white inside,
reddish or purplish outside. Any rich, leafy soil,
sun or part shade. Hardy to −20°C. Var. *nigra*
(Nichols) Rehd. is said to have larger flowers,
12 cm long, pale purple inside, and be hardier
than the ordinary variety. Both have long been
cultivated in Japan.

**M. denudata** Desrouss **'Purple Eye'**
(*Magnoliaceae*) A form or possibly hybrid of
*M. denudata* with a fine rounded pure white
flower, stained purple at the base. There is also
a pinkish red variety var. *purpurascens*, grown in
Japan, which we have not seen.

**M. 'Elizabeth'** A hybrid between *M.
acuminata* (L.) L., the Cucumber Tree, with
green flowers, and *M. denudata*, raised at the
Brooklyn Botanic Garden in 1950. Habit similar
to a robust *M. × soulangiana*. Our photograph
shows an original plant in bud, and does not do
it justice. When in full flower, it is a most
beautiful pale yellow.

*Magnolia 'Rustica Rubra' at Kew*

*Magnolia 'Norbertii'*

*Magnolia liliiflora*

*Magnolia denudata 'Purple Eye'*

*Magnolia 'Elizabeth'*

*Magnolia wilsonii* at Benmore, Argyll

**Magnolia sinensis** (Rehd. & Wils.) Stapf (*Magnoliaceae*)   Native of China, in northwestern Sichuan, growing in scrub and forest at 2000–2600 m, flowering in June. Deciduous shrub to 5 m in the wild, but more in gardens, of spreading habit. Leaves broadly obovate or elliptic-obovate, rounded with a short point at the apex, silky hairy on the veins beneath. Flowers 10–13 cm across, scented. Tolerant of chalky soil, and preferring partial shade. Most beautiful when in flower, with most of the flowers open at one time. Hardy to −15°C. Early summer.

**M. wilsonii** (Fin. & Gagnep) Rehd.   Native of China in western Sichuan and in N. Yunnan near Dali, growing in scrub and moist forest at 2300–3000 m, flowering in May and June. Deciduous shrub or small tree up to 8 m in the wild. Leaves elliptic-oblong to elliptic-lanceolate, acute at the apex, densely silky-hairy beneath. Any good soil, and tolerant of chalk. Shade or part shade. Hardy to −15°C.

**M. sieboldii** K. Koch (syn. *M. parviflora* Sieb. & Zucc.)   Native of Japan in S. Honshu, Shikoku and Kyushu where it is rare, and of Korea, growing in woods in the mountains, flowering from May to July. Large deciduous shrub to 4 m; leaves broadly ovate or obovate, 7–15 cm long, sparsely pubescent beneath. Flowers 8–10 cm across, scented. Best on neutral or acid soils. Sun or part shade. Hardy to −20°C. Early to late summer.

**M. 'Highdownensis'** Dandy   Raised at Highdown garden in Sussex.

**M. globosa** Hook. fil. & Thoms.   Native of the Himalayas from E. Nepal to Bhutan and Xizang in moist *Tsga* and *Abies* forest, at 2440–3400 m, flowering in May–July. Deciduous shrub or tree to 8 m. Leaves to 18 cm long, oval, with reddish hairs beneath. Flowers remaining cup-shaped, to 8 cm across, scented. Acid or neutral good soil; part shade. Hardy to −10°C. Summer.

**M. × thompsoniana** (Loud.) C. de Vos   A hybrid between *M. virginiana* and *M. tripetala*, found among seedlings in about 1808 by Mr Thompson, a nurseryman at Mile End, London. Deciduous shrub or small multi-stemmed tree to 4 m. Leaves 7.5–25 cm long, glaucous beneath. Flowers scented, to 9 cm long. Moist peaty soil; sun or part shade. Hardy to −20°C. Summer.

**M. ashei** Weatherby   Native of N.W. Florida and E. Texas, growing by streams and on hills in woods at 30–60 m, flowering in March–April. Deciduous shrub or small tree to 5 m, with huge thin leaves to 60 cm long, 30 cm across, silvery beneath, petals 10–14 cm long. Rich, leafy moist soil; shelter and part shade. Hardy to −15°C. Early summer.

**M. virginiana** L. Sweet Bay   Native of Massachusetts and Long Island south to Florida and west to S.E. Texas, in wet, acid sandy barrens and swamps, flowering in June–July. Semi-evergreen or deciduous shrub or tree to 20 m, usually around 10 m. Leaves 7–12 cm long, silvery beneath. Hardy to −20°C.

**M. cordata** Michx.   Native of N. and S. Carolina and Georgia, in mixed forests, flowering in April–June. Deciduous shrub or small tree to 10 m. Flowers 4–5 cm long; leaves 8–15 cm long, cuneate to rounded at the base. Hardy to −20°C. Early summer.

*Magnolia sinensis*

*Magnolia globosa*

*Magnolia sieboldii*

*Magnolia 'Highdownensis'* at Sandling Park, Kent

*Magnolia × thompsoniana*

*Magnolia ashei*

*Magnolia virginiana*

*Magnolia cordata* at Wisley

'Takeba'

'Tsueban'

'Tzepao'

'Buddha'

'Balderdash'

'Confucius'

'Exaltation'

'Tom Durrant'

$\frac{2}{3}$ life size. Specimens from the Savill Garden, Windsor, 15th March

An old temple at Ulu Ky in the foothills of the Lijiang mountains, Yunnan

**Camellia reticulata** Lindl. (*Theaceae*)  Native
of W. Yunnan, around Tenchung (Tengyueh)
in open pine forest and scrub at 2000 m,
flowering in April and May. An evergreen shrub
or small tree to 10 m, usually around 3 m.
Leaves 8–11 cm long; flowers with 8–10 petals,
about 10 cm across in a good form, pale pink to
crimson (p. 59). Long cultivated in China,
especially in Yunnan in temple courtyards, as
shown here, above Ulu Ky, near Lijiang. Lime-
free soil; part shade and shelter. Hardy to
−10°C. Spring.

**C. reticulata 'Takeba'**  A huge-flowered
camellia growing in the Savill Garden, Windsor
in a cool greenhouse.

**C. reticulata 'Tsueban'** (syns. 'Chrysanthenum
Petal', 'Juban')  A form of *C. reticulata*,
introduced from Kunming, China to the USA
by Descanso Gardens & R. Peer in 1948.
Slender open growth.

**C. reticulata 'Tzepao'** (syns. 'Purple Gown',
'Zipao')  A form of *C. reticulata*, introduced
from the Botanical Institute at Kunming, China
to the USA by Descanso Gardens and R. Peer in
1948. Compact growth. Free-flowering on a
compact bush.

**C. reticulata 'Buddha'**  A hybrid between *C.
reticulata* 'Early Peach Blossom' and *C. pitardii*
var. *yunnanica*. Introduced from Kunming,

China to the USA by Descanso in 1950.
Vigorous upright growth.

**C. reticulata 'Balderdash'**  A hybrid between
*C. reticulata* 'Wild Form' and *C. reticulata*
'Crimson Robe'. Raised in New Zealand in 1967
by Dr Jane Crisp of Tirau. Vigorous growth.

**C. reticulata 'Confucius'**  A hybrid between
*C. reticulata* and *C. pitardii* var. *yunnanica*.
Introduced from Kunming, China to the USA
by Descanso in 1950. Medium, compact,
upright growth.

**C. reticulata 'Tom Durrant'**  A hybrid
between *C. reticulata* 'Wild Form' and *C.
reticulata* 'Shot Silk'. Raised in New Zealand in
1966 by Dr Jane Crisp of Tirau. Medium,
bushy, upright growth.

**C. × williamsii 'Exaltation'**  A hybrid
between *C. × williamsii* and *C. japonica*
'Gauntletti', raised at the Savill Garden,
Windsor, England, in about 1966.

**C. reticulata 'Tataochung'** (syn. 'Crimson
Robe', 'Early Crimson')  A cultivar of *C.
reticulata*, introduced from Kunming, China to
the USA by Descanso & Peer in 1948, and to
Windsor in 1956.

*Camellia reticulata* in the temple courtyard

*Camellia reticulata 'Tataochung'*

C. 'Momoiro Wabisuke'

C. × williamsii
'J. C. Williams'

C. × williamsii 'St Ewe'

'Cornish Snow'

C. tsaii

C. fraterna

C. reticulata 'Mary Williams'

C. japonica 'Haku-Tsuru'

⅗ life size. Specimens from Savill Garden, Windsor, 4th April

Camellia japonica at Pengneep, Cornwall

Camellia 'Cornish Snow'

Camellia 'Fragrant Pink'

**Camellia japonica L.** (*Theaceae*) Camellia Native of Japan, in Honshu, Shikoku and Kyushu, growing in woods in the hills and down to sea level, flowering from February to June according to altitude. Three varieties are recognized in Japan; the lowland variety, with cup-shaped flowers and filaments joined for a half to a third of their length, and the upland variety, var. *decumbens* or subsp. *rusticana* (Honda) Kitam., with a more open flower and stamens joined only at the base. The third variety which has large fruits, like small apples, with a very thick wall to the capsule is var. *macrocarpa* Masam., found by mountain streams and on the coast in the south, in Yakushima and S. Sikoku. All three varieties can make small, slender trees or shrubs, with pinkish-red flowers.

**C. japonica 'Momoiro Wabisuke'** Wabisuke are a group of Japanese camellias popular in the 17th C, variously reported as sub-species of *japonica*, or of hybrid origin between *C. saluenensis* or *C. sinensis* and *C. japonica*. The flowers are usually rather small and campanulate, red, pink or white; the ovaries may be hairy.

**C. × williamsii** W. W. Sm. **'J. C. Williams'** A hybrid between *C. saluenensis* and *C. japonica*, raised at Caerhays in England by J. C. Williams in 1940. Vigorous, with horizontal branches and a very long flowering season. The first clone of × *williamsii* to be named. Hardy to −15°C.

**C. 'Cornish Snow'** A hybrid between *C. saluenensis* and *C. cuspidata*, raised by J. C.

Williams at Caerhays Castle, Cornwall, England in 1930. Open, upright growth, making a medium to large-sized bush.

**C. tsaii** Hu (*Theaceae*) Native of Yunnan, Burma and northern Vietnam at 1200–2400 m, introduced by George Forrest. Differs from *C. cuspidata* in its hairy twigs, floppier leaves with more teeth, and stalked flowers on the underside of the branches. It requires protection from frost. Hardy to −5°C.

**C. × williamsii 'St Ewe'** A hybrid between *C. saluenensis* and *C. japonica* raised at Caerhays in England by J. C. Williams before 1940. Vigorous, upright growth; very free-flowering.

**C. fraterna** Hance (*Theaceae*) Native of E. and C. China, in Zhejiang and Hubei near Ichang growing in valleys between 30–300 m, flowering in March. An evergreen shrub 1–2 m high, close to *C. cuspidata* (p. 65) but with sepals, shoots and pedicel all hairy. A tender graceful species with numerous small flowers, requiring protection from more than a few degrees of frost.

**C. reticulata** Lindl. **'Mary Williams'** A seedling of *C. reticulata* (see p. 57), raised at Caerhays, England by J. C. Williams, from seed collected by George Forrest in the wild near Tenchung (Tengyueh) in western Yunnan in 1932.

**C. japonica 'Haku-Tsuru'** (syns. 'White Crane', 'White Stork') Introduced in Japan in 1934 by Chugai Nursery, of Kobe, Japan. Vigorous, upright growth.

Camellia 'Vallée Knudsen'

**C. 'Vallée Knudsen'** A hybrid between *C. saluenensis* and *C. reticulata* 'Buddha', introduced in 1958 by Howard Asper of Escondido, California. Best grown in a cool greenhouse. Flowers around 12 cm across.

**C. 'Fragrant Pink'** A hybrid between *C. japonica* subsp. *rusticana* and *C. lutchuensis*, a species from the Liuku Islands, with scented flowers, raised by W. L. Akerman of Maryland in 1968. A colchicine-induced sport, possibly a tetraploid, called 'Fragrant Pink Improved', was produced in 1975. Small-flowered, but prolific with a long flowering period. Hardy to −5°C.

'Donckelarii'

'Tricolor'

'Mrs Tingley'

C. japonica seedling

'Devonia'

'Bright Buoy'

'Grace Bunton'

'Prof. Charles S. Sargent'

'Furo-an'

'Princess Charlotte'

'Rubescens Major'

$\frac{2}{3}$ life size. Specimens from Wisley, 11th April

*Camellia japonica 'Mrs Bertha A. Harms'*

*Camellia japonica 'Jupiter'* at the Hillier Arboretum

*Camellia 'Freedom Bell'*

*Camellia japonica 'Gertrude Preston'*

*Camellia japonica 'Yukimi-guruma'*

**C. japonica** L. (*Theaceae*)   This seedling *C. japonica* closely resembles the species as found commonly in the wild in Japan (see p. 59).

**C. japonica 'Donckelarii'**   There are many named strains of this variety, e.g. 'Tea Garden', 'Middleton No. 15', 'Cantelon', 'English', 'Camellia T', 'Tallahassee', 'Mary Robertson', 'Willie Davis' and 'Aileen'. Introduced from China to Belgium by Dr Franz von Siebold in 1834. Very popular as it blooms well both out of doors and under glass. Bushy growth.

**C. japonica 'Tricolor'** (syns. 'Waka-no-Ura', 'Sieboldii', 'Tricolor de Siebold')   A variety of *C. japonica* introduced from Japan *c.* 1830, by Dr Franz von Siebold. Vigorous, compact upright growth. Flowers variable in the amount of streaking even on the same plant. A pure white sport is 'Tricolor White', a red sport 'Lady de Saumarez'. Flowers cup-shaped when first open. Hardy to −15°C with shelter. (See also p. 66.)

**C. japonica 'Mrs Tingley'**   Raised in the USA in 1949 by Tuttle Bros. Nursery, Pasadena, California. Medium, compact growth.

**C. japonica 'Bright Buoy'**   Raised by L. E. Jury of New Plymouth, New Zealand, in 1975. Bushy, spreading growth. Not reliably hardy.

**C. japonica 'Grace Bunton'**   Raised in the USA in 1950 by W. J. Robinson and C. J. Hayes, Norfolk, Virginia. Vigorous, compact, upright growth.

**C. japonica 'Devonia'** (syns. 'Devoniensis', 'Devona')   A seedling introduced by Veitch Nurseries, Exeter, England and first described in the RHS *Journal* in 1900–1. One of the best whites for weather resistance.

**C. japonica 'Prof. Charles S. Sargent'**   A variety raised in the USA in 1925 by Magnolia Gardens and Nurseries, Johns Island, S. Carolina. Vigorous, compact, upright growth.

**C. japonica 'Furo an'** (syn. ?Taro-an)   A Japanese Higo camellia, with characteristic large-spreading boss of stamens, introduced to Britain in 1939, from Japan. Growth spreading. Early–mid-season flowering. Hardy to −15°C.

**C. japonica 'Princess Charlotte'**   An old variety, grown at Wisley, which varies on the same bush from white, through pale pink, to mid-pink, with many particoloured flowers. Early-flowering and hardy to −15°C.

**C. japonica 'Rubescens Major'** (syns. 'Paolina Guichardini', 'Princess Ann')   Introduced in France in 1895 by Guichard Soeurs, Nantes.

Compact, bushy habit. Flowers produced in mid-season.

**C. japonica 'Mrs Bertha A. Harms'**   Introduced in 1949 by J. H. Harms, of Portland, Oregon. Medium, open, upright growth.

**C. japonica 'Jupiter'** (syns. 'Juno', 'Sylva')   Introduced in England in about 1900 by William Paul of Cheshunt. Upright, vigorous growth. (See also p. 67.)

**C. 'Freedom Bell'**   Introduced in the USA in 1965 by Nuccio Nurseries, Altadena, California. Vigorous, upright compact growth. An inter-specific hybrid of unknown parentage.

**C. japonica 'Gertrude Preston'**   This plant is thought to be a seedling from *C. japonica* 'Apple Blossom'. It first flowered in about 1940. When fully open the flowers are slightly lighter in colour than the young blooms.

**C. japonica 'Yukimi-guruma'** (syn. 'Amabilis')   Makes a rather upright, loosely branched shrub.

'Contessa
Lavinia Maggi'

'Apollo'

'Mme de Strekaloff'

'Nobilissima'

'Debutante'

'Mathotiana Alba'

'Arejishi'

'Mrs Skottowe'

'Marguerite Gouillon'

'Apple Blossom'

⅖ life size. Specimens from Eccleston Square, 11th April

*C. japonica* 'Contessa Lavinia Maggi'  Raised in Italy by Conte Maggi and recorded in *Flore dess Serres* in 1858. Vigorous, upright growth. Sometimes branches bearing red flowers appear; these should be cut out as they will take over the whole bush if left.

*C. japonica* 'Mme de Strekaloff'  Introduced in Italy in 1855 by Cesare Franchetti, of Florence, Italy.

*C. japonica* 'Apollo' (syn. 'Amagashita')  One of a group of single and semi-double varieties introduced or raised by William Paul in about 1900. A vigorous grower, this is one of the camellias most suitable for growing outdoors as the flowers are fairly frost-resistant. Often confused with 'Jupiter', also raised by Paul, from which it differs chiefly in its deeper coloured petals and longer leaves.

*C. japonica* 'Nobilissima' (syn. 'Fuji-Yama')  Introduced from Japan to Belgium in about 1834 by M. Lefevre of Ghent. Vigorous, upright growth. The flowers are produced very early in the season.

*C. japonica* 'Debutante' (syn. 'Sara C. Hastie')  Parentage unknown. A variety raised in the USA in the early 1900s by Magnolia Gardens and Nurseries, Johns Island, South Carolina. Vigorous, upright growth. Flowers produced from early to mid-season.

*C. japonica* 'Mathotiana Alba'  A variety of *C. japonica*, raised by M. Mathot in Belgium, and described in 1858. It has broad, leathery leaves, sparse branching and is better grown indoors.

*C. japonica* 'Arejishi' (syn. 'Aloha')  An old Japanese cultivar, known since 1877 in Yokohama, and introduced to Europe in 1891. Early-flowering, with rather small flowers 8 cm across. Hardy to −15°C.

*C. japonica* 'Apple Blossom'  Introduced in the USA in 1930 by Coolidge Rare Plant Gardens, of Pasadena, California. An upright, compact bush. There is some confusion over this name as it applies to several other camellias also, notably a very pale pink single.

*C. japonica* 'Marguerite Gouillon'  This old variety was raised in Nantes, France, by Drouard Gouillon and described by Berlese in his *Monographie* in 1845. It is often confused with 'General Lamoricière' which is very similar, but is a deeper pink and has fewer stripes. 'Marguerite Gouillon' is a vigorous, upright grower which becomes rather spreading when older.

*C. japonica* 'Mrs Skottowe' (syns. 'Mrs Moore's Speckled', 'Queen Victoria's Blush')  A sport of 'Jubilee', raised in Australia in 1878 by Michael Guilfoyle of Double Bay, New South Wales, Australia.

*C. japonica* 'Coquettii' (syns. 'Coquette', 'Glen 40')  A seedling raised by M. Tourres of Mancheteaux, France, and first described in 1840. A vigorous upright grower. A sport called

Camellia japonica 'Coquettii'

Camellia japonica 'Baron Leguay'

Camellia japonica 'Duc de Bretagne'

Camellia japonica 'Kumasaka'

Camellia japonica 'Mathotiana Rosea'

Camellia japonica 'Augusto L. Gouveia Pinto'

'Coquettina' has deeper red flowers and sometimes streaks of white.

*C. japonica* 'Baron Leguay'  An old variety, raised in France in 1908 by Guichard Soeurs, of Nantes.

*C. japonica* 'Duc de Bretagne'  Raised in Nantes by Drouard Gouillon, this variety was illustrated and described by Verschaffelt in 1848. Vigorous branching habit, making a large spreading bush.

*C. japonica* 'Kumasaka' (syns. 'Lady Marion', 'Jeanne Kerr', 'Maiden', 'Sherbrooke', 'Kumasaka-Beni', 'Hollyhock')  Introduced in

Japan in 1896 by Tokyo Nurseries. Vigorous, compact growth.

*C. japonica* 'Mathotiana Rosea' (syns. 'Pink Beauty', 'Laura Polka', 'Warwick')  A sport of 'Mathotiana Alba'. Introduced in England in 1874 by James Veitch & Son, of Chelsea, London.

*C. japonica* 'Augusto L. Gouveia Pinto' (syn. 'Jack McCaskill', 'Portuguese Pink')  A sport of 'Mathotiana' said to have originated in Portugal around the end of the 19th century. Growth upright, open. A large-flowered variety, 10–11 cm across, best grown under glass.

'Bow Bells'

'Francis Hanger'

'Hiraethlyn'

'C. F. Coates'

'Sea Foam'

'Golden Spangles'

C. saluenensis

C. cuspidata

'Cornish Spring'

⅖ life size. Specimens from Wisley, 11th April

Camellia × williamsii 'Elizabeth Rothschild'

Camellia × williamsii 'Mary Christian' at Tregrehan, Cornwall

Camellia Haru Gasumi (Spring Misty)

**C. × williamsii 'Francis Hanger'** A hybrid between *C. japonica* 'Alba Simplex' and *C. saluenensis* raised by Francis Hanger in England. Suitable for growing against a shaded wall.

**C. × williamsii 'Bow Bells'** A cultivar originating from a cross between *C. japonica* and *C. saluenensis*, raised by J. C. Williams at Caerhays Castle, Cornwall in about 1925. 'Bow Bells' often comes into flower exceptionally early, and may bloom from mid-winter–late spring. Compact, bushy growth; suitable for a shady wall.

**C. × williamsii 'Hiraethlyn'** A hybrid between *C. saluenensis* and *C. japonica* (? possibly 'Flora') raised at Bodnant, N. Wales, in 1950. Vigorous, compact, upright growth.

**C. × williamsii 'C. F. Coates'** A hybrid between *C. saluenensis* and *C. japonica* 'Quercifolia', raised (?) at Kew Gardens, England in 1935. The peculiar 3-lobed leaves have led to this sometimes being called the 'Fishtail Camellia'.

**C. × williamsii 'Golden Spangles'** A form, with a variegated leaf, of 'Mary Christian'. It was first noticed, amongst a batch of plants labelled 'Mary Christian', at the RHS Garden, Wisley, in 1946, but it is not clear whether it arose as a separate seedling, or as a mutation.

**C. × williamsii 'Sea Foam'** A double white *C. × williamsii*, very successful in the camellia trial at Wisley.

**Camellia saluenensis** Stapf (*Theaceae*) Native of N.W. Yunnan, in the volcanic mountains of the Shweli river basin, N.W. of Tenchung (Tengyueh), and in the Yangtze valley, at 1800–2700 m in scrub on open rocky hillsides and along streams, flowering in May. Evergreen shrub from 2–5 m tall. Leaves dull green above, finely toothed, about 5 cm long. Flowers about 6 cm across, from white to red in the wild, March to May in gardens, and usually pink with a distinct trace of blue. Acid or non-chalky soil; some shade. Hardy to −10°C. The parent, with *C. japonica*, of the very popular × *williamsii* camellias.

**Camellia cuspidata** Veitch (*Theaceae*) Native of C. China, in W. Hubei and E. Sichuan, where it is common in open woods around Ichang. Evergreen shrub up to 3 m; leaves very elegant, to 6 cm long, coppery when young; flowers white, very numerous. Easily grown in open woodland, and as hardy as most other camellias, damaged only by temperatures below −10°C or cold, dry wind.

**C. 'Cornish Spring'** A hybrid between *C. japonica* 'Rosea Simplex' and *C. cuspidata*, raised by Miss G. Carlyon at Tregrehan, Cornwall, England, in 1950. Vigorous, upright, bushy growth, The flowers are produced mid–late season. Hardy to −10°C.

**C. × williamsii 'Elizabeth Rothschild'** A hybrid between *C. saluenensis* and *C. japonica* 'Adolphe Audusson', introduced in England in 1950 by Francis Hanger. Flowers produced mid–late season.

Camellia × williamsi 'Bowen Bryant'

**C. × williamsii 'Mary Christian'** This was one of the earliest × *williamsii* hybrids to be raised at Caerhays. It has an open, upright habit. Blooms are produced early to mid-season.

**C. Haru Gasumi** (syn. 'Spring Misty') A hybrid between *C. japonica* and *C. lutchuensis*. Introduced in the USA in 1981 by Dr Clifford Parks, of Chapel Hill, N.C. Hardy to −15°C.

**C. × williamsii 'Bowen Bryant'** A hybrid between *C. saluenensis* and *C. japonica*, raised by E. G. Waterhouse in Australia in 1960. Upright, vigorous growth. Hardy in northern England and Scotland, to −15°C.

# JAPONICA CAMELLIAS

'Lady Clare'

'Adolphe Audusson'

'Gloire de Nantes'

'Tricolor'

'Alba Simplex'

'Kouron Jura'

'La Pace Rubra'

'Jupiter'

'Bella Romana'

'Daikagura'

⅖ life size. Specimens from Valley Gardens, Windsor, 23rd April

Camellia japonica 'Little Bit'

Camellia japonica 'Adolphe Audusson' at Exbury, Hants

Camellia japonica 'Satanella'

**C. japonica 'Lady Clare'** (syns. 'Empress', 'Akashi-Gata', 'Nellie Bly') This was introduced to Europe from Japan in 1887 and distributed by L. van Houtte in Belgium. Rather loose, pendulous habit; the large flowers are freely produced.

**C. japonica 'Adolphe Audusson'** (syns. 'Audrey Hopfer', 'Adolphe') A variety of *C. japonica* introduced by M. Audusson, of Angers, France, in 1877. There are two variants of 'Adolphe Audusson' – 'Adolphe Audusson Special', which has predominantly white blooms, and 'Adolphe Audusson Variegated', a dark red form with white blotches or spots.

**C. japonica 'Gloire de Nantes'** Introduced by Guichard of Nantes in 1895, this is one of the hardiest and earliest-flowering camellias. It makes a medium-sized, compact bush.

**C. japonica 'Alba Simplex'** (syn. 'Snow Goose') An old variety, reported to be a seedling of 'Variegata' raised in 1813 at the Tooting Nursery, London. It was first recorded by Samuel Curtis in 1819 under the name 'flore albo simplici', and in 1822 it was illustrated in Loddiges' *Botanical Cabinet*, described as 'alba'. Paxton, in 1833, and other later writers described this variety as 'Alba Simplex', and this name has been retained to avoid confusion with all the other varieties named 'Alba'. It has a vigorous, upright habit.

**C. japonica 'Tricolor'** (syns. 'Waka-no-Ura', 'Sieboldii') A variety of *C. japonica* introduced from Japan by Dr F. von Siebold *c.* 1830. Vigorous, compact, upright growth. There are

many other forms of this variety including 'Dainty', 'Fred Sander', 'Jewel Bowdon', 'Blush Tri-color' and 'Chalk Pink'. (See also p. 61.)

**C. japonica 'Kouron Jura'** (syns. 'Konron-Koku' (which properly belongs to a *C. sasanqua* cultivar), 'Mt. Konlong Black') Introduced from Japan by Star Nursery, Sierra Madre, California in 1930, and to Britain by Sir James Horlick in 1939. Medium-sized bush; flowers particularly frost-resistant.

**C. japonica 'La Pace Rubra'** (syn. 'Red Pressii') A sport of 'La Pace', which (i.e. L.P.) was introduced in Italy in 1860 by M. Santareui, of Florence. Some branches revert to 'La Pace' and have white or rose-pink flowers, striped with crimson. Bushy, vigorous habit.

**C. japonica 'Jupiter'** (syns. 'Juno', 'Sylva') Introduced in England in about 1900 by William Paul of Cheshunt. Upright, vigorous growth. The variety grown as 'Sylva' in the southern USA is in fact 'Adolphe Audusson'. (See also p. 61.)

**C. japonica 'Bella Romana'** A variety of *C. japonica* raised by C. Lemaire in Rome in 1863. Vigorous, bushy growth. 'La Bella', with rose flowers splashed with white, is a sport of 'Bella Romana'.

**C. japonica 'Daikagura'** (syns. 'Idaten Shibori' (in error), 'Kiyosu') A Japanese variety, known since 1851. Very variable in colour, may be bright pink streaked white to white, variably streaked with deep pink, as shown here.

Camellia japonica 'Althaeiflora'

Flowers early, about 9 cm wide. We are not sure of the identification of this variety.

**C. japonica 'Little Bit'** Introduced in the USA in 1958 by Dr J. D. Lawson, Camelliana, Antioch, California. Medium, upright growth.

**C. japonica 'Satanella'** This plant was grown under the name 'Saturnia' until 1956, when it was renamed 'Satanella'.

**C. japonica 'Althaeiflora'** (syn. 'Rosette') A seedling of 'Anemoniflora' raised in 1819 by Alfred Chandler of Vauxhall Nursery, London. Strong upright growth, becoming spreading when older.

'Debbie'

'Donation'

'Inspiration'

'Caerhays'

'Captain Rawes'

'Haku Rakuten'

'Kimberley'

'Salutation'

'Leonard Messel'

'Magnoliaeflora'

$\frac{2}{3}$ life size. Specimens from Savill Garden, Windsor, 24th April

*Camellia reticulata 'Mouchang'*

*Camellia 'Harold L. Paige'*

*Camellia 'Royalty'*

*Camellia 'Salutation' at Borde Hill*

*Camellia × williamsii 'Anticipation'*

**C. × williamsii 'Debbie'**   A hybrid between *C. saluenensis* and *C. japonica* 'Debutante' raised by L. E. Jury in New Zealand in 1965. This vigorous camellia has a long flowering season, sometimes coming into bloom in mid-winter. The flowers weather well and drop from the bush when over.

**C. × williamsii 'Donation'**   A hybrid between *C. saluenensis* and *C. japonica* 'Donckelarii', raised by Col. R. S. Clarke at Borde Hill, England in 1941. Vigorous, erect growth to 3 m.

**C. 'Inspiration'**   A hybrid between *C. reticulata* and *C. saluenensis* raised by Francis Hanger, in England, in 1954. Very hardy to −15°C if sheltered, with dense, upright growth; very floriferous.

**C. williamsii 'Caerhays'**   A hybrid between *C. saluenensis* and *C. japonica* 'Lady Clare', raised at Caerhays Castle, Cornwall, England, by J. C. Williams in 1948. Rather spreading, pendulous habit of growth.

**C. reticulata 'Captain Rawes'** (syns. 'Guixia', 'Semi-Plena')   This variety of *C. reticulata* was introduced to England from Canton by Robert Fortune in 1820, and is named after Captain Richard Rawes of the East India Company, who is credited with introducing the original *C. reticulata* to Britain. Makes a large shrub, to 3 m or more.

**C. japonica 'Haku Rakuten'** (syn. 'Wisley White')   Introduced from Japan in 1929. The blooms are quite weather-resistant. Vigorous, upright growth, flowering from mid to late in the season.

**C. japonica 'Kimberley'** (syn. 'Crimson Cup') Introduced by Messrs Sander of Bruges, Belgium, in about 1900. Upright, vigorous growth.

**C. 'Salutation'**   A hybrid between *C. saluenensis* × *C. reticulata* 'Captain Rawes'

raised by Col. R. S. Clarke at Borde Hill, England in 1936. Vigorous, open, upright growth to 3 m. Very early flowering.

**C. 'Leonard Messel'**   A hybrid between a wild form of *C. reticulata* and *C. × williamsii* 'Mary Christian', raised by Mrs L. C. R. Messel at Nymans, England in 1958. Flowers in mid-season. Hardy to −15°C.

**C. japonica 'Magnoliaeflora'** (syns. 'Rose at Dawn', 'Hagoromo', 'Cho-no-Hagasane')   A Japanese variety imported into Italy in 1886, and thence to England in about 1890. The flowers are freely produced but are rather susceptible to frost damage, so a sheltered position is preferable. Compact growth, making a medium-sized bush. There is a white form, 'Magnoliaeflora Alba' (syn. 'Yobeki-dori') and a sport named 'Arthur Bolton' with blooms of a similar colour to the original plant, but with reflexed, wavy petals.

**C. reticulata 'Mouchang'**   A hybrid between *C. reticulata* 'Cornelian' and *C. reticulata* 'Moutancha'. Introduced in 1966 by H. Asper, Escondido, California. Best grown in a cool greenhouse. Hardy to −5°C.

**C. 'Harold L. Paige'**   A hybrid between *C. japonica* 'Adolphe Audusson' and *C. reticulata* 'Crimson Robe', introduced in the USA in 1972 by J. Osegueda, Oakland, California. Vigorous, spreading growth.

**C. 'Royalty'**   A hybrid between *C. japonica* 'Clarise Carleton' and *C. reticulata* 'Cornelian', introduced in the USA in 1968 by T. E. Croson, of Simi, California. Medium, upright growth.

**C. × williamsii 'Anticipation'**   A hybrid between *C. saluenensis* and *C. japonica* 'Leviathan', raised by Jury in New Zealand in 1962. A hardy upright grower, flowering well until late in the season.

*Camellia japonica 'Guilio Nuccio'*

*Camellia japonica 'Beni-otome' at Windsor*

*Camellia japonica 'Alexander Hunter'*

*Camellia × williamsii 'E. G. Waterhouse'*

*Camellia × williamsii 'Philippa Forwood'*

**Camellia japonica 'Beni-otome'** (syns. 'Cheerful', 'Cheerfulness', 'Lucida', 'Hi-otome') A *japonica* hybrid, introduced by S. Quin, McComb, Mississippi in 1884. Vigorous, upright, compact growth.

**C. japonica 'Guilio Nuccio'** Introduced in the USA in 1956 by Nuccio Nurseries, Altadena, California. Vigorous, upright growth. Flowers produced mid–late season.

**C. japonica 'Alexander Hunter'** A cultivar raised in about 1884 by Alexander Hunter, of Somersby, Sydney, New South Wales, Australia. It was later named by G. C. Linton Esq., who took over the property and was first listed commercially by Hazlewood Bros., N.S.W. in 1941. Upright, vigorous growth.

**C. × williamsii 'Philippa Forwood'** Introduced in England in 1940 by J. C. Williams. Vigorous, open growth. Often confused with *C.* 'J. C. Williams'. (For details of *C. × williamsii* see p. 59).

**C. × williamsii 'E. G. Waterhouse'** Occurred in 1954, as a self-sown seedling in the garden of Prof. E. G. Waterhouse of N.S.W. Australia. There is also a variegated form.

**C. japonica 'Desire'** Raised in 1977 by D. L. Feathers of Lafayette, California, USA. A vigorous grower. Flowers pale pink or in warm conditions almost white, with deeper pink edge.

**C. japonica 'William Bartlett'** Raised in Australia in 1958 by Hazlewood Bros., of

Eppling, N.S.W. Compact growth. Flowers produced in mid-season.

**C. japonica 'Margaret Davis'** A sport of 'Aspasia MacArthur'. Introduced in Australia in 1961 by A. M. Davis of Cammeray.

**C. japonica 'Bob Hope'** Raised by Nuccio Nurseries, California, USA in 1972. Slow-growing; compact. May be very dark red and produce semi-double flowers, showing a central ring of stamens.

**C. japonica 'Commander Mulroy'** Introduced in USA in 1961 by T. C. Patin, Hammond, LA. Medium-sized bush, upright growth; can be grown in a container. The flowers (which are a deeper pink when grown under glass) are produced in mid-season.

**C. japonica 'Berenice Perfection'** Introduced in USA in 1965 by Nuccio Nurseries, Altadena, California. Vigorous, upright growth. Flowers mid-season.

**C. japonica 'Annie Wylam'** Upright growth, making a medium-sized bush. A chance seedling, raised in USA in 1959 by W. E. Wylam, of Pasadena, California. A.M. 1981.

**C. japonica 'Paul Jones Supreme'** Raised by Waterhouse in Australia in 1968.

**C. japonica 'Adolphe Audusson Variegated'** (syn. 'F. M. Vyematsu') A variegated sport of 'Adolphe Audusson'.

*Camellia japonica 'William Bartlett'*

*Camellia japonica 'Desire'*

*Camellia japonica 'Margaret Davis'*

*Camellia japonica 'Bob Hope'*    *Camellia japonica 'Commander Mulroy'*    *Camellia japonica 'Berenice Perfection'*

*Camellia japonica 'Annie Wylam'*    *Camellia japonica 'Paul Jones Supreme'*    *Camellia japonica 'Adolphe Audusson Variegated'*

*Camellia japonica 'Madge Miller'*

*Camellia japonica* (p. 59) at the Hillier Arboretum

*Camellia japonica 'Sea Foam'*

**C. japonica 'Madge Miller'** (syn. 'Chandleri Alba') A recent American introduction. The flowers are produced in mid-season and stand up well to bad weather.

**C. japonica 'Sea Foam'** Of unknown parentage, raised in the USA in 1959 by J. T. Weisner. Upright growth.

**C. japonica 'Grand Slam'** Introduced in the USA in 1962 by Nuccio Nurseries, Altadena, California. When grown in a cool greenhouse the flowers are much larger than if grown outdoors (the specimen illustrated was grown under glass). A very popular variety in America.

**C. 'Howard Asper'** A hybrid between *C. reticulata* 'Cornelian' and *C. japonica* 'Coronation'. Introduced in the USA in 1963 by H. Asper of Escondido, California. Vigorous growth. Hardy to −5°C.

**C. japonica 'Erin Farmer'** Introduced in the USA in 1962 by Mr and Mrs H. E. Ashby of Charleston, S. Carolina. Thick petals, and flowers with some scent.

**C. japonica 'Dobrei'** (syns. 'Dobreei', 'Dobreyi') This camellia was first described by Berlese in the *Annals de la Société Centrale d'Horticulture de France* in 1849. Upright, vigorous habit.

**C. japonica 'Matterhorn'** Raised by David Feathers in California in 1976. Introduced in the USA in 1981. Upright bush, well clothed with dark green foliage. Flowers mid–late in the season.

**C. × williamsii 'Senorita'** A hybrid between *C. saluenensis* and *C. japonica* 'Herine', raised by Les Jury in New Zealand in 1975. Very free-flowering; blooms are produced mid–late season.

**C. × williamsii 'Laura Boscawen'** Raised by D. L. Feathers, of California, USA and introduced in England by Trehane Camellias in 1985. A stiff, twiggy bush, this camellia is best grown outdoors, as under glass the flowers lose their clarity of form. Very free-flowering.

**C. 'Jury's Yellow'** A hybrid between *C. saluenensis* × *C. japonica*) and *C. japonica* 'Gwenneth Morey' raised by Les Jury in New Zealand in 1976. Upright growth, making a compact, medium-sized bush.

**C. × williamsii 'Ballet Queen'** A hybrid between *C. saluenensis* and *C. japonica* 'Leviathan' raised by Les Jury in New Zealand in 1976. Mid–late season.

**C. japonica 'Mrs D. W. Davis'** Introduced in 1954 by D. W. Davis of Seffner, Florida, USA. A vigorous grower and in America makes an erect and compact bush. In England it tends to have a more spreading habit when grown outdoors, and the flowers are easily damaged in bad weather; it is best grown under glass, when its huge, beautiful flowers can be seen to perfection. (There are three sports: 'Mrs D. W. Davis Peony' (loose peony-form blooms); 'Mrs D. W. Davis Descanso' (full peony form); and 'Mrs D. W. Davis Special', which has double the number of rows of petals.)

**C. × williamsii 'Joan Trehane'** A hybrid between *C. saluenensis* and *C. japonica* 'Herine', raised by Les Jury (no. 8), in New Zealand and introduced by D. Trehane & Son, Wimborne, Dorset, UK in 1980. Flowers weather well, and are produced mid–late season. Good grower; bush spreading.

*Camellia japonica 'Grand Slam'*

*Camellia 'Howard Asper'*

*Camellia japonica 'Erin Farmer'*

*Camellia japonica 'Dobrei'*

*Camellia japonica 'Matterhorn'*

*Camellia 'Jury's Yellow'*

*Camellia × williamsii 'Senorita'*

*Camellia × williamsii 'Laura Boscawen'*

*Camellia × williamsii 'Ballet Queen'*

*Camellia japonica 'Mrs D. W. Davis'*

*Camellia × williamsii 'Joan Trehane'*

73

Vaccinium angustifolium
var. laevifolium

Corylopsis sinensis

Corylopsis platypetala
var. levis

Menziesia ciliicalyx

Vaccinium caespitosum

Enkianthus perulatus

Illicium anisatum

Sambucus racemosa 'Plumosa Aurea'

Ribes alpinum

⅓ life size. Specimens from Wisley, Surrey, 24th April

*Menziesia ciliicalyx var. purpurea*

*Menziesia pentandra* at Balbithan, Aberdeenshire

*Vaccinium atrococcum*

*Illicium henryi*

*Chamaedaphne calyculata*

**Corylopsis sinensis** Hemsl. The finest species, native of W. China, described fully on p. 47.

**Corylopsis platypetala** Rehd. & Wilson var. **levis** Rehd. & Wilson (*Hamamelidaceae*) Native of China, in W. Hubei and W. Sichuan (var. *levis*), growing in forest and scrub at 1300–2600 m flowering in April and May. Leaves ovate or broadly ovate, 4.5–10 × 4–7 cm soon glabrous beneath. Raceme 3–5 cm long, flowers 8–20 pale greenish-yellow, rotate, scented; petals 3–4 mm across, anthers shorter than the petals, yellow. Leafy, moist soil; sheltered position with semi-shade. Hardy to −15°C. Early spring.

**Menziesia ciliicalyx** Maxim.
(*Ericaceae*) Native of S. Honshu, in scrub and woods in the hills and mountains, flowering in May and June. Deciduous shrub to 1 m. Flowers 1.3–1.7 cm long, pale yellow or greenish, with glandular–pilose pedicels. Capsule erect. Acid soil; shade or part shade. Hardy to −20°C.

**Menziesia ciliicalyx** Maxim. var. **purpurea** Makino Native of C. Honshu, in scrub in the mountains, flowering in June. Deciduous shrub to 1.5 m, spreading. Pedicels with long glandular and eglandular hairs. Sepals 1–2 mm long. Flowers 5-lobed, (4-lobed in *M. purpurea* Maxim. Acid soil; part shade. Hardy to −20°C. Spring (c.f. p. 148).

**Menziesia pentandra** Maxim. (*Ericaceae*) Native of Sakhalin, the S. Kurile islands, and Japan, south to Kyushu, in mountain scrub, flowering in May and June. Deciduous shrub to 1.5 m. Flowers 3–6 in an umbel, 5–7 mm long. Moist acid soil. Hardy to −25°C.

**Enkianthus perulatus** (Miq.) C. K. Schneid. (*Ericaceae*) Native of S. Honshu, Shikoku and Kyushu, in scrub and woods in the mountains, flowering in April. Deciduous shrub to 2 m. Leaves obovate or elliptic-ovate, 2–4 cm long, acute, serrulate. Flowers *c*. 8 mm long. Acid soil; part shade. Hardy to −20°C.

**Sambucus racemosa** L. (*Caprifoliaceae*) Native of Europe from Belgium and Spain eastwards to Siberia and well naturalized in parts of Scotland, growing in woods, mainly in the mountains. Flowers yellowish- to greenish-white; fruit red. Deciduous shrub up to 4 m. **'Tenuifolia'** has deeply dissected leaves; **'Plumosa Aurea'** has golden leaves, dissected halfway to the midrib on strong-growing, vegetative shoots. Any soil; sun or part shade. Hardy to −25°C.

**Ribes alpinum** L. (*Grossulariaceae*) Mountain Currant Native of Europe from Wales and northern England to Russia, Bulgaria and Morocco, growing in rocky places in the mountains, on limestone, flowering from April to June. Hardy to −25°C.

**Vaccinium angustifolium** Ait. var. **laevifolium** House (*Ericaceae*) Lowbush Blueberry Native of Newfoundland, east to Saskatchewan south to Virginia and Iowa in dry acid hills and rocks, flowering in April–June. Deciduous suckering shrub to 60 cm high. Leaves to 3.5 cm long, glabrous. Flowers 6–10 mm, white or pink tinged. Berries blue, with glaucous bloom. Acid soil; sun or part shade. Hardy to −30°C and below. Spring.

**Vaccinium caespitosum** Michx. (*Ericaceae*)

Dwarf Bilberry Native of Alaska to California and Colorado east to Labrador and New Hampshire, on rocky or gravelly banks, in open woods and alpine scrub, flowering in May–June. Deciduous shrub to 30 cm. Fruit black with glaucous bloom. Hardy to −30°C.

**Vaccinium atrococcum** (Gray) Keller (*Ericaceae*) Black Highbush Blueberry Native of New England, Ontario and Indiana south to Florida and Arkansas, in swamps and pine barrens, wet woods and the edges of lakes, flowering in March–May, a week or more earlier than *V. corymbosum*. Deciduous shrub to 2 m. Leaves woolly, opening after the flowers. Calyx not glaucous. Berries black, shining, or whitish. Wet, acid soil. Hardy to −25°C.

**Illicium anisatum** L. (syn. *I. religiosum* Sieb. & Zucc.) (*Magnoliaceae*) Native of S. China, Japan and Taiwan, growing in scrub and forest at low altitudes. Small evergreen tree or large shrub 2–10 m tall. Much planted near Buddhist shrines and temples. Hardy to −10°C. Spring.

**Illicium henryi** Diels (*Magnoliaceae*) Native of Hubei and Sichuan, growing on cliffs and in scrub in gorges, at 300–1300 m, flowering in May and June. An evergreen shrub up to 2 m. Hardy to −10°C in a sheltered position.

**Chamaedaphne calyculata** Moench. (*Ericaceae*) Leather leaf Native of the northern hemisphere from Siberia and Hokkaido, to British Columbia and Newfoundland, south to New Jersey and Illinois, in wet bogs, and pine barrens, flowering in April–June. Straggling evergreen shrub to 1.5 m. Fruit a dry capsule 4 mm wide. Hardy to −25°C or lower. Spring.

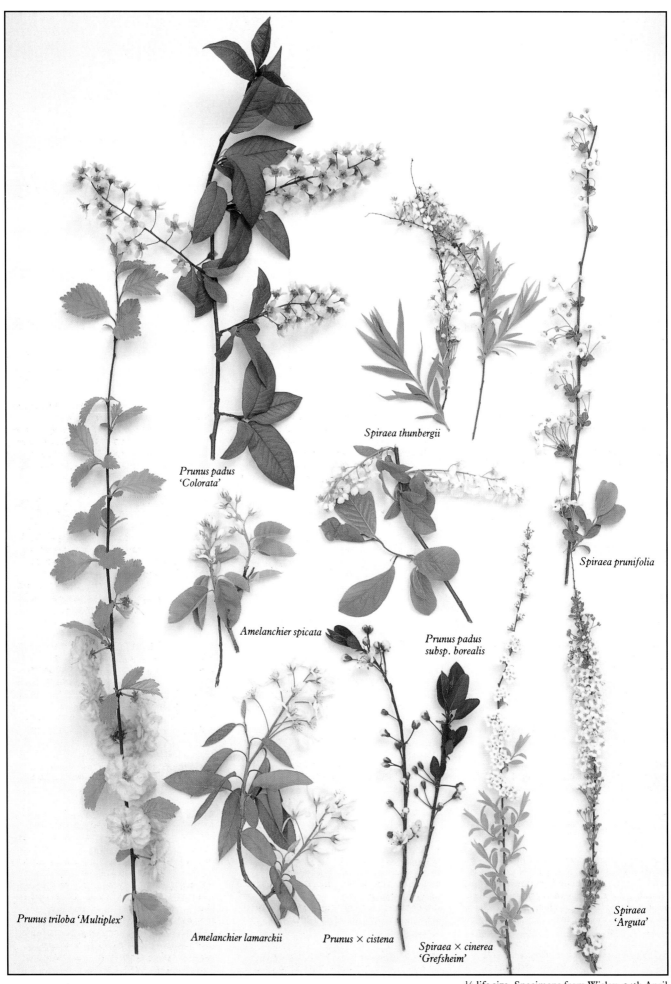

*Spiraea thunbergii*

*Prunus padus
'Colorata'*

*Spiraea prunifolia*

*Amelanchier spicata*

*Prunus padus
subsp. borealis*

*Prunus triloba 'Multiplex'*

*Spiraea
'Arguta'*

*Amelanchier lamarckii*

*Prunus × cistena*

*Spiraea × cinerea
'Grefsheim'*

⅓ life size. Specimens from Wisley, 24th April

*Prunus padus* in Aberdeenshire

*Spiraea media*

*Spiraea arcuata* in China

**Prunus padus** L. (*Rosaceae*) Bird Cherry
Native of Europe from Ireland and Scotland
where it is common, eastwards, but absent from
the Mediterranean area, and commonest in the
mountains. From Europe it extends eastwards
across Siberia to Korea, and Hokkaido in N.
Japan, flowering from May to July according to
altitude. In Europe two subspecies are
recognized; subsp. *padus* is tree-like, up to 27 m
with scented flowers, pendent racemes of fruit
and leaves glabrous except for tufts in the axils
of the veins; 'Watereri' is a particularly large
clone of this subspecies. Subsp. *borealis* is a
shrub up to 3 m, with leaves hairy beneath, and
almost scentless flowers in erect or horizontal
racemes. It is found in Scandinavia, Finland
and in the mountains from C. Europe
eastwards. Easily grown and good in cold
upland areas. Hardy to −30°C. Late spring.

**Prunus padus** L. 'Colorata' A shrub or small
tree, flowering at a young age, with spreading
racemes of pale pink flowers and purple leaves
and stems, fading to dark green in summer.

**Prunus triloba** Lindl. (syn. *P. triloba*
'Multiplex') (*Rosaceae*) Native of China and
N. Korea; in its double form, shown here, long
cultivated, and introduced to Europe by Robert
Fortune in 1855. It is usually grown as a wall
shrub, up to 3 m high, and should be pruned
hard soon after flowering to within 4 or 5 buds
of the previous year's wood. The leaves are
deciduous, often 3-lobed, but unlobed in
'Petzoldii', a clone with only 10 petals. Any soil,
sun or light shade. Hardy to −20°C. Spring.

**Prunus × cistena** (Hansen) Koehne (*Rosaceae*)
A hybrid between *Prunus* 'Pissardii' and *P.
pumila* or *P. besseyi* raised by Dr N. E. Hansen
at the South Dakota State Experimental Station
soon after 1900. It makes a low multi-stemmed
deciduous shrub up to 2 m high, with purple
leaves and dark purple fruit. Any soil; full sun.
Hardy to −30°C. Spring.

**Spiraea thunbergii** Blume (*Rosaceae*) Native
of N. China, though widely naturalized in S.

Japan, growing on rocky hillsides, flowering in
March and April. A deciduous or semi-
evergreen shrub up to 1.5 m high, the most
graceful of this group of spiraeas, and the
earliest to flower. Leaves pale green, narrowly
lanceolate, glabrous. In cool climates this
requires a warm autumn, and a sheltered
position to flower freely, as the buds are formed
on well-ripened long shoots formed during the
summer. Any soil. Hardy to −20°C. Spring.

**Spiraea prunifolia** Sieb. & Zucc. (syn. *S.
prunifolia* 'Plena') (*Rosaceae*) Native of E.
China, Korea and Taiwan, on sunny hillsides at
up to *c.* 1500 m, but in its double form (shown
here) long cultivated both in China and Japan,
from whence it was introduced by Siebold in
*c.* 1800. A deciduous shrub up to 2 m high, with
arching branches, obovate leaves, and flowers in
groups of 3–6. Any soil; full sun. Hardy to
−20°C. Spring.

**Spiraea × cinerea** Zab. **Grefsheim** (syn.
*Spiraea* 'Arguta Compacta') (*Rosaceae*)
Probably a hybrid between *S. hypericifolia* and
*S. cana*, which appeared at the Grefsheim
nursery in Norway, and was introduced into
cultivation in 1954. *S.* 'Arguta Compacta' is
very similar if not identical. It makes a
deciduous, twiggy shrub up to 1.5 m high, with
lanceolate leaves, silky hair beneath. Any soil;
full sun. Hardy to −20°C. Spring.

**Spiraea arguta** Zab. (*Rosaceae*) A hybrid of
uncertain parentage, but thought to be *S.
thunbergii* × *S.* × *multiflora* (*S. hypericifolia* × *S.
crenata*), known since 1884. It forms a
spreading, twiggy shrub up to 2.5 m high, with
narrowly oblanceolate leaves, and flowers in
clusters on the upper sides of the arching
branches. Pruning (soon after flowering) should
aim to remove the faded flowers and encourage
strong shoots from below the flowered portion
of the stem. Any soil; full sun. Hardy to −20°C.
Spring.

**Spiraea media** Franz Schmidt (*Rosaceae*)
Native of C. Europe in Austria eastwards to

Siberia, Korea and Japan, growing in scrub on
rocky slopes, flowering in April–May. A
deciduous, upright shrub up to 2 m high; leaves
to 5 cm long, with few shallow teeth near their
apex. Flowers in racemes. Hardy and easily
grown in a sunny well-drained place; any soil.
Hardy to −35°C. Spring.

**Spiraea arcuata** Hook. fil (*Rosaceae*) Native
of the Himalayas from N.W. India to S.W.
China, growing as a low thicket or in scrub,
from 2000–4500 m, flowering in May–July. A
low deciduous shrub up to 1.8 m, but usually
*c.*1 m; flowers 6–8 mm across, pink in bud,
with stamens longer than the petals; leaves
6–15 mm long, entire or lobed, with blunt teeth.
Photographed here in Yunnan near Lijiang in
May. Any soil; full sun. Hardy to −15°C.
Spring.

**Amelanchier spicata** (Lam.) K. Koch
(*Rosaceae*) Native of North America, but not
now known there wild. Cultivated in Europe
since the 18th C. and now naturalized in N.
Europe, from Belgium and Norway to Russia. A
deciduous suckering upright shrub to 8 m high,
forming thickets. Inflorescence erect, dense;
petals 6–10 mm long, obovate, ciliate at apex.
Any soil; full sun. Hardy to −25°C. Spring.

**Amelanchier lamarckii** F. N. Schroeder (syn.
*A.* × *grandiflora* Rehder, *A. canadensis* hort.)
(*Rosaceae*) Native of North America, but not
now known wild there, though close to *A. laevis*
Wieg. Grown in Europe since the 18th C. and
now naturalized in N.W. Europe from S.
England to Holland, Germany and Sweden. It
usually grows in damp acid woods or scrub on
sandy soil, flowering in April or May. It makes a
deciduous spreading shrub or tree up to 10 m,
not suckering, with leaves copper-coloured on
opening (at the same time as the flowers), silky-
hairy beneath when young, colouring red or
orange in autumn. Inflorescence lax, often
nodding. Petals 10–15 mm long, oblanceolate,
glabrous. Easily grown on acid or neutral soils,
and seeding freely, the fruits being eaten by
birds. Hardy to −25°C. Spring.

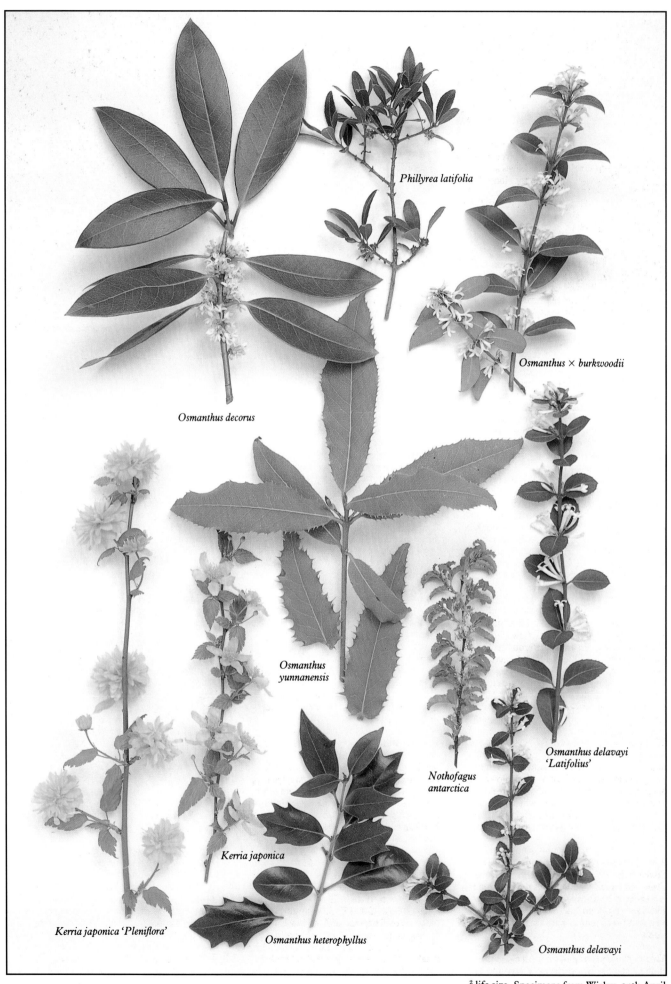

Phillyrea latifolia

Osmanthus × burkwoodii

Osmanthus decorus

Osmanthus
yunnanensis

Nothofagus
antarctica

Osmanthus delavayi
'Latifolius'

Kerria japonica

Kerria japonica 'Pleniflora'

Osmanthus heterophyllus

Osmanthus delavayi

⅔ life size. Specimens from Wisley, 24th April

***Phillyrea latifolia*** L. (*Oleaceae*)  Native of
Portugal and the Mediterranean region in
evergreen woods and scrub, often on limestone,
flowering in March–May. Evergreen shrub or
small tree to 15 m, very elegant when old.
Leaves lanceolate to elliptical, 20–70 cm long.
Flowers greenish. Fruit bluish-black, globose.
Any soil; full sun. Hardy to −15°C.

***Osmanthus decorus*** (Boiss. & Bal.) Kasapligil
(*Oleaceae*)  Native of N.E. Turkey and W.
Georgia, growing in mixed forests and on the
sides of gorges, at 1000–1600 m, flowering in
May. Evergreen shrub to 4 m. Leaves 4.5–
17 cm long. Flowers fragrant, 5 mm long. Fruit
egg-shaped, deep purple, often freely produced
in gardens. Any soil; sun or shade. Hardy to
−20°C.

***Osmanthus* × *burkwoodii*** (Burkwood &
Skipwith) P. S. Green (syn × *Osmarea b.*)
(*oleaceae*)  A hybrid between *O. decorus* and *O.
delavayi*, raised before 1928 by Messrs
Burkwood and Skipwith at Kingston-on-
Thames, Surrey. Evergreen shrub to 3 m.
Leaves to 5 cm long. Flowers scented, in April.
Any soil, good on chalk; sun or shade. Hardy to
−20°C.

***Osmanthus delavayi*** Franch. (*Oleaceae*)
Native of Yunnan, on dry hillsides in scrub and
forest, often on limestone, flowering in April–
May. Evergreen, spreading shrub to 2.5 m and
more across. Leaves ovate to elliptic-ovate,
1–2.5 cm long. Flowers to 1.5 cm long, scented.
Any well-drained soil; sun or part shade. Hardy
to −15°C. **'Latifolius'** is taller-growing, with
larger, broader leaves.

***Osmanthus yunnanensis*** P. S. Green (syn. *O.
forrestii* Rehd.) (*Oleaceae*)  Native of Yunnan
and Sichuan, at 2500–3000 m, by streams, on
the edges of woods and in dry scrub, flowering
in February. Evergreen large shrub or small tree
to 10 m. Leaves 10–20 cm long. Flowers in
clusters of 15–20 in leaf axils, each 5 mm long,
with reflexed petals, sweet-scented, creamy
white. Fruits to 1.5 cm long. Any soil; part
shade and shelter. Hardy to −10°C.

***Osmanthus heterophyllus*** (G. Don) P. S.
Green (*Oleaceae*)  Native of S. Honshu,
Shikoku, Kyushu and Taiwan, flowering in
October–December. Evergreen rounded shrub
to 3 m, rarely to 10 m in the wild. Leaves
variable, to 5 cm long. Flowers white, 4–5 mm
long, sweetly-scented. Fruits to 15 mm long,
purplish-black. Any soil; sun or shade. Hardy
to −15°C. **'Purpureus'** is said to be the hardiest
variety.

***Nothofagus antarctica*** (Forst.) Oerst.
(*Fagaceae*)  Native of S. Chile and Argentina,
in the subalpine zone of the Andes above the
evergreen forest, or in frost pockets, flowering
in spring. Deciduous shrub or small tree to
35 m. Leaves aromatic, sticky when young, to
3 cm long. Moist soil; sun or part shade. Hardy
to −15°C. A very attractive small tree with
bright green leaves.

***Kerria japonica*** DC. (*Rosaceae*)  Native of
China, from W. Sichuan eastwards to Japan, by
rivers and on rocks in gorges in the mountains,
flowering in April–May. Deciduous shrub to
2 m. Leaves 3–7 cm long. Flowers 2.5–5 cm
across. Any soil; sun or part shade. Hardy to
−20°C.

***Kerria japonica*** **'Pleniflora'**  An old garden
variety, long grown in China and Japan, and

*Osmanthus delavayi* at Kew

*Nothofagus antarctica*

*Orixa japonica* '*Variegata*'

introduced to Europe in 1805. Taller than the
single form, to 3 m. Flowers in late spring and
often again in autumn.

***Orixa japonica*** Thunb. **'Variegata'** (*Rutaceae*)
Native of Honshu, Shikoku, Kyushu, S. Korea
and N. China, east to Hubei, in woods, scrub
and on cliffs at up to 1300 m, flowering in
April–May. Deciduous, bushy shrub to 2 m.
Leaves foetid, obovate to elliptic, to 12 cm long.
Male and female flowers on separate plants. Any
soil; sun or part shade. Hardy to −15°C. The
variegated form is lower growing, to 1.5 m.

***Sibiraea altaiensis*** (Maxim.) C. K. Schneider
(syn. *S. laevigata* (L.) Maxim.)
(*Rosaceae*) Native of six localities in
Yugoslavia, then of E. Kazakstan (over 5000
miles to the east) and E. Siberia, south to W.
Sichuan, on limestone cliffs and rocky hills, at
up to 4500 m, flowering in May and June.
Deciduous shrub to 2 m. Leaves to 8 cm long.
Petals 2.5 mm. Any soil; full sun. Hardy to
−25°C and below.

*Sibiraea altaiensis*

*Prunus bucharica* at Amankutan, near Samarkhand, C. Asia

*Exochorda albertii* near Dushanbe

*Exochorda serratifolia*

*Prunus bifrons*

*Prunus spinosissima*

*Atraphaxis pyrifolia*

**Prunus bucharica** (Korsh.) Hand.-Mazz. (syn. *Amygdalus bucharica* Korsh.) (*Rosaceae*)
Native of Central Asia in the Kizil Kum, the Tien Shan, the Pamir-Alai, and N. Afghanistan, on rocky limestone hills to 2600 m, flowering in March and April. Spiny, deciduous shrub to 3 m. Leaves oval-elliptic or oblong, 3–4 cm long, sometimes greyish. Flowers pink or white, to 4 cm across. Well-drained soil; full sun. Hardy to −20°C.

**Prunus spinosissima** (Bunge) Franch. (syn. *Amygdalus spinosissima* Bunge) (*Rosaceae*)
Native of the Kizil Kum, Tien Shan, Pamir-Alai, N. Iran and Afghanistan, in rocky places in the mountains at 700–2600 m, flowering in April. Low, spiny, deciduous shrub to 1 m and more across. Leaves elliptic-obovate to oblanceolate, to 2 cm long. Flowers pale pink, 1.5–2 cm across. Fruit oval to rounded. Dry, well-drained soil; full sun. Hardy to −20°C.

**Prunus bifrons** Fritsch (syn. *Cerasus erythrocarpa* Nevski) (*Rosaceae*)   Native of Kashmir to Afghanistan and Central Asia, in the Tien Shan, the Pamir-Alai and the Kopet Daǧ, on rock ledges and cliffs at 1000–3000 m, flowering in April and May. Very twiggy, deciduous, shrub to 1.5 m. Leaves 1–1.5 cm long. Flowers about 1.2 cm across. Fruit red. Poor, well-drained soil; full sun. Hardy to −20°C.

**Exochorda albertii** Regel (syn. *E. korolkowii* Lav.) (*Rosaceae*)   Native of the Pamir-Alai from Samarkhand southeast to Dushanbe, in mountain scrub on steep slopes flowering in April–June. Deciduous shrub to 4 m. Leaves 4–7 cm long, oval-oblong. Flowers 3–4 cm wide. Good, well-drained soil; full sun. Hardy to −20°C. Early summer. This is one of the parents of the popular hybrid 'The Bride' (see next page).

**Exochorda serratifolia** Moore (*Rosaceae*)
Native of Korea and N.E. China. Deciduous shrub to 2 m, flowering in May. Leaves 3–7 cm long, elliptic, toothed towards apex. Flowers *c*.4 cm across. Any well-drained, good soil; full sun. Hardy to −20°C. Early summer.

**Atraphaxis pyrifolia** Bunge (*Polygonaceae*)
Native of the mountains of Central Asia, Afghanistan and N. Pakistan on dry hillsides, at 1500–2650 m, flowering in May–July. Twiggy, deciduous shrub to 1 m. Leaves 1–2 cm long, short-stalked. Flowers *c*.7 mm long. Dry, well-drained soil; full sun. Hardy to −20°C. Most *Atraphaxis* species are low desert shrubs, with pink or white flowers on thread-like stems. They need dry soil or a desert climate.

Prunus tenella 'Firehill'

Prunus incana

Prunus incisa

Exochorda 'The Bride'

Chaenomeles 'Nivalis'

Prunus divaricata

Chaenomeles cathayensis

Chaenomeles 'Rowallane'

Chaenomeles × superba

Chaenomeles japonica

Chaenomeles speciosa 'Phylis Moore'

Chaenomeles 'Boule de Feu'

⅓ life size. Specimens from Kew, 9th May

**Prunus tenella** Batsch. var. **gesslerana** Rehd. **'Firehill'** (syn. *Amygdalus nana* L.) (*Rosaceae*) Native of E. Austria and Czechoslovakia south to Bulgaria and east to the Caucasus, on dry, grassy steppes, flowering in May. Var. *gesslerana* is a large-flowered (to 2.5 cm across), richly coloured form; a white form is also known. A low suckering deciduous shrub to 1.5 m. Leaves lanceolate, to 7 cm long. Any well-drained soil; full sun. Hardy to −25°C.

**Prunus incana** (Pallas) Batsch. (syn. *Cerasus incana* (Pallas) Spach    Native of N. and C. Turkey, the Caucasus and N.W. Iran, on dry, rocky limestone slopes and cliffs, at 360–2400 m, flowering in April–June. Deciduous shrub to 2 m, often prostrate. Leaves elliptic to narrowly lanceolate, to 4 cm long, whitish, hairy below. Flowers to 17 mm across, in late spring. Fruit dark red, sub-globose. Hardy to −20°C.

**Prunus divaricata** Ledebour    Native of S.E. Europe, from Yugoslavia and Bulgaria, eastwards to Turkey, Syria, the Caucasus and C. Asia, in open woods and on rocky slopes up to 2450 m, flowering in April–May, with the leaves. Deciduous shrub to small tree to 10 m, sometimes spiny. Leaves ovate-elliptic to obovate, sometimes hairy beneath, 4–6 cm long. Flowers up to 2.5 cm across. Fruit globose to ovoid-oblong, damson-like, yellow, red or purple. Any soil; sun. Hardy to −25°C. This is the wild form of P. 'Pissardii', the commonly planted, purple-leaved flowering plum.

**Prunus incisa** Thunb. (syn. *Cerasus incisa* (Thunb.) Loisel)    Native of C. and W. Honshu, in woods in the mountains, flowering in April–June. Deciduous shrub to rarely small tree to 10 m. Leaves obovate or ovate, 3–5 cm long. Any soil; sun or part shade. Hardy to −20°C.

**Exochorda × macrantha 'The Bride'** (*Rosaceae*)    A hybrid between *E. racemosa* and *E. korolkowii*, raised by Grootendorst in about 1938. Spreading deciduous shrub to 1.5 m high and more across, with pendulous branches. Any soil; sun or part shade and warm position. Hardy to −20°C.

**Chaenomeles × superba** Rehd.    A hybrid of *C. japonica* and *C. speciosa* which makes a vigorous, but generally small shrub. This cross has given rise to many of the garden hybrids grown today.
**'Boule de Feu'**    Raised by Barbier of Orléans in 1913, this makes a shrub up to 2.8 m high. The flowers are followed by fragrant fruits.
**'Rowallane'**    Raised at Rowallane, Co. Down, in 1920. Normally a low spreading shrub, it grows to 1.3 m high against a wall.

**Chaenomeles cathayensis** C. K. Schneid. Native of W. Hubei, and perhaps elsewhere in C. China, in scrub and hedges, and commonly cultivated, flowering in March and April. Deciduous shrub to 3 m. Leaves finely and sharply serrate, 3–11 cm long, pubescent beneath when young. Flowers pink. Any soil; sun and benefits from wall protection. Hardy to −20°C.

**Chaenomeles japonica** (Thunb.) Lindl. (syn. *Cydonia japonica* Pers., *Pyrus japonica* Thunb.) 'Japonica'    Native of Honshu and Kyushu, in woods in the mountains, at low altitudes, flowering in April and May. Deciduous, spreading shrub to 1 m, more across. Leaves pale green, glabrous. Flowers orange-scarlet,

*Prunus tenella 'Firehill'* at Kew

*Chaenomeles speciosa 'Simonii'*

*Chaenomeles speciosa 'Moerloosii'*

2.5 cm across. Fruit 3 cm across. Any soil; sun or part shade. Hardy to −20°C.

**Chaenomeles × californica** Weber **'Enchantress'**    A cultivar of *C. × californica* which is a hybrid raised in California by W. B. Clarke, by crossing *C. cathayensis* with *C. × superba*. A free-flowering, erect shrub.

**Chaenomeles speciosa** (Sweet) Nakai (*Rosaceae*)    Native of C. China, but long cultivated both there and in Japan, so that its natural distribution is obscure. Deciduous shrub to 2 m and more across, with spines. Leaves glabrous. Flowers to 3.5 cm aross, scarlet, pink or white, in spring. Any soil; warm position. Hardy to −20°C.
**'Nivalis'**    A strong-growing variety raised by Lémoine *c.* 1880.
**'Phylis Moore'**    Raised at Knap Hill, Surrey, and named after the wife of the Keeper of Glasnevin Botanic Garden.
**'Simonii'**    A low-growing cultivar, up to 80 cm high.
**'Moerloosii'**    Raised in the 1850s by Moerloos of Belgium.

*Chaenomeles × californica 'Enchantress'*

*Parriotiopsis
jacquemontiana*

*Amelanchier
bartramiana*

*Amelanchier alnifolia*

*Elaeagnus multiflora*

*Amelanchier
humilis*

*Prinsepia uniflora*

*Prunus persica
'Sagami Shidare'*

*Prunus persica
'Kurokawa-Yaguchi'*

*Prunus persica 'Stellata'*

*Prunus persica
'Sansetsu Shidare'*

⅔ life size. Specimens from Kew, 25th April

**Prinsepia uniflora** Batalin (*Rosaceae*) Native of China, in N. Shaanxi, where it was collected by Purdom and Farrer. Flowering in April or May. A deciduous shrub up to 2 m high, with long arching branches and purplish-red or crimson fruit. Any soil; sun. Hardy to −20°C. Spring. *P. utilis* Royle (p. 33) differs in being very stiff and spiny, with black hanging fruit, ripe in April and May, from flowers produced in autumn.

**Amelanchier bartramiana** (Tausch) Roem. (*Rosaceae*) Native of North America from Labrador to Minnesota and south to Pennsylvania, flowering in April and May. A deciduous shrub up to 2.5 m, distinct from other species in its few-flowered (1–5) umbel-like inflorescence. Petals *c.*8 mm long. Fruit purplish-black. Any soil; sun or part shade. Hardy to −30°C.

**Amelanchier alnifolia** Nutt. (*Rosaceae*) Native of Saskatchewan south to Colorado and Idaho, flowering in May. A low deciduous shrub up to 2 m, with broadly oval leaves densely woolly. Petals *c.*10 mm long. Fruit black. Any soil; sun. Hardy to −20°C.

**Amelanchier humilis** Wieg. (*Rosaceae*) Native of North America, from Vermont eastwards to Alberta, south to New York and Iowa, flowering in May. A stoloniferous deciduous shrub up to 1.25 m, forming thickets. Leaves 2.5 cm long, acute, coarsely toothed to below the middle with 3–5 teeth per cm. Petals *c.*8 mm long. Fruit black. Any soil; sun or light shade. Hardy to −25°C. Spring.

**Amelanchier ovalis** Med. (*Rosaceae*) Service-berry Native of Belgium south to Portugal and east to Turkey and the Caucasus, growing in rocky places and woods, usually on limestone, flowering in April and May. An erect deciduous shrub up to 3 m, distinguishable from the American species by its short styles (*c.*1 mm) which are separated, not joined at their base. Leaves woolly beneath when young. Less graceful than *A. lamarckii* (p. 77), but with longer-lasting flowers, and a more compact woolly infloresence. Any well-drained soil; sun. Hardy to −20°C. Spring.

**Parrotiopsis jacquemontiana** (Decne.) Rehd. (*Hamamelidaceae*) Native of the W. Himalayas from Afghanistan to N.W. India, growing in undergrowth in the forests from 1500–2100 m, flowering in May. A large shrub or small tree up to 8 m; leaves deciduous, when mature 4–8 cm long. Flowers very small, surrounded by 4–6 large white bracts. Easily grown, but liable to damage by late frosts; in cultivation flowers continue to be produced until mid-summer. Any soil; sun or part shade. Hardy to −20°C. Spring.

**Elaeagnus multiflora** Thunb. (*Elaeagnaceae*) Native of Japan and N. China from Jiangxi to W. Hubei and Sichuan, growing in scrub and open woods in the mountains at 600–1800 m, flowering in April and May. A deciduous shrub up to 3 m, with elliptic to lanceolate leaves, up to 6 cm long, with white and brown scales beneath. Flowers in groups of 1–3, with pedicels 1–5 cm long. Fruits red, 1.5 cm long, pendulous, edible; twigs brown, scaly. Easily cultivated, but less showy in flower than *E. umbellata*. Any soil; sun or light shade. Hardy to −20°C. Spring.

**Prunus persica** Batsch (*Rosaceae*) Ornamental Peach Probably originally native of N. China,

*Prunus lusitanica* at Longleat, Wiltshire

*Amelanchier ovalis*

*Prunus cerasus*

and cultivated there for over a thousand years for both flower and fruit. They may now be seen planted along the road from the airport to Beijing (Peking). These Japanese varieties are spectacular in flower; and may be identical to clones imported in the 19th C. and given Latin cultivar names; other flowering clones have been raised in Europe and in California. 'Kurokawa – Yaguchi' (pink; semi-double); 'Sagami Shidare' (deep pink; semi-double); 'Sansetsu Shidare' (white; semi-double); 'Stellata' is distinct in its narrow petals and curious rather than beautiful, unless flowering exceptionally well. Any soil, preferably not acid; full sun and a warm position. Hardy to −20°C. Spring.

**Prunus lusitanica** L. (*Rosaceae*) Portugal Laurel Native of S.W. France, Spain and Portugal, with subspecies in the Azores and the Canaries, growing in forests, flowering in April–May. Subsp. *azorica* has broader leaves and

fewer-flowered inflorescences; subsp. *hixa*, from the Canaries, has long-tipped, acuminate leaves. An evergreen shrub or small tree with leaves 8–13 cm long. A good species in cultivation, hardier and more tolerant of chalk than *P. laurocerasus*, and very good for a low windbreak. Any soil; sun or part shade. Hardy to −20°C. Early summer.

**Prunus cerasus** L. (*Rosaceae*) Sour Cherry Native range unknown. Now found semi-wild throughout Europe and Asia. A deciduous shrub or small tree up to 8 m, freely suckering, commonly naturalized in hedges, distinguished from *P. avium* L. by flowering a week or two later, and by its broadly campanulate hypanthium and spreading, not reflexed, sepals. A double-flowered form, 'Rhexii', is commonly cultivated; it has been known since the 16th C. Any soil. Sun or part shade. Hardy to −20°C. Spring.

Exochorda giraldii
var. wilsonii

Holboellia coriacea

Zanthoxylum
piperitum

Actinidia kolomikta

Akebia quinata

Dipelta ventricosa

Schisandra glaucescens

Akebia trifoliata

Schisandra rubriflora

Ponciris trifoliata

Akebia ×
pentaphylla

⅓ life size. Specimens from Kew and Wisley, 19th May

**Holboellia coriacea** Diels (*Lardizabalaceae*)
Native of China, especially in W. Hubei,
growing in scrub and gorges, from 600–1300 m,
flowering in May. An evergreen climber to 5 m,
with male and female flowers in separate
inflorescences, the male white, the female
purplish; both sweetly and heavily scented, with
fleshy sepals. Easily cultivated on a sheltered
wall. Any soil, sun or shade. Hardy to −15°C.
Spring. *H. fargesii* Réaub. from W. Hubei, with
5–9 leaflets, grows at higher altitudes than *H.
coriacea* and should be hardier.

**Exochorda giraldii** Hesse var. **wilsonii** Rehder
(*Rosaceae*)   Native of W. Hubei on cliffs from
600–1300 m, flowering in May. Deciduous
shrub to 3.25 m, upright or somewhat
spreading; petals *c*.2.5 cm long. *E. giraldii*
Hesse is known from Shaanxi and is reported to
be distinct in its slender red petioles. Both need
well-drained soil; sun. Hardy to −20°C. Late
spring.

**Actinidia kolomikta** Maxim. (*Actinidiaceae*)
Native of N.E. and W. China, Korea and
Japan, growing in coniferous forests, climbing
to 10 m, flowering in May and June. The
flowers are white, about 1 cm across, sweetly
scented like Lily of the Valley. Hardy to −25°C.
Late spring.

**Actinidia chinensis** Planch. (*Actinidiaceae*)
Chinese Gooseberry, Kiwi fruit   Native of
most of China, commonest in W. Hubei, S.
Sansu and W. Sichuan, growing in scrub and
oak forest at 200–2400 m, flowering in June. A
robust deciduous climber to 8 m, shoots densely
reddish-hairy; leaves large, up to 20 cm across,
broadly heart-shaped. Flowers opening creamy
white, deepening with age, male and female on
separate plants. Any soil; sun or part shade.
Hardy to −15°C. Summer.

**Dipelta ventricosa** Hemsl. (*Caprifoliaceae*)
Native of W. Sichuan, growing in woods and
scrub at 1200–2700 m, flowering in May–June.
A deciduous shrub to 4 m high. Any soil; sun or
part shade. Hardy to −20°C. Spring.

**Zanthoxylum piperitum** DC (*Rutaceae*) Japan
Pepper   Native of N. China, Korea and Japan,
growing in scrub in the mountains and in
hedges, flowering in April–June. Deciduous
shrub to 2 m high; fruit reddish, with black
seeds which are used in Japan as pepper. The
female flowers are shown here. Any soil; warm
position. Hardy to −15°C.

**Schisandra glaucescens** Diels (*Schisandraceae*)
Native of W. Hubei, in rocky woods and scrub
at 1600–2300 m, flowering in May–June.
Deciduous climber to 6 m, with leaves thin in
texture, and glaucous beneath. Flowers orange;
fruits scarlet. Late spring.

**Schisandra rubriflora** (Franch.) Rehd. & Wils.
(syn. *S. grandiflora* var. *rubriflora* Schneid.)
(*Schisandraceae*)   Native of the Himalayas from
Assam westwards to China, growing in scrub
and forest to 3000 m, flowering in June.
Deciduous twining climber to 8 m or more. The
male and female flowers are on separate plants
and should be planted nearby to ensure a good
crop of the hanging chains of scarlet fruit, which
may consist of up to 80, 2–seeded fleshy carpels
(p. 265). Any soil; sun or shade. Hardy to
−15°C. Spring.

*Schisandra* in the Lijiang Mountains, Yunnan

**Ponciris trifoliata** Rafin. (syn. *Aegle sepiaria*)
(*Rutaceae*)   Native of N. China and Korea. A
spreading shrub to 3 m high, with green, spiny
twigs, flowering in spring; fruits yellow, like
small oranges, to 5 cm across. Only flowers
freely after a warm autumn. Leaves deciduous,
trifoliate. Any soil. Hardy to −15°C.

**Akebia quinata** Decne (*Lardizabalaceae*) Native
of Japan, in Honshu and southwards, in China
as far west as Hubei, and Korea, growing in
scrub and hedges in the mountains, flowering in
April–May. A usually evergreen climber, up to
6 m. Inflorescence with female flowers at the
base, male at the apex, the pedicels of the female
flowers at an acute angle with the inflorescence
axis. Any soil; sun or shade; usually trained on a
wall or pergola. Hardy to −15°C.

**Akebia trifoliata** (Thunb.) Koidz. (syn. *A.
lobata* Decne) (*Lardizabalaceae*)   Native of
Japan, as far north as Hokkaido, and China west
to Hubei and W. Sichuan, growing in rocky
places and scrub to 1800 m, flowering in April–
May. A deciduous (or partly evergreen) climber
to 10 m or more, with 3 shallowly lobed leaflets.
Fruit sausage shaped, to 12 cm long, edible.
Easily grown but probably not as hardy as *A.
quinata*. Hardy to −10°C.

**Akebia × pentaphylla** Makino
(*Lardizabalaceae*)   The hybrid between *A.
quinata* and *A. trifoliata* known wild in Japan. It
is intermediate between the parents, with often
5 wavy-edged leaflets, and inflorescences closer
to *A. quinata*.

**Stauntonia hexaphylla** Decne (*Lardizabalaceae*)
Native of Japan, Korea and Taiwan, growing in
forests, reaching at least 10 m in height. Male
and female flowers are produced on separate
inflorescences, and are sweetly scented. The
purple fruits are about 3 cm long, sweet and
edible, but produced only in warm climates.
The leathery, evergreen leaves have 3–7 leaflets.
Hardy to −10°C.

**Lardizabala biternata** Ruiz & Pavon
(*Lardizabalaceae*)   Native of Chile, common in
the central region of the coast and inland,
growing in forests. A climber to about 4 m with
evergreen leaves with 3–9 leaflets. Male and
female flowers on separate plants. The male
flowers are shown here; the female are solitary,
and may produce small, sausage-shaped fruit.
Hardy to −10°C. Spring.

*Stauntonia hexaphylla*

*Actinidia chinensis (male)*

*Lardizabala biternata*

Berberis heterophylla

B. buxifolia

B. empetrifolia

B. pallens

B. linearifolia

B. replicata

B. × stenophylla

B. darwinii

B. wardii

B. thunbergii

B. thunbergii 'Aurea'

B. thunbergii 'Atropurpurea Nana'

⅔ life size. Specimens from Kew, 25th April

**Berberis heterophylla** Juss. ex Poir (*Berberidaceae*)  Native of S. Chile. Evergreen or partly deciduous shrub to 1.5 m. Leaves to 2.5 cm long. Flowers to 1.5 cm across. Berries blue, globose. Any soil; full sun or part shade. Hardy to −15°C perhaps. Spring.

**B. buxifolia** Lam.  Native of S. Chile and S. Argentina on open slopes and scrub in the hills, flowering in November. Evergreen shrub to 2 m, with arching branches. Leaves to 1.7 cm long, greyish beneath. Flowers 1.4–1.6 cm across. Berries globose, blue with a bloom. Any soil; full sun. Hardy to −15°C. Late spring.

**B. empetrifolia** Lam.  Native of S. Chile and S. Argentina to Tierra del Fuego, on rough ground near the sea, up to 1300 m, flowering in November. Dwarf, often prostrate evergreen to 60 cm high. Leaves 10–20 mm long. Flowers c.1.5 cm across. Berries blue, with a bloom. Moist, well-drained soil; full sun. Hardy to −15°C. Spring.

**B. pallens** Franch.  Native of W. Yunnan at 3300 m, flowering in May. Deciduous or semi-evergreen shrub to 2 m. Leaves 3–5 cm, Flowers c.12 mm across. Any soil; full sun. Hardy to −15°C.

**B. linearifolia** Phil.  Native of Chile and C. Patagonia, in damp woodland, at 1000–2000 m, flowering in November. Evergreen, upright shrub to 3 m. Leaves to 4 cm long, 6 mm wide. Flowers to 18 cm across. Fruit black, bloomed, egg-shaped. Moist soil; full sun. Hardy to −10°C. Spring.
**'Orange King'**  Has larger, deeper orange flowers than most cultivars.

**B. replicata** W. W. Sm.  Native of W. Yunnan, at 1500–3300 m, in scrub on open hillsides, flowering in December–February. Evergreen shrub to 2 m. Leaves 2–3.5 cm long. Flowers 4–12 together, c.6 mm across. Berries blue-black, to 8 mm long. Sun or part shade. Hardy to −15°C. Spring, often early.

**B. × stenophylla** Lindl.  Hybrids between *B. empetrifolia* and *B. darwinii* first raised in about 1860. Evergreen shrubs to 3 m with numerous arching branches. Leaves variable. Flowers in groups or racemes of 4–14, rarely solitary.
**'Crawley Gem'**  Has flowers in racemes of 7–14, reddish outside. Any soil; full sun. Hardy to −15°C. Spring. Very popular for its ease of growth, hardiness and free-flowering.

**B. darwinii** Hook.  Native of S. Chile and S. Argentina, in the Patagonian mountains, flowering in November. Much branched, evergreen shrub to 1.5 m. Leaves 10–20 mm long. Flowers in racemes of 10–30, to 1.4 cm across. Berries blue, with a bloom. Soil preferably moist and acid; full sun. Hardy to −15°C. Spring.

**B. wardii** Schneid.  Native of the Naga hills in Assam, at c.3000 m, in open grassy places among scrub. Evergreen, dense shrub to 1.5 m. Leaves 2–3 cm long. Flowers in groups of 2–5, c.1.4 cm across, on red pedicels. Any soil; full sun. Hardy to −10°C. Spring.

**B. thunbergii** DC  Native of S. Japan, flowering in April. Low-growing, deciduous, spiny shrub to 1 m. Leaves to 3.5 cm long. Flowers 6 mm across. Fruits red, elliptic, 7–10 mm long. Any soil; full sun. Hardy to −25°C. Spring, and pretty in autumn when fruiting freely. Numerous varieties are

cultivated; shown here are:
**'Aurea'**  A dwarf variety, to 50 cm with yellowish leaves, brightest in full sun, and **'Atropurpurea Nana'** (syn. 'Crimson Pygmy') A popular variety, raised in 1942, to 40 cm high. Other varieties such as 'Pink Queen' and 'Rose Glow' have pink-variegated leaves.

**B. montana** Gay  Native of C. Chile and C. Argentina at c.1000 m, flowering in January and February. Erect, much-branched, deciduous shrub to 4 m, with stout 3-pointed spines. Leaves 10–20 mm long, obovate, entire. Flowers in groups of 2–3, 1.5–2 cm across. Berries blue, with a bloom. Any soil; full sun. Hardy to −15°C. Late spring.

**B. valdiviana** Phil.  Native of Chile, from Concepçion to Valdivia, at 200–800 m, flowering in September (?). Evergreen shrub to 4 m, with spines at the nodes. Leaves 2–7.5 cm long, sometimes with spiny teeth. Flowers, up to 30 in hanging racemes to 7.5 cm long. Fruits ovoid, purple. Good on chalk; sun or part shade. Hardy to −15°C. Late spring.

*Berberis stenophylla 'Crawley Gem'*

*Berberis montana*

*Berberis linearifolia 'Orange King'*

*Berberis valdiviana*

*Mahonia repens 'Rotundifolia'*

*Berberis × ottawensis 'Superba'*

*Mahonia × wagneri 'Undulata'*

*Mahonia aquifolium*

*Mahonia nevinii*

*Mahonia fremontii*

**Mahonia repens** Lindl. **'Rotundifolia'** This clone or hybrid of *M. repens* has rounded leaflets with small spines; it makes an upright shrub 1–1.5 m high. The wild form of *M. repens*, from British Columbia along the east of the Sierras to New Mexico, grows in dry, open woods. It is a suckering shrub with upright stems to 20 cm high. Leaflets 5, dull green above and beneath, with 8–20 bristles on each edge; and short, dense racemes to 8 cm long. Any dryish soil; full sun or part shade. Hardy to −15°C, with shelter. Spring.

**Mahonia × wagneri 'Undulata'** *M. × wagneri* (Jouni) Rehd. is the name proposed for hybrids between *M. pinnata* and *M. aquifolium*. 'Undulata' is a fine clone, probably of this cross, of unknown origin. It makes an upright evergreen shrub to 2 m, with glossy, wavy leaves and rich yellow flowers. The lowest pair of leaflets are near the base of the petiole, as in *M. pinnata*. Hardy to −15°C. Spring.

**Mahonia aquifolium** Nutt. (*Berberidaceae*) Oregon Grape Native of northernmost California to British Columbia and Idaho, in *Pseudotsuga* and mixed conifer woods up to 2000 m, flowering March–May. Evergreen, suckering shrub to 2 m, usually *c*.1.5 m. Leaves 10–25 cm long with 5–9 leaflets, glossy above and beneath, the lowest pair 2–4 cm above the base of the leaf stalk. Flowers 16 mm across. Fruits blue, with a grey bloom. Any soil; sun or shade. Hardy to −20°C. Spring.

**Mahonia nevinii** Gray Native of S. California, in sandy or stony places in sage bush scrub or chaparral, flowering in March–April. Evergreen shrub to 4 m, large and rounded in the wild, rather loose and floppy in cultivation in N. Europe. Leaves 4–8 cm long with 3–5 leaflets. Flowers in a loose raceme. Berries red to orange. Well-drained, dry soil in a hot position; full sun. Hardy to −10°C perhaps. Spring.

**Mahonia fremontii** Torr. Native of S.E. California, east to Utah, Colorado and Arizona, in Pinyon-pine and Juniper or Joshua tree (*Yucca*) woodland, growing on dry rocks, at 1000–1500m, flowering in May–June. Upright, stiff shrub to 2 m. Leaves with 3–7 leaflets, each with spreading spines; flowers 3–9 in loose racemes; fruits reddish, dry, inflated and spongy when ripe. Well-drained soil; full sun and hot position. Hardy to −10°C. Spring.

**Berberis × ottawensis** Schneid. **'Superba'** (*Berberidaceae*) A hybrid between *B. thunbergii*, probably 'Atropurpurea', and *B. vulgaris*, raised in Holland before 1943. Deciduous spreading shrub to 2 m high and wide. Leaves reddish; flowers yellow with red markings, in hanging clusters of 5–10. Any soil; sun or part shade. Hardy to −25°C. Late spring.

*Berberis temolaica*

*Berberis dumicola* at Ulu-Ky, Lijiang in Yunnan

**Berberis temolaica** Ahrendt Native of S.E.
Xizang, on open grassy slopes and in scrub at
4000–4500 m, flowering in June. Deciduous
shrub to 2 m, with arching branches, usually
rather sparsely branched in cultivation. Stems
pruinose; leaves 20–45 mm long, often spiny on
the margins; bluish-green, white beneath.
Flowers *c*.1.5 cm across. Fruits red, with white
bloom. Any soil; sun or part shade. Hardy to
−15°C. Late spring. Once established it is best
to prune this species heavily so a good crop of
white stems is produced. If left unpruned, the
bush becomes very straggly.

**Berberis dumicola** Schneid. Native of N.W.
Yunnan, in scrub and open pine forest at 2000–
3000 m flowering in April–May. Evergreen
shrub to 1.5 m. Young shoots red; leaves
5–9.5 cm, with 20–40 teeth, green beneath.
Flowers in groups of 10–30, *c*.1.2 cm across.
Berries blue. Any soil; sun or part shade. Hardy
to −15°C. Spring.

**Berberis gyalaica** Ahrendt Native of S.E.
Xizang, in the Pome district, on dry hillsides
and in open scrub at 3000–3500 m, flowering in
July, fruiting in October. Shown here is the
type of var. *maximiflora* Ahrendt, L. S. & E.
15826. Deciduous shrub to 3 m. Leaves obovate
to elliptic, sessile, not spined, to 3 cm. Panicles
8–16 cm long; pedicels 2–5 mm. Flowers *c*.8 cm
across. Berries black, bloomed. Any soil; sun or
part shade. Hardy to −15°C. A bushy shrub.

**Berberis chinensis** Poir Native of the
Caucasus, with the related *B. crataegina* DC in
Turkey, growing in open rocky places,
flowering in May–June. Deciduous arching and
spreading shrub to 3 m; leaves oblanceolate to
obovate, to 4 cm long, entire or finely toothed.
Fruits deep red, 1 cm long. Any soil; sun or part
shade. Hardy to −25°C. Spring.

**Berberis verruculosa** Hemsl. & Wilson
Native of W. Sichuan, near Kangding
(Tachienlu), at 1200–4000 m. Evergreen, dense
shrub to 1.5 m. Leaves 12–22 mm long, with
2–4 spines, greyish beneath. Pedicels 4–7 mm
long. Flowers 2 cm across, if opened. Any soil;
shade or part shade. Hardy to −20°C. Early
summer.

**Berberis 'Bunch o' Grapes'** A hybrid of the
Polyanthae section from the Himalayas, with
reddish, globose fruit in large bunches. A
deciduous shrub to 2 m or more. Any soil; full
sun. Hardy to −20°C. Summer-flowering,
autumn-fruiting. 'Sibbertoft Coral' is somewhat
similar.

*Berberis gyalaica*

*Berberis chinensis*

*Berberis verruculosa*

*Berberis 'Bunch o' Grapes'*

# PAEONIES

*Paeonia suffruticosa* cultivar in Beijing

*Paeonia lutea* var. *ludlowii*

*Paeonia lutea* × *delavayi*

*Paeonia* × *lemoinei* 'Argosy'

*Paeonia* 'Anne Rosse'

**Paeonia suffruticosa** Andrews (*Paeoniaceae*)
Moutan, Tree Paeony   Native of Gansu and
probably also N. Sichuan and Shaanxi, growing
in scrub in the mountains, flowering in May.
The form shown here, 'Joseph Rock', was
introduced by Rock from a lamasery garden in
S.W. Gansu and said to have been brought from
the Min Shan, a limestone range, in the same
area that the wild moutan was seen by Farrer
and Purdom, about 65 km N.E. of Wudu.
Deciduous spreading shrub to 2 m high, and
more across. Flowers *c*.12 cm across, in early
summer. Rich well-drained soil, and good on
chalk; warm position. Hardy to −20°C. Many
cultivars are known, and have been grown in
China since the 4th century and in Japan and
Bhutan. Most have double or semi-double
flowers in shades of deep red to pink or white,
up to 30 cm across.

**P. × lemoinei** Rehd. **'Argosy'**   A hybrid
between *P. lutea* and *P. suffruticosa* raised by
Professor A. P. Saunders of Clinton, New York.
The flowers, 18 cm across, tend to sit down
among the leaves, though in this character they
are an improvement on the earliest *P.* ×
*lemoinei* hybrids raised in France. Newer
hybrids such as 'Tria' and 'Artemis' hold their
flowers better.

**P. lutea** Franch. (*Paeoniaceae*)   Native of
Yunnan, especially in the mountains above Dali,
flowering in May. Low deciduous shrub to 1 m.
Flowers 5–10 cm across, often yellow and red in
the wild. Well-drained, good soil; warm
position. Hardy to −15°C. Late spring – early
summer.

**P. lutea** Franch. var **ludlowii** Stern & Taylor
(*Paeoniaceae*)   Native of S.E. Xizang, near the
Tsangpo gorges, at 3000–3500 m, flowering in
June. Deciduous shrub to 2.5 m. Flowers 10–
13 cm across. Easily raised from seed which is set
in abundance. Any soil; full sun and shelter.
Hardy to −20°C. Late spring.

**P. lutea × delavayi**   Probable hybrids between
*P. lutea* and *P. delavayi* were reported by George
Forrest in the wild in Lijiang. They varied from
yellow with crimson blotches at the base, to
brownish orange. Similar hybrids are found in
cultivation, varying in the proportions of yellow
and crimson in the flowers. Those shown here
have *P. lutea* var. *ludlowii* as one parent.

**P. 'Anne Rosse'**   A hybrid between *P. delavayi*
and *P. lutea* var. *ludlowii* raised by the Earl of
Rosse before 1961. A robust shrub to 2 m tall;
flowers 10 cm across, in April–May.

**P. delavayi** Franch. (*Paeoniaceae*)   Native of
N. Yunnan in the Lijiang range, growing in
scrub and open rocky places on limestone at
*c*.3000 m, flowering in May. Deciduous shrub,
with bare weak stems surmounted by deeply
divided leaves. Flowers 5–10 cm across, deep
purplish-red. Well-drained, good soil; sun.
Hardy to −20°C. Early summer.

**P. potaninii** Komar. f. **alba** F. C. Stern
(*Paeoniaceae*)   Native of N.W. Yunnan and W.
Sichuan, on rocky hillsides at 3000–3600 m,
flowering in June. The original form, called *P.
delavayi* var. *angustiloba* Rehder & Wilson, has
deep purplish-crimson flowers like *P. delavayi*.
The white form, shown here, is more commonly
cultivated. There does not appear, however, to
be a white form of ordinary *P. delavayi*. The
yellow form of *P. potaninii*, from Yunnan, is
called var. *trollioides* (Stapf) F. C. Stern. Low
suckering shrub to 1 m, forming spreading
patches. Leaves to 25 cm long, 30 cm across,
with narrower segments than *P. delavayi*.
Flowers *c*.5 cm across. Any well-drained soil;
full sun. Hardy to −20°C. Early summer.

*Paeonia suffruticosa 'Joseph Rock'* at Kew

*Paeonia potaninii 'Alba'*

*Paeonia delavayi* near Lijiang, Yunnan

*Paeonia lutea var. lutea*

Genista hispanica

Sophora tetraptera
'Otari Gnome'

Coronilla emerus

Sophora microphylla

Cytisus emeriflorus

Cytisus x praecox
'Allgold'

Piptanthus nepalensis

Chamaecytisus ratisbonensis

Cytisus scoparius var. andreanus

Chamaecytisus purpureus

$\frac{2}{3}$ life size. Specimens from Kew, 19th May

*Sophora microphylla* at Logan

*Piptanthus tomentosus* in Lijiang, Yunnan

*Lygos sphaerocarpa*

*Piptanthus tomentosus*

*Teline linifolia*

**Coronilla emerus** L. (*Leguminosae*) Scorpion Senna   Native of S. Norway and Czechoslavakia south to Spain, Greece and Crete, in scrub and rocky limestone hills, flowering in March–May. Evergreen shrub to 2 m. Leaves with 2–4 pairs of obovate leaflets. Flowers 14–20 mm; pod 5–10 cm, on a slender 2–5 cm-long stalk. Any well-drained soil; full sun. Hardy to −20°C. Late spring.

**Genista hispanica** L.   See next page. A useful dwarf shrub for the top of a sunny wall.

**Sophora microphylla** Ait. (*Leguminosae*) Kowhai Native of both islands of New Zealand, in open forest and in damp rocky places, flowering from July to October. Deciduous shrub; the leaves appearing with the flowers. Any soil; full sun and shelter. Hardy to −10°C. See also p. 26. Early summer.

**Sophora tetraptera** J. S. Miller (*Leguminosae*) Kowhai   Native of New Zealand, in North Island, on the edges of forest, in open woods and damp or rocky places, flowering in July–September. Deciduous or semi-deciduous shrub or tree to 8 m. Leaves with 10–20 pairs of often elliptical leaflets. Flowers with standard shorter than or equalling the wings. Any soil; sheltered position or on a wall in full sun. Hardy to −10°C. Shown here: the cv. **'Otari Gnome'** in bud. Early summer.

**Cytisus × praecox 'Allgold'**   The original clone of this hybrid between *C. multiflorus* and *C. purgans* proved to be fertile, and several cultivars have been raised from it; 'Allgold' was raised in Holland by A. G. Brand of Boskoop in 1963. Other cultivars have been raised in deep yellow, pink and white. Early summer.

**Cytisus emeriflorus** Rchb. (*Leguminosae*) Native of S. Switzerland and N. Italy in the Alps around Lago di Como and Lugano. Deciduous shrub to 60 cm. Leaves with 3 leaflets, 10–20 cm long. Flowers in groups of 1–4, 10–12 mm long. Any well-drained soil. Full sun. Hardy to −20°C.

**Cytisus scoparius** (L.) Link var. **andreanus** (Puissant) Dipp. (*Leguminosae*)   A variety of the common broom (p. 166) in which the wings are crimson, found wild in Normandy in about 1884. Many of the richly-coloured cultivars were raised from this. Early summer.

**Chamaecytisus purpureus** (Scop.) Link (*Leguminosae*)   Native of S. Austria and N.W. Italy to N. Yugoslavia and Albania, on subalpine limestone rocks and in scrub, flowering in May–June. Deciduous, non-spiny subshrub to 30 cm with arching branches. Leaves 3-foliate; leaflets obovate, 2 cm long. Flowers 15–25 mm long, from white to dark purple in gardens. Any well-drained soil, but not too dry; full sun. Hardy to −20°C. This is one half of the remarkable chimaera +*Laburnocytisus adami*. Late spring.

**Piptanthus nepalensis** (Hook.) D. Don (syn. *P. laburnifolius* (D. Don) Stapf) (*Leguminosae*) Native of the Himalayas from N. India to Yunnan and Sichuan, at 2000–3600 m, flowering in March–May. Deciduous upright shrub to 2 m. Leaves dark green and shining, the leaflets 3–10 cm long. Flowers 2.5–3 cm long, opening with the leaves. Pods to 13 cm, flat, hanging. Any well-drained soil; sun or part shade. Hardy to −15°C but often breaking again from the base if cut down. Spring.

**Piptanthus tomentosus** Franch. (*Leguminosae*) Native of Yunnan, growing in open woods and scrub on limestone at *c*.3000 m, flowering in May. Deciduous shrub to 2 m. Distinguished from *P. nepalensis* by its very silky-hairy leaves. Any soil; sun or part shade. Hardy to −15°C.

**Chamaecytisus ratisbonensis** (Schaeffer) Rothm. (*Leguminosae*)   Native of C. Europe from Poland and Austria to S. Russia. A low shrub to 45 cm. Leaflets 3. Flowers 16–22 mm long. Full sun. Hardy to −25°C.

**Lygos sphaerocarpa** (L.) Heywood (*Leguminosae*) Retama   Native of E. Portugal, C. and S. Spain and N. Africa, on dry sandy or gravelly hills, flowering in April–May. Evergreen, leafless shrub to 2 m. Flowers in dense racemes, 5–8 mm long; pod 7–9 mm, one-seeded. Well-drained soil, dry in summer; full sun. Hardy to −10°C. Other species of *Lygos* are white-flowered.

**Teline linifolia** (L.) Webb. & Berth. (*Leguminosae*)   Native of the western Mediterranean region in the Balearic Islands, S. France, Spain and N. Africa, in woods and scrub on acid soil, flowering in April–May. Evergreen shrub to 1.5 m. Leaflets 10–15 mm, linear-oblanceolate, glabrous above, silky below. Flowers in terminal heads, 10–18 mm long. Well-drained acid soil, sun. Hardy to −10°C.

95

*Caragana tragacanthoides*

*Caragana tragacanthoides* in Ferghana, C. Asia

*Sophora mollis* in Tashkent Botanic Garden

**Caragana tragacanthoides** (Pall.) Poir.
(*Leguminosae*)    Native of C. Asia, N.W.
Xizang, Gansu, W. Mongolia, N. Pakistan
(Karakoram), on screes and rocks at 1800–
3300 m, flowering in May. Spiny low spreading
shrub to 1 m, the central rib of the leaf
becoming spiny. Leaves with 2–3 pairs of
leaflets, silky-hairy, especially beneath. Flowers
2–3 cm long. Any dry, well-drained soil; full
sun. Hardy to −25°C. perhaps.

**Caragana arborescens** Lam.    Native of
Siberia, C. Asia, and N.W. Mongolia, growing
by rivers, on rocky slopes or on the edges of
forest, flowering in May–June. Deciduous
shrub to 3 m, or small tree rarely to 7 m. Leaves
with 4–7 pairs of elliptic or ovate leaflets.
Pedicels 2–6 cm long. Any well-drained soil, full
sun. Hardy to −30°C or lower. Late spring. A
pendulous form is often grafted as a standard,
making a small rather ungainly, weeping tree.

**Caragana brevispina** Royle    Native of
Kashmir to C. Nepal, in scrub at 2400–3200 m,
flowering in May and June. Deciduous shrub to
3 m. Leaflets 8–16, ovate to oblong, 8–20 mm
long. Flowers often flushed with orange,
2–2.5 cm long. Any well-drained soil; full sun.
Hardy to −20°C.

*Caragana arborescens*

*Caragana brevispina*

*Genista lydia*

*Ulex gallii* on Dartmoor

**Sophora mollis** (Royle) Graham (*Leguminosae*) Native of the Pamir Alai, east to C. Nepal, on rocks in dry valleys at 1200–2000 m, flowering in March–April. Deciduous upright shrub to 2 m. Leaflets 1.2–2.5 cm long when mature, ovate to elliptic. Flowers 1.2–2.5 cm long. Pod winged, with 4–10 seeds, narrowed between the seeds. Any well-drained, dry soil. Full sun. Hardy to −15°C.

**Genista lydia** Boiss. (*Leguminosae*)    Native of Yugoslavia, Bulgaria, Greece and Turkey, on rocks and screes, flowering in April–May. Deciduous shrub to 1 m, branches often arching downwards. Leaves 3–10 mm, linear-oblanceolate. Flowers in short racemes on side branches, 10–12 mm long. Any well-drained soil; full sun. Hardy to −15°C.

**Genista hispanica** L.    Native of S.W. France and N. and E. Spain, on rocky hills and in scrub, flowering in April–May. Deciduous spreading shrub to 50 cm high, forming rounded mounds. Spines on short side shoots. Leaves 6–10 mm, single. Flowers 6–11 mm long, in short dense terminal racemes. Any well-drained soil; full sun. Hardy to −20°C.

**Anthyllis hermanniae** L. (*Leguminosae*) Native of the Mediterranean region from Corsica eastwards on rocky hills, flowering in May–June. Deciduous twiggy shrub to 50 cm. Leaves simple or 3-foliolate, 1–2 cm long, oblanceolate. Flowers *c*.5 mm long. Any well-drained soil; full sun. Hardy to −10°C.

**Ulex gallii** Planchon (*Leguminosae*)    Native of the Atlantic coast of Europe from Scotland and Ireland to Brittany and N.W. Spain, on sandy and rocky acid heaths, flowering in July–September. Evergreen spiny shrub to 1 m. Differs from common Gorse, *U. europaeus*, in its late flowering, deeper yellow flowers and narrower bracteoles 1.5 mm wide, and from the autumn-flowering *U. minor* Roth, by its longer calyx more than 10 mm, and standard 12.5–16 mm. Acid soil; full sun. Hardy to −15°C.

**Ulex europaeus** L. Gorse    Native of W. Europe from Scotland to Spain, N. Africa and Italy, on sandy heathland and hills, flowering in April–June, and intermittently through autumn and winter. Evergreen, spiny shrub to 2.5 m. Leaves reduced to scales or small spines. Flowers 15–20 mm long, sweetly and heavily scented. Pod black, hairy. Acid or neutral soil; full sun. Hardy to −20°C, and sprouting from the base if cut down.

**Ononis speciosa** Lag. (*Leguminosae*)    Native of S. and S.E. Spain, and N. Africa, growing on dry hillsides and in scrub, flowering in May. Glandular sticky evergreen shrub to 1 m. Leaflets 15–23 mm elliptical to suborbicular. Flowers 15–20 mm long. Any well-drained, dry soil; full sun. Hardy to −10°C, perhaps.

*Genista hispanica*

*Anthyllis hermanniae*

*Ononis speciosa* in Spain

*Ulex europaeus* and *Cytisus scoparius* (in distance) in Scotland

# HONEYSUCKLES

Kolkwitzia amabilis

Lonicera quinquelocularis

Lonicera involucrata

Lonicera bracteolaris

Lonicera maackii var. podocarpa

Lonicera tomentella

Lonicera pyrenaica

Chionanthus virginicus

Chionanthus retusus

⅔ life size. Specimens from Kew, 10th June

Lonicera korolkowii at Milling House, Gloucestershire

Lonicera tartarica 'Hack's Red'

Lonicera implexa in S. Spain

Lonicera japonica

Lonicera henryi

**Lonicera quinquelocularis** Hardw.   Native of the Himalayas from Afghanistan east of Yunnan, at 1800–3000 m, in forests, scrub and hedges, flowering in May–July. Large shrub or small spreading tree to 5 m. Fruit whitish, translucent with purplish seeds. Hardy to −15°C. Early summer.

**Kolkwitzia amabilis** Graebn. (*Caprifoliaceae*) Beauty Bush   Native of Shaanxi (Shensi), and W. Hubei, and apparently rare. Deciduous shrub to 2.5 m. Any soil; full sun. Hardy to −20°C. Early summer.

**Lonicera involucrata** (Richards) Banks Twinberry   Native of W. North America from Alaska south to Mexico, in moist places in the mountains at 1800–3000 m and along the coast below 1000 m, in California, and along the Great Lakes to Quebec, usually on limestone by water, in woods, flowering June–August. Deciduous shrub to 1 m. Hardy to −25°C.

**Lonicera bracteolaris** Boiss. & Bhuse.   Native of Soviet Georgia. Hardy to −20°C.

**Lonicera tomentella** Hook. f. & Thoms. Native of Sikkim, in rather dry valleys, at 2500–3500 m, flowering in June. Deciduous, upright shrub to 4 m. Fruit blue-black. Hardy to −15°C. Summer.

**Lonicera maackii** Maxim. var. **podocarpa** Franch.   Native of W. Hubei and Zhejiang (Chekiang) in scrub and hedges, at 900–1500 m, flowering in May–June. Deciduous, spreading shrub to 4 m. Any soil; full sun. Hardy to −15°C.

**Lonicera pyrenaica** L.   Native of the Pyrenees, N.E. Spain and the Balearic islands, on limestone rocks, flowering in May–June. Twiggy, deciduous shrub to 1 m. Flowers 12–15 mm (to 20 mm in var. *majoricensis*). Fruit red. Hardy to −15°C.

**Chionanthus virginicus** L. (*Oleaceae*) Fringe Tree   Native of Florida and Texas, north to New Jersey, Ohio and Missouri, in damp woods and scrub, flowering in April–June. Deciduous, dioecious shrub or small tree to 9 m. Moist, rich soil; sun. Hardy to −25°C. Late spring.

**Chionanthus retusus** Lindl. & Paxton (*Oleaceae*)   Native of China, Taiwan, Korea and S. Honshu in forests and on cliffs, flowering in April–May. Deciduous shrub to 2–3 m; leaves on young plants toothed. Hardy to −15°C. Late spring.

**Lonicera korolkowii** Stapf.   Native of C. Asia, Afghanistan and N. Pakistan, in scrub on dry hills, flowering in June–July. Deciduous shrub

to 3 m. Flowers 1.5 cm long. Fruits red. Hardy to −20°C.

**Lonicera tartarica** L. (*Caprifoliaceae*)   Native of the Caucasus eastwards to the Altai, and naturalized in W. Europe and E. North America, in scrub and dry hills, flowering in May–June. Deciduous upright shrub to 4 m. Any soil; sun. Hardy to −25°C. 'Hack's Red' is one of the darkest-flowered of many cultivars.

**Lonicera implexa** Aiton   Native of the whole Mediterranean region, and Portugal, in rocky places and scrub, flowering in April–June. Evergreen, twining shrub to 4 m. Flowers 2.5–4.5 cm long. Fruit pinkish-red. Hardy to −10°C, perhaps.

**Lonicera japonica** Thunb.   Native of China, west to W. Hubei, of Taiwan, Korea and Japan and commonly naturalized in E. North America, in scrub and woods, flowering in May–July. Twining shrub to 6 m; flowers scented, 3–4 cm long. Fruit black. Any soil; part shade. Hardy to −20°C.

**Lonicera henryi** Hemsl.   Native of W. Hubei where it is very common, and W. Sichuan, in scrub at 1200–2300 m, flowering in June–July. Twining evergreen shrub to 4 m. Flowers 2 cm long, fruit black. Hardy to −20°C.

*Abelia triflora*

*Dipelta floribunda*

*Jasminum beesianum*

*Lonicera chaetocarpa*

*Lonicera × americana*

*Lonicera × americana*

*Lonicera caprifolium*

*Lonicera × brownii 'Fuchsioides'*

*Lonicera × tellmanniana*

½ life size. Specimens from University Botanic Garden, Cambridge, 20th May

**Dipelta floribunda** Maxim. (*Caprifoliaceae*)
Native of W. Hubei and Shaanxi, in woods and
open scrub at 1200–1800 m, flowering in May–
July. Deciduous shrub to 5 m. Bracts shield-like,
attached by their centre. Flowers 3 cm long. Any
soil. Hardy to −20°C.

**Jasminum beesianum** Forrest & Diels
(*Oleaceae*)   Native of Yunnan and W. Sichuan,
growing in hedges, on grassy banks between
paddy fields, and in ravines, at 1000–2000 m
flowering in May–August. Deciduous twining
shrub to 3 m. Leaves to 5 cm long. Flowers deep
to pale pink. Hardy to −15°C.

**Abelia triflora** R. Br. ex Wall. (*Caprifoliaceae*)
Native of the W. Himalayas from Afghanistan to
C. Nepal, in dry scrub and rocky slopes, at
1500–4200 m, flowering in May–July.
Deciduous shrub to 4 m. Branches with bristly
hairs. Flowers 8 mm across. Wonderfully
scented. Hardy to −15°C.

**Lonicera × americana** (Mill.) K. Koch
Presumed to be a hybrid between *L. caprifolium*
and *L. etrusca*, found wild in S. France. Less
climbing than either species, making a twiggy,
scrambling shrub to 10 m. Upper 1–3 pairs of
leaves fused. Hardy to −20°C. Late spring.

**Lonicera chaetocarpa** Rehder (*Caprifoliaceae*)
Native of W. Sichuan, Gansu and E. Xizang, in
scrub and on cliffs at 2000–3500m, flowering in
June–July. Deciduous upright shrub to 2 m.
Fruits orange-red, surrounded by pale bract .
Any soil; sun. Hardy to −25°C.

**Lonicera caprifolium** L. (*Caprifoliaceae*) Native
of Austria and Czechoslovakia, south to Romania
and Turkey, and naturalized in W. Europe, in
hedges and scrub, flowering in May–June.
Climbing shrub to 3 m. Upper pairs of leaves
fused. Full sun. Hardy to −20°C.

**L. × brownii** (Reg.) Carr. **'Fuchsioides'**   A
hybrid between *L. sempervirens* and *L. hirsuta*.
Very close to *L. sempervirens*, but deciduous,
with shorter, minutely glandular flowers *c*.4 cm
long, from late spring to early autumn. Hardy to
−15°C.

**L. × tellmanniana** Spaeth.   A hybrid between
L. *tragophylla* and *L. sempervirens*, raised in
Budapest around 1920. Deciduous shrub to 6 m.
Flowers about 5 cm long; yellow or orange.
Flowers well in shade. Hardy to −10°C.

**Lonicera tragophylla** Hemsl. (*Caprifoliaceae*)
Native of W. Hubei and common near Ichang, in
scrub and woods, at 900–1800 m, flowering in
June–August. Deciduous twining shrub to 6 m.
Leaves glaucous beneath, the upper pair united.
Flowers yellow, 7–8 cm long. Any soil, with
shade at the root. Hardy to −20°C.

**Lonicera etrusca** G. Santi (*Caprifoliaceae*)
Native of the Mediterranean region and S.
Switzerland, east to S.E. Turkey and Israel, in
hedges and scrub, flowering from June onwards.
Deciduous, climbing shrub to 10 m; upper
leaves fused. Flowers 3.5–4.5 cm long. Any soil;
sun or part shade. Hardy to −15°C.

**Lonicera periclymenum** L. (*Caprifoliaceae*)
Honeysuckle   Native from Ireland and S.
Sweden, southwards to N. Africa, in woods,
scrub and hedges, flowering in June–August.
Deciduous climbing shrub to 4 m. Leaves all
separate. Sun or part shade. Hardy to −20°C.
**'Graham Thomas'** is a very free-flowering form,
found in a hedge in Warwickshire.
**'Belgica'** is a form known since before 1789.

*Lonicera tragophylla* at Spetchley Park

*Lonicera × tellmanniana*

*Lonicera etrusca*

*L. periclymenum 'Graham Thomas'*

*L. periclymenum 'Belgica'*

*Dipelta yunnanensis* in Lijiang, Yunnan

*Abelia floribunda* at Trebah, Cornwall

*Abelia umbellata* at Crathes Castle

**Lonicera tangutica** Maxim. (*Caprifoliceae*)
Native of Gansu, W. Sichuan and N. Yunnan,
in open woods, rocky places and scrub at 1800–
3300 m, flowering in May–June. Spreading,
deciduous, elegant shrub to 2 m. Leaves
obovate to elliptic, 1.5–3 cm long, ciliate;
flowers in pairs hanging on slender stalks
1.5–3 cm long. Bracts very narrow, about
equalling the ovaries. Fruits red, attractive on
their slender stalks. Any good soil; sun or part
shade. Hardy to −15°C. Late spring.

**Abelia floribunda** Decne. (*Caprifoliaceae*)
Native of Mexico in the Veracruz, Puebla and
Oaxaca districts at *c.*3300 m. Evergreen shrub
to 2.5 m or to 6 m in cultivation. Leaves ovate,
shining, 2–4 cm long. Flowers 3–5 cm long, on
previous year's shoots. Any good soil; full sun.
Hardy to −10°C with shelter. Early summer.

**Abelia umbellata** (Graeb. & Buch.) Rehd.
Native of W. Hubei and E. Sichuan, in woods at
1200–1800 m, flowering in June. Deciduous
spreading shrub to 3 m, with stiffly hairy twigs.
Leaves rather leathery, lanceolate, or elliptic,
4–8 cm long, toothed, sometimes hairy on the
veins beneath; petioles swollen at the base.
Sepals *c.*17 mm. Flowers with tube 15–18 mm,
lobes 3 mm, scented. Style as long as the tube.
Any soil; sun or part shade. Hardy to −15°C.
Early summer. A rare shrub; an old specimen,
shown here, growing well at Crathes Castle
Garden, Aberdeenshire. Distinct in its small
flowers in groups of 5–7, swollen petiole bases
and short style.

**Dipelta yunnanensis** Franch. (*Caprifoliaceae*)
Native of N.W. Yunnan, in *Pinus yunnanensis*

forest and scrub on hills at 2500–3000 m,
flowering in May. Deciduous shrub to 4 m,
usually *c.*2 m. Leaves ovate-lanceolate,
acuminate, pubescent on the midrib beneath,
5–12 cm long. Flowers, on stalks 2–5 cm long,
whitish, flushed pink, orange in the throat,
2–2.5 cm long; bracts cordate, (not as large as in
*D. ventricosa*), enlarging in fruit. Any good soil;
sun or part shade. Hardy to −15°C. Late
spring.

**Leycesteria crocothyrsos** Airy Shaw
(*Caprifoliaceae*)   Native of Assam, at 1800 m in
the Delei valley on steep sheltered rocks, in
dense thickets, flowering in May. Deciduous
shrub to 2 m. Leaves 5–12.5 cm long, ovate-
lanceolate, acuminate, hairy on the margins and
beneath. Flowers in a hanging raceme to 18 cm
long, each 2 cm long, yellow; fruit slightly
bristly. Any well-drained moist soil; sun or part
shade. Hardy to −15°C. Summer. Rare in
cultivation, but established in a terrace wall at
Logan, on the W. coast of Scotland.

**Weigela praecox** (Lemoine) Bailey
(*Caprifoliaceae*)   Native of Korea and N.E.
China (Heilongjiang), and E. Siberia (Ussuri
region). A spreading or erect deciduous shrub to
2 m; leaves elliptic to obovate, 5–8 cm long,
acuminate, hairy above and beneath. Flowers
somewhat nodding, in groups of 3–5 on short
lateral shoots. Calyx divided to about the
middle, hairy, with lanceolate lobes. Any soil;
full sun. Hardy to −20°C. Late spring.

**Weigela middendorfiana** (Trautv. & C. A.
Mey.) K. Koch   Native of N. China, E.
Siberia, Korea, Hokkaido and N. Honshu,

*Lonicera tangutica* in Lijiang, Yunnan

*Leycesteria crocothyrsos*

*Weigela praecox*

*Weigela middendorfiana* with leaves of *Podophyllum emodi*

forming low thickets in the mountains, flowering in July. Deciduous shrub to 1.5 m. Leaves oblong or narrowly ovate, acute or acuminate, hairy beneath, 5–8 cm long. Flowers in pairs, in axils of upper leaves; calyx deeply 2-lobed. Flowers 3.5–4 cm long, with a short narrow tube at the base, on stalks *c*.3 cm long. Anthers in a tight group. Capsules smooth. Any moist, well-drained soil; sun or part shade. Hardy to −20°C, but susceptible to late frost. Spring. The rather similar *W. maximowiczii* (S. Moore) Rehd. is a taller, more elegant shrub, with smaller sessile flowers and a long narow tube at the base of the corolla. It is confined to mountains in C. Honshu.

**Weigela 'Gustave Mallet'** An old cultivar, raised by Billard at Fontenay-aux-Roses in 1868, probably by crossing *W. coraiensis* and *W. florida*. An upright deciduous shrub to 2 m, flowering in early summer. Hardy to −20°C. Best in rich moist soil, pruned after flowering to encourage strong new shoots. About 170 cultivars have been named, in shades of red, pink or white. 'Dame Blanche' and 'Bristol Snowflake' are good whites; 'Eva Rathke' and 'Eva Supreme' good dark reds.

**Weigela florida** (Bge) DC. **'Foliis Purpureis'** (*Caprifoliaceae*) A brownish-purple-leaved form of *W. florida*, variably reported to have been 'raised in France from Chinese seed' (Bean quoting *Revue Horticole*) or 'found in Holland' (Krussman). A rather low-growing variety, to 1.5 m, of stiff upright growth.
*W. florida* Is native of Kyushu, Korea and N.E. China. A deciduous shrub to 3 m or more. Leaves ovate to obovate, acuminate, glabrous above, hairy on the veins beneath. Calyx divided to about the middle, glabrous. Flowers *c*.3 cm long. Any soil; sun or part shade. Hardy to −20°C. Early summer.

**Sambucus nigra** L. **'Pulverulenta'** (syn. 'Albopunctata') (*Caprifoliaceae*) A remarkable form of the common Elder, with young leaves almost pure white; the older green splashed with white. Photographed in the shrubbery at West Dean, Sussex. A very striking white shrub, to 3 m, at its best in mid-summer. Known in England since 1740.

**Sambucus racemosa** L. **'Tenuifolia'** A form of *S. racemosa* with very finely cut leaves, purplish when young. It makes a low bush, to 1 m, like a Japanese maple, but can have bright red berries. Raised from 'Plumosa', which originated in Russia before 1886.

*Weigela 'Gustave Mallet'*

*Weigela florida 'Foliis Purpureis'*

*Sambucus racemosa 'Tenuifolia'*

*Sambucus nigra 'Pulverulenta'*

R. cyanocarpum

R. stewartianum

R. stewartianum
F.26922

R. stewartianum
F.24891

R. eclectum
K.W.21006

R. fulgens

R. eclectum var.
bellatulum F.21770

R. meddianum F.24104

R. mallotum Farrer 815

½ life size. Specimens from the Valley Gardens, Windsor, 25th March

**Rhododendron cyanocarpum** (Franch.) W. W. Smith (ss. *Thomsonia*) (*Ericaceae*) Native of W. Yunnan, above Dali on edges of forest, open meadows, and rocky ravines, at 3000–4000 m, flowering in May. Evergreen shrub to 3.8 m, with rough bark. Moist, acid soil; light shade. Hardy to −15°C. Spring.

**R. stewartianum** Diels (ss. *Thomsonia*) Forrest 21841 (cream); 26922 (pale pink); 24891 (pink) Native of W. Yunnan, N.E. Upper Burma and S.E. Xizang, on rocky slopes and among bamboo at 3000–4250 m, flowering in May–June. Evergreen shrub to 2.5 m. Moist, acid soil; light shade. Hardy to − 10°C or −15°C.

**R. eclectum** Balf. fil. & Forrest var. **eclectum** (ss. *Thomsonia*) Kingdon Ward 21006 Native of S.E. Xizang, N.W. Yunnan, S.W. Sichuan, and N.E. Upper Burma, on rocky slopes, in scrub and bamboo thickets at 3000–4000 m, flowering in May–June. Evergreen shrub to 3 m. Moist, acid soil; light shade. Hardy to − 10°C or −15°C. Early spring.

**E. eclectum** var. **bellatulum** Balf. fil. ex. Tagg (ss. *Thomsonia*) Forrest 21770 Grows in the same habitats as var. *eclectum* but only in N.W. Yunnan, and differs in its longer petioles, 8–30 mm not 4–10 mm, and broader leaves.

**R. fulgens** Hook. fil. (ss. *Fulgensia*) Native of the E. Himalayas from E. Nepal to Bhutan, N.E. India and S. Xizang, growing in mixed forest and scrub, at 3200–4300 m, flowering in May–June. Evergreen shrub to 4.5 m; bark smooth, peeling. Moist, acid soil and some shade. Hardy to − 10°C to −15°C. Early spring.

**R. meddianum** Forr. (ss. *Thomsonia*) Forrest 24104 Native of N.E. Upper Burma and W. Yunnan, on open rocky slopes and in scrub, at 2700–3600 m, flowering in June. Evergreen shrub to 1.8 m. Var. *atrokermesinum* Tagg is a larger shrub with finer flowers, but is usually more tender. Moist, acid soil; light shade. Hardy to − 10°C to −15°C. Early spring.

**R. mallotum** Balf. fil. & Kingdon Ward (ss. *Neriiflora*). Farrer 815 Native of W. Yunnan and N.E. Upper Burma, just W. of the Salween, on cliffs, rocky hillsides and among bamboo scrub at 3350–3650 m, flowering in April–May. Evergreen shrub to 6.5 m. Moist, acid soil. Hardy to − 10°C to −15°C.

**R. beanianum** Cowan (ss. *Neriiflora*) Native of N.E. Upper Burma in the Seinghku Valley, and the Delei Valley on the border of India (NEFA) and Xizang, in bamboo forests, on sheltered rocks and open alpine slopes at 3000–3500 m, flowering in June. Evergreen shrub to 3 m. Leaves to 9 cm long, densely red-brown, velvety below. Moist, acid soil; semi-shade. Hardy to − 10°C to −15°C. Early spring.

**R. haematodes** Franch. (ss. *Neriiflora*) Native of W. Yunnan, above Dali and in the far northwest, on rocky alpine slopes and in scrub at 3650– 4450 m, flowering from May–July. Evergreen shrub to 1.5 m. Leaves fawn to red-brown, woolly beneath. Moist, acid soil; some shade. Hardy to −15°C. Early summer.

**R. pseudochrysanthum** Hayata (ss. *Maculifera*) Native of Taiwan, in the undergrowth of conifer forests and on open slopes to the summit of Mt. Morrison, at 1800–4000 m. Evergreen shrub to 3 m, but usually to 1 m. Moist, acid soil; sun or shade. Hardy to −15°C. A beautiful, compact-growing, neat shrub. Spring.

*Rhododendron mallotum* at Wakehurst Place

*Rhododendron beanianum* at Nymans

*Rhododendron haematodes*

*Rhododendron pseudochrysanthum*

R. strigillosum

R. pachytricum
W. 1522

R. uvariifolium L.S. & E. 15817

R. barbartum
Smythe 1962

R. fulvum F. 24110

R. principis L.S. & E. 15831

R. lanigerum

½ life size. Specimens from the Valley Gardens, Windsor, 25th March

Rhododendron argyrophyllum subsp. nankingense 'Chinese Silver'

Rhododendron pachytrichum at Boaxing, Sichuan

Rhododendron bureavii at Inverewe

**Rhododendron strigillosum** Franch. (ss. *Maculifera*)   Native of Sichuan and N.E. Yunnan, in scrub and forest and on cliffs at 2200–3350 m, flowering in April–June. Evergreen shrub to 2.5 m. Moist, acid soil; some shade. Hardy to −10°C to −15°C.

**R. uvariifolium** Diels (ss. *Fulva*). L. S. & E. 15817   Native of N.W. Yunnan, S.E. Xizang and S.W. Sichuan, on open rocky limestone slopes, in scrub and conifer forest, at 3000–4000 m, flowering in May–June. Evergreen shrub to 10 m. Moist, non-chalky soil, light shade. Hardy to −10°C to −15°C.

**R. pachytrichum** Franch. (ss. *Maculifera*) Wilson 1522   Native of Sichuan and N.E. Yunnan, in scrub and open coniferous forest, at 2500–3600 m, flowering in May. Evergreen shrub to 6 m. Leaves to 15 cm long, with branched hairs on the midrib and few stalked glands on the petiole. Acid soil. Hardy to −15°C. Early spring.

**R. barbatum** Wall. ex. G. Don (ss. *Barbata*) coll. J. S. Smythe 1962   Native of the Himalayas from N. India from Uttar Pradesh eastwards, to Bhutan and S. Xizang, in forest and scrub at 2700–3700 m, flowering from April to June. Evergreen shrub to 9 m, with greyish, peeling bark. Moist, acid soil, some shade. Hardy to −10°C to −15°C. Early spring.

**R. fulvum** Balf. fil. & W.W. Sm. (ss. *Fulva*) Forrest 24110   Native of W. Yunnan, S.E. Xizang and N.E. Upper Burma, on rocky slopes, in scrub and in open conifer forest, at 3000–4700 m, flowering in May–June.

Evergreen shrub to 8 m or more. Moist, acid soil, shade. Hardy to −10°C to −15°C . Early spring.

**R. lanigerum** Tagg (ss. *Arborea*)   Native of S. Xizang in the Tsangpo gorge and N.E. India, in the Delei Valley, in conifer and bamboo forest at 2550–3350 m, flowering in May. Evergreen shrub to 6 m. Leaves whitish to pale brown, felted beneath. Moist, acid soil; light shade. Hardy to −10°C to −15°C. Early spring.

**R. principis** Bur. & Franch. (incl. *R. vellereum*) (ss. *Taliensia*) L. S. & E. 15831   Native of E. Xizang, especially in the Tsangpo valley, in open conifer forest, on dry rocky hillsides and cliffs, often on limestone, at 2900–3950 m, flowering in May. Evergreen shrub to 6 m. Moist, non-chalky soil, light shade. Hardy to −15°C. Early spring.

**R. argyrophyllum** Franch. subsp. **nankingense** (Cowan) Chamberlain **'Chinese Silver'** (ss. *Argyrophylla*)   Native of Guizhou on rocky slopes at *c.*1250 m and in Sichuan, flowering in April–May. Evergreen shrub to 12 m. Leaves silvery when young. Acid soil, some shade. Hardy to −15°C. Other subspecies of *R. argyrophyllum* have smaller leaves and flowers. Late spring.

**R. bureavii** Franch. (ss. *Taliensia*)   Native of N. Yunnan, in open conifer forest and scrub, at 3350–4250 m, flowering in May. Evergreen shrub to 3 m; leaves densely covered with red-brown felt beneath. Moist, acid soil; some shade. Hardy to −10°C. Valued for its beautiful foliage. Spring.

Rhododendron bureavii

Rhododendron strigillosum

R. lutescens
(long-leaved form)

R. lutescens

'Golden Oriole Talavera'

'Silkcap'

'Seta'

'Nestor'

'Cilipinense'

'Praecox'

R. johnstoneanum
(yellow form)

'Portia'

'Choremia'

$\frac{2}{5}$ life size. Specimens from the Valley Gardens, Windsor, 24th March

**R. lutescens** Franch. (ss. *Triflora*)   Native of
C. Sichuan, on hillsides in scrub, in hedges and
edges of forest at 1750–3000 m, flowering in
April–May. Evergreen or partly deciduous
shrub to 6 m, leaves reddish when young. Non-
chalky soil, moist when growing; sun or shade
and somewhat heat and drought tolerant. Hardy
to −10°C. Early spring.

**R. 'Golden Oriole Talavera'** (*R. moupinense* ×
*R. sulfureum*)   Raised by J. C. Williams before
1947. Evergreen shrub to 1 m; bark red-brown,
peeling. Hardy to −10°C. Early spring.

**R. 'Seta'** (*R. moupinense* × *R. spinuliferum*)
Raised by Lord Aberconway around 1933.
Evergreen shrub to 1.5 m, more across. Hardy
to −10°C. Early spring.

**R. 'Nestor'** (*R. barbatum* × *R. thomsonii*)
Raised by Sir Edmund Loder before 1969.
Evergreen shrub to 3 m or more. Moist, acid
soil; part shade. Hardy to −10°C. Early spring.

**R. 'Silkcap'** (*R. leucaspis* × *R.* 'Cilpinense')
Raised at Windsor before 1951. Evergreen
shrub to 1.5 m. Acid soil. Hardy to −10°C.
Early spring.

**R. johnstoneanum** Hutch. (ss. *Maddenia*)
Native of N.E. India in Manipur and Nagaland,
in open scrub, forest margins and epiphytic, at
1850–3100 m, flowering in April–May. Height
up to 4.5 m. Flowers scented. Acid soil, moist
when growing; sun or shade. Hardy to −5°C to
−10°C. Late spring.

**R. 'Praecox'** (*R. dauricum* × *R. ciliatum*)
Height to 1.5 m, more across. Raised by Isaac
Davies, near Liverpool in about 1853. Acid or
neutral soil; sun or part shade. Hardy to −15°C,
but flowers very frost-tender. Early spring.

**R. 'Cilpinense'** (*R. ciliatum* × *R. moupinense*)
Height to 1 m, more across. Moist, acid or
neutral soil. Some shade. Hardy to −10°C, but
flowers very frost-tender. Early spring.

**R. 'Choremia'** (*R. arboreum* × *R. haematodes*)
Raised by Lord Aberconway before 1933.
Evergreen shrub to 5 m or more. Acid soil; part
shade. Hardy to −15°C. Early spring.

**R. 'Portia'** (*R. neriiflorum* × *R. strigillosum*)
Raised by Lord Aberconway before 1935.
Evergreen shrub to 5 m. Hardy to −15°C.

**R. caucasicum** Pallas (ss. *Pontica*)   Native of
the Caucasus, where it is common, forming low
thickets above 2000 m, of N.E. Turkey from
Trabzon eastwards, and in Georgia, in alpine
meadows and on the upper limits of birch
forest, at 2000–3000 m, flowering from May to
July. Evergreen shrub to 1.5 m. Leaves to
7.5 cm long, with brownish, thin velvet below.
Moist, acid soil. Hardy to −20°C. Spring.

**R. leucaspis** Tagg (ss. *Boothia*)   Native of S.
Xizang in the Tsangpo gorge on grassy slopes
and in scrub at 2450–3050 m. Height to 1 m.
Some shade. Hardy to −10°C. Early spring.

**R. 'Rosa Mundi'** (*R. caucasicum* hybrid?)
Height to 1 m; very slow growing. Compare
with *R. caucasicum*. Hardy to −20°C.

**R. 'Elizabeth'** (*R. forrestii* var. *repens* × *R.
griersonianum*)   Height to 2 m, with spread of
3 m or more. Flowers to 7.5 cm across. Raised
by F. C. Puddle at Bodnant in *c.* 1933. Moist,
acid soil. Hardy to −15°C. Spring.

*Rhododendron caucasicum* near Mt Elbrus, Caucasus

*Rhododendron caucasicum*

*Rhododendron caucasicum*

*Rhododendron* 'Rosa Mundi'

*Rhododendron leucaspis*

*Rhododendron* 'Elizabeth'

*R. calophytum (pale form)*

*R. calophytum*

*R. oreodoxa*
*W. 4245*

*R. montroseanum*

*R. arboreum*
*var. roseum*

*R. sutchuenense*

¼ life size. Specimens from the Valley Gardens, Windsor, 4th April

*Rhododendron calophytum* at Boaxing, Sichuan

*Rhododendron vernicosum* at Lijiang on limestone

**Rhododendron calophytum** Franch. (ss. *Fortunea*) Native of C. and E. Sichuan and N.E. Yunnan, in forests, scrub and on hillsides of bamboo at 1800–4000 m, flowering in May and June. Large evergreen shrub or tree to 12 m. Style with large flat stigma. Var. *openshawianum* (Rehder & Wilson) Chamberlain differs in its shorter, narrower leaves to 18.5 cm, cuspidate at apex, and fewer-flowered inflorescence. Both these are found in the region of Omei Shan. Moist, acid soil; shade or half-shade. Hardy to −20°C. Early spring.

**R. orerodoxa** Franch. (ss. *Fortunea*) Wilson 4245 Native of Sichuan, N.W. Yunnan, Gansu, Shaanxi and Hubei, in forests especially on mountain ridges, at 2650–4150 m, flowering in May and June. Evergreen shrub to 5 m. Ovary glabrous in var. *oreodoxa*; var. *fargesii* has glandular pedicels and ovary; var. *shensiense* has glandular ovary and reddish-hairy pedicels. Often very free-flowering in gardens. Moist, acid or non-chalky soil; sun or part shade. Hardy to −20°C. Early spring.

**R. montroseanum** Davidian (syn. *R. mollyanum* Cowan & Davidian) (ss. *Grandia*) Native of S. Xizang, where it is common in the Tsanpo gorge in rain forest from 2400–2700 m, flowering in May. Evergreen shrub to 15 m. Leaves to 30 cm or more, silvery beneath. Moist, acid soil, with shelter and shade. Hardy to −10°C. Early spring.

**R. arboreum** Smith var. **roseum** Lindl. (ss. *Arborea*) Native of the Himalayas from E.

Nepal to Bhutan and C. Xizang, in forests and on rocky hillsides, at 2750–3650 m, flowering from March to May. Evergreen shrub to 30 m, usually tree-like. Leaves to 11 cm long, white or fawn beneath. Moist, acid soil; sun or part shade. Hardy to −10°C to −15°C, and usually hardier than red-flowered *R. arboreum*. Early spring.

**R. sutchuenense** Franch. (ss. *Fortunea*) Native of N. Sichuan, Shaanxi, Hubei, Guizhou and Guangxi in forests at 1600–2500 m, flowering in April and May. Evergreen shrub to 5 m. Style with small stigma. Moist, acid soil, some shade. Hardy to −20°C. Early spring.

**R. vernicosum** Franchet (ss. *Fortunea*) Native of N. Yunnan, S.W. Sichuan and S. Gansu, in scrub, conifer and mixed forest, and open rocky slopes, at 2600–3650 m, flowering from April to July. A very variable species. Evergreen shrub to 8 m, but usually less and rounded. Flowers 3.5–5 cm, pale pink to purplish-pink. Moist, not chalky soil; some shade. Hardy to −15°C to −20°C (see also p. 143). Spring.

**R. orbiculare** Decne (ss. *Fortunea*) Native of S. and C. Sichuan around Boaxing and southwards, and N.E. Guangxi, in conifer forest and on rocks, at 2500–4000 m, flowering in May and June. Evergreen shrub to 15 m, but for long forming a rounded bush to 3 m; leaves to 10 cm long, and almost as wide. Moist, acid or neutral soil; sun or half-shade. Hardy to −15°C, but petioles broken easily by strong winds. Spring.

*Rhododendron oreodoxa* at Boaxing

*Rhododendron orbiculare*

R. burmanicum
'Elizabeth David'

'Jane Hardy'

'Ashcombe'

'Countess of Haddington'

R. ciliicalyx
K.W.21081

R. roseatum

'William Wright Smith'

$\frac{2}{5}$ life size. Specimens from Sandling Park, 4th April

**Rhododendron 'Jane Hardy'** (*R. nuttallii* (L. & S. 12117) × *R. lindleyi* (L. & S. 7244))   Raised by G. A. Hardy at Sandling Park, Kent in 1981. Evergreen shrub to 2 m or more. Well-drained acid soil, in sun or part shade. Hardy to −5°C.

**R. 'Countess of Haddington'** (*R. ciliatum* × *R. dalhousiae* var. *dalhousiae*]   Evergreen shrub to 1.5 m. Flowers scented. Well-drained acid soil; some shade. Hardy to −7°C. Spring.

**R. roseatum** Hutch. (ss. *Maddenia*) incl. *R. parryae* 'A.M. form' shown here.   Native of northeastern Burma and western Yunnan, growing in forests and epiphytically on rocks and trees. An evergreen shrub up to 5 m, with reddish, peeling bark. Hardy to −5°C.

**R. burmanicum** Hutch. (ss. *Maddenia*) Native of W. Burma, growing on Mt. Victoria on the edges of forest, and in exposed places at *c.*3000 m, flowering in March and April. An evergreen shrub up to 2 m. Flowers scented. Shown here the clone **'Elizabeth David'**. Well-drained, acid soil; sun or part shade. Hardy to −10°C for brief periods. Good in California around San Francisco.

**R. veitchianum** Hooker (ss. *Maddenia*) incl. *R. cubitii* Hutch.   Shown here is the clone **'Ashcombe'**, not typical of wild *R. veitchianum*. Native of Burma, Laos and Thailand, usually growing as an epiphyte or on rocks in deciduous or evergreen forest at 1200–2400 m, flowering in March–May. Height up to 2 m. Flowers usually scented, from early spring to mid-summer in gardens. Drought-tolerant, but needs shade. Hardy to −5°C with shelter.

**R. ciliicalyx** Franch. (ss. *Maddenia*) Kingdon Ward 21081   Native of N. and C. Yunnan, especially around Dali, at *c*.2400 m, on rocky hillsides, flowering in May. Height to 2 m. Flowers to 6 cm, white or pink. Well-drained, acid soil, well-watered while growing; sun or part shade. Hardy to −10°C for short periods.

**R. 'William Wright Smith'** (*R. nuttallii* × *R. veitchianum*)   Raised at the Royal Botanic Garden, Edinburgh before 1960. Hardy to −5°C.

**R. pachypodum** Balf. fil. W. W. Sm. (ss. *Maddenia*)
Native of northeast Burma to Yunnan, on steep, grassy slopes, cliffs, scrub and edges of forest, at 1800–4000 m, flowering in May–June. Evergreen shrub to 7 m, but often *c*.1 m. Flowers to 10 cm long, sometimes fragrant. Well-drained soil, not chalky, watered in summer; heat-tolerant if shaded. Hardy to −5°C to −10°C. Spring.

**R. dalhousiae** Hooker fil. (ss. *Maddenia*) Native of the Himalayas from C. Nepal to Bhutan and S. Xizang, epiphytic on trees, or on rocks in the forest, at 1800–2450 m, flowering in May. Evergreen shrub up to 3 m, of sparse growth. Calyx lobes not ciliate (ciliate in *R. lindleyi*). Flowers to 10.5 cm long (with red lines in var. *rhabdotum*). Very well-drained soil; heat- and drought-resistant with shade. Hardy to −5°C. Grows well outside in Cornwall and S.W. Scotland. Spring or summer.

**R. edgeworthii** Hooker fil. (ss. *Edgeworthia*) syn. *R. bullatum* Franch.   Native of the eastern Himalayas from Sikkim to Yunnan, growing on trees and on rocks at 2000–3300 m, flowering in April–June. Leaves with thick reddish felt beneath. Flowers scented. Very well-drained, not chalky soil; some shade. Hardy to −5°C to −10°C. Spring.

*Rhododendron pachypodum* above Dali Lake, Yunnan

*Rhododendron edgeworthii* at Bodnant

*Rhododendron dalhousiae*

*Rhododendron pachypodum*

subsp. *xanthocodon*
*L.S. & T.6590*

*R. cinnabarinum*

*Rhododendron cinnabarinum*
*subsp. xanthocodon*

*'Alison Johnstone'*

*R. cinnabarinum*

*R. russatum R.18462*

*R. racemosum F.21965*

*R. ciliatum*

*R. cinnabarinum var.*
*purpurellum L.S. & T.6349*

*R. rubiginosum R.24301*

*R. spinuliferum*

*R. augustinii*

$\frac{2}{5}$ life size. Specimens from Windsor Great Park, 23rd April

Rhododendron cinnabarinum var. roylei at Crarae

Rhododendron cinnabarinum at Minterne

Rhododendron cinnabarinum subsp. tamaense K.W.21021

**Rhododendron cinnabarinum** Hooker fil. subsp. **cinnabarinum** (ss. *Cinnabarina*)   Native of the Himalayas from E. Nepal to S. Xizang growing in forest and scrub at 2700–4000 m, flowering in May and June. Evergreen shrub to 7 m, usually *c*.3 m, of open growth. Moist, acid soil; shade or half-shade. Hardy to −10°C to −15°C. Early summer.

**R. cinnabarinum** var. **roylei** (Hooker fil.) hort. Flowers are large and deep crimson. Plants of this type are exceptionally good in western Scotland, e.g. at Benmore and Crarae. Hardy to −10°C.

**R. cinnabarinum** Hooker. fil. subsp. **tamaense** (Davidian) Cullen  Kingdon Ward 21021   Native of N. Burma, in the northern part of the Triangle, in scrub and the edges of forest at 2750–3200 m, flowering in June. A low, semi-evergreen or nearly deciduous shrub to 2 m. Hardy to −10°C.

**R. cinnabarinum** subsp. **xanthocodon** (Hutch.) Cullen (syn. *R. concatenans* Hutch.) L. S. & T. 6560   Native of Bhutan, S. Xizang and N.E. India, on hillsides and in forests, at 3050–3950 m, flowering in April–June. More compact than subsp. *cinnabarinum*; leaves broader; flowers more open, yellow to orange or purple. Hardy to −15°C.

**R. russatum** Balf. fil. & Forr. (ss. *Lapponica*) Rock 18462   Native of N. Yunnan and S.W. Sichuan, on the edges of forest and in mountain meadows at 3400–4300 m, flowering in June. Evergreen shrub to 2 m. Acid soil; sun. Hardy to −20°C or below. Late spring.

**R. cinnabarinum** subsp. **xanthocodon** (Hutch.) Cullen var. **purpurellum** (Cowan) L. S. & T. 6349A   The purple-flowered form of subsp. *xanthocodon*, from S. Xizang.

**R. 'Alison Johnstone'** (*R. cinnabarinum* subsp. *xanthocodon* × *R. yunnanense*)   Raised at Trewithen, Cornwall. Hardy to −15°C.

**R. racemosum** Franch. (ss. *Scabrifolia*) Forrest 21965   Native of Yunnan and S.W. Sichuan in scrub, rocky slopes and forest edges, often on limestone, at 2750–4300 m, flowering in May and June. Evergreen shrub to 3 m, upright. Dry soil, possibly chalk-tolerant; sun. Hardy to −20°C. Late spring.

**R. ciliatum** Hooker fil. (ss. *Maddenia*)   Native of the Himalayas from E. Nepal to S. Xizang, in forests and on rocks and steep slopes, at 2400–4000 m, flowering in May and June. Evergreen shrub to 2 m and more across. Moist soil, not chalky; sun or part shade. Hardy to −10°C.

**R. rubiginosum** Franch. (ss. *Heliolepida*) Rock 24301   Native of Yunnan, S.W. Sichuan, S.E. Xizang and N.E. Burma, in scrub, on rocks and in open forest, at 2500–3500 m, flowering in May. Evergreen shrub to 10 m or more. Acid or non-chalky soil, somewhat drought-tolerant. Sun or part shade. Hardy to −10°C or −15°C. Spring.

**R. augustinii** Hemsl. subsp. **augustinii** (ss. *Triflora*)   Native of E. Sichuan and Hubei, in rocky places in full sun and on the edges of forest at 1300–3000 m, flowering in May. Evergreen shrub to 10 m. Leaves with fine, stiff

Rhododendron keysii

down on the upper side. Acid soil, on the dry side. Hardy to −10°C or −15°C, the paler-flowered forms usually hardier. Spring.

**R. spinuliferum** Franch. (ss. *Scabrifolia*) Native of C. and S. Yunnan, especially around Kunming, at 1800–2500 m, in scrub and open forest, flowering from February to May. Evergreen shrub to 2 m. Acid or laterite soil; sun. Heat resistant but tender. Hardy to −10°C.

**R. keysii** Nutt. (ss. *Cinnabarina*)   Native of the Himalayas from Sikkim and Bhutan, where it is common, to N.E. India and S. Xizang in forest and scrub, at 2440–3650 m, flowering in June–July. Evergreen shrub to 6 m. Flowers to 2.5 cm long. Moist, acid soil; half shade. Hardy to −10°C or −15°C. Late spring to summer.

*R. albrechtii*

*R. albrechtii*

*R. albrechtii*

*R. reticulatum*

*R. campylocarpum K.W.8256*

*R. pentaphyllum*

*R. selense var. selense R.11111*

*R. thomsonii L.S. & H.21285*

*R. selense var. probum F.21878*

*R. neriiflorum F.6780*

*R. williamsianum*

½ life size. Specimens from Windsor Great Park, 23rd April

*Rhododendron pentaphyllum* in March

*Rhododendron callimorphum var. myiagrum*

*Rhododendron quinquefolium*

*Rhododendron sanguineum var. didymoides*

*Rhododendron sanguineum var. haemaleum*

**Rhododendron albrechtii** Maxim. (s. *Azalea*) Native of Japan from C. Honshu, to C. Hokkaido, in the mountains and forests at *c*.1000 m, flowering in May and June. Deciduous shrub to 3 m; leaves to 10 cm long, obovate to broadly lanceolate, sparsely hairy beneath. Moist, acid soil; sun or part shade. Hardy to −20°C or more. Spring.

**R. reticulatum** D. Don ex G. Don (s. *Azalea*) Native of Japan from S. Hokkaido to Kyushu, in scrub and in open forest, at 100–1800 m, flowering in March–June. Deciduous shrub to 8 m; leaves 4–7 cm, broadly ovate to rhombic, pale green and almost glabrous beneath. Acid soil; sun or part shade. Hardy to −10°C, and best in climates with warm summers. Spring.

**R. campylocarpum** Hook. fil. subsp. **campylocarpum** (ss. *Campylocarpa*) Kingdon Ward 85256  Native of the Himalayas from E. Nepal to Bhutan, S.E. Xizang and N.E. India, in open mixed forest, scrub, and stony hillsides at 3000–4600 m, flowering in May–June. Evergreen shrub or small tree to 4 m. Moist, acid soil; some shade but best in the open in cool areas. Hardy to −10°C to −15°C. Spring.

**R. pentaphyllum** Maxim (s. *Azalea*)  Native of Japan from C. Honshu to Shikoku and Kyushu, in deciduous forest at 1000–2000 m, flowering in April and May. Deciduous shrub to 8 m; twigs often reddish-brown, leaves 2.5–4.5 cm long, elliptic, acute. Moist, acid soil; sun or part shade. Hardy to −15°C. Early spring.

**R. thomsonii** Hooker fil. (ss. *Thomsonia*) L. S. & H. 21285  Native of the Himalayas from E.

Nepal to Bhutan and S.E. Xizang (subsp. *lopsangianum*), in *Abies* forest and *Rhododendron* scrub, at 3000–3800 m, flowering in May–June. Evergreen shrub or small tree to 3.5 m. Flowers waxy, to 5 cm long; calyx well developed, green or reddish. Moist, acid soil; half shade. Hardy to −10°C. Spring.

**R. selense** Franch. subsp. **selense** (ss. *Selensia*) var. **selense** Rock 11111 and var. **probum** Forrest 21878  Native of N.W. Yunnan and S.E. Xizang, on stony slopes, in open conifer forest and in scrub, at 3350–4550 m, flowering in June and July. Evergreen shrub to 5 m. Flowers to 4 cm, white to pink or yellowish. Moist, acid soil; sun or part shade. Hardy to −15°C. Spring.

**R. neriiflorum** Franch. (ss. *Neriiflora*) incl. *R. euchaites* Balf. fil. & Forr. Forrest 6780  Native of W. Yunnan, S.E. Xizang and N.E. Upper Burma, in pine forest, on rocks and in scrub, at 2750–3350 m, flowering in May–June. Evergreen shrub or small tree to 6 m. Flowers waxy, to 4.5 cm. Moist, acid soil; shade or half shade. Hardy to −10°C or −15°C. Spring.

**R. williamsianum** Rehd. & Wils. (ss. *Williamsia*)  Native of C. Sichuan, on scrub-covered cliffs in the Wa-Shan at 2800 m, where it is rare, flowering in June. A rounded evergreen shrub to 2 m high and more across. Moist, humus-rich, not chalky soil in full sun or part shade. Hardy to −10°C or −15°C, but susceptible to late frosts. Spring.

**R. callimorphum** Balf. fil. & W. W. Smith var. **myiagrum** (Balf. fil. & Forr.) Chamberlain

Native of W. Yunnan, in scrub and on rocky hillsides and cliffs, at 3000–4000 m, flowering in June. Evergreen shrub to 2 m, leaves glaucous with minute glands beneath. Var. *callimorphum* differs only in its pink flowers. Moist, acid soil; sun or part shade. Hardy to −10°C to −15°C. Spring.

**R. quinquefolium** Bisset & Moore (s. *Azalea*) Native of Japan from C. Shikoku to N. Honshu, in mountains and forests at *c*.1000 m, flowering in May–June. Deciduous shrub to 6 m, leaves 4–5 cm long, rhombic or obovate-elliptic, hairy beneath. Moist, acid soil; sun or part shade. Hardy to −15°C. Spring.

**R. sanguineum** Franch. var. **didymoides** (Tagg. & Forr.) Chamberlain (ss. *Neriiflora*) Differs from var. *haemaleum* in its yellow and pink, or pink flowers, and glandular ovary. Other varieties have white, yellow or pink flowers.

**R. sanguineum** Franch. var. **haemaleum** (Balf. fil & Forr.) Chamberlain (ss. *Neriiflora*) Native of S.E. Xizang and N.W. Yunnan, on rocky slopes, in meadows and in scrub at 3000–4500 m, flowering in May–August. Evergreen shrub to 1.5 m or more. Leaves to 8 cm, silvery to greyish beneath. Moist, cool, acid soil; some shade. Hardy to −15°C. One of the darkest flowered of all Rhododendrons; var. *sanguineum* has brighter crimson flowers. Spring.

**Rhododendron yunnanense** Franch. (ss. *Triflora*)   Native of N.E. Burma, W. Yunnan, W. Sichaun and Guizhon, in scrub, open forest and cliffs at 2100–3950 m, flowering in April–May. A beautiful and very common species around Dali and on limestone near Lijiang. Evergreen or deciduous shrub to 6 m. Flowers white to pale mauve, usually spotted. Acid or slightly alkaline soil. Hardy to −10°C to −15°C.

**Taxillus tibetanus** (*Loranthaceae*)   Native of Yunnan growing as a parasite on *Rhododendron yunnanense*, flowering in May. Flowers in umbels. Fruits orange, fleshy. A beautiful mistletoe, worth cultivating if seed should be collected in future.

**R. oreotrephes** W.W. Sm. (ss. *Triflora*) Native of N.W. Yunnan where it is common, S. & S.E. Xizang and S.W. Sichuan, growing in scrub, forests and on rocky slopes, sometimes on limestone at 2750–4250 m, flowering in May and June. Evergreen or semi-deciduous shrub to 8 m. Hardy to −15°C. Spring.

**R. polylepis** Franch. (ss. *Triflora*)   Native of W. Sichuan, in woods, bamboo thickets and scrub, at 2000–3000 m, flowering in May. Evergreen shrub to 6 m. Flowers 2.5–3 cm across. Acid soil; sun or part shade. Hardy to −15°C. Spring.

**R. concinnum** Hemsl. (ss. *Triflora*) incl. *R. pseudoyanthinum* Balf. fil. ex Hutch.   Native of Sichuan where it is widespread and W. Hubei, on rocks and in forests and scrub, at 2300–4500 m. Flowering in May–July. Evergreen shrub to 2 m. Flowers 2–3 cm, purple to reddish. Hardy to −15°C. Spring.

**R. davidsonianum** Rehd. & Wils. (ss. *Triflora*) c.v. **'Ruth Lyon'**   Native of S.W. and C. Sichuan, on cliffs, in scrub and the edges of forest, at 2000–3300 m, flowering in May–June. Evergreen shrub up to 5 m. Flowers pink to lavender. Acid or non-chalky soil; sun or part shade. Hardy to −10°C to −15°C. Spring.

**R. ambiguum** Hemsl. (ss. *Triflora*)   Native of C. Sichuan in scrub and on rocky slopes at 2600–4500 m, flowering in May, on Mount Omei, June at higher elevations. Evergreen shrub to 5 m. Acid or non-chalky soil; sun or part shade. Hardy to −25°C.

**R. keiskii** Miq. (ss. *Triflora*)   Native of Japan from C. Honshu south to Yakushima, on hills, rocky hillsides or as an epiphyte, at 600–1850 m, flowering in April and May. Evergreen shrub to 3 m, but with dwarf forms frequent in cultivation. Acid soil; sun or part shade. Hardy to −15°C to −20°C. Early spring.

*Rhododendron yunnanense* between Dali and Lijiang, Yunnan

*Rhododendron yunnanense*

*Taxillus tibetanus*

*Rhododendron oreotrephes*

*Rhododendron polylepis*

*Rhododendron polylepis* at Boaxing, Sichuan

*Rhododendron concinnum*

*Rhododendron ambiguum* at Benmore, Argyll

*Rhododendron davidsonianum* 'Ruth Lyon'

*Rhododendron keiskii*

R. taliense L.S.6612

R. irroratum 'Polka Dot'

R. arboreum subsp. cinnamomeum

R. niveum

R. roxieanum var. oreonastes

R. crinigerum Rock 59067

Cooper 5763

S.S.W. 9107

R. campanulatum

¼ life size. Specimens from Windsor Great Park, 24th April

**R. roxieanum** Forrest (incl. var. *oreonastes* Balf. fil. & Forr.) (ss. *Taliensia*)  Native of S.E. Xizang, N.W. Yunnan and S.W. Sichuan, in pine forest, and on rocky slopes at 3050–4250 m, flowering in June and July. Evergreen shrub to 2.5 m, often smaller; leaves linear to elliptic, in extreme forms as shown here (var. *oreonastes*) up to 15 times as long and as wide. Acid soil; part shade. Hardy to −15°C. Spring.

**R. crinigerum** Franch. (ss. *Glischra*) Rock 59067/10982  Native of N.E. Yunnan and S.E. Xizang, and N.E. Upper Burma, in open pine forests and on rocky slopes at 3350–4000 m, flowering in June and July. Evergreen shrub to 5 m. Moist, acid soil; some shade. Hardy to −10°C to −15°C. Spring.

**R. campanulatum** D. Don (ss. *Campanulata*) Cooper 5736; S.S.W. 9107  Native of the Himalayas from Kashmir to Bhutan, in mixed forest and scrub at 2700–3500 m, flowering from April–June. Evergreen shrub to 4.5 m. Moist, acid, soil; part shade. Hardy to −10°C to −20°C. Early to late spring. Subsp. *aeruginosum* from Bhutan and Sikkim at 3800–4500 m, with intermediates in E. Nepal, has striking bluish leaves, and always lilac or purplish flowers. It is a dwarf shrub to 2.5 m. Hardy to −20°C.

**R. arboreum** subsp. *zeylanicum* (Booth) Tagg (ss. *Arborea*)  Native of mountains in Sri Lanka, around Nuwara Eliya and Adams Peak at 2000–2500 m, in forest and grassy places, flowering in November. Evergreen shrub to 12 m; leaves 8–11 cm long, with spongy brown fur beneath. Moist, acid soil; sun or part shade. Hardy to −5°C to −10°C. Spring. Grows well in Cornwall, England, and should be heat-tolerant as well. A related subspecies, subsp. *nilagiricum* is found in the Nilgiri, Anaimalai and Palni hills in S. India, especially at Ootacamund and Kodaikanal, in grassy scrub, at around 2000 m.

**R. venator** Tagg (ss. *Venatora*)  Native of S.E. Xizang in the Tsangpo gorge near Pemakochung at around 2500 m, in scrub, wet places and on rocks. Evergreen shrub to 3 m. Moist, acid soil; shade or part shade. Hardy to −10°C to −15°C. Early summer.

**R. aberconwayi** Cowan (ss. *Irrorata*)  Native of N.E. Yunnan, on mountain summits, flowering in June: a rare species, little collected. Evergreen shrub to 2.5 m; leaves elliptic, stiff, 3–6 × 1.1–2.2 cm, glabrous when mature. Moist, acid soil; part shade or sun. Hardy to −20°C and below. 'His Lordship' (shown here) white with crimson spots.

**R. micranthum** Turcz. (ss. *Micrantha*)  Native of Korea and northern China from Heilongjiang west to Gansu and Sichuan, in scrub and on grassy slopes at 1000–2600 m. Evergreen shrub to 2 m. Flowers 5–8 mm long, with a short tube 1–3 mm at the base, more like a *Ledum* (p. 151), than a *Rhododendron*, from late spring to mid-summer. Acid soil; sun or half shade. Hardy to −20°C.

**R. taliense** Franch. (ss. *Taliensia*) Ludlow and Sheriff 6612  Native of W. Yunnan, on the Dali mountains in mountain meadows, in scrub and on cliffs at 3050–3650 m, flowering in May and June. Evergreen shrub to 4 m. Moist, acid soil; part shade. Hardy to −15°C. Spring.

**R. arboreum** subsp. *cinnamomeum* (Wall. ex Lindl.) Tagg (syn. *R. campbelliae* Hook. fil.) (ss. *Arborea*)  Native of E. Nepal, N. Bengal and Sikkim, in open forest and on rocky hillsides at 2750–3650 m, flowering from March–May. Evergreen shrub or tree to 50 m. Moist, acid soil; part shade. Hardy to −10°C. Spring. Var. *roseum* Lindley differs in its narrower leaves, whitish beneath without loose red-brown velvet.

**R. irroratum** Franch. subsp. *irroratum* (ss. *Irrorata*)  Native of W. & C. Yunnan and S.W. Sichuan, in scrub and coniferous forest at 2500–3500 m, flowering in April and May. Evergreen shrub to 9 m. Flowers often heavily spotted and particularly so in **'Polka Dot'** (shown here) and 'Spatter Paint'. Acid soil; sun or part shade. Hardy to −10°C to −15°C. Early to late spring.

**R. niveum** Hooker fil. (ss. *Arborea*)  Native of the Himalayas in Sikkim and Bhutan, in mixed forest with bamboo and *Tsuga*, at 2900–3650 m, flowering in May and June. Very rare in the wild. Evergreen shrub or small tree to 6 m. Moist, acid soil; shade or half shade. Hardy to −10°C to −15°C. Spring.

*subsp. zeylanicum* at Newara Eliya

*Rhododendron arboreum var. roseum* at Windsor

*Rhododendron venator*

*Rhododendron aberconwayi 'His Lordship'*

*Rhododendron aberconwayi*

*Rhododendron micranthum*

R. rex subsp.
rex Rock 03800

R. wightii

R. macabeanum

R. falconeri

R. lacteum

R. rex subsp. fictolacteum F.22020

⅓ life size. Specimens from Windsor Great Park, 24th April

*Rhododendron macabeanum* at Nymans K.W.7724

*Rhododendron lacteum* at Windsor

**Rhododendron rex** Lévl. subsp. **rex** (ss. *Falconera*) Rock 03800    Native of S. Sichuan and N.E. Yunnan, in conifer forest and on shaded slopes on limestone, at *c*.3500 m, flowering in May. Evergreen shrub or small tree to 12 m; leaves 12–37 cm long, grey or fawn beneath. Flowers white, flushed pink with a crimson blotch, to 4.5 cm long. Moist acid, or non-chalky soil, in shade or half shade. Hardy to −15°C with shelter. Spring.

**R. wightii** Hooker fil. (ss. *Taliensia*)    Native of the Himalayas from E. Nepal to Bhutan, N.E. India and S.E. Xizang, growing in scrub and forest and on rocky ridges at 3350–4550 m, flowering in May and June. Evergreen shrub to 4 m; leaves 5–14 cm long, softly brown-velvety beneath. Flowers to 4.5 cm, pale yellow, in cultivation usually in a lopsided truss, in spring. Moist, acid soil. Hardy to −15°C.

**R. macabeanum** Watt ex Balf. fil. (ss. *Grandia*)    Native of N.E. India in Manipur and Nagaland, on the summits of hills and in mixed forest at 2500–3000 m, flowering in May. Evergreen tree to 15 m; leaves 14–30 cm long and up to 18.5 cm wide, rounded, white to greyish, furry beneath. Flowers pale to bright lemon yellow, to 7.5 cm long. A very fine species for a sheltered position in sun or part shade, acid soil. Hardy to −10°C to −15°C. Spring.

**R. falconeri** Hooker fil. (ss. *Falconera*)    Native of the Himalayas from E. Nepal to Bhutan and N.E. India, in mixed and deciduous forest at 2700–3750 m, flowering in April and May. Evergreen, large shrub or tree to 12 m; leaves 20–35 cm long, densely reddish, velvety beneath, wrinkled with impressed veins above. Flowers to 5 cm long, creamy-white to pale yellow, waxy. Moist, acid soil; shade, or half shade and shelter from cold winds. Hardy to −10°C to −15°C. Spring.

**R. lacteum** Franch. (ss. *Taliensia*)    Native of W. Yunnan, on the Dali mountains and westwards, in conifer forest, scrub and rocky

hillsides at 3700–4000 m, flowering in May. Evergreen shrub to 7.5 m; leaves 8–17 cm long, softly greyish-brown velvety beneath. Flowers to 5 cm long. Difficult to cultivate well, and said to grow best in a warm but partly shaded, rather dry situation, in acid or non-chalky soil. Hardy to −15°C. Spring.

**R. rex** subsp. **fictolacteum** (Balf. fil.) Chamberlain (ss. *Falconera*) Forrest 22020 Native of W. Yunnan, where it is common, S.E. Xizang and N.E. Burma, in conifer forest and *Rhododendron* scrub, at 3000–4000 m, flowering in May. Differs from subsp. *rex* in having thick, brown to red-brown, not fawn indumentum on the leaves beneath, and somewhat smaller leaves, to 3 cm, and flowers to 5 cm long. Where the two species grow together in the wild, intermediates are found. A third subspecies, *arizelum* (Balf. fil. & Forrest) Chamberlain, with broader leaves and pale yellow flowers, is found further west in W. Yunnan, S.E. Xizang and N.E. Burma. Hardy to −15°C. Spring.

**R. semnoides** Tagg & Forrest (ss. *Falconera*) Rock 25393)    Native of S.E. Xizang and N.W. Yunnan, growing in *Rhododendron* forest at 3700–4000 m, flowering in June. Evergreen shrub to 6 m; leaves to 24 cm long, whitish to buff beneath. Flowers *c*.15 in a truss, white to pale pink, 4–5 cm long. Very close to *R. basilicum*, differing mainly in the shape of the hairs (strongly fimbriated) and in the white rather than pale yellow flowers. Moist, acid soil; shelter and half-shade. Hardy to −10°C to −15°C. Spring.

**R. hodgsonii** Hooker fil. (ss. *Falconera*) Native of the Himalayas from E. Nepal to Bhutan and S.E. Xizang, growing in *Abies* forest, scrub and among bamboo, at 3000–4000 m, at higher altitudes than *R. falconeri*, flowering in April and May. Evergreen large shrub or tree to 11 m; leaves to 24 cm long, silvery to brownish, matted beneath. Flowers to 4 cm long, pink to purple or reddish, waxy. Moist, acid soil; shade and shelter from cold wind. Hardy to −15°C. Early spring.

*Rhododendron semnoides*

*Rhododendron hodgsonii*

*Rhododendron 'Cornish Cross'* at Windsor

*Rhododendron 'Temple Belle'*

*Rhododendron × loderi 'Pink Diamond'*

*Rhododendron 'Pink Glory'*

**Rhododendron 'Cornish Cross'** (*R. thomsonii ×
R. griffithianum*)    Raised by Samuel Smith,
head gardener, at Penjerrick, Cornwall in about
1920. Evergreen shrub to 7 m; bark purplish,
peeling. Flowers waxy, to 13 cm wide. Moist,
acid soil; some shade and shelter. Hardy to
−12°C. Spring.

**R. 'Temple Belle'** (*R. orbiculare × R.
williamsianum*)    Raised at the Royal Botanic
Gardens, Kew, in around 1916. Rounded
evergreen shrub to 1.5 m. Moist, acid soil or
neutral soil; part shade. Hardy to −20°C.
Spring.

**R. 'Pink Glory'** (*R. irroratum × R.* 'Loderi')
Raised at Leonardslee before 1937. Evergreen
shrub to 6 m. Moist, acid soil. Hardy to−15°C.

**R. 'Loderi Pink Diamond'** (*R. griffithianum ×
R. fortunei*) Raised by Sir Edmund Loder around

1901. Evergreen shrub to 7 m. Flowers 15 cm
wide, fragrant. Moist, acid or neutral soil; some
shade and shelter. Hardy to −15°C. Late spring.

**R. 'Jocelyne'** (*R. lacteum × R. calophytum*)
Raised by Rothschild before 1942. Evergreen
shrub to 3 m. Leaves 20 cm long, velvety
beneath. Moist, acid soil. Hardy to −20°C. Early
spring.'

**R. 'Crest'** (*R.* 'Lady Bessborough' × *R. wardii*
KW4170)    Raised by Lionel de Rothschild at
Exbury before 1940. Evergreen shrub to 2 m.
Moist, acid or neutral soil; part shade. Hardy to
−20°C. Spring.

**R. 'Roza Stevenson'** (*R.* 'Loderi Sir Edmund' ×
*R. wardii* KW5736)    Raised by Mr and Mrs J.
B. Stevenson at Tower Court before 1968.
Evergreen shrub to 3 m. Moist, acid soil; part
shade. Hardy to −20°C. Spring.

**R. 'Moonshine Bright'** (*R.* 'Adriaan Koster' ×
*R. wardii*)    Raised by Francis Hanger at
Wisley in 1946. Evergreen shrub to 2 m. Moist,
acid soil; part shade. Hardy to −20°C. Spring.

**R. 'Carita'** (*R.* 'Naomi' × *R. campylocarpum*)
Raised by Rothschild at Exbury before 1935.
Evergreen shrub to 5 m. Moist, acid soil; part
shade. Hardy to −15°C. Spring.

**R. 'Moonstone'** (*R. campylocarpum × R.
williamsianum*)    Raised by J. C. Williams at
Caerhays before 1933. Rounded evergreen
shrub to 1.5 m. Moist, acid or non-chalky soil;
part shade. Hardy to −20°C. Spring.

**R. 'Cowslip'** (*R. williamsianum × R. wardii*)
Raised by Lord Aberconway before 1937.
Rounded evergreen shrub to 1 m. Moist, acid or
non-chalky soil; part shade. Hardy to −15°C.
Spring.

*Rhododendron 'Jocelyne'*

*Rhododendron 'Moonshine Bright'*

*Rhododendron 'Carita'*

*Rhododendron 'Crest'*

*Rhododendron 'Roza Stevenson'*

*Rhododendron 'Moonstone'*

*Rhododendron 'Cowslip'*

*Rhododendron 'Lady Rosebery' at Bodnant*

*Rhododendron 'Conroy'*

*Rhododendron 'Conyan'*

*Rhododendron 'Minterne Cinnkeys'*

*Rhododendron 'Alison Johnstone'*

**Rhododendron 'Lady Rosebery'** (*R. cinnabarinum* × *R.* 'Royal Flush' (pink form)) Raised by Rothschild before 1931. Upright evergreen shrub to 2.5 m. Leaves up to 10 cm long, scaly. Flowers waxy, about 7.5 cm long. Moist, acid soil; part shade. Hardy to −10°C. Spring. 'Lady Chamberlain' is similar, but has more orange flowers. 'Salmon Trout' is a clone of this cross.

**R. 'Conroy'** (*R. cinnabarinum roylei* group × *concatenas* group) Raised by Lord Aberconway before 1937. Bushy evergreen shrub to 2 m. Leaves up to 7.5 cm long, scaly. Flowers waxy, about 7 cm long. Moist, acid soil; part shade. Hardy to −15°C. Spring.

**R. 'Conyan'** (*R. cinnabarinum* × *R. concinnum* var. *pseudoyanthinum*) Raised by J. B. Stevenson before 1953. Bushy evergreen shrub to 2 m. Leaves up to 7.5 cm long, scaly. Flowers waxy, about 6.5 cm long. Moist, acid soil; part shade. Hardy to −15°C. Spring. There are three named clones of this cross, 'Conyan Apricot', 'Conyan Pink' and 'Conyan Salmon'.

**R. 'Minterne Cinnkeys'** (*R. cinnabarinum* × *R. keysii*) Raised by Lord Digby at Minterne in 1931). Evergreen shrub to 3 m. Leaves to 12 cm long, scaly. Flowers in clusters of up to 30, *c*.3.5 cm long, waxy. Moist, acid soil; part shade. Hardy to −15°C. Late spring.

**R. 'Alison Johnstone'** (*R. yunnanense* × *R. cinnabarinum* subsp. *xanthocodon*) Raised by G. H. Johnstone before 1945. Evergreen shrub to 2 m. Leaves bluish-green, to 7.5 cm long. Flowers 4 cm across. Moist, acid soil; sun or part shade. Hardy to −15°C. Spring.

**R. 'Electra'** (*R. augustinii* subsp. *chasmanthum* × *R. augustinii* subsp. *augustinii*) Raised by Lionel de Rothschild before 1937. Evergreen shrub to 4 m. Leaves 6.4 m long. Flowers 6 cm across. Acid soil, well drained; sun or part shade. Hardy to −15°C. Spring.

**R. 'Saint Tudy'** (*R. impeditum* × *R. augustinii*) Raised by E. J. P. Magor before 1950. Evergreen shrub to 2 m. Flowers 5 cm across, about 14 in a truss. Acid or non-chalky soil; sun or part shade. Hardy to −20°C. Spring.

**R. 'Blue Diamond'** (*R.* 'Intrafast' × *R. augustinii*) Raised by Crossfield before 1935. Evergreen shrub to 2.5 m. Leaves up to 3.5 cm. long, scaly beneath. Flowers 4.5 cm across. Acid or non-chalky soil; sun or part shade. Hardy to −20°C. Spring. More than one clone, of the same parentage, has this name.

**R. 'Bo-Peep'** (*R. lutescens* × *R. moupinense*) Raised by Rothschild before 1934. Evergreen shrub to 1.5 m. Flowers 5 cm across. Acid soil; sun or part shade. Hardy to −15°C. Early spring.

**R. 'Fragrantissimum'** (*R. edgeworthii* × *R. formosum*) Raiser unknown, before 1868. Leggy evergreen shrub to 1 m or more. Leaves to 8.5 m long, hairy, and scaly beneath. Flowers to 10 cm across, very fragrant. Acid, well-drained soil; sun or part shade. Can be grown in a cold greenhouse and plunged outside in part shade in summer. Hardy to −10°C with shelter. Spring.

*Rhododendron 'St Tudy'*

*Rhododendron augustinii 'Electra' at Crarae*

*Rhododendron 'Blue Diamond'*

*Rhododendron 'Bo-peep'*

*Rhododendron 'Fragrantissimum'*

127

'Mrs E. C. Stirling'

'Professor Hugo de Vries'

'Cynthia'

'Bulstrode Park'

'Snow Queen'

'Britannia'

'Loder's White'

'Daydream'

'Lord Roberts'

'Goldsworth Yellow'

⅖ life size. Specimens from Sandling Park, 2nd June

**Rhododendron 'Mrs E. C. Stirling'** (*R. griffithianum* × unknown)   Raised by J. Waterer before 1906. Evergreen shrub to 3 m. Flowers 7 cm across. Acid soil; sun or part shade. Hardy to −20°C. Late spring.

**R. 'Professor Hugo de Vries'** (*R.* 'Pink Pearl' × *R.* 'Doncaster')   Raised by Major A. E. Hardy at Sandling Park, Kent before 1958. Evergreen shrub to 2 m or more. Acid soil; sun or part shade. Hardy to −20°C.

**R. 'Bulstrode Park'** (*R. griffithianum* hybrid × **R.** 'Sefton')   Raised in Holland by C. B. van Nes and Sons. Evergreen shrub to 2 m. Acid soil; part shade. Hardy to −20°C.

**R. 'Cynthia'** (syn. 'Lord Palmerston') (*R. catawbiense* × *R. griffithianum*)   Raised by Standish and Noble before 1856. Evergreen shrub to 10 m. Leaves 16 cm long, flowers 7.5 cm across. Acid soil; sun or part shade. Hardy to −25°C.

**R. 'Snow Queen'** (*R.* 'Halopeanum' × *R.* 'Loderi')   Raised by Sir Edmund Loder before 1934. Evergreen shrub to 2 m or more. Buds deep pink. Acid soil; shade or part shade. Hardy to −15°C.

**R. 'Loder's White'** (*R.* ('Album Elegans. × *griffithianum*) × *R.* 'White Pearl')   Raised by J. M. Mangles before 1884. Evergreen shrub to 5 m. Leaves to 18 cm long. Flowers 10 cm across, pale pink in the bud. Acid soil; sun or part shade. Hardy to −15°C.

**R. 'Britannia'** (*R.* 'Queen Wilhelmina' × *R.* 'Stanley Davies')   Raised by C. B. van Nes and Son before 1921. Evergreen shrub to 1.2 m. Leaves to 27 cm long; palish green. Flowers 7.5 cm across. Hardy to −20°C.'

**R. 'Lord Roberts'** (Parentage unknown). Probably raised by Messrs. Fromow at Chiswick, before 1900. Evergreen shrub to 2 m. Leaves crinkled. Flowers 5 cm across; sun or part shade. Hardy to −25°C.

**R. 'Daydream'** (*R.* 'Lady Bessborough' × *R. griersonianum*)   Raised by L. de Rothschild before 1936. Evergreen shrub to 2 m. Flowers 7.5 cm across, opening carmine pink, fading to yellowish. Hardy to −15°C.

**R. 'Goldsworth Yellow'** (*R.* 'Jacksonii' or *R. caucasicum* × *R. campylocarpum*)   Raised by W. C. Slocock before 1917. Evergreen shrub to 1.5 m. Leaves yellowish-green, 12 cm long. Flowers 6.5 cm across. Hardy to −25°C.

**R. 'Pink Pearl'** (*R.* 'George Hardy' × *R.* 'Broughtonii' or perhaps 'Cynthia')   Raised by T. Waterer and Sons before 1896. Evergreen shrub to 3 m. Leaves 12.5 cm long. Hardy to −20°C. Late spring.

**R. 'Alice'** (*R. griffithianum* × unknown) Raised by J. Waterer before 1920. Evergreen shrub to 3 m. Flowers 9.5 cm across. Hardy to −20°C..

**R. 'Beauty of Littleworth'** (Unknown × *R. griffithianum*)   Raised by J. H. Mangles before 1884. Evergreen shrub to 4 m or more; leaves to 20 cm long; flowers 15 to 18 in a large truss, 12 cm across, shaded mauve in the bud. Acid soil; some shade and shelter. Hardy to −20°C.

**R. 'May Day'** (*R. haematodes* × *R. griersonianum*)   Raised by A. M. Williams before 1932. Evergreen shrub to 1.5 m. Leaves to 15 cm long, with light brown velvety hairs beneath. Flowers 7.5 cm across, waxy. Moist, acid soil; partly shaded. Hardy to −15°C. There are several slightly different clones of this cross.

¼ life size. Specimens from Eccleston Square, 14th May

**R. 'Queen Elizabeth II'** (*R.* 'Idealist' × *R.* 'Crest')   Raised at Windsor before 1967. Evergreen shrub to 3 m. Leaves 14 cm long, glabrous beneath. Flowers 11.5 cm across. Acid soil; part shade. Hardy to −20°C.

**R. 'Mrs A. T. de la Mare'**   (Sir Charles Butler, a form of *R. fortunei* x 'Halopeanum' (*maximum* × *griffithianum*) or 'White Pearl') Raised by C. B. van Nes before 1958. Flowers 7.5 cm across, fragrant, pale pink in the bud. Acid soil; sun or part shade. Hardy to −25°C.

**R. 'Goldfort'** (*R.* 'Goldsworth Yellow' × *R. fortunei*)   Raised by Slocock before 1937. Evergreen shrub to 2 m. Leaves pale green to 15 cm long. Flowers 7.5 cm across, about 12 in a truss. Hardy to −25°C.

**R. 'Sun of Austerlitz'** (*R. arboreum* × unknown)   Of unknown origin, known since 1868. Evergreen shrub to 2 m or more. Acid soil; sun or part shade. Hardy to −20°C.

**R. 'Mount Everest'** (*R. campanulatum* × *R. griffithianum*)   Raised by W. C. Slocock before 1930. Evergreen shrub to 4 m. Leaves to 15 cm. Flowers 7 cm across, slightly fragrant. Very free flowering, and one of the best white hybrids at Wisley, and in London. Hardy to −15°C.

**R. 'The Honourable Jean Marie de Montague'** (*R. griffithianum* × unknown) Raised by C. B. van Nes and Sons before 1958. Compact evergreen shrub to 1.5 m. Leaves oblanceolate, to 22 cm long, deep green. Flowers 7 cm across. Acid soil; sun or part shade. Hardy to −20°C.

129

'Arthur Bedford'

'Mrs Lionel
de Rothschild'

'G. A. Sims'

'Thunderstorm'

'Anthony Waterer'

'Mrs Davis Evans'

'Frank
Galsworthy'

'Sappho'

'Sigismund Rucker'

'Mrs Furnival'

'Purple Splendour'

²/₅ life size. Specimens from Sandling Park, 2nd June

**Rhododendron 'Arthur Bedford'** (*R. ponticum* × mauve seedling) Raised by Th. Lowinsky before 1936. Evergreen shrub to 2 m. Acid soil; sun or part shade. Hardy to −25°C. Early summer.

**R. 'Mrs Lionel de Rothschild'** Raised by A. Waterer before 1931. Evergreen shrub to 2 m. Flowers pale pink in the bud; white when fully open, to 9 cm across. Hardy to −15°C.

**R. 'G. A. Sims'** Raised by Waterer's at Knap Hill, before 1938. Evergreen shrub to 2 m. Leaves to 18 cm long. Flowers in a truss of up to 16, 6.5 cm across. Hardy to −20°C.

**R. 'Anthony Waterer'** Raised by A. Waterer before 1900. Evergreen shrub to 2 m. Acid soil; sun or part shade. Hardy to −20°C.

**R. 'Thunderstorm'** (*R.* 'Doncaster' × unknown) Raised by W. C. Slocock in 1930. Evergreen shrub to 3 m. Leaves to 17.5 cm long. Flowers dark red with white filaments and anthers. Acid soil; sun or part shade. Hardy to −20°C.

**R. 'Sappho'** Raised by Waterer's at Knap Hill, before 1867. Evergreen shrub to 3 m. Leaves to 17 cm across. Flowers about 7.5 cm across. Hardy to −20°C.

**R. 'Mrs Davies Evans'** Raised by A. Waterer before 1915. Evergreen shrub to 3 m. Flowers to 7.5 cm across, 16–20 in a dense truss. Acid soil; sun or part shade. Hardy to −20°C.

**R. 'Frank Galsworthy'** (*R. ponticum* × unknown) Raised by A. Waterer before 1900. Evergreen shrub to 2 m and more across. Leaves *c.*15 cm long. Hardy to −20°C.

**R. 'Sigismund Rucker'** Raised by A. Waterer before 1872. Evergreen shrub to 3 m. Flowers *c.*6 cm across, in late May or early June. Acid soil; sun or part shade. Hardy to −20°C.

**R. 'Mrs Furnival'** (*R. griffithianum* hybrid × *R. caucasicum* hybrid) Raised by A. Waterer before 1920. Evergreen shrub to 2 m. Leaves to 10 cm long. Flowers 10–14 in a truss, 7.5 cm across. Acid soil; sun or part shade. Hardy to −20°C.

**R. 'Purple Splendour'** (*R. ponticum* × unknown) Raised by A. Waterer before 1900. Evergreen shrub to 2 m. Leaves to 15 cm long. Flowers up to 15 in a truss, 7.5 cm across. Acid soil; sun or part shade. Hardy to −20°C. Early summer.

**R. 'Susan'** (*R. campanulatum* × *R. fortunei*) Raised by J. C. Williams at Caerhays castle before 1948. Evergreen shrub to 4 m. Leaves 14 cm long. Flowers to 9 cm across. Moist, acid soil; part shade. Hardy to −20°C. Late spring.

**R. 'Nick Skelton'** Evergreen shrub to 2 m. Acid soil; sun or part shade. Hardy to −20°C. Late spring.

**R. 'W. F. H.'** (*R. haematodes* × *R.* 'Tally Ho') Raised by Whittaker in 1941, and named after W. F. Hamilton, head gardener at Pylewell Park, Hants. Evergreen shrub to 2 m. Flowers *c.*5.5 cm long. Moist, acid soil; part shade. Hardy to −15°C.

**R. 'Cunningham's White'** (*R. caucasicum* × *R. ponticum* f. *album*) Raised by Cunningham in 1830. Bushy evergreen shrub to 3 m. Flowers 5 cm across. Acid or non-chalky soil, and said to be good on limestone in wet areas. Sun or part shade. Hardy to −25°C.

'Susan'    'Nick Skelton'    'W. F. H.'    'Scarlett O'Hara'    'Cunningham's White'    'Mrs G. W. Leak'    'Crest'

¼ life size. Specimens from the Hillier Arboretum, 14th May

**R. 'Scarlett O'Hara'** (*R. thomsonii* × *R.* 'Langley Park') Raised by Sir James Horlick around 1932. Evergreen shrub to 2 m. Flowers waxy, *c.*6 cm long. Moist, acid soil; part shade. Hardy to −15°C.

**R. 'Mrs G. W. Leak'** (*R.* 'Coombe Royal' × *R.* 'Chevalier Felix de Sauvage') Raised by M. Foster and Sons around 1916. Evergreen shrub to 2 m. Leaves around 20 cm long. Flowers 9 cm across. Acid soil; sun or part shade. Hardy to −20°C. Late spring.

**R. 'Crest'** (syn. 'Hawk Crest') (*R. wardii* × *R.* 'Lady Bessborough') Raised by Lionel de Rothschild around 1940. Evergreen shrub to 2 m. Flowers 10 cm across. Moist, acid or neutral soil; part shade. Hardy to −20°C. Late spring.

*Rhododendron* 'Cynthia' (p. 127)

'Chanticleer'

'Blue Danube'

'Hatsugiri'

'Day Spring'

'Katsura-no-hama' W.29

'Didpa'

'Hinamoyo'

'Mimi'

'Hershey's Red'

'Eddy'

'Ho-o' W.9

'Orange Beauty'

'Kure-no-Yuki' W.2

'Iro-Hayama' W.8

'Palestrina'

½ life size. Specimens from the Valley Gardens, Windsor, 18th May

# EVERGREEN AZALEAS

*Kurume* azaleas at Sandling Park

*'Vuyk's Scarlet'*

*'John Cairns'*

*'Jeanette'*

*'Mother's Day'*

**Evergreen azaleas** are nearly all low, spreading shrubs to 2 m high at the most, and more across, with small dark green, ovate leaves, and brightly coloured flowers in shades of red, mauve or white. Many were selected by the Japanese in the 19th century, from *R. kiusianum* and *R. kaempferi* and their hybrids; these are known as Kurume azaleas, and fifty of the best were introduced by E. M. Wilson to America in 1918. In the mid-20th century numerous hybrids were raised at Glenn Dale, Maryland, by the Plant Introduction Station, and new hybrids are at present being made mainly in southeastern USA.

**'Chanticleer'** A hybrid evergreen azalea of complex parentage, raised by B. Y. Morrison at Glenn Dale, Maryland, after 1935. Dense habit, very free-flowering. Hardy to −25°C.

**'Blue Danube'** A hybrid evergreen azalea of uncertain parentage raised by A. Vuyk in Boskoop, in about 1921. Hardy to −20°C.

**'Day Spring'** A hybrid evergreen azalea of complex parentage, raised at Glenn Dale, Maryland, before 1961. Hardy to −25°C.

**'Hatsugiri'** A Kurume azalea introduced from Japan around 1915. Low growth to 1 m. Hardy to −20°C.

**'Katsura-no-hama'** (Wilson No. 27) A Kurume azalea, introduced by E. H. Wilson from Japan in 1918. Hardy to −20°C.

**'Kure-no-Yuki'** (Wilson No. 2, syn. 'Snowflake') A Kurume azalea, introduced by E. H. Wilson from Japan in 1918. Bushy growth to 1 m. Hardy to −20°C.'

**'Didpa'** A hybrid evergreen azalea, of unknown origin.

**'Hershey's Red'** A Kurume hybrid azalea raised by Ralph Hershey in Gap, Pennsylvania. Hose-in-hose flowered. Hardy to −25°C.

**'Hinamoyo'** (Commonly mis-spelt 'Hinomayo') A Kurume azalea introduced from Japan to Holland in 1910. Bushy growth to 1.5 m. One of the best and most free-flowering of all evergreen azaleas. Hardy to −20°C.

**'Mimi'** A hybrid evergreen azalea, of unknown origin.

**'Eddy'** A hybrid evergreen azalea, *R. kaempferi* × 'Apollo' (Indica) raised by Lionel de Rothschild at Exbury before 1944. Tall growth, to 2 m. Hardy to −15°C.

**'Ho-o'** (Wilson No. 9 syn. 'Apple Blossom') A Kurume azalea introduced by E. H. Wilson from Japan in 1918. Hardy to −20°C.

**'Orange Beauty'** A hybrid evergreen azalea, the Kurume 'Hinode-Giri' × *R. kaempferi* raised by C. B. Van Nes before 1945. Bushy growth to 1 m. Hardy to −20°C.

**'Iro-Hayama'** (Wilson No. 8 syn. 'Dainty') A Kurume azalea, introduced by E. H. Wilson from Japan in 1918. Bushy growth to 1.5 m. Hardy to −20°C.

**'Palestrina'** A hybrid evergreen azalea, *R. kaempferi* × 'Malvaticum' raised by A. Vuyk in Boskoop, before 1926. Growth to 1.1 m, with large, rather pale leaves. Very free-flowering. Hardy to −20°C.

**'Vuyks Scarlet'** A hybrid evergreen azalea of uncertain parentage raised by A. Vuyk in Boskoop, before 1954. Low growth to 1 m. Hardy to −20°C.

**'John Cairns'** A hybrid evergreen azalea, 'Malvaticum' × *kaempferi*, raised in Holland in about 1920. Hardy to −20°C.

**'Jeanette'** A hybrid evergreen azalea, *R. kaempferi* × 'Malvaticum' raised in Holland before 1920. Hardy to −20°C.

**'Mother's Day'** A hybrid evergreen azalea, probably the Kurume Minode-Giri × an Indica azalea, raised by van Hecke in Belgium before 1970. Low, spreading growth to 1.5 m. Hardy to −20°C.

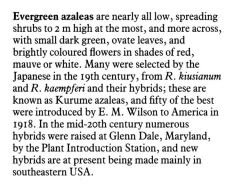

*R. schlippenbachii*

*R. scabrum*

*R. kiusianum*

*R. vaseyi*

*R. kaempferi*

*R. kiyosumense*

*R. canadense f. albiflorum*

*R. canadense*

$\frac{2}{3}$ life size. Specimens from the Valley Gardens, Windsor, 13th May

*Rhododendron microphyton* near Kunming, Yunnan

*Rhododendron luteum* by the Georgian Military Highway

*Rhododendron sinense*

**Rhododendron schlippenbachii** Maxim. (s. *Azalea*)   Native of Korea, N.E. China from inner Mongolia to Heilongjiang and eastern Siberia, on hillsides and forming undergrowth in woods, at 300–1845 m, flowering in May–June. Deciduous shrub to 5 m. Leaves thin, obovate, 5–9 cm long. Acid soil; light shade and protection from late frost. Hardy to −30°C.

**R. scabrum** D. Don (s. *Azalea*)   Native of the Liukiu Islands, especially Okinawa, in scrub, grassland and open pine forest, flowering in March–April. Evergreen shrub to 2 m. Leaves leathery. Acid or non-chalky soil; sun- and heat-tolerant. Hardy to −10°C. Spring.

**R. kiusianum** Makino (s. *Azalea*)   Native of Kyushu, especially Mt. Kirishima, on mountains at 600–1700 m, in meadows, forming low thickets and among dwarf pines, flowering in May–June. Low evergreen or semi-deciduous shrub around 1 m high. Flowers mauve to pink or white. Acid soil; sun or part shade. Hardy to −15°C. Spring.

**R. vaseyi** A. Gray (s. *Azalea*) Pinkshell Azalea Native of western North Carolina, in ravines and swamps and on mountain slopes at 1000–1800 m. Flowering in May. Deciduous shrub to 5 m; leaves elliptic or elliptic-oblong, 5–12 cm long. Moist, or even wet acid soil; sun or light shade. Hardy to −25°C. Spring.

**R. kaempferi** Planch. (s. *Azalea*) (syn. *R. obtusum* var. *kaempferi* Wilson)   Native of Hokkaido, Honshu, Shikoku and Kyushu, in open woods and scrub and on sunny, grassy hillsides and mountain sides at up to 1600 m, flowering in April–June. Evergreen or, in cold

areas, deciduous shrub to 3 m. Acid soil; sun or light shade. Hardy to −20°C. Spring. Shown here is the clone **'Semperflorens'**.

**R. kiyosumense** Makoin (s. *Azalea*)   Native of S. central Honshu, in woods in the mountains, flowering in April and May. Deciduous shrub to 2 m. Leaves broadly rhombic, 3–6 cm long. Acid soil; sun or light shade. Hardy to −15°C. Spring.

**R. canadense** (L.) Torr. (s. *Azalea*) Rhodora Native of E. Quebec and Newfoundland south of N. New Jersey and N.E. Pennsylvania, on bogs, wet hillsides and on rocky hills, flowering from March–July. Deciduous shrub to 1 m, rarely to 2 m. Moist acid soil and tolerant of waterlogging; sun or light shade. Hardy to −30°C. Forma **albiflorum** Rehder is a beautiful white-flowered form.

**R. luteum** Sweet (s. *Azalea*)   Native of Poland, Austria and Yugoslavia south to Turkey and the Caucasus, in mountain meadows, sometimes on limestone, in beech, or open coniferous forest, up to 2200 m, flowering in April–July. Deciduous shrub to 3.5 m. Flowers sweetly scented, sticky with glands. Acid or non-chalky soil, and tolerant of drought under trees. Hardy to −30°C. Early summer.

**R. sinense** Maxim. (syn. R. *molle* Sieb. & Zucc.) (s. *Azalea*)   Native of Japan from S.W. Hokkaido, south to Shikoku and C. Kyushu, in the mountains, in open forest, scrub and in wet bogs, flowering in May and June. Deciduous shrub to 3 m; leaves to 10 cm long, hairy above, often glaucous beneath. Flowers usually orange-red, but sometimes pink, scarlet or deep yellow,

*Rhododendron amagianum*

scented. Acid or non-chalky soil; sun or part shade. Hardy to −30°C. Early summer.

**R. microphyton** Franch. (s. *Azalea*)   Native of Yunnan and S.W. Sichuan, in open pine forest, cliffs and scrub at 1800–3000 m, flowering in April–May. A small evergreen shrub usually c. 1 m. Leaves to 5 cm long. Flowers to 2 cm across, pinkish to white, dotted red. Acid soil. Hardy to −10°C. Spring.

**R. amagianum** Makino (s. *Azalea*)   Native of Japan, on Amagi and Higane Mts. in Izu southwest of Tokyo, flowering in June and July. Deciduous shrub to 5 m; leaves 5–8 cm long, rhombic, in threes at the ends of the twigs. Acid soil; part shade. Hardy to −15°C.

R. prinophyllum

R. occidentale var. sonomense

R. flammeum

R. periclymenoides

R. atlanticum
from Choptank River

R. atlanticum

R. minus var.
chapmannii

R. minus var. minus

R. minus var. carolinianum

⅔ life size. Specimens from the Valley Gardens, Windsor, 25th May

**Rhododendron flammeum** (Michx.) Sarg. (syn. *R. speciosum* (Willd.) Sweet) (s. *Azalea*) Oconee Azalea   Native of S. Carolina and Georgia, on shady bluffs and in open woods, and on sand hills, flowering in late April–May. Deciduous shrub to 2 m. Acid soil; sun or light shade. Hardy to −15°C. Early summer.

**R. prinophyllum** (Small) Millais (s. *Azalea*) (syn. *R. roseum* Rehder & Wilson)   Native of S.W. Quebec and C. Vermont, south to S.W. Virginia and W. Tennessee, in dry woods and rocky slopes, and on the edges of swamps, flowering in May–June. Differs from *R. periclymenoides* in its densely hairy branchlets, and usually bright pink, very fragrant, flowers.

**R. occidentale** A. Gray (s. *Azalea*)   Native of S. California to Oregon, on stream banks and in moist places in coniferous forest, among Douglas Fir Redwoods and *Sequoiadendron*, and in mixed evergreen forest, up to 2700 m, flowering from April to August. Deciduous shrub to 3 m. Very variable, the largest, flowered forms coming from near the coast. Var. **sonomense**, from the Napa range in Sonoma County, N. California, differs in its smaller leaves 2–2.5 cm long, and pink flowers with a salmon-pink blotch. Damp acid or non-chalky soil. Hardy to −20°C.

**R. atlanticum** (Ashe) Rehder (s. *Azalea*) Dwarf Azalea   From Choptank River, Delaware. Native of S. New Jersey to South Carolina, along the coastal plain in wet pine barrens and sandy open woods, flowering in April–early June. Deciduous suckering shrub to 1 m. Flowers white to pinkish, purple or yellowish, very fragrant. Acid, damp or even wet soil; sun or light shade. Hardy to −25°C.

**R. periclymenoides** (Michx.) (s. *Azalea*) (Sleumer syn. *R. nudiflorum* (L.) Torr.) Pinxter-Flower, Purple Honeysuckle.   Native of C. New York and Pennsylvania, east to Ohio and south to North Carolina, in dry open woods and along streams, flowering in March–May. Deciduous shrub to 2 m. Hardy to −25°C.

**R. minus** Michx. var. **minus** (ss. *Caroliniana*) incl. *R. carolinianum* Rehder   Native of Georgia, Alabama, N. & S. Carolina and Tennessee, in woods and on hillsides, flowering in May. Spreading evergreen shrub to 2 m or more. Flowers white to pinkish-purple. Hardy to −25°C. Traditionally *R. carolinianum* was considered smaller and montane, *R. minus* larger and lowland.

**R. minus** Michx. var. **chapmannii** (A. Gray) Duncan & Pullen (ss. *Caroliniana*)   Native of Florida, in open sandy pine forest and on the dry banks of creeks, flowering in April. Hardy to −10°C to −15°C. Early summer.

**R. bakeri** Lemm. & McKay (s. *Azalea*) 'Camps Red' (syn. *R. cumberlandense* E. L. Br.) Native of E. Kentucky, Tennessee, N. Georgia and Alabama, especially on the Cumberland plateau, in oak woods, flowering in June and July. Deciduous shrub to 2 m. Flowers after the leaves. Acid soil; light shade. Hardy to −25°C.

**R. albiflorum** Hooker (s. *Candidastrum*) Native of Alberta to British Columbia, south to Oregon and east to W. Montana, in wet woods and alpine scrub at 1200–2200 m, flowering in June–August. Deciduous shrub to 2 m, often with horizontal branches. Flowers 1.5–2 cm across, mildly citrus-scented. Acid, well-drained soil; light shade. Hardy to −25°C.

**R. arborescens** (Pursh) Torr. (s. *Azalea*) Smooth Azalea   Native of Pennsylvania to E. Kentucky, south to Georgia and Alabama, mainly in the Appalachians, on the banks of streams, and swamps, flowering in June and July. Deciduous shrub to 3 m, rarely to 6 m. Flowers white, very fragrant. Acid soil; light shade. Hardy to −20°C or lower. Summer.

**R. viscosum** (L.) Torr. var. **glaucum** Torr. (s. *Azalea*) Swamp Honeysuckle, Clammy Azalea Native of Massachusetts south to Virginia, on the coastal plain, scattered among the typical form (p. 142). Flowers white, suffused red outside, especially in bud, or red. Damp, acid soil. Hardy to −25°C. Summer.

*Rhododendron bakeri* at Windsor

*Rhododendron albiflorum* in the Cascades

*Rhododendron arborescens*

*Rhododendron viscosum var. glaucum*

'Satan'

'Klondyke'

'Bright Straw'

'Brazil'

'Persil'

'Balzac'

'Toucan'

'Strawberry Ice'

'George Reynolds'

'Corringe'

'Sunte Nectarine'

'S. T. Coleridge'

'Anthony Koster'

'Queen Emma'

'Christopher Wren'

'Oxydol'

'Jeanne Oosthock'

'Koster's Brilliant Red'

⅝ life size. Specimens from Sandling Park and Windsor Great Park, 25th May

*'Berry Rose'*

*Mollis* Azaleas at Sandling Park

*'Spek's Orange'*

*'George Reynolds'*

## Mollis – Knap Hill – Exbury Azaleas

The early 'Mollis' azaleas were raised from *Rhododendron japonicum* and *R. molle* in the mid-19th century. Vast numbers were grown in Belgium and Holland for winter colour in Victorian conservatories. Their colours were soft, from yellow to orange-red, their flowers rather small, fragrant and bell-shaped. They are still found forming scented shrubberies in old gardens. Some of the paler, stronger-scented varieties may have *R. viscosum* in their ancestry.

The Knap Hill azaleas, with brighter colours and larger, more open flowers, were raised by the Waterer family at the Knap Hill Nursery in Surrey from the late 19th century until about 1939. They combined *R. molle* with several American species, such as *R. calendulaceum*, *R. viscosum* and *R. arborescens*. Further breeding along the same lines was continued at Exbury by Lionel de Rothschild, originally using azaleas bred at Knap Hill.

Mollis, Knap Hill and Exbury azaleas are easily grown in acid or neutral soil, in sun or part shade; they are heat-tolerant in summer, and hardy to −20°C. All are deciduous shrubs, to 3 m high after several years, with good autumn colour.

**Rhododendron 'Satan'**   A deciduous azalea raised at Messrs Waterer's Knap Hill Nursery before 1925, but named by W. C. Slocock and Sons after 1945. Compact habit to 1.5 m; leaves

green when young. Early summer.

**'Klondyke'**   A Knap Hill deciduous azalea, raised by Lionel de Rothschild at Exbury in 1947.

**'Bright Straw'**   A Knap Hill deciduous azalea raised at Exbury around 1934.

**'Brazil'**   A Knap Hill deciduous azalea, raised by Lionel de Rothschild at Exbury around 1934.

**'Balzac'**   A Knap Hill deciduous azalea, raised by Lionel de Rothschild at Exbury before 1934.

**'Persil'**   A deciduous azalea raised at Messrs Waterer's Knap Hill Nursery before 1925, but named by W. C. Slocock and Sons after 1945.

**'Toucan'**   A deciduous azalea raised at Messrs Waterer's Knap Hill Nursery before 1931, named in 1941.

**'Strawberry Ice'**   A Knap Hill deciduous azalea, raised by Lionel de Rothschild at Exbury and distributed by Waterer's of Bagshot in 1947. 'Cecile' is very similar.

**'George Reynolds'**   A deciduous azalea raised at Messrs Waterer's Knap Hill Nursery before 1936. This was the parent of many of the

Exbury strain of Knap Hill azaleas, notable for its tall habit and large flowers of thick texture and good scent.

**'Sunte Nectarine'**   A Knap Hill deciduous azalea, raised by Lionel de Rothschild at Exbury before 1934.

**'Corringe'**   A Knap Hill deciduous azalea, raised by Lionel de Rothschild at Exbury before 1934.

**'Samuel Taylor Coleridge'**   A 'Mollis' deciduous azalea, raised by Kersbergen in Boskoop.

**'Anthony Koster'**   A 'Mollis' deciduous azalea, raised in Holland, and introduced by M. Koster and Sons in 1892.

**'Christopher Wren'** (syn. 'Goldball').   A 'Mollis' azalea, raised by L. J. Endtz and Co. in Boskoop.

**'Jeanne Oosthock'** (syn. 'Merrouw G. van Noordt')   A 'Mollis' deciduous azalea, raised by P. van Noordt and Son in Boskoop.

**'Queen Emma'**   Syn. 'Koningin Emma', 'Dr Nolans'   A 'Mollis' deciduous azalea raised by K. Weselenburg and Sons, in Hazerswonde, Holland.

**'Oxydol'**   A Knap Hill deciduous azalea, raised at Exbury around 1947.

**'Koster's Brilliant Red'**   A 'Mollis' deciduous azalea raised by M. Koster and Sons in Holland in around 1918. Originally this name was given to a strain of seedlings of uniform colour, produced by hand pollination, a forerunner of modern F1 hybrid strains. Flowers with little scent. Upright growth to 1.8 m.

**'Spek's Orange'**   A 'Mollis' deciduous azalea raised by Jan Spek before 1948.

**'Berry Rose'**   A Knap Hill azalea raised by Lionel de Rothschild at Exbury before 1934.

'Narcissiflora'

'Phoebe'

'Norma'

'Corneille'

'Flora'

'Murillo'

'Solion'

'Freya'

'Glory of Littleworth'

'Fanny'

'Double Damask'

'Pallas'

'Gloria Mundi'

'Nancy Waterer'

'Irene Koster'

'Exquiseta'

½ life size. Specimens from Sandling Park, 25th May

'Freya' at Sandling Park

'Coccinea Speciosa'

'Glory of Littleworth'

Rhododendron vaseyi 'White Find'

**Deciduous azaleas**
The first azalea hybrids were made in Belgium in the 1820s, by crossing the east European *R. luteum* with American species such as *R. calendulaceum* and *R. periclymenoides*. They are generally taller than the Mollis-Knap Hill group, with smaller, paler but more elegant and sweetly scented, flowers. They make open deciduous shrubs to 3 m high and wide. These are known collectively as 'Ghent' hybrids; double-flowered Ghent hybrids, some of which involved crosses with Mollis azaleas, are called 'Rusticas'.

Another group, the so-called Occidentale hybrids, originated at Knap Hill as crosses between Ghent azaleas and *R. occidentale* from California. They are mainly pale-coloured, late flowering. *R. occidentale* was also crossed with Mollis azaleas by M. Koster and Sons, producing pale-coloured but earlier flowering azaleas. With their *R. occidentale* parentage, these hybrids should be heat- and drought-tolerant.

**'Norma'**   A Rustica azalea, raised by C. Vuylsteke in 1888. Double, scented flowers; Ghent × Mollis azalea. Compact deciduous growth to 1.5 m. Hardy to −25°C.
**'Narcissiflora'**   A double-flowered Ghent azalea raised by L. van Houtte before 1871. Flowers scented. Upright growth to 2.5 m. Hardy to −25°C.
**'Phoebe'**   A double-flowered Ghent azalea. Upright growth to 2.5 m. Hardy to −25°C.
**'Corneille'**   A double-flowered Ghent azalea raised by C. Vuylsteke around 1890. Upright growth to 2.5 m. Hardy to −25°C.
**'Freya'**   A Rustica azalea, raised by C.

Vuylsteke in 1888. Double, scented flowers; Ghent × Mollis azalea. Compact growth to 1.5 m. Hardy to −25°C.
**'Flora'**   A Ghent azalea, known since 1875. Growth to 2.5 m. Hardy to −25°C.
**'Murillo'**   A Rustica azalea, raised by C. Vuylsteke in 1888. Double, scented flowers; Ghent × Mollis azalea. Compact growth to 1.5 m. Hardy to −25°C.
**'Double Damask'**   A deciduous azalea raised at Messrs Waterer's Knap Hill Nursery. Height to 2 m. Hardy to −20°C.
**'Solion'**   A double-flowered deciduous azalea of unknown origin. Hardy to −20°C.
**'Fanny'** (syn. 'Pucella')   A deciduous Ghent azalea, of unknown origin. Bushy growth to 2.5 m. Hardy to −25°C.
**'Pallas'**   A deciduous Ghent azalea raised in Belgium before 1875. Bushy growth to 2.5 m.
**'Gloria Mundi'**   A deciduous Ghent azalea, raised by L. Seneclause in 1846. Bushy growth to 2.5 m. Hardy to −25°C.
**'Nancy Waterer'**   A deciduous azalea, raised at Messrs Waterer's Knap Hill Nursery before 1867, a cross, it is thought, between a Ghent-type azalea and *R. molle*, and the first of the Knap Hill azaleas to be named. Hardy to −20°C.
**'Irene Koster'**   A deciduous azalea raised by Koster and Co. A hybrid of *R. occidentale* × a Mollis azalea. Flowers scented. Height to 2.5 m. Hardy to −20°C.
**'Exquiseta'**   A deciduous azalea raised by M. Koster and Sons in 1901. A hybrid of *R. occidentale* × a Mollis azalea. Flowers scented. Height to 2.5 m. Hardy to −20°C.
**'Coccinea Speciosa'**   Close to *R. calendulaceum*, and known in England before

1843. Little scent. Tall-growing to 2.5 m in layers. Generally considered an early Ghent azalea.
**'Glory of Littleworth'**   An Azaleodendron, raised by Henry Mangles before 1908, of unknown parentage but presumably a yellow deciduous azalea crossed with a hardy evergreen rhododendron. An upright and sometimes leggy, semi-deciduous shrub to 2 m. Acid soil; full sun or part shade. Hardy to −20°C.
**R. vaseyi 'White Find'**   A clone of *R. vaseyi* (p. 135) collected in the wild in North Carolina. It has white, green-spotted flowers and good yellow autumn colour. Hardy to −25°C. White-flowered plants, f. *album*, also appeared among seedlings raised in the Arnold Arboretum and at Kew.

R. viscosum

R. griersonianum

R. brachyanthum
subsp. hypolepidotum

R. brachycarpum

R. wardii F.19467

R. heliolepis
F.15933

R. ponticum

R. decorum K.W.4487

½ life size. Specimens from Windsor Great Park, 19th June

*Rhododendron vernicosum* Yu. T.T.13961 at Benmore

*Rhododendron fortunei subsp. discolor* at Windsor

*Rhododendron vernicosum*

*Rhododendron glaucophyllum*

*Rhododendron auriculatum* in August

**Rhododendron viscosum** (L.) Torr. (s. *Azalea*) Swamp Honeysuckle, Clammy Azalea  Native of Maine south to S. Carolina and Georgia, in swamps and moist pine barrens on the coastal plain, flowering in June–August. Deciduous shrub to 5 m. Flowers white to pink, fragrant. Moist or wet acid soil. Sun or part shade. Hardy to −20°C and below. Summer.

**R. griersonianum** Balf. fil. & Forr. (ss. *Griersoniana*)  Native of W. Yunnan and N.E. Upper Burma, in coniferous and mixed forest, and in scrub at 2150–2700 m, flowering in June. Evergreen shrub to 3 m; young shoots and pedicels sticky with glandular hairs. Acid soil; tolerant of more drought and sun than most species. Hardy to −10°C. Summer.

**R. brachyanthum** Franch. subsp. **hypolepidotum** (Franch.) Cullen (ss. *Glauca*) Rock 11172  Native of N.E. Burma, N.W. Yunnan and S.E. Xizang, on rocky hillsides and scrub, and sometimes epiphytic, at 2050–4000 m, flowering in July. Evergreen shrub to 2 m; leaves aromatic, glaucous beneath, with scattered scales (or with few or no scales in subsp. *brachyanthum*, from near Dali, Yunnan). Acid soil, with extra good drainage; sun or part shade. Hardy to −20°C. Summer.

**R. brachycarpum** D. Don ex G. Don subsp. **brachycarpum** (ss. *Pontica*)  Native of Korea (where it is mainly replaced by subsp. *fauriei*) and Japan from Hokkaido to C. Honshu and Shikoku, usually above 2000 m in conifer forest and subalpine scrub, flowering in June–August. Evergreen shrub to 3 m. Leaves greyish felted beneath (except in subsp. *fauriei*). Acid soil; sun

or part shade. One of the hardiest species, to −25°C or lower in some forms. Summer.

**R. wardii** W. W. Sm. (incl. *R. litiense* Balf. fil. & Forr.) (ss. *Campylocarpa*) Forrest 19467  Native of S.E. Xizang, N.E. Yunnan and S.W. Sichuan, in pine forest, scrub and open mountainsides, sometimes in swamps or on limestone cliffs, at 3000–4300 m, flowering in June–July. Evergreen shrub to 8 m; flowers yellow to white (var. *puralbum*). Acid or non-chalky soil; part shade. Hardy to −20°C in hardiest forms. Early to mid-summer.

**R. heliolepis** Franch. (ss. *Heliolepida*) Forrest 15933.  Native of Yunnan, S.W. Xizang and N.E. Burma, in scrub and forest at 2500–3700 m, flowering in July–August. Evergreen shrub to 3 m. Flowers white or pink, rarely purplish. Acid soil; sun or part shade. Hardy to −20°C. Late summer.

**R. ponticum** L. (ss. *Pontica*)  Native of the W. Caucasus, N. Turkey, Bulgaria, Lebanon, S.W. Spain and S. Portugal (and of W. Ireland before the last Ice Age), in *Abies* and *Fagus* forest, *Pinus* forest (in Lebanon) and in scrub, at up to 1800 m, flowering in May–July. Evergreen shrub to 5 m. Acid or neutral soil; sun or shade. Hardy to −15°C. Summer.

**R. decorum** Franch. (ss. *Fortunea*) KW4487  Native of N.E. Burma and Yunnan, Sichuan and W. Guizhou, in open forest, scrub and bare limestone pavement at 2500–3600 m, flowering in May–June. Evergreen shrub to 6 m. Flowers fragrant. Non-chalky soil, and both drought-and heat-tolerant; sun or part shade. Hardy to

−15°C or lower in the hardiest forms. Summer.

**R. vernicosum** Franch. (ss. *Fortunea*) Yu. T. T. 13961 ?Loch Eck  Native of N. Yunnan, S.W. Sichuan and ?Gansu, in scrub, coniferous and mixed forest and on open rocky slopes, at 2600–3650 m, flowering in April–July. Very variable (see p. 111). Evergreen shrub to 8 m, but usually less. Flowers pale pink to purplish-pink, rarely white, fragrant. Moist, not chalky soil; some shade. Hardy to −15°C to −20°C. Late spring.

**R. fortunei** Lindl. subsp. **discolor** (Franch.) Chamberlain (ss. *Fortunea*)  Native of much of China from Sichuan eastwards, in scrub and open forest, at 1100–2100 m, flowering in May–June. Evergreen shrub or small tree to 10 m. Flowers white to pink, fragrant. Acid soil; part shade. Hardy to −20°C. Summer.

**R. glaucophyllum** Rehd. (ss. *Glauca*)  Native of the Himalayas from E. Nepal to Bhutan and S. Xizang, growing on rocky slopes and in open forest, at 2750–3650 m, flowering in May. Evergreen shrub to 2 m, but usually *c.*1 m. Leaves glaucous beneath. Acid soil; part shade. Hardy to −20°C with shelter, from cold winds. Spring.

**R. auriculatum** Hemsl. (ss. *Auriculata*)  Native of E. Sichuan, W. Hubei and E. Guizhou, in open forest, on ridges and rocky slopes at 500–2300 m, flowering in July. Evergreen large shrub or tree to 6 m. Flowers white or pale pink, greenish in the throat, fragrant. Acid soil; shade or part shade and shelter. Hardy to −15°C and heat-tolerant. Late summer.

'Lascaux'

'Amor'

'Romany Chal'

'Biscuit Box'

'Jalisco Goshawk'

'Kilimanjaro'

'Grosclaude'

'Tensing'

'Tally Ho'

⅖ life size. Specimens from Windsor Great Park, 19th June

**R. 'Amor'** (*R. griersonianum* × *R. thayerianum*)
Raised by J. B. Stevenson in 1927. Evergreen
shrub to 2 m. Hardy to −15°C. Mid summer.

**R. 'Lascaux'** (*R. 'Fabia'* × *R. wardii, Litiense*
group) Raised by Francis Hanger at Wisley,
Surrey in 1947. Evergreen shrub to 1.5 m. Acid
soil. Hardy to −15°C. Mid summer.

**R. 'Romany Chal'** (*R. 'Moser's Maroon'* × *R.*
*facetum*) Raised by Lionel de Rothschild
before 1932. Evergreen shrub to 3 m. Moist,
acid soil; some shade. Hardy to −15°C. Mid
summer.

**R. 'Biscuit Box'** (*R. fortunei* subsp. *discolor* ×
*R. elliottii*) Raised by Francis Hanger at
Wisley, before 1960. Evergreen shrub to 3 m or
more. Acid soil; part shade. Hardy to −15°C.
Mid summer.

**R. 'Jalisco Goshawk'** (*R. 'Dido'* × *R. 'Lady
Bessborough'*) Raised by Lionel de Rothschild
around 1942. Evergreen shrub to 2 m. Flowers
with a small non-petaloid calyx (unlike other
clones of 'Jalisco'). Acid soil; part shade. Hardy
to −15°C. Mid summer.

**R. 'Kilimanjaro'** (*R. elliottii* × *R. 'Dusky
Maid'*) Raised by Lionel de Rothschild before
1943. Evergreen shrub to 2 m. Acid soil; part
shade. Hardy to −15°C. Mid summer.

**R. 'Grosclaude'** (*R. haematodes* × *R. facetum*)
Raised by Lionel de Rothschild in 1941.
Compact shrub to 1.5 m. Moist, acid soil; some
shade. Hardy to −15°C. Mid summer.

**R. 'Tensing'** (*R. 'Fabia'* × *R. 'Romany Chai'*)
Raised by Francis Hanger at Wisley before
1953. Evergreen shrub to 1.5 m. Acid soil; part
shade and shelter. Hardy to −15°C. Close to *R.*
*griersonianum* of which both its parents are
offspring. Early summer.

**R. 'Tally Ho'** (*R. griersonianum* × *R. facetum*)
Raised by J. J. Crossfield before 1933.
Evergreen shrub to 2.5 m. Acid soil; part shade.
Hardy to −10°C. Early summer.

**R. 'Polar Bear'** (*R. diaprepes* × *R. auriculatum*)
Raised by J. B. Stevenson before 1926.
Evergreen shrub to 9 m. Leaves to 20 cm or
even 30 cm long. Flowers 11 cm across,
fragrant. Acid soil; part shade. Hardy to −20°C.
Late summer.

**R. 'Rothenberg'** (*R. 'Diane'* × *R.*
*williamsianum*) Raised by J. Bruns before
1972. Compact evergreen shrub to 1.5 m.
Leaves very glossy. Acid or chalk-free soil;
part shade. Hardy to −20°C. A very good
hybrid, both for foliage and flower. Summer.

**R. 'Joanita'** (*R. lacteum* × *R. campylocarpum*
subsp. *caloxanthum*) Raised by Lionel de
Rothschild before 1942. Compact evergreen
shrub to 1.5 m. Acid soil; some shade. Hardy to
−15°C. Early summer.

**R. 'Queen's Wood'** (*R. souliei* × *R.*
*aberconwayi*) Raised by T. H. Findlay at
Windsor before 1972. Evergreen shrub to 2 m.
Leaves broadly elliptic. Acid soil; some shade.
Hardy to −20°C. Early summer.

**R. 'Vintage Rose'** (*R. yakushimanum* ×
('Eclipse' × 'Fusilier')) Raised by J. Waterer,
Sons and Crisp before 1975. Low spreading
evergreen shrub to 1 m high. Acid soil; sun or
part shade. Hardy to −15°C. Early summer.

Rhododendron 'Polar Bear' at Wakehurst in August

Rhododendron 'Rothenberg'

Rhododendron 'Joanita'

Rhododendron 'Queen's Wood'

Rhododendron 'Vintage Rose'

R. dichroanthum
subsp. scyphocalyx

R. 'Moonstone'

R. wardii L.S. & E.15764

R. triflorum

R. ponticum

R. souliei

R. cerasinum
K.W.11011

R. yakushimanum

R. smirnowii

⅔ life size. Specimens from Windsor Great Park, 19th June

*Rhododendron yakushimanum* at Windsor

*Rhododendron souliei* at Windsor

**Rhododendron dichroanthum** Diels subsp. **scyphocalyx** (Balf. fil. & Forrest) Cowan, including subsp. *herpesticum* (Balf. f. & Ward) Cowan: (ss. *Neriiflora*) Forrest 27051 Native of N.E. Upper Burma and W. Yunnan, on rocky slopes and in bamboo scrub at 3600–4550 m, flowering in July. Evergreen shrub to 2 m. Flowers waxy, 3.5–5 cm long. Moist, acid soil; part shade. Hardy to −15°C. Summer.

**R. 'Moonstone'** (*R. campylocarpum* × *R. williamsianum*) Raised by J. C. Williams before 1933. Evergreen, rounded shrub to 1.5 m. Flowers *c*.6.5 cm across, 3–5 in a truss. Acid or non-chalky soil; part shade. Hardy to −20°C. Spring to summer.

**R. wardii** W. W. Sm. (ss. *Campylocarpa*) L. S. & E. 15764 (see also p. 141.) This clone, with primrose yellow flowers and a deep blotch has been named 'Meadow Pond', when exhibited by the Crown Estate Commissioners from Windsor. *R. wardii* is very widespread and variable in the wild, with bell-shaped to nearly flat flowers, sometimes unmarked. It differs from *R. campylocarpum*, also yellow-flowered, in its glandular style and well-developed calyx, 5–15 mm long.

**R. ponticum** L. (ss. *Pontica*) (see p. 141.) In its three main areas of distribution, *R. ponticum* has been given different names, subsp. *ponticum* around the Black Sea, subsp. *baeticum* in Spain and Portugal, and var. *brachycarpum* Boiss. in Lebanon, but the morphological distinctions among the three have been shown to be trivial or inconstant.

**R. triflorum** Hooker fil. (ss. *Triflora*) Native of the Himalayas from E. Nepal to Bhutan and S. Xizang (where it is common), in scrub, forest and mountainsides at 2400–3650 m, flowering in April and May. Straggly evergreen shrub to 7 m, with reddish-brown, peeling bark. Flowers pale yellow, sometimes (in S. Xizang) with dark red spots, 4–5 cm across. Acid soil. Hardy to −15°C. Early summer.

*Rhododendron cerasinum*

*Rhododendron maximum 'Summer Time'*

**R. souliei** Franch. (ss. *Campylocarpa*) Native of W. Sichuan and N.E. Yunnan, on rocky mountain summits and in forest at 2700–4500 m, flowering in June. Evergreen shrub to 5 m. Flowers nearly flat, 5–7.5 cm across, pale pink or white flushed pink. Well-drained, acid soil; sun or part shade. Hardy to −20°C. Early summer.

**R. yakushimanum** Nakai (ss. *Pontica*) (syn. *R. metternichii* var. *yakushimanum* Ohwi) Native of Yakushima Island, S. Kyushu, at 1200–1800 m, in rainforest as an epiphyte on ancient *Cryptomeria*, on rocky granite bluffs and on the edges of sphagnum bog, flowering in May. Evergreen shrub to 2.5 m, less in exposed sites. Flowers 3-4 cm long, pale pink to almost white. Acid soil; sun or part shade. Hardy to −25°C. Late spring. A very easy species in spite of its restricted distribution in the wild. The parent of many new dwarf hybrids.

**R. cerasinum** Tagg (ss. *Thomsonia*) Kingdon Ward 11011 Native of N.E. Upper Burma and S.E. Xizang, in coniferous forest and dense

scrub, at 3000–3800 m, flowering in June. Evergreen shrub to 3.7 m. Flowers pendulous, on pedicels 15–25 mm long, waxy, crimson to scarlet or white edged pink, with dark nectaries, 3.5–4.5 cm long. Moist, acid soil; some shade. Hardy to −15°C. Late spring.

**R. smirnowii** Trautv. (ss. *Pontica*) Native of N.E. Turkey near Artvin, on hillsides and in *Picea* forest, on acid and basic igneous rock, at 1525–2200 m, flowering in June and July. Evergreen shrub to 4 m. Leaves woolly beneath. Flowers pink to white flushed pink, 3.4 cm across. Acid or non-chalky soil; sun or part shade. Hardy to −25°C. Late spring.

**R. maximum** L. (ss. *Pontica*) **'Summer Time'** Rosebay Native of Nova Scotia south to Georgia and Alabama, in damp places along streams and in the edges of bogs and ponds as well as mountain slopes at up to 900 m, flowering in June and July. Evergreen shrub to 10 m. Flowers 3.5–4 cm across, pale pink or white to purplish. Moist, acid soil; sun or part shade. Hardy to −30°C and below. Summer.

*Enkianthus cernuus var. marsudae*

*Menziesia ciliicalyx var. purpurea*

*Enkianthus cernuus f. rubens*

*Enkianthus chinensis*

*Enkianthus campanulatus var. palibinii*

*Enkianthus campanulatus*

*Vaccinium corymbosum*

*Vaccinium corymbosum*

*Vaccinium corymbosum*

*Leucothoë fontanesiana*

*Gaultheria hookeri*

*Berberis calliantha*

*Berberis hookeri Farrer 1030*

*Berberis hookeri Schilling 1089*

⅖ life size. Specimens from Sandling and Windsor, 1st June

Gaultheria shallon and Davidia involucrata

Enkianthus cernuus f. rubens

Vaccinium ovatum

Agapetes serpens

Arctostaphylos patula

**Enkianthus cernuus** (Sieb. & Zucc.) Makino (*Ericaceae*) Native of S.E. Honshu, Kyushu and Shikoku, in woods in the mountains, flowering in May–June. Deciduous shrub to 3 m. Leaves obovate. Flowers white, or red in f. **rubens** (Maxim.) Ohwi and var. **matsudae** (komatsu) Mak, from S.C. Honshu, which has an exserted style. Hardy to −20°C.

**Enkianthus campanulatus** (Miq.) Nichols (*Ericaceae*) Native of S.E. Hokkaido, Honshu (rare in the southeast) and Shikoku (var. *sikokianus* Palib.), flowering in June–July. Deciduous shrub to 5 m. Leaves elliptic-obovate to obovate, hairy along the nerve axils beneath, sometimes pilose above, colouring orange and red in autumn. Flowers 8–12 mm long, pale greenish with pink veins, to reddish in var. **palibinii** (Craib) Bean (from C. Honshu) pollinated by wasps.

**Enkianthus chinensis** Franch. (*Ericaceae*) Native of W. Hubei, Sichuan, Yunnan and N.E. Burma, in forest, on cliffs and rocks, at 1600–2000 m, flowering in May–June. Deciduous shrub to 6 m. Leaves glabrous but otherwise hardly different from the Japanese *E. campanulatus*. Flowers usually yellowish, veined pink, with reflexed lobes; the pale form shown here collected by Kingdon Ward in the Burma 'Triangle'. Acid soil; part shade. Hardy to −10°C. Early summer.

**Menziesia ciliicalyx** (Miq.) Maxim. var. **purpurea** Makino (syn. *M. multiflora* var. *purpurea* (Makino) Ohwi) (*Ericaceae*); see also p. 75 This beautiful variety is confined to the district of Hakone, S.E. of Tokyo. Var.

*multiflora* (Maxim) Makino has pale pink flowers with long spreading ciliate sepals 4–6 mm long, and is common on Hokkaido, Honshu and Shikoku, but rare in gardens.

**Leucothoë fontanesiana** (Steud.) Sleumer (syn. *L. editorum* Fern. & Schub., *L. catesbei* Gray) (*Ericaceae*) Native of Virginia to Georgia and Tennessee, in damp woods in the mountains flowering in May. Evergreen shrub to 1.5 m, with arching branches forming a spreading clump. 'Rainbow' with pink, yellow and orange flecked leaves is often cultivated. Acid soil. Hardy to −20°C.

**Berberis hookeri** Lem. (*Berberidaceae*) Farrer 1030 and Schilling 1089 Native of the Himalayas from Nepal to Bhutan in *Tsuga* and *Rhododendron* forest, at 3000–3500 m, flowering in April–June. Evergreen, bushy shrub to 1.5 m. Hardy to −15°C. Early summer.

**Berberis calliantha** Mulligan (*Berberidaceae*) Native of S.E. Xizang, near Pemakochung in the Tsangpo Gorge growing in marshes at 2500 m. Evergreen, dense shrub to 1 m. Flowers to 2.5 cm across. Hardy to −10°C. Early summer.

**Gaultheria hookeri** C. B. Clarke (*Ericaceae*) Native of E. Nepal east to Yunnan, growing in forests at 2700–3000 m, flowering in May–June. Evergreen shrub to 1 m, with bristly-hairy branches. Flowers *c.*4 mm long. Acid soil; shade. Hardy to −10°C.

**Gaultheria shallon** Pursh (*Ericaceae*) Salal (see p. 151).

**Vaccinium corymbosum** L. (*Ericaceae*) Highbush Blueberry Native of Nova Scotia and Quebec west to Wisconsin and Alabama, south to Florida, in swamps, wet meadows, pine barrens and mountain woods, flowering in May–June, fruiting June–August. Deciduous shrub to 4.5 m. Fruit deep blue with a greyish bloom. Acid soil; sun or part shade. Hardy to −25°C. Late spring.

**Vaccinium ovatum** Pursh (*Ericaceae*) California Huckleberry Native of California north to British Columbia, on dry rocky slopes and sandy, heathy places near the sea to 800 m, flowering March–May. Low, much-branched evergreen shrub to 2.5 m. Flowers 5–7 mm long. Fruit 6–9 mm, black. Hardy to −15°C. Early summer.

**Agapetes serpens** (Wight) Sleumer (*Ericaceae*) Native of E. Nepal to Bhutan and N. Assam, on mossy banks in forest or as an epiphyte at 1500–3000 m, flowering in February–June. Lax evergreen shrub from a woody tuber with spreading and hanging branches to 2 m long. Flowers 2.5 cm, whitish in 'Nepal Cream' introduced by Roy Lancaster. Moist, acid soil; shade. Hardy to −5°C. Spring.

**Arctostaphylos patula** Greene (*Ericaceae*) Native of California north to Oregon, Nevada and Utah, in open places in mixed conifer forest, flowering in April–June. Evergreen shrub to 2 m, with smooth reddish bark, and swollen fire-resistant rootstock. Leaves not glaucous; dark or bright green, rounded. Well-drained soil, dry in summer. Hardy to −10°C or less. Spring.

Gaultheria shallon

× Gaulnettya wisleyenis

Pernettya mucronata

Zenobia pulverulenta

Kalmia latifolia

Kalmia latifolia

Kalmia angustifolia 'Rubra'

Vaccinium stamineum

Leucothoë davisiae

½ life size. Specimens from Windsor and Wisley, 19th June

*Fothergilla major* at Wisley

*Lyonia ovalifolia* in Dali, Yunnan

**Gaultheria shallon** Pursh (*Ericaceae*) Salal
Native of California north from Santa Barbara,
to British Columbia, in Redwood forests and
other woods and scrub in the coast ranges at up
to 800 m, flowering in April–July. Evergreen,
low, suckering shrub to 2 m high, usually *c*.1 m.
Fruit, formed by the fleshy calyx, purple. Acid
soil; part shade or full shade. Hardy to −20°C.

× **Gaulnettya wisleyensis** Marchant (*Ericaceae*)
'Wisley Pearl' A hybrid between *Gaultheria
shallon* and *Pernettya mucronata*, which arose
spontaneously in the wild garden at Wisley
before 1929. The specimens here were from the
type locality! Evergreen shrub to 1.5 m,
suckering. Leaves to 3.7 cm long, tough,
rugose. Fruit pinkish-purple, fleshy (p. 262).
Acid, moist soil. Hardy to −20°C. Summer.

**Pernettya mucronata** (L.) Gaud. (*Ericaceae*)
Native of S. Chile and S. Argentina forming
dwarf scrub on moist, acid soil, flowering in
October–December. Evergreen bushy shrub to
2 m. Leaves to 2 cm long, with a spiny point.
Flowers 5 mm long, white or pink tinged.
Berries variously coloured, white or red or
purple (see p. 262), showy in winter. Acid,
moist soil; sun or part shade. Hardy to −20°C.
Early summer.

**Zenobia pulverulenta** (Bartr.) Pollard
(*Ericaceae*) Native of S.E. Virginia to S.
Carolina, in damp, sandy or peaty heaths and
pine barrens, flowering in June. Deciduous
shrub to 3 m. Leaves 2–7 cm long, covered with
a powdery bloom. Flowers 6–8 mm long, with
very good scent, on shoots of the preceding
year. Acid soil, moist; sun or part shade. Hardy
to −10°C. Early summer.

**Kalmia latifolia** L. (*Ericaceae*) Mountain laurel
Native of New England, Quebec, New York
State and Ohio south to Louisiana and W.
Florida, in deciduous forest often among rocks
on acid soil, flowering from May to July in the
north. Evergreen shrub to 3 m, rarely to 10 m.
Leaves oblanceolate, to 10 cm long. Flowers to
2.5 cm across, usually pale pink but sometimes

crimson, purplish-brown or white. Acid soil;
part shade or full sun in cooler climates. Hardy
to −30°C. Summer. Many cultivars from North
America are now likely to become commoner, as
they are propagated by tissue culture.

**Kalmia angustifolia** L. 'Rubra' (*Ericaceae*)
Lambkill, Sheep Laurel Native of Labrador,
Manitoba and Newfoundland south to Virginia
and Georgia in the mountains, growing in acid
bogs, heaths, open woods, and pine barrens,
flowering from late May to August (in the
north). Small lax evergreen shrub to 1 m.
Leaves oblong to elliptic-lanceolate, to 5 cm
long. Flowers to 13 mm across, usually deep
pink or crimson, rarely white. Moist, acid soil;
sun or part shade. Hardy to −30°C. 'Rubra' is a
deep pink form, frequent in cultivation.
Summer.

**Vaccinium stamineum** L. (*Ericaceae*)
Deerberry Native of Massachusetts, Ontario
to Indiana south to Missouri, Florida and
Louisiana, in dry woods and scrub, flowering in
March–May. Deciduous shrub to 3 m. Leaves
variable in shape and size, to 10 cm long.
Flowers white, greenish or purplish, to 8 mm
long, with exserted anthers. Fruit green, pale
orange, purple or blue, ripe in July–September.
Acid soil; part shade. Hardy to −25°C.
Summer.

**Leucothöe davisiae** Torr. (*Ericaceae*) Native
of C. and N. California, from Fresno Co.
northwards to Oregon, in bogs and swamps at
1000–2500 m, flowering in June–August.
Evergreen shrub to 1.5 m. Leaves glabrous,
3–6 cm long. Acid, moist soil; sun or part shade.
Hardy to −20°C. Summer.

**Lyonia ovalifolia** (Wall.) Drude (*Ericaceae*)
Native of the Himalayas from Pakistan east to
Yunnan, Sichuan and Hubei; in Japan on
Honshu, Shikoku and Kyushu, and in Taiwan;
common on hills, in scrub and on the edges of
oak, pine and *Rhododendron* woods, in sunny
places, flowering in April–June. A deciduous or
half-evergreen shrub or small tree to 10 m, with

*Ledum glandulosum subsp. columbianum*

bark peeling in vertical strips; often only 1 m
high as here. Leaves 8–15 cm long, often hairy
beneath when young. Flowers 8–10 mm in
racemes 5–14 cm long. Capsule 4–5 mm across.
Acid soil; sun or part shade. Hardy to −10°C.

**Fothergilla major** (Sims) Lodd.
(*Hamamelidaceae*) Native of Georgia,
flowering in May. Deciduous shrub to 3 m.
Leaves 5–10 cm long, glabrous above, glaucous
and stellate-pubescent beneath, orange-yellow
in autumn. Flower spikes to 5 cm long, with
conspicuous white stamens to 14 mm long.
Acid, moist soil; sun or part shade. Hardy to
−20°C. Early summer.

**Ledum glandulosum** Nutt. **subsp.
columbianum** (Piper) C. L. Hitchc. (*Ericaceae*)
Native of N. Califorinia from Santa Cruz Co.
north to Washington, near the coast in wet,
peaty places and open pine and Redwood forest,
below 1000 m, flowering in May and June.
Evergreen, leggy shrub to 2 m. Leaves 3–6 cm
long, whitish beneath. Inflorescence rounded,
dense; flowers 1.2–1.8 cm across. Acid, moist
soil; sun or part shade. Hardy to −15°C. Early
summer.

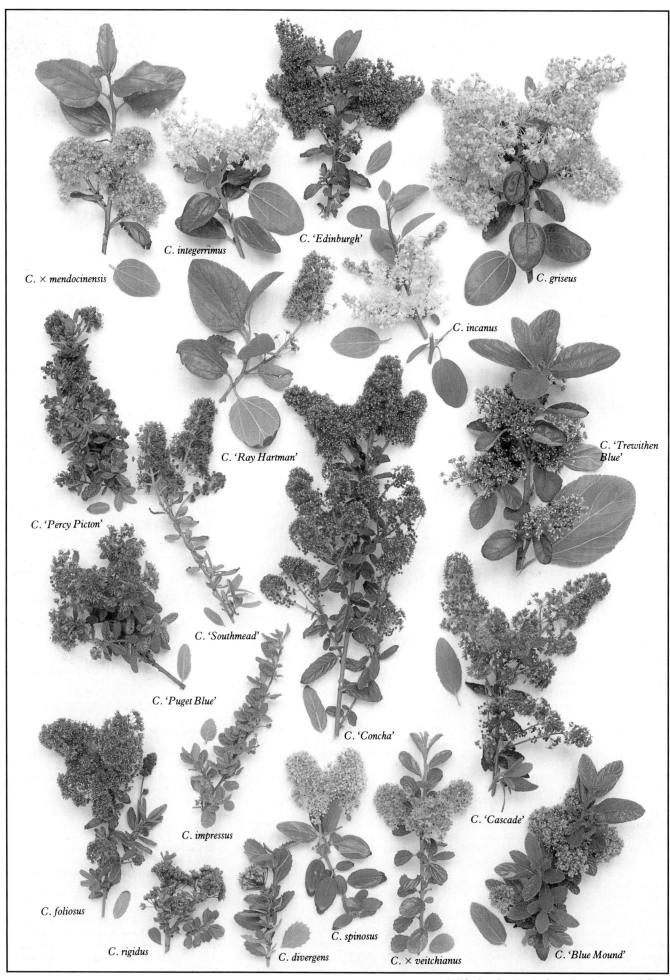

C. × mendocinensis

C. integerrimus

C. 'Edinburgh'

C. griseus

C. incanus

C. 'Ray Hartman'

C. 'Trewithen Blue'

C. 'Percy Picton'

C. 'Southmead'

C. 'Puget Blue'

C. 'Concha'

C. 'Cascade'

C. impressus

C. foliosus

C. rigidus

C. divergens

C. spinosus

C. × veitchianus

C. 'Blue Mound'

½ life size. Specimens from Cannington, 10th June

Ceanothus 'Concha' at Cannington, Somerset

Ceanothus purpureus

Ceanothus in N. California

**Ceanothus** (*Rhamnaceae*)   Found throughout North America, but with most, and the more beautiful, species in California, near the coast. Easily grown, late spring or early summer flowering, but susceptible to wet in summer, so should not be irrigated. Fast-growing, but short-lived even when not killed by cold winters. (See also p. 252.)

**C.** × **mendocinensis** McMinn   A hybrid between *C. velutinus* and *C. thyrsiflorus*; to 4 m.

**C. integerrimus** Hook. & Arn.   Native of S. California north to Washington, on dry slopes and hills in pine forest, and mixed evergreen forest at 300–2000 m, in the Coast Ranges, flowering in May and June. Semi-deciduous shrub to 4 m. Flower clusters 4–15 cm long, white to pink or dark blue. Hardy to −10°C.

**C. 'Edinburgh'**   A hybrid of *C. griseus* perhaps with *C. papillosus*, which originated at Edinburgh Botanic Gardens. Hardy to −10°C.

**C. griseus** (Trel.) McMinn   Native of California from Santa Barbara Co. north to Mendocino Co., in the Coast Ranges in pine forest and coastal scrub, flowering from March to May. Evergreen shrub to 3 m. Flowers in dense clusters 2–5 cm long, violet-blue. Hardy to −5°C. to −10°C. A form from Yankee Point, var. *horizontalis*, makes a wide-spreading bush with pale blue flowers.

**C. 'Ray Hartman'**   Evergreen shrub or small tree to 6 m and as much across. A hybrid of *C. arboreus*. Hardy to −10°C.

**C. incanus** Torr. & Greene   Native of California from Santa Cruz Co. north to Siskiyou Co. in open places in redwood and mixed forest in the outer coast ranges at up to 1000 m, flowering in April and May. Evergreen shrub to 4 m; branches spiny and glaucous. Flowers white in dense clusters 3–6 cm long. Hardy to −10°C.

**C. arboreus** Greene **'Trewithen Blue'**   Native of Santa Cruz, Santa Rosa and Santa Catalina islands, off the south California coast, in scrub on hills, flowering in February–May. Evergreen large shrub or small tree to 7 m. Leaves to 8 cm long. Flower clusters to 12 cm long, pale blue in the wild. Hardy to −5°C.

**C. 'Percy Picton'**   A hybrid, perhaps, of *C. impressus* and *C. papillosus*. Dense, evergreen, to 3 m.

**C. 'Southmead'**   Perhaps a hybrid between *C. griseus* and *C. dentatus*. Evergreen, to 3 m.

**C. 'Concha'**   Dense evergreen shrub to 2 m and as much or more across. Leaves 2.5 cm long. Flower buds reddish; petals deep blue. Hardy to −10°C.

**C. 'Puget Blue'**   Sometimes listed as a form of *C. impressus* from which it differs in its longer, narrower leaves to 2 cm long, with *c.*48 glandular teeth, possibly showing the influence of *C. papillosus*. Dense, evergreen shrub to 5 m, with support. Very free-flowering. Any soil and tolerant of clay; full sun. Hardy to −10°C.

**C. impressus** Trel.   Native of S. California from Santa Barbara Co. to San Luis Obispo Co., in evergreen scrub, flowering in March and April. Dense evergreen shrub to 2 m. Flower clusters narrow, to 2.5 cm long. Flowers deep blue. Hardy to −10°C.

**C. foliosus** Parry   Native of California from Santa Cruz Co., north to Humboldt Co., and in San Diego Co., with var. *medius* south to St Luis Obispo Co., growing in evergreen scrub below 1200 m in the coast ranges, flowering from March to May. Evergreen shrub to 1 m high. Flower clusters simple and to 2.5 cm long, or compound and longer. Hardy to −5°C.

**C. rigidus** Nutt.   Native of the Monterey peninsula in California, on sandy hills and valleys, flowering in February–April. Bushy, twiggy shrub to 2 m tall, more across. Flowers in few-flowered umbels. Hardy to −5°C. There is a white-flowered form 'Snowball' in cultivation in California.

**C. divergens** Parry   Native of California in the Napa Valley near Calistoga, in scrub and open woods, flowering in February–March. Subsp. *confusus* (J. T. Howell) Abrams is more widespread in Sonomona and Lake Co., also. A low evergreen shrub with arching branches, to 1.5 m high. Flowers in small umbels. Hardy to −10°C.

**C. 'Cascade'**   A form or hybrid of *C. thyrsiflorus*, with arching branches. Hardy to −10°C.

**C. spinosus** Nutt. Red-Heart, Greenbark ceanothus   Native of California, from San Luis Obispo Co., southwards, on dry slopes and in scrub below 1000 m in mountains near the coast, flowering in February–May. Large evergreen shrub to 6 m with green bark; spiny branches. Flowers pale blue to white, in large compound clusters to 15 cm long. Hardy to −5°C.

**C.** × **veitchianus** Hook.   Probably a hybrid between *C. griseus* and *C. rigidus* collected near Monterey. Evergreen to 3 m.

**C. 'Blue Mound'**   A low spreading evergreen, possibly a hybrid between *C. thyrsiflorus* var. *repens* and *C. papillosus*.

**C. purpureus** Jeps.   Native of California, in the Napa range, on dry rocky hills at up to 500 m, flowering in February–April. Evergreen shrub to 2 m. Flowers deep blue to purple, in umbels. Hardy to −5°C.

153

W. floribunda 'Macrobotrys'

W. venusta

W. floribunda 'Issai'

W. sinensis 'Black Dragon'

W. floribunda 'Rosea'

W. sinensis

¼ life size. Specimens from Cannington, 10th June

154

Wisteria floribunda 'Alba'

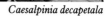

Wisteria × formosa at Cannington

Caesalpinia decapetala

**Wisteria floribunda** (Willd.) DC.forma **macrobotrys** (Neubert) Rehd. & Wils. (*Leguminosae*) Native of Japan, on Honshu, Shikoku and Kyushu, where it is common in thickets and woods and along streams in the mountains flowering in May–July. The name *macrobotrys* is used for cultivated forms which have extra long racemes of flowers, sometimes to 150 cm long, and many cover ⅛ acre. Woody, climbing deciduous shrub to 20 m, self-standing to c.2 m, twining clockwise. Leaflets 11–19. Racemes in the wild to 60 cm long. Flowers 2 cm across, scented. Any good soil. Full sun and requiring wall heat in summer in cool climates. Hardy to −20°C. Early summer.
**W. floribunda 'Rosea'** A pale pinkish form, known since 1903. Racemes to 45 cm long.
**W. floribunda 'Alba'** Flowers white or very pale mauve. Racemes 30–40 cm.
**W. floribunda 'Issai'** A form of *W. floribunda* or possibly a hybrid with *W. sinensis* or *W. venusta*, which flowers well as a young plant. Racemes about 30 cm long. Several clones were introduced by K. Wada from Japan, under this name, according to 'Bean' ed. 8. It twines clockwise.

**Wisteria sinensis** Sweet (*Leguminosae*) Chinese Wisteria Native of W. Hubei and E. Sichuan, and probably elsewhere in China, on cliffs and in woods, flowering in April–May. Woody climbing deciduous shrub to 40 m, covering large trees if allowed, twining anticlockwise. Leaflets 7–13; racemes 16–30 cm long, bluish-lilac. In early summer in gardens, often with a second, poorer crop of flowers two months later. Pruning should cut back the current year's growth to about 5 cm, in late summer. Sparrows

or other birds frequently eat the young buds, and they are the commonest cause of poor flowering on established plants. Any soil; full sun or part shade. Hardy to −15°C. Early summer.
**W. 'Black Dragon'** A double-flowered dark purple cultivar.

**Wisteria × formosa** Rehder A hybrid between *W. sinensis* and *W. floribunda* in which all the flowers of a raceme open together. The original cross, made in 1905, used *W. floribunda* 'Alba', and had 9–15 leaflets, racemes 25 cm long with flowers pale violet, 2 cm long.

**Wisteria venusta** Rehd. & Wils. (*Leguminosae*) A white-flowered cultivar, long grown in Japan, recognized by its velvety-hairy leaves, short, broad racemes, 10–15 cm long, and flowers 2.5–3 cm across, open at the same time. The wild form with purple flowers, var. *violacea* Rehder, syn. *W. brachybotrys* Sieb. & Zucc. is rather rare in W. Honshu, Shikoku and Kyushu, in mountains and hills, flowering in May–July. It twines anticlockwise. Woody deciduous climber to 10 m or more. Any good soil; sun. Hardy to −20°C.

**Caesalpinia decapetala** (Roth.) Alston, (syn. *C. sepiaria* Roxb.) (*Leguminosae*) Native of the Himalayas from Pakistan to China, Japan (var. *japonica*) and S.E. Asia, scrambling in scrub, on rocky slopes and in gorges, at up to 2200 m, flowering in March–May. Deciduous, partly climbing shrub to 7 m (or 2 m in var. *japonica*); branches with backward curving prickles. Leaves to 38 cm long, doubly pinnate with 5–10 pinnae, each with 8–12 pairs of leaflets. Flowers

Mucuna sempervirens

in upright racemes to 40 cm, each 2–3 cm across, in early summer. Hardy to −10°C.

**Mucuna sempervirens** Hemsl. (*Leguminosae*) Native of W. Hubei and E. Sichuan where it is common and elsewhere in China, and of Kyushu, where it is very rare, on cliffs and in gorges, or growing over bamboos, at up to 300 m, flowering in April. A rampant evergreen climber to 12 m or more. Leaflets 3, with prominent reticulate veins, the terminal leaflet 7–15 cm long. Flowers evil-smelling, waxy, rich in honey, produced mainly on the old wood, the curved keel 6–8 cm long. Pods 40 cm long, 7-seeded, velvety. Any soil; warm position with support. Hardy to −5°C.

*Syringa vulgaris*

*S. vulgaris 'Aurea'*

*S. oblata var. oblata*

*S. microphylla 'Superba'*

*S. × chinensis*

*S. laciniata*

*S. persica 'Alba'*

*S. 'William Judd'*

*S. × henryi*

½ life size. Specimens from Kew, 30th May

**Syringa oblata** Lindl. (*Oleaceae*)    Native of N. China, whence it was introduced by Robert Fortune in 1856. Deciduous shrub to 4 m high, with scented flowers in panicles to 12 cm long. Foliage bronze when young; turns red in autumn. Liable to frost damage. Any good soil. Hardy to −25°C. Late spring.

**S. microphylla** Diels **'Superba'**    Native of N. China, in N. Hubei; 'Superba' is a selection made in France in 1934. It makes a rounded bush up to about 2 m high. Very free-flowering, with scented blooms, 1 cm long. Any soil; full sun. Hardy to −25°C. Late spring and often again in late summer.

**S. × chinensis** Willd. (syn. 'Rouen lilac') A hybrid between *S. laciniata* and *S. vulgaris*, raised in the Botanic Garden at Rouen *c.* 1777. A bush up to 5 m high. Hardy to −35°C.

**S. × persica 'Alba'**    A white form of *S. × persica* raised in 1770, this grows up to *c.*2 m high. Leaves sometimes pinnate or lobed. Flowers scented. Hardy to −25°C.

**S. laciniata** Miller    Native of of Gansu, but long-grown in Kabul, Afghanistan, and sometimes confused with the entire-leaved *S. afghanica* Schneid. Perhaps one parent of *S. × persica*. Deciduous bushy shrub to 2 m. Leaves variably pinnate with 3–9 lobes. Flowers in broad panicles. Any soil; full sun. Hardy to −25°C. Late spring.

**S. × diversifolia** Rehder 'William H. Judd' A hybrid between *S. oblata* var. *giraldii* and *S. pinnatifolia*. A medium-sized shrub, with white scented flowers in panicles up to 11 cm long.

**S. × henryi** C. K. Schneider    A hybrid between *S. villosa* and *S. josikaea* raised by Louis Henry of Paris in 1896. Makes a shrub up to 3.5 m high. Late spring.

**S. reflexa** C. K. Schneider    Native of W. Hubei, at 1500–3000 m. Introduced by E. H. Wilson in 1910. Deciduous shrub up to 4 m high, with flowers in narrow panicles to 20 cm long. Any good soil; full sun. Hardy to −20°C. Late spring.

**S. × josiflexa 'Guinevere'**    Miss Isabella Preston of Ottawa raised a group of hybrids from the cross *S. josikaea* × *S. reflexa* in 1920; 'Guinevere' was the first of these. It makes a medium-sized shrub and bears scented flowers in late spring.

**S. julianae** C. K. Schneider (syn. *S. verrucosa* Schneid.)    A native of W. Hubei on mountain tops at *c.*2500 m, flowering in June. Introduced by E. H. Wilson in 1900. A deciduous shrub up to 2 m high, with very scented flowers in panicles up to 10 cm long. Any good soil; full sun. Hardy to −20°C. Late spring.

**S. sweginzowii** Koehne & Lingelsh    Native of W. Sichuan, collected by E. H. Wilson in 1904 in ravines at *c.*2400 m, flowering in June. Vigorous deciduous shrub to 4 m. Leaves ovate to oblong, 5–10 cm long. Panicles to 20 cm long. Flowers 13 mm long, pale pink with a red throat. Any soil; full sun. Hardy to −15°C.

**S. vulgaris** L.    Native of N. C. Romania, Yugoslavia, Bulgaria, C. Albania and N.E. Greece, in scrub on rocky hills, flowering in April–May. Deciduous shrub to 4 m. Leaves 4–8 cm long. Flowers pale mauve, or white (f. **alba**) in the wild. **'Aurea'** is a variety with yellowish leaves.

Syringa reflexa at Kildrummy, Scotland

Syringa reflexa

Syringa × josiflexa 'Guinevere'

Syringa sweginzowii

Syringa julianae

# LILACS

'John Dunbar'

'Lucie Baltet'

'Charles Joly'

'Volcan'

'Sensation'

'Mme Florent Stepman'

'Edith Cavell'

'Mme Felix'

'Mme A. Buchner'

'Mrs Edward Harding'

'Primrose'

'Firmament'

'Hugo Koster'

'Katherine Havemeyer'

⅝ life size. Specimens from Kew, 30th May

'Maréchal Foch'

'Blue Hyacinth'

'Buffon'

'Maud Notcutt'

'Esther Staley'

'Souvenir de Alice Harding'

$\frac{2}{5}$ life size. Specimens from Kew, 30th May

**Syringa vulgaris** cultivars There are hundreds of garden varieties of *S. vulgaris*, the common lilac; those illustrated here bear scented flowers in late spring (unless otherwise noted below) and thrive in full sun. They like good well-drained soil, will do well on chalk, but will not tolerate very acid conditions. No regular pruning is required, but dead-heading improves the plant. Lilacs take 2–3 years to become established after transplanting; until then they are unlikely to be true to form and colour.

**'John Dunbar'** Raised in the USA, named after John Dunbar of Dept. of Parks, Rochester, New York.
**'Lucie Baltet'** Raised by Baltet of Troyes, France, in the late 19th century; now uncommon. Good scent.
**'Charles Joly'** An upright shrub, raised by Lémoine in 1896. The heavily scented flowers are freely borne from mid-late summer.
**'Volcan'** Raised by Lémoine of Nancy, France, in 1899.
**'Mme Felix'** A cross between 'Marie Legraye' and an unnamed seedling raised by Felix and Dykhuis of Holland in 1924. Free-flowering; used for forcing and as a cut flower.
**'Mme Antoine Buchner'** A tall shrub, with a rather 'open' habit, raised by Lémoine in 1909. The very fragrant flowers are borne from mid-late summer.
**'Sensation'** An unusual lilac, with a rather loose habit, raised by De Maarse of Boskoop in 1938. The flowers are produced in mid-summer; they sometimes revert to plain white.
**'Edith Cavell'** Raised and introduced by Lémoine of Nancy, France, in 1916.
**'Mme Florent Stepman'** Introduced by F.

Stepman-De Messemaeker of Brussels in 1908; a cross between 'Dr Lindley' and 'Marie Legraye'.
**'Mrs Edward Harding'** A tall shrub with a rather loose habit, raised by Lémoine in 1923. The scented flowers (which fade to pink soon after opening) are freely produced in late summer.
**'Primrose'** A sport from 'Marie Legraye' introduced by De Maarse of Holland *c.* 1949. Makes a compact shrub with flowers freely produced in summer.
**'Firmament'** A medium-sized bush, introduced by Lémoine in 1932. The scented flowers appear in early summer.
**'Hugo Koster'** Introduced by Koster of Boskoop, Holland in 1914. Flowers freely produced and very sweetly scented. Suitable for forcing.
**"Katherine Havemeyer"** Introduced by Lémoine in 1922, makes a compact shrub with very fragrant flowers (liable to fading) produced in summer.
**'Maréchal Foch'** A tall, vigorous shrub, raised by Lémoine in 1924. The large flower heads are produced in early summer.
**'Maud Notcutt'** Raised by Notcutt of Suffolk, England, in 1956. Vigorous, rather upright habit. Large flower heads (up to 30 cm long) produced in summer.
**'Souvenir d'Alice Harding'** Raised by Lémoine in 1938. Flowers produced in early summer.

**S. × hyacinthiflora 'Blue Hyacinth'** *S. × hyacinthiflora* is a hybrid between *S. oblata* and *S. vulgaris* first raised by Lémoine of France in 1876. More recently W. B. Clarke of California

'Lucie Baltet'

has repeated the cross and obtained several clones, of which 'Blue Hyacinth' is one. Flowers appear in spring.
**S. × hyacinthiflora 'Buffon'** A form of *S. × hyacinthiflora*, raised by Lémoine in *c.* 1921. The slightly scented flowers are produced in spring.
**S. × hyacinthiflora 'Esther Staley'** Raised by W. B. Clarke in 1948. Flowers pinkish.

*Cotinus coggygria*

*Artemisia arborescens 'Powis Castle'*

*Cotinus coggygria 'Notcutt's Variety'*

**Artemisia arborescens** L. **'Powis Castle'**
(*Compositae*) Tree Wormwood   Native of the
Mediterranean region from S. Portugal
eastwards to S. Turkey, growing on cliffs and
rocky hillsides, especially on limestone, at up to
800 m, flowering in May–September. Evergreen
shrub to 1 m high, and more across; leaves
aromatic, 1–3 pinnatisect flower heads 6–7 mm
across, in a large branching inflorescence. Well-
drained soil; full sun. Hardy to −10°C. **Powis
Castle**   Shown here on the great walls
supporting the terraced garden at Powis, where
it originated as a seedling, is an exceptionally
hardy form, or possibly a hybrid with *A.
absinthum*, with leaves 1–3 pinnatisect,
flowering only in warm summers. Any soil and
full sun, but hardiest in poor, well-drained soil.
Hardy to −10°C. to −15°C.

**Cotinus coggygria** Scop. (*Anacardiaceae*)
Smoke Bush   Native of Europe from S.E.
France, eastwards to C. Ukraine and Turkey to
the Himalayas, C. China var. *pubescens* Engler
and E. China near Qingdao (Tsingtan) var.
*cinerea* Engler. It grows on rocky hillsides and
limestone rocks, most commonly on foothills of
mountains at up to 1300 m, flowering in April–
July, and brilliant in autumn colour. A
deciduous shrub to 5 m. Leaves 3–8 cm long,
ovate or obovate, glaucous, or purplish when
young in var. *purpureus*, deep purple in 'Foliis
Purpureis', and deep reddish-purple in
**'Notcutt's Variety'** (syn. 'Royal Purple'),
shown here. Flowers about 3 mm across, with 5
minute petals. Inflorescence much branched
and with long purplish hairs. Dry soil, well
drained. Full sun. Hardy to −20°C.

**Phlomis fruticosa** L. (*Labiatae*)   Native of the
Mediterranean region from Sardinia eastwards to
S.W. Turkey, on cliffs and rocky limestone hills
up to 1000 m, flowering from April to July.
Evergreen shrub to 1 m or 2 m in cultivation;
leaves 3–9 m long. Flowers in 1–2 whorls.
Bracteoles obovate, or lanceolate, not glandular.
Dry, well-drained soil, without water or with
little water in summer. Full sun. Hardy to −10°C.

**Phlomis bourgaei** Boiss. (*Labiatae*)   Native of
S.W. Turkey, in scrub, open pine forest, and on
limestone or serpentine rocks at up to 1000 m,
flowering in April–August. Evergreen shrub to
1.5 m; leaves greenish above, greyish beneath,
3–16 cm long. Flowers in 1–2 whorls, 12–20
flowered. Differs from *P. fruticosa* in its
subulate, stellate-hairy, sticky glandular
bracteoles. Dry, well-drained soil, without water
in summer and tolerant of summer drought. Full
sun. Hardy to −10°C.

**Paliurus spina-christi** Miller (*Rhamnaceae*)
Christ's Thorn   Native of the Mediterranean
region from Spain and France eastwards to C.
Asia, and N. China, on dry hills and in hedges up
to 3000 m, flowering in April–July, and
conspicuous fruit from August to October. A
deciduous shrub to 3 m, with crooked twigs.
Leaves 2–4 cm long ovate, with spiny stipules.
Flowers with 5 petals; fruits 1.8–3 cm in
diameter, with a wavy wing. Dry soil, and
tolerant of drought in summer, full sun. Hardy
to −15°C.

**Euphorbia dendroides** L. (*Euphorbiaceae*)
Native of the Mediterranean region, from the

Isles de Hyères in S. France, southwards, and
eastwards to Israel, growing on rocky, usually
limestone slopes and cliffs near the sea, at up to
400 m, flowering from March–May. An
evergreen shrub to 2 m; leaves 2–6.5 cm long.
Glands shortly 2–horned. Seeds 2.5–3 mm, pale
grey. Dry, well-drained soil, without water in
summer. Full sun. Hardy to −5°C.

**Euphorbia mellifera** Aiton (*Euphorbiaceae*)
Native of Madeira, N. Tenerife and N. La
Palma, in laurel forest at around 500–1000 m,
flowering in February to April. Now almost
extinct in the wild. Evergreen shrub or small
tree to 15 m high. Leaves to 10 cm long.
Flowers with brownish glands, in late spring.
Well-drained but rich, moist, leafy soil; sun or
part shade. Hardy to −10°C, but often self-
seeding when killed by cold.

**Euphorbia acanthothamnos** Heldr. & Sart.
(*Euphorbiaceae*)   Native of the E.
Mediterranean region, in Greece, Crete, Turkey
and the islands, on rocky limestone and
serpentine slopes and hills up to 300 m,
flowering from March to May. A deciduous,
rounded shrub to 35 cm tall, spiny with the
hardened rays of the previous season's
inflorescence. Leaves 0.5–2 cm long. Root
tuberous. Flowers scented of honey. Dry, well-
drained soil, without water in summer, moist in
winter and spring. Full sun. Hardy to −10°C.

*Paliurus spina-christi*

*Phlomis fruticosa* at Monemvasia, S. Greece

*Phlomis bourgaei* in Turkey

*Euphorbia dendroides*

*Euphorbia mellifera*

*Euphorbia acanthothamnos* in S. Turkey

*Euphorbia mellifera* at Kerdalo

Cistus × skanbergii

Cistus salviifolius

Cistus creticus

Cistus 'Anne Palmer'

Cistus palhinhae

Cistus × purpureus

Cistis × corbariensis

Cistus × purpureus
'Betty Taudevin'

Cistis × pulverulentus

Cistus × anguilari

½ life size. Specimens from Chelsea Physic Garden, 20th June

*Cistus* × *skanbergii* Lojac. (*Cistaceae*)  A hybrid between *C. monspeliensis* and *C. parviflorus* originally found on Lampedusa, but also known from Greece. Evergreen shrub to 60 cm. Leaves greyish-green. Flowers around 3 cm across, in branched cymes. Full sun and tolerant of summer drought. Hardy to −10°C.

*Cistus salviifolius* L. (*Cistaceae*)  Native of the Mediterranean region, Portugal, S.W. France and S. Switzerland, eastwards to N.E. Turkey, on dry hills in scrub and open woods on limestone, up to 500 m, flowering from March to May. Evergreen shrub to 50 cm and more across. Flowers solitary or up to 4 in a cyme, 3–5 cm across. Sepals 5, the outer pair larger. Full sun and tolerant of summer drought. Hardy to −10°C. Early summer.

*Cistus creticus* L. (*Cistaceae*) (syn. *C. incanus* subsp. *creticus* (L.) Heywood)  Native of the eastern Mediterranean from Greece, the Crimea and Georgia to S. Turkey, in scrub and open woods on dry hills up to 1000 m, flowering from March to June. Evergreen shrub to to 1 m. Flowers 1–7 in a cyme, 3–5 cm across, with 5 sepals. Full sun and tolerant of summer drought. Hardy to −15°C. Summer.

*Cistus* 'Anne Palmer'  A hybrid between *C. crispus* and *C.* 'Paladin' (*C. palhinhae* × *C. ladanifer*), raised by Capt. Collingwood Ingram at Benenden, Kent before 1960. Any well-drained soil in full sun. Hardy to −10°C with shelter.

*Cistus* × *purpureus* Lam.  A hybrid between *C. creticus* and *C. ladanifer*, known since 1790. Evergreen shrub to 2.5 m. Flowers 6–8 cm across. Well-drained soil; full sun and shelter from cold, dry wind. Hardy to −10°C.

*Cistus purpureus* 'Betty Taudevin (syn. 'Betty Tandeville')  An improved cultivar of *C.* × *purpureus*, raised by Messrs Taudevin in Willaston, Cheshire before 1952. Flowers deeper pink than in the original, with purplish stems.

*Cistus* × *pulverulentus* Pourr. (syn. *C. crispus* hort. non L.)  A hybrid between *C. albidus* and *C. crispus*, found in the wild. Evergreen shrub to 1 m. Well-drained soil, full sun and shelter from cold, dry wind. Hardy to −10°C.

*Cistus* × *anguilari* Pau  A hybrid between *C. ladanifer* and *C. populifolius*, found in the wild. Evergreen shrub to 2 m. Flowers unspotted in the form originally introduced into cultivation, but spotted in *C.* × *anguilari* 'Maculatus', raised around 1936, from the spotted form of *C. ladanifer*. Well-drained soil; full sun and shelter from cold, dry wind. Hardy to −10°C.

*Cistus libanotis* L. (*Cistaceae*)  Native of S.W. Portugal and S.W. Spain, growing in sandy soil under pines near the coast, flowering in March. Evergreen bushy shrub to 1.5 m. Flower stalks and sepals more or less glabrous and sticky. Flowers up to 12 in an umbel-like cyme, 2–3 cm across, with 3 sepals. Well-drained soil; full sun. Hardy to −10°C. Spring.

*Cistus parviflorus* Lam. (*Cistaceae*)  Native of S.E. Italy and Greece, eastwards to S. Turkey and Cyprus, in scrub on limestone hills up to 100 m, flowering in March and April. Evergreen shrub to 1 m, more across. Flowers 1–6 in a cyme, 2–3 mm in diameter, with a short style. Any well-drained soil; full sun. Hardy to −10°C. Early summer.

*Cistus crispus* in S.E. Spain; Gibraltar on the horizon

*Cistus libanotis*

*Cistus crispus*

*Cistus crispus* L. (*Cistaceae*)  Native of the W. Mediterranean and Portugal, in scrub on dry hills and in open pine woods up to 1000 m, flowering in March and April. Evergreen shrub to 60 cm, more across. Flowers 3–4 cm across with crinkled petals and 5 hairy sepals. Full sun and tolerant of summer drought. Hardy to −10°C. Early summer.

*Cistus* × *corbariensis* Pourr.  A hybrid between *C. populifolius* and *C. salviifolius* found in the wild. Evergreen shrub to 1 m; leaves ovate, cordate, 2–5 cm long. Flowers 3.5 cm across. Well-drained soil; full sun and shelter from cold, dry, wind. Hardy to −15°C.

*Cistus palhinhae* Ingram (*Cistaceae*)  Native of S.W. Portugal, especially on Cape St Vincent, on bare limestone cliff tops, flowering in February to April. Evergreen shrub to 50 cm and more across, forming in the wild a compact mound. Leaves 2–6 cm long, very sticky, dark green above. Flowers 7–10 cm across, usually unspotted, with 3 sepals and a 6–10-celled ovary. Hardy to −5°C. Early summer.

*Cistus parviflorus*

*Cistus monspeliensis*

*Cistus albidus*

*Cistus 'Silver Pink'*

*Cistus 'Alan Fradd'*

*Cistus laurifolius*

*Cistus ladanifer*

× *Halimiocistus wintonensis*
'*Merrist Wood Cream*'

*Cistus populifolius*

½ life size. Specimens from Wisley, 21st June

*Halimium atriplicifolium* near Ronda

*Cistus populifolius* near Ronda in S. Spain

*Halimium ocymoides*

*Halimium lasianthium subsp. formosum*

**Cistus monspeliensis** L. (*Cistaceae*)   Native of
S. Europe from Portugal to Greece, North
Africa and the Canaries, growing in scrub on
dry hills, flowering in March–May. Evergreen
shrub to 1.5 m. Flowers 2–3 cm across, with 5
sepals, the outer pair cuneate at the base. Well-
drained soil; full sun. Hardy to −10°C.
Summer.

**Cistus albidus** L. (*Cistaceae*)   Native to S.W.
Europe from Portugal to N. Italy and N.W.
Africa, growing in scrub and open pine forest,
flowering in April–June. Evergreen shrub to
1.5 m. Leaves softly grey, 2–5 cm long. Flowers
4–6 cm across. Well-drained soil; full sun.
Hardy to −15°C. Summer.

**Cistus 'Silver Pink'**   A hybrid, probably
between *C. creticus* and *C. laurifolius*, which
originated as a chance seedling in Hillier's
nursery in around 1910. Evergreen shrub to
1 m. Leaves greyish-green, lanceolate, to 7.5 cm
long. Flowers about 4 cm across. Well-drained
soil; full sun. Hardy to −15°C. Said to grow
better and be hardier on good, rather than poor,
acid soil. Summer.

**Cistus laurifolius** L. (*Cistaceae*)   Native of the
Mediterranean region from Morocco and
Portugal to Italy, in N. Greece, and in the
western half of Turkey, in mountains and open
pine forest at up to 1200 m, flowering in May–
July. Evergreen shrub to 3 m. Leaves leathery.
Flowers 3–6 cm across. Well-drained soil; full
sun. Hardy to −20°C. Summer.

**Cistus × purpureus** Lam. **'Alan Fradd'**   A
form of *C × purpureus* (p. 163), named after a
Sussex nurseryman. Hardy to −10°C.

**Cistus ladanifer** L. (*Cistaceae*)   Native of S.
France, Spain, Portugal and N. Africa, growing
on dry, usually granite hills at up to 1000 m,
flowering in April–June. Evergreen shrub to
2.5 m. Leaves and branches very sticky and
aromatic. Flowers 5–10 cm across, solitary with
or without a purple blotch. Ovary 10-celled.
Well-drained soil, full sun. Hardy to −10°C.
Summer.

**Cistus populifolius** L. (*Cistaceae*)   Native of S.
France, Spain, Portugal and N.W. Africa, on
dry rocky hills on limestone and acid rock at up
to 1000 m, flowering in April–June. Evergreen
shrub to 2.5 m, slightly aromatic and sticky.
Leaves ovate, cordate, to 10 cm long. Flowers
nodding with red sepals in bud, 4–6 cm across.
Well-drained soil, full sun. Hardy to −15°C.
Summer.

**× Halimocistus wintonesis** O. & E. F. Warb.
**'Merrist Wood Cream'**   A hybrid between
*Halimium ocymoides* and *cistus salviifolius* raised
at Merrist Wood Horticultural College,
Guildford in 1970. A low spreading evergreen
shrub to 50 cm, flowers about 5 cm across, in
May and June. Well-drained soil; full sun.
Hardy to −10°C.

**Halimium ocymoides** (Lam.) Willk. (*Cistaceae*)
Native of Spain, Portugal and Morocco, on
heaths, sandy places and open pine woods,
flowering in April–June. Evergreen shrub to

1 m. Leaves on sterile shoots silvery, obovate, to
1.5 cm long; on flowering shoots, obovate to
lanceolate, 1.2–3 cm long, green. Flowers
2.5–3.5 cm across . Well-drained soil; full sun.
Hardy to −15°C. Late spring.

**Halimium lasianthium** (Lam.) Spach, subsp.
**formosum** (Curtis) Heywood (*Cistaceae*)
Native of S. Portugal, in the Algarve, in open
woods and scrub, flowering in April–May.
Evergreen shrub to 1 m. Leaves greyish, to 4 cm
long. Flowers 4–6 cm across. Well-drained soil;
full sun. Hardy to −15°C. Late spring.

**Halimium atriplicifolium** (Lam.) Spach
Native of S. & C. Spain, in open pine forest and
on mountain rocks at up to 1000 m, flowering in
April and May. The largest *Halimium*, up to
1.5 m, with ball inflorescence covered in
reddish-purple glandular hairs. Leaves silvery
1–4 cm long. Sepals 3; flowers 4–5 cm across,
usually spotted at the base. Full sun and well-
drained soil. Hardy to −10°C.

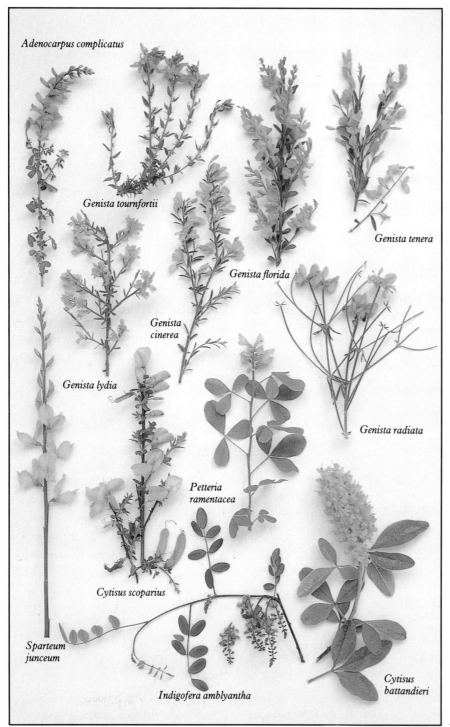

Adenocarpus complicatus

Genista tournfortii

Genista tenera

Genista florida

Genista cinerea

Genista lydia

Genista radiata

Petteria ramentacea

Cytisus scoparius

Sparteum junceum

Indigofera amblyantha

Cytisus battandieri

⅕ life size. Specimens from Wisley, 21st June

*Lupinus arboreus* at Salt Point, N. California

**Adenocarpus complicatus** (L.) Gray (*Leguminosae*) Native of N.W. France and Madeira south to N. Africa, Italy, Sicily, Greece and Turkey, in open woods, scrub, and on hillsides, flowering from April to June. Deciduous shrub to 4 m, without spines. Any well-drained soil; full sun or part shade. Hardy to −10°C. Summer.

**Genista tournfortii** Spach (*Leguminosae*) Native of Spain, Portugal and N. Africa, on heaths and in open pine woods, flowering in May. Low, much-branched evergreen shrub. Well-drained soil; full sun. Hardy to −15°C. Summer.

**Genista florida** L. (*Leguminosae*) Native of Morocco, Spain and N. Portugal, in scrub of *Erica* and *Cistus* and open woods at up to 1000 m, flowering in May and June. Evergreen shrub to 3 m. Hardy to −15°C. The Moroccan plants are said to be more silvery than those from Europe. Summer.

**Genista tenera** (Jacq.) O. Kuntze (syn. *G. virgata* (Ait.) Link non Willd.) (*Leguminosae*) Native of Madeira and Tenerife, on dry, sunny rocks and cliffs at up to 1200 m, flowering in March–July. Deciduous shrub to 4 m. Hardy to −10°C.

**Genista lydia** Boiss. (*Leguminosae*) Native of Yugoslavia and Bulgaria, south to Turkey and Syria, on rocky limestone hills flowering from April to June. Spreading evergreen shrub to 1 m. Leaves simple, 3–10 mm long, on unwinged stems. Well-drained soil; full sun and best planted where the branches can hang down. Hardy to −15°C. Early summer.

**Genista cinerea** (Vill.) DC. (*Leguminosae*) Native of S. France, Portugal and N. Africa, east to Italy, in woods and scrub on hillsides, at up to 1800 m in S. Spain, flowering in May and June. Erect shrub to 3.5 m. Hardy to −15°C.

**Genista radiata** (L). Scop. (*Leguminosae*) Native of the S. Alps from France to W. Yugoslavia and in S.W. Romania and C. Greece, on limestone hills, flowering in May and June. Bushy shrub to 1 m. Hardy to −15°C.

**Genista aetnensis** (Biv.) DC. (*Leguminosae*) Mount Etna Broom Native of Sicily and Sardinia, on dry hills at up to 1800 m, flowering in June. Large shrub or small tree to 5 m in the wild, or 10 m in cultivation, with weeping rush-like branches. Flowers about 12 mm across. Hardy to −15°C. Summer. A very beautiful and elegant, late-flowering shrub.

**Spartium junceum** L. (*Leguminosae*) Spanish Broom Native of Portugal and the Mediterranean region east to Israel, in scrub and on hillsides and roadsides, usually on limestone, flowering from May to August. Shrub to 3 m or more with glaucous, cylindrical twigs. Any soil; in full sun. Hardy to −10°C.

**Petteria ramentacea** (Sieber) C. Presl (*Leguminosae*) Native of S. Yugoslavia and N. Albania, in mountain scrub, flowering in May. Deciduous shrub to 2 m. Hardy to −15°C. Early summer.

**Cytisus scoparius** (L.) Link, (syn. *Sarothamnus scoparius* (L.) Wimmer ex. Koch). (*Leguminosae*) Broom Native of W. Europe from Ireland and Portugal, north to S. Sweden and east to the Ukraine, and of N. Africa, in open woods, on heaths, hills and river banks, usually on acid, sandy soil, flowering in May and June. Shrub to 2 m, with dark green ribbed twigs. Flowers 1.6–1.8 cm long, rich yellow, occasionally pale yellow or reddish in the wild, with many cultivars from nearly white to deep red, scented. Seed pods black when ripe, opening explosively in hot sun. Well-drained, acid or non-chalky soil. Hardy to −20°C.

**Cytisus battandieri** Maire (*Leguminosae*) Native of Morocco, in the Middle Atlas, around Azrou and Ifrane at 1500–2000 m, and in the Rif, growing in sandy, acid soil in oak and cedar forest, flowering in June. Semi-evergreen shrub to 4 m, usually rather spindly and often trained on a wall. Flowers scented, somewhat like pineapple. Well-drained light soil; full sun. Hardy to −15°C.

**Indigofera amblyantha** Craib (*Leguminosae*) Native of W. Hubei, where it is common, in scrub on hillsides at 1000–1800 m, flowering from May to July, and into autumn. Deciduous shrub to 2 m. Leaflets 7–11. Flowers pale pink to reddish, 6–7 mm long, in erect inflorescences which continue to grow and flower through the summer. Well-drained soil; sun and a warm situation with summer water. Hardy to −20°C.

**Lupinus arboreus** Sims (*Leguminosae*) Tree Lupin Native of the Pacific coast from S. California north to Oregon, on stable sand dunes, coastal scrub and Pine forest below 30 m, flowering from March to June. Naturalized by the sea in S. England and Ireland. Evergreen shrub to 2.5 m, much branched. Flowers sometimes white ('Snow Queen'), or shades of blue. Well-drained soil; full sun and good in coastal gardens. Hardy to −15°C. Summer. Plants naturalized near the coast have mostly less silky leaves and longer racemes of flowers than the wild form.

**Colutea arborescens** L. (*Leguminosae*) Bladder Senna Native of S. and C. Europe from France and Austria south to N. Africa, in woods, scrub and dry limestone hills, flowering from May to July. Deciduous shrub to 6 m. Leaflets 4–5 pairs, broadly elliptical, ovate or obovate, to 3 cm long. Flowers yellow, 16–20 mm long; pods inflated 5–7 × 3 cm. Well-drained soil; full sun or part shade. Hardy to −20°C. Summer.

**Colutea × media** Willd. (*Leguminosae*) A hybrid between *C. arborescens* (above) and *C. orientalis* Miller, an orange-red flowered species from the Caucasus. A variable shrub to 3 m. Leaves usually greyish with 11–13 more rounded leaflets. Flowers usually orange-yellow, with narrowly lanceolate calyx lobes. Well-drained soil. Hardy to −20°C.

**Sesbania punicea** Benth. (*Leguminosae*) Native of Brazil, but naturalized from Florida to S. Texas and in parts of S. Africa, in waste places in rich soil, flowering in April and May and again in autumn. Evergreen shrub to 3 m, with pendulous racemes of flowers to 2 cm across. Seed pods strikingly 4-winged. Hardy to −10°C, or for cool greenhouse.

**Amicia zygomeris** DC. (*Leguminosae*) Native of W. Mexico, in the western Cordillera, in woods and by rivers at 1800–2500 m. Deciduous subshrub to 2 m or more. Leaves with 4 leaflets around 6 cm long: stipules leafy, usually purple, 2 cm across. Flowers 2 cm long, yellow-veined purple. Any soil in a warm sheltered position in full sun. Cut down by frost in winter, but growing quickly again from the rootstock. Hardy to −10°C with protection for the root. Late summer.

*Genista aetnensis* at Goatcher's Nurseries, Washington, Sussex

*Colutea arborescens*

*Colutea × media*

*Amicia zygomeris*

*Sesbania punicea*

*Indigofera kirilowii* at the University Botanic Gardens, Cambridge

*Indigofera heterantha*

*Sophora davidii*

**Indigofera kirilowii** Maxim. (*Leguminosae*)
Native of Heilonjiang (N.E. China), Korea, and
N. Kyushu, in grassy places and scrub,
flowering in May–July. Deciduous shrub to
1.5 m, with spreading branches. Leaflets 7–11,
pubescent on both sides, suborbicular to
obovate or elliptic, mucronate, 1–3 cm long.
Flowers *c.* 2 cm long, in dense racemes to
12 cm, with peduncle longer than petiole. Any
soil; full sun. Hardy to −20°C. Summer.

**I. heterantha** Wall. ex Brandis (syn. *I.
gerardiana* Baker)   Native of the Himalayas
from Afghanistan to W. China, often forming
dense scrub at 1500–3000 m on dry sunny
slopes, flowering in May–June. Deciduous
much-branched shrub to 2.5 m. Leaves with
13–21 small leaflets, 1–1.5 cm long, variable in
shape but usually rounded or emarginate, with
few appressed hairs on both sides. Flowers in
dense, upright, short-stalked racemes 7–15 cm
long, with minute bracts. Any soil; full sun.
Hardy to −15°C, but flowering after being cut
to the ground in winter. Mid–late summer.

**Sophora davidii** (Franch.) Skeels (syn. *S.
viciifolia* Hance) (*Leguminosae*)   Native of W.
Hubei, W. Sichuan and Yunnan, in dry, rocky
places and arid valleys, often covering large
areas, flowering in April–June. Much-
branched, upright deciduous shrub to 2.5 m.
Leaves 2–6 cm long, with 13–19 leaflets.
Flowers 1.6–2 cm long, in 6–12 flowered
racemes, pale blue to dark violet-blue. Any
well-drained, dry soil, good on chalk; full sun.
Hardy to −20°C. Early summer. Requires wall
protection to flower well, but has made a good
bushy shrub at Kew near the large *Pinus pinea*.

**Campylotropus polyantha** (Franch.) A. K.
Schindl. (*Leguminosae*)   Native of Yunnan, and
Sichuan, on dry hillsides in scrub at 1500–
2600 m, flowering in May. Deciduous, rather
upright or arching shrub to 2 m. Leaves with 3
leaflets *c.* 1 cm long. Flowers in short, upright
racemes. Any soil; full sun. Hardy to −10°C.
Late spring.

**Desmodium tiliaefolium** (D. Don) G. Don
(*Leguminosae*)   Native of the Himalayas east to
W. Sichuan, in scrub and among rocks by rivers
flowering in May–August. Deciduous subshrub
to 2 m, with long shoots springing up from the
base. Leaflets 3, the terminal obovate to rhombic
ovate, 5–10 cm long. Flowers about 1.2 cm long,
crimson to purple, pale mauve or pink; pod
5–7 cm long, 6–9 seeded. Any soil; sun and
shelter. Hardy to −15°C, but flowering from the
ground in one year. Late summer to autumn. *D.
praestans* Forrest, from Yunnan and S. Sichuan,
is a taller shrub, with leaves usually with one
larger leaflet. Numerous other species are found
in W. China.

**Lespedeza bicolor** Turcz. (*Leguminosae*) Native
of Japan, Korea, E. Siberia and N. China, in
grassy places and scrub, flowering in July–
October. Deciduous subshrub to 1.8 m, with
annual arching stems. Leaflets 3, elliptic, to 4 cm
long. Flowers in slender racemes, 12–17 mm
long. Any soil; part shade. Hardy to −25°C.
Autumn. The very similar *L. thunbergii* (DC.)
Nakai has often narrower leaflets, and lowest
calyx teeth longer than the tube (shorter in *L.
bicolor*). An elegant, late-flowering, broom-like
plant for moist or dry shade. Sun and dry soil are
said to produce earlier flowering.

*Campylotropus polyantha* at Lijiang

*Desmodium tiliaefolium* at Boaxing, Sichuan

*Lespedeza bicolor* in Japan in October

*Ononis fruticosa*

*Dorycnium hirsutum*

*Carmichelia flagelliformis*

**Dorycnium hirsutum** (L.) Ser.   Native of the Mediterranean, S. Portugal and S. Turkey on dry rocky hills and roadside banks, flowering in June–August. Evergreen shrub to 6 cm, covered with long white hairs. Flowers 10–12 mm across, white or pink. Pod 6–12 mm long, reddish. Well-drained soil; full sun. Hardy to −15°C.

**Ononis fruticosa** L. (*Leguminosae*)   Native of N. Africa, Spain, the central Pyrénées and S.E. France (the Cévennes), growing in dry, rocky places, usually on limestone, flowering in May–

August. Sticky-leaved, dwarf shrub to 1 m. Leaves with 3 leaflets 7–25 mm long. Flowers 1–2 cm long. Well-drained soil; full sun, with shelter. Hardy to −15°C. Summer.

**Carmichelia flagelliformis** Colenso (*Leguminosae*)   Native of both islands of New Zealand, in scrub, dry rocky streambanks and edges of forest, flowering in October–November. Evergreen, usually leafless, erect, shrub to 2 m. Twigs rounded, not flattened. Leaves minute with 3–5 leaflets. Flowers

c.3 mm across. Well-drained soil; full sun. Hardy to −10°C. Spring. Most other *Carmichelia* species have flattened stems, equally small, scented flowers (up to 6 mm in *C. grandiflora* Benth. & Hook fil.); they are usually tender, but *C. petriei*, *C. enysii* and *C. grandiflora* are reported to be the hardiest. *C. williamsii* T. Kirk is distinct from the others in its solitary or few, yellowish, brown-veined flowers to 2.5 cm long. Found along the N.E. coast of N. Island and on the offshore islands.

*Robinia hispida*

*Robinia kelseyi* at the University Botanic Gardens, Cambridge

*Amorpha canescens*

*Amorpha fruticosa*

*Robinia viscosa*

*Erythrina crista-galli*

**Erythrina crista-galli** L. (*Leguminosae*) Native of Brazil. In very mild climates a shrub or small tree to 5 m, with thick branches and trunk, but will flower on annual shoots if the woody base of the plant is protected from frost. Flowers up to 5 cm long in inflorescence to 30 cm or more long. Any soil; full sun with wall protection in cool climates. Hardy to −10°C with protection. Summer.

**Robinia viscosa** Vent. (*Leguminosae*) Clammy Locust Native, but uncommon from West Virginia south to Alabama, in dry, open woods and scrub at up to 1200 m. Deciduous shrub or tree to 9 m. Branches and petioles sticky. Racemes dense, 6–16 flowered. Well-drained soil; sun or part shade. Hardy to −25°C. Early summer.

**Robinia hispida** L. Rose-Acacia Bristly Locust Native of Virginia and Tennessee south to Alabama, in dry woods and scrub in the hills. Deciduous shrub to 3 m. Branches brown, bristly; calyx bristly. Recemes loose, 3–8 flowered. Seed pod bristly. Any well-drained soil; full sun. Hardy to −20°C. Early summer.

**Robinia kelseyi** Hutchins Native of North Carolina, on wooded hills and ridges. Deciduous shrub or small tree to 3 m. Racemes loose, 5–8 flowered. Seed pods covered with purple hairs. Well-drained soil; full sun. Hardy to −15°C. Early summer.

**Amorpha canescens** Pursh (*Leguminosae*) Lead Plant Native of C. North America, in sandy woods and by streams. Deciduous shrub to

*Asimina triloba*

*Aesculus parviflora* at Wakehurst Place, Sussex

1.1 m; leaves with no petiole and 15–45 leaflets 7–20 mm long. Flowers numerous. Sun or part shade. Hardy to −25°C and below. Late summer.

**Amorpha fruticosa** L. False Indigo   Native of C. and E. North America, in moist scrub, on river banks and in flood plains. Deciduous shrub to 4 m. Leaves with leaflets variable in size and shape, to 6 cm long. Any sandy soil; sun or part shade. Hardy to −25°C. Summer.

**Asimina triloba** (L.) Dunal (*Annonaceae*) Native of C. and E. North America, growing in rich moist soil in valleys, flowering in April and May. Deciduous shrub or small tree to 12 m. Flowers 4.5 cm across, appearing before or with the leaves. Fruit elongated, brown or black, sweet with good flavour, like its relative, the Custard Apple (*Anona*). Any moist soil; sun or part shade. Hardy to −20°C. Early summer.

**Aesculus parviflora** Walt.   Native of Georgia and Alabama south to Florida, on wooded bluffs and rich woods, along streams. Deciduous suckering shrub to 4 m, eventually forming a large clump. Leaflets 5–7, to 20 cm long. Inflorescence to 30 cm long. Sun or part shade. Hardy to −20°C. Summer.

**Aesculus californica** (Spach) Nutt. California Buckeye   Native of C. California, growing in scrub, on the edges of oak and pine woods below 1000 m in the Coast Ranges and foothills of the Sierra Nevada. Deciduous shrub to 7 m; leaflets 5–7, to 15 cm long; inflorescence to 20 cm long, with pale pink or white flowers. Fruit brownish, pear-shaped, not spiny. Seeds very large. Any well-drained soil, dry in summer; full sun. Hardy to −10°C. Summer.

**Aesculus pavia** L. (*Hippocastanaceae*) Red Buckeye   Native of S.E. North America, in moist woods and along streams. Deciduous shrub or small tree to 6 m, usually to 4 m. Leaves 18–32 cm long, with 5–7 leaflets, of thin texture. Flowers red. Fruits smooth. Any soil; sun or deciduous shade. Hardy to −15°C. Early summer.

**Cephalanthus occidentalis** L. (*Rubiaceae*) Honeyballs, Button Bush   Native of Canada, North America, C. America and Cuba, in swamps and wet places by lakes and streams, flowering in June–August. Shrub to 6 m. Leaves opposite or 3 together. Flowers 15 mm long, stalkless, scented, in spherical balls. Damp or waterlogged soil; full sun. Hardy to −25°C.

*Aesculus californica* in North California

*Cephalanthus occidentalis*

*Aesculus pavia*

*Rubus odoratus*

*Rubus* × 'Tridel Benenden'

*Rubus odoratus* × 'Tridel'

*Rubus neo-mexicanus*

*Rubus deliciosus*

**Rubus odoratus** L. (*Rosaceae*) Thimble-berry Native of S. Quebec and Ontario, south to Georgia and Tennessee, in moist woods and scrub, flowering in June–September. Deciduous, suckering shrub to 2 m. Leaves 3–5 lobed, 10–30 cm across. Flowers 3–6 cm across with a glandular calyx. Fruit red, rather dry. Any moist soil; shade or part shade. Hardy to −30°C. Mid-late summer.

**Rubus odoratus** × 'Tridel' This hybrid has the habit of *R. odoratus*, but larger paler mauve-pink flowers.

**Rubus 'Tridel Benenden'** A hybrid between *R. trilobus*, a Mexican mountain species, and *R. deliciosus*, raised by Capt. Collingwood Ingram at Benenden, Kent in 1950. Deciduous shrub with reddish arching canes to 4 m. Leaves to 9 cm long. Flowers to 5 cm across. Any good soil; sun or part shade. Hardy to −20°C. Early summer.

**Rubus neo-mexicanus** Gray (*Rosaceae*) Native of New Mexico, Arizona and N. Mexico (Sonora), growing in canyons in the mountains.

Erect deciduous shrub to 2 m, close to *R. deliciosus*, but the leaves with an acute terminal lobe, and more deeply 3–5 lobed, pubescent beneath. Flowers to 5 cm across. Hardy to −15°C.

**Rubus spectabilis** Pursh (*Rosaceae*) Salmon Berry Native of N.W. California north to Alaska, in damp woods and Redwood forest, flowering in March-June. Deciduous shrub with upright, branching canes to 4 m. Leaves with 3 leaflets, the middle 4–10 cm long. Flowers 1–4, 1.5–2 cm long. Fruit red, orange or yellow. Moist soil; part shade. Hardy to −25°C. Summer. The double-flowered form is growing in the garden at Crathes Castle, Aberdeenshire.

**Rubus biflorus** Buch.–Ham. (*Rosaceae*) Native of the Himalayas from N. Pakistan to Sichuan and Gansu, in scrub and on the edges of forest at 1800–2100 m, flowering in May. Deciduous shrub with arching canes to 3.5 m with a white bloom. Leaves with 3–5 leaflets, white beneath. Flowers 2–8 in loose bunches, 2–2.5 cm across, nodding. Fruit yellow or orange. Any soil; sun or part shade. Hardy to −15°C, perhaps.

Spring-flowering. Good for its white canes in winter.

**Rubus amabilis** Focke (*Rosacea*) Native of Nepal to W. Sichuan, Hubei and Gansu, scrambling on the forest floor at 1300–3800 m, flowering in May–June. Deciduous shrub to 2 m long. Leaves 10–20 cm long, with 7–11 leaflets. Flowers solitary, nodding, 4–5 cm across. Fruit red. Moist, leafy soil; part shade. Hardy to −20°C. Spring–summer.

**Rubus deliciosus** Torr. (*Rosaceae*) Native of the Rocky Mountains in New Mexico, Oklahoma, Colorado and Wyoming, in scrub and rocky slopes, flowering in May–June. Deciduous shrub to 3 m, with arching stems. Leaves unlobed or with rounded lobes, becoming glabrous beneath. Flowers 3.8–6 cm across. Fruit dark red, to 1.5 cm across. Well-drained soil; full sun. Hardy to −20°C. Summer.

**Rubus tricolor** Focke (*Rosaceae*) Native of Yunnan and Sichuan, on steep banks and in scrub at 1000–2000 m, flowering in June–July. Creeping, semi-evergreen shrub, covering large

*Rubus spectabilis*

*Pyracantha rogersiana* near Lijiang, Yunnan

*Rubus spectabilis* with double flowers

*Niellia thibetica*

*Rubus tricolor*

areas, growing as much as 1 m per year. Stems reddish, bristly. Leaves 6–10 cm long. Flowers to 2.5 cm across. Moist soil; part shade. Hardy to −15°C. Summer.

**Pyracantha rodgersiana** (A. B. Jacks) Chitt. (*Rosaceae*)  Native of N.W. Yunnan, in scrub and hedges at 2500 m, flowering in May. Evergreen or semi-deciduous shrub to 4 m. Leaves oblanceolate, obtuse, glabrous beneath, 1.5–3.5 cm long, serrulate. Inflorescence glabrous. Fruit 6 mm reddish-orange (see p. 262). Any good soil; full sun. Hardy to −15°C. Late spring; fruiting throughout the winter.

**Niellia thibetica** Franch. (*Rosaceae*)  Native of W. Sichuan, in scrub and among rocks by streams at 1600–2600 m, flowering in May–July. Deciduous shrub with arching stems to 2 m. Leaves 5–8 cm long, hairy beneath, serrate and lobulate. Flowers 8 mm long, in dense racemes 4–8 cm long. The closely related *N. longiracemosa* Hemsl. has leaves not lobulate, nearly glabrous beneath, and racemes to 15 cm long. Any soil; sun or part shade. Hardy to −20°C. Summer.

*Rubus biflorus* in Lijiang

*Rubus amabilis* in Boaxing

Viburnum
buddleifolium

Viburnum 'Park Farm'

Viburnum carlesii 'Aurora'

Viburnum 'Anne Russel'

Viburnum furcatum

Viburnum lantanoides

Viburnum × carlcephalum

Viburnum carlesii 'Diana'

Viburnum carlesii
var. bitchiuense

½ life size. Specimens from the Hillier Arboretum, 14th May

*Viburnum lantanoides* at Windsor

*Xanthoceras sorbifolium*

**Viburnum buddleifolium** Wright (*Caprifoliaceae*)    Native of C. China, to W. Hubei in scrub, flowering in May. Deciduous, upright shrub to 2 m. Leaves oblong-lanceolate, 8–15 cm, greyish beneath. Flowers 8 mm across, the corolla lobes longer than the tube (cf. *V. cotinifolium* p. 177). Any soil; full sun. Hardy to −20°C. Early summer.

**Viburnum carlesii** Hemsl.    Native of Korea and Tsushima Is. (Kyushu) in scrub, flowering in April–May. Deciduous, rounded shrub to 1.5 m. Leaves broad, ovate, 3–10 cm long, densely pubescent beneath, with 5–7 pairs of veins. Flowers 1–1.4 cm across, scented, in a rounded head 5–7 cm wide. Any soil; sun or part shade. Hardy to −20°C. Late spring. Three selections from Korean seed were raised and named by Leslie Slinger, at the Slieve Donard Nursery, Northern Ireland: **'Aurora'**, with pinkish flowers; **'Diana'**, more vigorous with pinkish flowers; and 'Charis', flowers white (not shown).

**Viburnum carlesii** var. **bitchiuense** (Mak.) Nakai    Native of Korea, and isolated areas in Honshu and Shikoku growing in scrub, flowering in April-May. Differs from var. *carlesii* in its narrower leaves with longer 4–8 mm (vs. 3–5 mm) petioles, and smaller flowers, with a longer tube. Height to 2.5 m. Hardy to −20°C.

**Viburnum 'Anne Russel'**    A backcross of *V.* × *burkwoodii* to *V. carlesii*, raised by L. R. Russel at Windlesham, Surrey in 1951. More upright in habit than *V. carlesii*, with scented flowers 16 mm across. Early spring.

**Viburnum × burkwoodii 'Park Farm'**    A hybrid between *V. carlesii* and *V. utile*, raised in around 1925. The clone 'Burkwoodii' has somewhat smaller clusters of paler flowers. A deciduous shrub to 2.5 m; leaves ovate to lanceolate; flowers scented, 12 mm across, in spring. Any soil; full sun. Hardy to −20°C. Hardier and faster-growing than *V. carlesii*.

**Viburnum × carlcephalum** Burkw.    A hybrid between *V. carlesii* and *V. macrocephalum*. Deciduous shrub to 2 m high. Flowers in large, globose heads to 13 cm wide; pinkish in bud, opening pure white, slightly scented. Hardy to −20°C. Spring. More robust, but less beautiful than *V. carlesii*.

**Viburnum × juddii** Rehd.    A hybrid between *V. carlesii* var. *carlesii* and var. *bitchiunense*. Close to var. *carlesii*, but with more oblong

leaves, larger and looser heads of smaller flowers, and with signs of hybrid vigour. Rounded shrub to 2 m high; flowers *c.*6 mm across; scented in spring.

**Viburnum lantanoides** Michx. (syn. *V. alnifolium* Marsh.) Hobble-bush    Native of Ontario and Prince Edward Is. south to Georgia and Tennessee (in the mountains), in damp woods and shady valleys, flowering in May–June. Deciduous shrub to 3 m; often layering to form a thicket. Similar to *V. furcatum* (q.v.) but differing in having fertile flowers with rounded corolla lobes and longer stamens. Moist, preferably acid soil; shade or part shade. Hardy to 30°C. Early summer.

**Viburnum furcatum** Bl.    Native of Taiwan, Japan, Korea and Sakhalin, in damp woods and scrub in the mountains, flowering in May, fruiting in October. Upright, deciduous shrub to 2 m. Leaves 7–15 cm long, with 7–10 pairs of nerves. Flowers in a flat head 7–15 cm across; fertile flowers with acute lobes; stamens short. Acid soil; part shade. Hardy to −25°C. Early summer. See p. 259 for fruit.

**Viburnum davidii** Franch.    Native of W. Sichuan in woods at 1800–2600 m, flowering in June; fruiting in October. Evergreen shrub to 1 m, with ascending branches forming a mound. Leaves elliptic, 5–14 cm long, 3-nerved. Flowers small, dirty white, in flat heads 5–8 cm across. Fruit blue, 6 mm long. Any soil; sun or part shade. Hardy to −15°C. *Not* beautiful unless very well grown. 'Femina' is a free-fruiting selection.

**Xanthoceras sorbifolium** Bunge (*Sapindaceae*) Native of N. China. Deciduous, erect shrub to 6 m. Leaves pinnate, to 20 cm long, with 9–17 toothed leaflets each 4–6.5 cm long. Flowers 2.5–3 cm across, with 5 petals, yellowish then reddish at their base, in panicles up to 20 cm long, opening with the leaves. Any soil; full sun and a warm, dry situation. Hardy to −20°C. Early summer. Best with warm summers and dry springs without late frost.

**Symplocos paniculata** (Thunb.) Miq. (*Symplocaceae*)    Native of the Himalayas from Pakistan to China, Korea, Japan and S.E. Asia, to the Philippines, growing in scrub and woods at up to 2700 m, flowering in April–June. Deciduous shrub to 4 m. Leaves rugose, 4–7 cm long. Flowers 8–10 mm across; fruit usually blue, sometimes white. Acid soil; full sun. Hardy to −10°C. Early summer; fruit ripe in autumn, remaining on the leafless branches.

*Symplocos paniculata*

*Viburnum davidii*

*Viburnum × juddii*

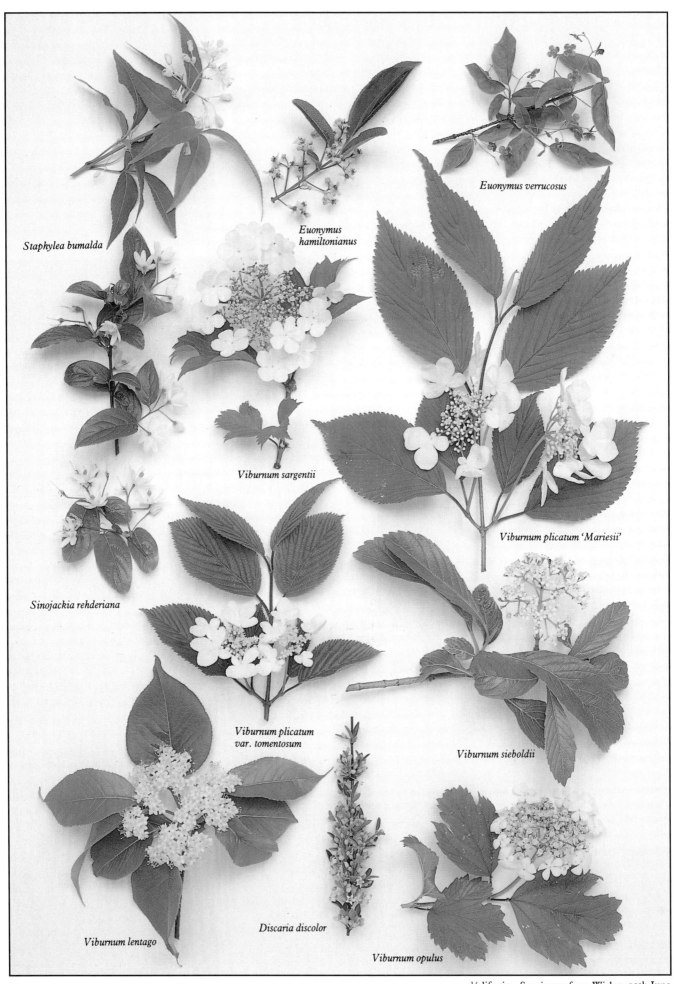

Staphylea bumalda

Euonymus
hamiltonianus

Euonymus verrucosus

Viburnum sargentii

Viburnum plicatum 'Mariesii'

Sinojackia rehderiana

Viburnum plicatum
var. tomentosum

Viburnum sieboldii

Viburnum lentago

Discaria discolor

Viburnum opulus

½ life size. Specimens from Wisley, 11th June

**Staphylea bumalda** (Thunb.) (*Staphyleaceae*)
DC. Native of Japan, Korea and China west to
W. Hubei growing in woods and by streams up to
1300 m, flowering in May–June. Shrub to 2.5 m.
Leaflets 3; flowers open after leaves. Fruit
usually 2–lobed, with recurving points. Any soil;
sun or part shade. Hardy to −25°C. Early
summer.

**Euonymus hamiltonianus** Wall. (*Celastraceae*)
Native of the Himalayas from Afghanistan east to
N. Burma with varieties in China, E. Siberia and
Japan, growing in scrub and woods up to
2700 m, flowering in April–July. Very variable,
but may be a small tree to 5 m or more. Leaves to
10 cm long. Flowers 7–8 mm across, 4–parted;
fruit 4–lobed, red. Any soil; sun or part shade.
Hardy to −15°C. Clones (e.g. 'Red Elf') have
been chosen for good fruiting and autumn colour.

**Euonymus verrucosus** Scop. Native of N.
Italy and Poland east and south to Turkey and
the Caucasus in scrub and woods, flowering in
May–June. Bushy, deciduous shrub to 3 m, with
green, warty branches. Leaves to 6 cm long.
Flowers 4–parted; black seeds only partly covered
by orange avil. Any soil; sun. Hardy to −25°C.

**Sinojackia rehderiana** Hu (*Styracaceae*) Native
of Guangdong, Hunan and Kiangxi, flowering in
April. Deciduous shrub or small tree to 6 m.
Leaves 6–9 cm long. Flowers 8–12 mm long.
Fruit cylindrical, beaked, 2.5 cm long. Any soil;
full sun. Hardy to −10°C. Early summer.

**Viburnum sargentii** Koehne (syn. *V. opulus* var.
*calvescens* (Rehd.) Hara) (*Caprifoliaceae*) Native
of E. Siberia, N. and W. China and Japan, in
scrub, woods and by rivers, flowering in June–
July. Similar to *V. opulus*, but leaves usually have
longer petioles and a longer central lobe, often
white-pubescent beneath. Any moist soil; sun or
part shade. Hardy to −30°C. Summer.

**Viburnum plicatum** Thunb. var. **tomentosum**
(Thunb.) Miq. Native of S.W. Honshu,
Shikoku and Kyushu, Taiwan and W. China
(e.g. Omei Shan) in scrub in mountains up to
1800 m, flowering in April–June. Deciduous
shrub to 3 m. Leaves 4–10 cm long. Flower
heads 6–10 cm across. Fruits at first red, finally
black. Any moist soil; sun or part shade. Hardy
to −25°C. Early summer.

**Viburnum plicatum** Thunb. **'Mariesii'**
A selection of *V. plicatum*, lower-growing, with
more horizontal branching and larger flower
heads, with sterile flowers to 4.5 cm wide.
'Lanarth' is coarser; 'Rowallane' and 'Cascade'
are neater, smaller growing, with equally large
flower heads. All do best in good, moist soil in
part shade. Hardy to −20°C. A poor fruiter.

**Viburnum plicatum** Thunb. **'Pink Beauty'**
A small, low-growing variety; flowers opening
white, soon becoming pink. A good fruiter.

**Viburnum plicatum** Thunb. var. **plicatum,**
(syn. *V. tomentosum* Thunb. var. *sterile*) Japanese
Snowball This is the sterile form of *V.
plicatum*, long grown in Japan and China,
brought to Europe in 1844 by Robert Fortune.

**Viburnum opulus** L. Guelder Rose Native of
England and Ireland, south to Algeria and east to
Siberia, in hedges, fens and by rivers, flowering
in June–July. Deciduous shrub to 4 m. Leaves
3–lobed, pubescent or glabrous beneath. Sterile
flowers with large petals; fertile 4–7 mm across,
but in 'Sterile' and the Snowball tree (var. *roseum*
L.), all sterile in a round cluster. Any moist soil;

*Viburnum plicatum 'Mariesii' at Eccleston Square*

*Viburnum plicatum var. plicatum*

*Viburnum plicatum 'Pink Beauty'*

*Viburnum opulus 'Sterile'*

*Viburnum cotinifolium*

good on chalk. Hardy to −30°C. Summer.
Berries red, in autumn and winter.

**Viburnum sieboldii** Miq. Native of Japan, in
Honshu southwards, in scrub on low hills,
flowering in April–May. Deciduous shrub to
10 m. Leaves 6–12 cm long, shiny above, foetid
when bruised. Flower head 7–10 cm across;
flowers 8 mm across. Fruit *c*.1 cm long, red,
finally black. Any moist soil; part shade. Hardy
to −15°C. Early summer.

**Viburnum lentago** L. Sheep-berry, Alisier
Native of Canada in Manitoba and Hudson Bay,
south to Georgia, Missouri and Colorado, on
wood edges and by streams, flowering in May–
June. Deciduous shrub to 10 m. Leaves
5–10 cm long; flower heads 6–12 cm across;

berries black. Any moist soil; sun or part shade.
Hardy to −30°C. Early summer.

**Viburnum cotinifolium** D. Don Native of the
Himalayas from Afghanistan to Bhutan, in
scrub, forest and by streams at 1800–3600 m,
flowering in April–May. Deciduous shrub to
4 m. Leaves white-woolly beneath, 5–12 cm
long. Flowers *c*.8 mm across, not scented. Any
soil, including chalky; full sun. Hardy to
−15°C. Spring.

**Discaria discolor** Dusen (*Rhamnaceae*) Native
of the Andes in S. Argentina and S.E. Chile,
flowering in November–December. Spiny
shrub to 2 m, and as wide. Leaves opposite,
5–18 mm long. Flowers scented. Any well-
drained soil; full sun. Hardy to −15°C.

*Styrax wilsonii* at Baoxing, Sichuan in late May

**Reevesia pubescens** Mast. (*Sterculiaceae*)
Native of the E. Himalayas from Sikkim to
Guizhou and W. Sichuan, in warm valleys in
scrub and forest at 1200–3300 m. Small
evergreen tree or shrub to 6 m; in the wild a tree
to 20 m. Flowers with style 2.5 cm long. Any
soil; sun. Hardy to −10°C with shelter. Summer.

**Styrax wilsonii** (*Styracaceae*)   Native of W.
Sichuan, in scrub on rocky hillsides and by
streams at 1300–1700 m, flowering in May.
Deciduous shrub to 3 m. Leaves 1.5–3 cm on
the flowering shoots, larger on the growing
shoots. Flowers in racemes of 3–5, 1.3–1.5 cm
long. Any soil; full sun. Hardy to −15°C,
perhaps. Late spring. So free-flowering in
cultivation, that it is often short-lived.

**Styrax limpritchii** Lingelsh (syn. *S.
lankongensis* W. W. Sm.)   Native of Yunnan
and Sichuan at 1300–2000 m, in scrub and on
rocky hillsides, flowering in May–July.
Deciduous shrub to 3 m. Leaves 3–6.5 cm.
Flowers 2–6 in a short raceme. Any soil; full
sun. Hardy to −10°C perhaps. Photographed
above Dali Lake.

**Styrax officinalis** L.   Native of the
Mediterranean, in S. France and Italy, east to
Israel and California from Shasta Co. southwards
in the Coast Ranges and Sierra foothills, on dry
rocky slopes, often limestone, below 1500 m,
flowering in March–May. Deciduous shrub or
small tree to 7 m. Leaves 3–5 cm long; flowers
12–18 mm long. Well-drained soil; hot position,
dry in summer. Hardy to −10°C. Spring. One
of the few, or only?, species to be native in both
California and Europe.

**Styrax serrulatus** Roxb.   Native of the
Himalayas, from Nepal to Burma and N.
Thailand at 300–1200 m. Deciduous much-
branched shrub to 3 m. Hardy to −10°C.

**Wattakaka sinensis** (Hemsl.) Stapf
(*Asclepiadaceae*)   Native of W. Hubei, Sichuan
and Yunnan, on scrub in rocky places, at 30–
2400 m, flowering in May–July. Deciduous
climber to 2.5 m. Leaves softly hairy beneath.
Flowers 1.5 cm across, in rounded heads 8–9 cm
across, pink or white. Seed pods to 7 cm long.
Any soil; full sun. Hardy to −15°C. Summer.

**Styrax obassia** Sieb. & Zucc.   Native of Japan,
where it is rather common, Korea and N.E.
China, growing in scrub in the mountains,
flowering in May–June. Deciduous shrub to 10 m.
Leaves ovate to ovate-orbicular, 10–20 cm wide,
broader than the closely related *S. hemsleyana*
Diels from W. China. Flowers 2 cm long. Any
good soil; sun or part shade. Hardy to −20°C.

**Pterostyrax hispida** Sieb. & Zucc. (*Styracaceae*)
Native of W. Hubei and W. Sichuan, and of
Honshu, Shikoku and Kyushu, in woods in the
mountains at up to 2300 m, flowering in June.
Deciduous shrub or small tree to 5 m. Flowers
6–8 mm long in a hanging panicle 10–20 cm long.
Moist, acid soil, part shade. Hardy to −20°C.
Summer.

**Halesia carolina** L. (*Styracaceae*) Carolina
Silverbell   Native of West Virginia south to E.
Texas, in moist woods along streams in the
mountains, flowering in April–May. Deciduous
shrub to 10 m (or tree to 24 m in var. *monticola*).
Any moist soil. Hardy to −25°C.

*Styrax limpritchii*

*Styrax serrulatus*

*Pterostyrax hispida* at Wisley

*Wattakaka sinensis* at Baoxing, Sichuan

*Styrax officinalis* in S. Turkey

*Halesia carolina*

*Reevesia pubescens* at Wakehurst

*Styrax obassia*

Cornus kousa var. chinensis

Physocarpus opulifolius
'Dart's Gold' see p.41

Stewartia serrata

Trochodendron aralioides

Styrax japonica var. fargesii

Cornus kousa

Cornus rugosa

Cornus mas
'Variegata'

Cornus mas var. aurea

Cornus controversa 'Variegata'

Cornus sanguinea see p. 271

$\frac{2}{3}$ life size. Specimens from Kew, 19th June

Cornus alternifolia 'Argentea' at the Savill Gardens, Windsor

Cornus florida in New Jersey

Cornus 'Ormonde'

Cornus 'Eddie's White Wonder'

Cornus capitata

**Stewartia serrata** Maxim (*Theaceae*)   Native of E. and S. Honshu, Shikoko and Kyushu in mountain woods, flowering in June–July. Deciduous shrub or tree to 10 m. Leaves 3–7 cm long. Flowers 5–6 cm across; ovary and capsule glabrous. Acid soil. Hardy to −15°C.

**Styrax japonica** Sieb. & Zucc. (*Styracaceae*) Native of all Japan, where it is common, Korea, China, Taiwan and the Philippines, in woods, scrub, and by streams in the mountains, flowering April–June. Deciduous shrub or small tree to 10 m. Flowers pendulous from the horizontal branches. **Fargesii** is a name that has been given to plants from China.

**Trochodendron aralioides** Sieb. & Zucc. (*Trochodendraceae*)   Native of Japan, from Honchu southwards, Taiwan and Korea, usually as an epiphyte on the lower part of *Cryptomeria* trunks, flowering in May–June. Evergreen tree to 20 m or more, but in cultivation usually a shrub to 3 m. Fruit 5–10 lobed. Hardy to −10°C. Late spring.

**Cornus rugosa** Lam. (*Cornaceae*) Round-leaved Dogwood   Native of Quebec east to Manitoba and south to Virginia and Illinois, flowering in late May–July. Fruits light blue or pale greenish.

**Cornus kousa** Buerg. ex Hance.   Native of Japan, where it is common in Honshu and southwards, of Korea and C. and W. China to Sichuan in woods and scrub in the mountains, flowering in June–July. Deciduous shrub or small tree to 6 m, with layered branches. Any soil except chalk. Hardy to −20°C. Summer.

Var. **chinensis** Osborn differs from the Japanese variety, if at all, in having leaves without brown hairs in the vein axils beneath.

**Cornus controversa** Hemsl.   Native of all Japan, Korea and China west to Yunnan, in woods, scrub and hedges in the mountains at up to 2000 m in W. China, flowering in May–June. Large, deciduous shrub or tree to 16 m, with an upright trunk and layers of horizontal branches. Leaves alternate, to 12 cm long. **'Variegata'** was introduced by Barbier in France in 1896. Hardy to −20°C.

**Cornus mas** L. See also p. 37.

**Cornus nuttallii** Audub. Pacific Dogwood Native of California, rare in the south, common in the north, to British Columbia and east to Idaho, in open, mixed woods and scrub in the mountains below 1800 m, flowering April–July, and sometimes again in September. Deciduous shrub or small tree to 25 m. Flowers with 4–7 white or pink bracts, 4–7 cm long. Hardy to −15°C. Fruit p. 271.

**Cornus florida** L. Flowering Dogwood   Native of Ontario east to Maine and south to Florida and E. Texas, in deciduous woods and fields, at up to 1500 m, flowering in April–June. Deciduous shrub or small tree to 10 m, less in the open. Flowers with white or pink bracts, the whole to 10 cm across. Acid soil; sun or part shade. Hardy to −25°C. Fruit p. 271.

**Cornus capitata** Wall.   Native of the Himalayas from N.W. India east to Sichuan and Hubei, in woods and scrub at 1200–3400 m,

Cornus nuttallii

flowering in May–July. Deciduous shrub or tree to 9 m. Leaves leathery to 7.5 cm long, glaucous beneath. Bracts 4 or 5, to 4.5 cm long. Fruits hemispherical. Any soil; sun. Hardy to −10°C.

**Cornus 'Eddie's White Wonder'**   A hybrid between *C. florida* and *C. nuttallii*. Easier to grow than *C. nuttallii*. Hardy to −15°C.

**Cornus 'Ormonde'**   A form or hybrid of *C. nuttallii*, originating at the Royal Botanic Gardens, Kew. A free-flowering shrub to 4 m.

**Cornus alternifolia** L. **'Argentea'**   The green-leaved normal form (Pagoda Dogwood) is native from New Brunswick east to Minnesota, south to Georgia and Missouri, in dry deciduous woods and on rocky slopes. Hardy to −25°C.

Staphylea pinnata

Stewartia
malacodendron

Stephanandra tanakae

Stewartia
pseudocamellia

Diervilla sessilifolia

Calycanthus occidentalis

Elaeagnus angustifolia

Carpenteria californica

⅓ life size. Specimens from Kew, 4th July

*Stewartia monadelpha* at the High Beeches, Sussex

**Staphylea pinnata** L. (*Staphyleaceae*) Bladder Nut   Native of France and Italy east to Poland, Romania and Turkey, and naturalized in England, in scrub and woods flowering in May–June. Deciduous shrub to 5 m. Petals 6–10 mm long, pinkish; sepals greenish-white. Hardy to −20°C. Early summer.

**Staphylea holocarpa** Hemsl. '**Rosea**'   Native of W. Hubei, Sichuan and Yunnan, in scrub and on the edges of woods at 1300–2500 m, flowering in May, before the leaves expand. Deciduous shrub or small tree to 10 m. Hardy to −25°C. Late spring.

**Staphylea colchica** Stev.   Native of S.W. Transcaucasia in Adzharya and Abkhazya, in forests at up to 1200 m, flowering in May. Deciduous shrub to 4 m. Leaflets 3 on flowering shoots, 5 on growing shoots, 4–6 cm long. Hardy to −20°C. Late spring.

**Stewartia malacodendron** L. (*Theaceae*) Silky Camellia   Native of Virginia, Tennessee and Arkansas, south to Florida and W. Louisiana, in moist woods, flowering in June. Deciduous shrub or small tree to 10 m. Flowers 8–10 cm across; styles united. Acid moist soil; part shade. Hardy to −15°C. Late summer.

**Stewartia pseudocamellia** Maxim.   Native of Honshu, Shikoku and Kyushu, in forests in the mountains, flowering in July. Deciduous shrub or small tree to 10 m, with bark peeling in large patches. Flowers 6–7 cm across, rather cup-shaped. Hardy to −20°C. Late summer.

**Stewartia ovata** (Car.) Weatherby Mountain Camellia   Native of Virginia and Kentucky south to Georgia and Alabama, in woods and by streams flowering in May–August. Deciduous shrub or small tree to 5 m. Flowers 6–7.5 cm across (to 10 cm across in var. *grandiflora* from Georgia). Styles 4, separate. Hardy to −20°C. Late summer.

**Stewartia monadelpha** Sieb. & Zucc.   Native of S. Honshu, Shikoku, Kyushu and Quelpart Is., in *Cryptomeria* forests in the mountains, flowering in July–August. Deciduous shrub or small tree to 25 m, with smooth flaky bark. Flowers 2–3.5 cm across. Hardy to −15°C. Late summer.

**Elaeagnus commutata** Bernh. (*Elaeagnaceae*) Silverberry   Native of Quebec west to Alaska south to Utah, South Dakota and Minnesota, on dry chalky slopes, flowering in June and July. A deciduous shrub to 4 m, suckering to form thickets. Leaves wavy-edged, silvery on both sides, 2–10 cm long. Any dry soil; full sun. Hardy to −40°C.

**Elaeagnus angustifolia** L. Oleaster   Native of C. Asia, but widely planted for hedges and naturalized in North America, S. and E. Europe and Turkey east to Pakistan. Often found along streams, flowering in April–June. Deciduous shrub or spreading tree to 7 m. Flowers 8–10 mm, heavily and sweetly scented. Hardy to −40°C.

**Calycanthus occidentalis** Hook. & Arnott. (*Calycanthaceae*) Spice Bush   Native of California, in the N. Coast ranges, and the foothills of the Sierra Nevada by streams, ponds and in wet places, below 1200 m, flowering in April–August. Deciduous rounded shrub to 3 m. Hardy to −15°C.

*Staphylea colchica*

*Elaeagnus commutata*

*Staphylea holocarpa* 'Rosea'

**Carpenteria californica** Torr. (*Saxifragaceae*) Native of California, between the San Joaquin and King rivers in Fresno Co., on dry granite hills, flowering in May–July. Evergreen shrub to 4 m or sprawling. Flowers 5–8 cm across. Hardy to −15°C. Summer.

**Diervilla sessilifolia** Buckl. (*Caprifoliaceae*) Bush Honeysuckle   Native of Virginia and Tennessee, south to Georgia and Alabama, in woods in the mountains, flowering in June–August. Deciduous suckering shrub to 1.5 m with arching branches. Hardy to −25°C.

**Stephanandra tanakae** Fr. & Sav. (*Rosaceae*) See p. 207.

*Stewartia ovata* var. *grandiflora*

D. × hybrida 'Mont Rose'

D. discolor

D. gracilis

D. gracilis 'Grandiflora'

D. scabra 'Candidissima'

D. × elegantissima
'Fasciculata'

D. longifolia 'Veitchii'

D. ×
elegantissima 'Rosealind'

½ life size. Specimens from Wisley, 21st June

**Deutzia glomeruliflora** Franch. (*Saxifragaceae*)
Native of Sichuan and Yunnan, in moist scrub
and on shady cliffs at 1800–3500 m, flowering in
May–June. Deciduous shrub to 3 m, with
arching branches. Leaves 1.5–4 cm long. Any
good moist soil; full sun or part shade. Hardy to
−20°C. Shown here var. **forrestiana** Zaikonn;
the rounded heads of flowers are typical of this
variety.

**D. × hybrida** Lémoine '**Mont Rose**'   A hybrid
between *D. longifolia* and *D. discolor* or perhaps
*D. purpurascens*, introduced in 1925. An upright
shrub to 1.5 m. Hardy to −20°C.

**D. discolor** Hemsl. (syn. *D. longifolia* var.
*farreri* Airy-Shaw)   Native of S. Gansu, S.
Shaanxi and W. Hubei, at 1150–2400 m,
flowering in May–June. Deciduous shrub to
1.5 m; leaves 6–9 cm long. Flowers white. Hardy
to −15°C.

**D. gracilis** Sieb. & Zucc.   Native of Japan, in S.
Honshu, Shikoku and Kyushu, in scrub in the
mountains, flowering in May–June. Deciduous
shrub to 1 m, with arching branches. Petals
c.10 mm long. Any soil; sun or part shade. Hardy
to −20°C, but sometimes damaged, as are other
species, by late frosts which cause the plant to
produce minute flowers. Late spring.
'**Grandiflora**' is a larger form, said to be *D.
gracilis × D. sieboldiana*.

**D. scabra** Thunb. '**Candidissima**' (syn. *D.
crenata* Sieb. & Zucc.)   Introduced by Froebel
in 1868. Flowers pure white, almost spherical.

**D. × elegantissima** (Lémoine) Rehd.
'**Fasciculata**'   A hybrid between *D.
purpurascens* and *D. sieboldiana* raised by
Lémoine in 1911. An upright shrub to 2 m.

**D. × elegantissima** '**Rosealind**'   Raised at
Slieve Donard before 1926. An upright shrub to
1.5 m; flowers the deepest pink of this group.

**D. longifolia** Franch.   Native of W. Sichuan,
where it is common in scrub at 1500–2750 m,
flowering in June. Deciduous shrub to 1.5 m.
Flowers pinkish. Calyx lobes lanceolate. Shown
here the clone or variety '**Veitchii**', with large
flowers. Hardy to −15°C. Summer.

**D. calycosa** Rehd.   Native of Yunnan, in scrub
and open forest at 2700 m, flowering in May–
June. SBEC 435 seems to belong to var.
**longisepala** Zaikonn, described from the
Shangchang Mts. Deciduous upright shrub to
2 m. Leaves greyish beneath. Any soil; sun or
part shade. Hardy to −15°C. Late spring.

**D. mombeigii** W. W. Sm.   Native of Yunnan,
in open scrub at 3300 m, flowering in June–July.
Deciduous shrub to 2 m. Leaves white beneath
with dense many-rayed scales. Any soil; full sun.
Hardy to −15°C. See also p. 187.

**D. grandiflora** Bunge   Native of N. China,
from Hebei, near Beijing west to N. Shaanxi,
Hubei and 'Mongolia', forming low thickets on
dry hills, flowering in April–May. Suckering
shrub to 1.5 m. Flowers 1–3 together, 2.5–3 cm
across. Well-drained soil; full sun. Hardy to
−20°C. Spring.

**D. ningpoensis** Rehd. (syn. *D. chunii* Hu)
Native of Anhui and Zhejiang (Chekiang) in the
Ningpo mountains at 150–1500 m, flowering in
June–July. Graceful shrub to 2 m, distinguished
by its narrow leaves, to 16 mm wide, small
flowers to 6 mm long, and late-summer flowering.

*Deutzia glomeruliflora* near Lijiang, Yunnan

*Deutzia calycosa* SBEC 435

*Deutzia mombeigii*

*Deutzia grandiflora*

*Deutzia ningpoensis*

Deutzia glauca

D. scabra
'Flore Pleno'

Philadelphus 'Dame Blanche'

Deutzia scabra

Philadelphus intectus

Deutzia mombeigii

Deutzia
setchuenensis

Deutzia pulchra

Philadelphus 'Burfordensis'

Philadelphus 'Virginal'

½ life size. Specimens from Kew, 28th June

# DEUTZIA AND PHILADELPHUS

**Deutzia glauca** Cheng (*Saxifragaceae*) Native of E. China, in Anhwei and Jiangxi in scrub in the hills at 350–1000 m, flowering in May. Deciduous shrub to 2 m. Leaves 5–8 cm long. Flowers 10–17 mm long. Hardy to −15°C.

**Deutzia scabra** Thunb. (syn. *D. crenata* Sieb. & Zucc.) Native of Japan, Korea and E. China, in scrub and at the edges of woods, flowering in May–July. Deciduous shrub to 3 m, with brown peeling bark. Petals *c.*15 mm long. Leaves rough. Hardy to −20°C.
**'Flore Pleno'** Introduced by Robert Fortune from Japan in 1861. Flowers pinkish outside.

**Deutzia mombeigii** W. W. Sm. See p. 185. Leaves often lanceolate, 1.5–4 cm long.

**Deutzia setchuenensis** Franch. Native of E. and W. Sichuan, and W. Hubei, in scrub at 900–1500 m. Deciduous shrub to 2 m. Flowers *c.*1 cm across. Good soil; sun or part shade. Hardy to −15°C. Summer.

**Deutzia pulchra** Vidal Native of N. Luzon and Taiwan in the mountains. Deciduous tall shrub. Flowers 12 mm long. Hardy to −15°C.

**Deutzia compacta** Craib (syn. *D. hookeriana* (Schneid.) Airy-Shaw) Native of the Himalayas from Nepal to N.W. Sichuan. Deciduous shrub to 2 m. Flowers *c.*15 mm across. Hardy to −15°C. Summer.

**Deutzia corymbosa** R. Br. Native of W. Himalayas, from Kashmir to Nepal, in scrub at 2000–3000 m, flowering in June–July. Deciduous shrub to 3 m. Flowers *c.*15 mm across. Anthers large, yellow. Hardy to −15°C.

**Deutzia × kalmiiflora** Lémoine A hybrid between *D. purpurascens* and *D. parviflora* raised in about 1900 by Lémoine at Nancy.

**Philadelphus intectus** Beadle (*Saxifragaceae*) Native of Kentucky, Tennessee and Oklahoma, with var. *pubigerius* in Arkansas, on rocky hillsides, flowering in June. Deciduous shrub to 5 m. Flowers 3 cm across. Hardy to −15°C.
**P. 'Dame Blanche'** Raised by Lémoine in 1920. Low growing, with arching branches. Flowers 8 mm long, well scented. Hardy to −25°C.
**P. 'Virginal'** Raised by Lémoine in around 1909. Upright gaunt shrub to 2.5 m. Flowers double, scented, 4–5 cm across.
**P. 'Burfordensis'** Said to be a sport of 'Virginal', raised at Burford Court, Surrey. Tall, robust, upright deciduous shrub to 3 m, forming dense columns of flowers to 7.5 cm across.

**Philadelphus coronarius** L. Syringa, Mock Orange Native of S. Austria and Italy, on rocky hills and screes, flowering in May–June. Deciduous shrub to 2 m. Flowers fragrant. Hardy to −25°C. Early summer.

**Jamesia americana** Torr. & Gray (*Saxifragaceae*) Native of New Mexico, west to California, north to Wyoming, in canyons and by streams at 2200–3600 m, flowering in May–June. Deciduous many-stemmed shrub to 1.5 m. Flowers 1.5 cm across, rarely pink. Full sun. Hardy to −20°C. Early summer.

**Fendlera wrightii** (Gray) Hell. (*Saxifragaceae*) Native of W. Texas, New Mexico, Arizona and Mexico, in canyons and on rock ledges at 1000–2200 m, flowering in May–June. Deciduous shrub to 2 m, with arching branches. Flowers *c.*2 cm across. Well-drained soil; full sun. Hardy to −20°C. Early summer.

*Jamesia americana*

*Deutzia corymbosa*

*Deutzia × kalmiiflora*

*Deutzia compacta*

*Fendlera wrightii*

*Philadelphus coronarius* at Crathes Castle, Aberdeenshire

Philadelphus 'Beauclerk'

Philadelphus × lemoinei 'Avalanche' in Eccleston Square

Philadelphus 'Bicolore'

Philadelphus 'Sybille'

Philadelphus 'Conquête'

**Philadelphus microphyllus** Gray
(*Saxifragaceae*)   Native of the Rockies from
Utah and Colorado, west to California and south
to Arizona and New Mexico at 1200–3000 m in
sunny, rocky canyons and Pinyon-juniper
woodland, flowering May–August. Delicate,
rounded twiggy shrub to 1.5 m. Leaves to 2 cm
long. Flowers 2–2.5 cm across, scented. Any
dry soil; full sun. Hardy to −20°C. Summer.

**P. × lemoinei** Lémoine **'Avalanche'**   Raised
by Lémoine in 1896, by crossing *P. coronarius*
and *P. microphyllus*. Deciduous shrub to 2 m
with arching branches. Flowers scented, to
2.5 cm across, usually in 7s. Any good soil; sun
or part shade. Hardy to −15°C. Summer.

**P. 'Beauclerk'**   Raised in 1938 by the Hon.
Lewis Palmer by crossing 'Sybille' with
'Burfordensis' (pollen). Spreading deciduous
shrub to 2 m, more across. Flowers scented, to
7.5 cm across, with reflexed petals, just pinkish
at the base.

**P. 'Bicolore'**   Raised by Lémoine at Nancy in
1918. Spreading shrub to 1 m. Flowers solitary
or in 3s, cup-shaped, 4.5–5 cm across, scented.

**P. delavayi** L. Henry   Native of Yunnan, S.E.
Xizang, S.W. Sichuan and N.E. Burma, at 700–
3800 mm, in scrub and by streams, flowering in
June. Upright, deciduous shrub to 3 m. Leaves
to 10 cm long. Flowers to 4 cm across, scented.
Twigs and calyx purple in var. **calvescens**
Rehd. (syn. f. *melanocalyx* or 'Nymans
Variety') shown here. Hardy to −15°C. Early
summer.

**P. 'Sybille'**   Raised by Lémoine in 1913.
Spreading shrub to 1 m. Flowers 4–5 cm across,
scented.

**P. 'Conquête'**   Raised by Lémoine in 1903.
Spreading deciduous shrub to 1 m. Flowers
variably double.

**P. subcanus** var. **magdalenae** (Koehne) S. Y.
Hu.   Native of N. Yunnan and W. Sichuan, in
hedges and scrub at 1500–3000 m, flowering in
May–June. Upright, deciduous shrub with
arching branches to 4 m. Leaves with short
appressed hairs, denser beneath. Ovary and
sepals brownish outside. Any soil. Full sun.
Hardy to −15°C. Early summer.

**P. tomentosus** Wall. ex G. Don.   Native of
Kashmir to S.E. Xizang, in scrub and open
forest at 1800–3300 m, flowering in May–July.
Upright, deciduous shrub to 3 m. Leaves hairy,
densely greyish below, rarely glabrous. Any soil;
sun. Hardy to −15°C. Summer.

**P. incanus** Koehne   Native of W. Hubei,
Shaanxi and W. Honan, in scrub and by streams
at 600–2300 m, flowering in June–July. Tall,
open, deciduous shrub to 3.5 m with dense,
appressed hairs. Flowers scented, c.2.5 cm
across. Any soil. Hardy to −20°C. Late summer.

**P. purpurascens** (Koehne) Rehder   Native of
W. Sichuan, S.E. Xizang and N. Yunnan in
alpine scrub at 2750–3200 m, flowering in June–
July. Spreading shrub to 2 m. Leaves small, to
5 cm long, hairy on the ribs beneath. Flowers to
2.7 cm across, often with a purple calyx. Hardy
to −15°C. Early summer.

*P. tomentosus* at Cambridge Botanic Gardens

*Philadelphus subcanus var. magdalenae* above Dali, Yunnan in May

*Philadelphus subcanus var. magdelenae*

*Philadelphus delavayi var. calvescens*

*Philadelphus incanus* at Nymans

*Philadelphus purpurascens* at Crathes Castle, Aberdeenshire

*Philadelphus microphyllus*

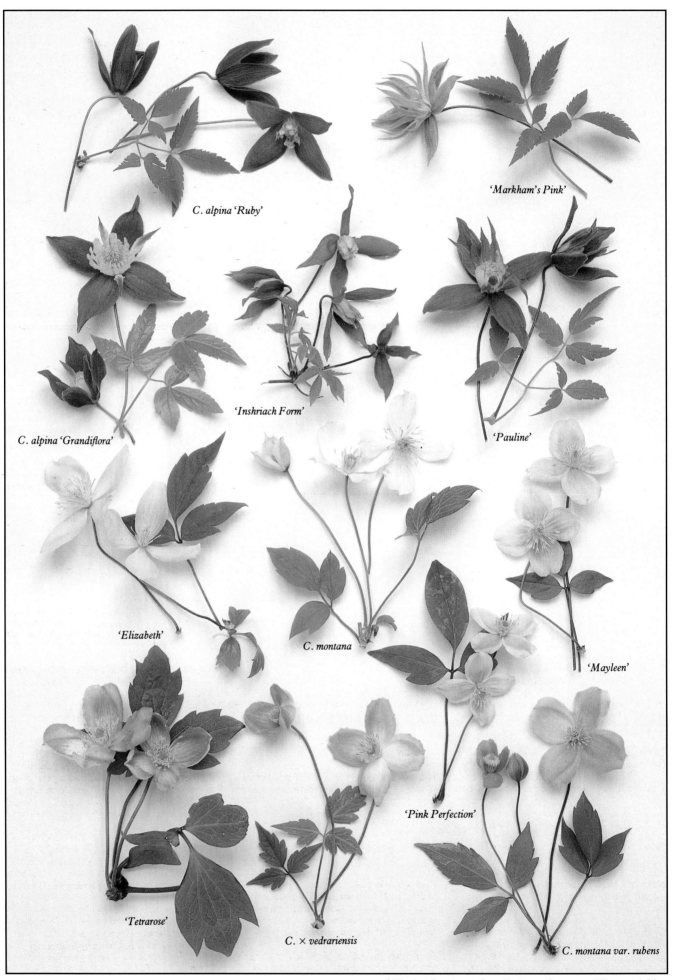

C. alpina 'Ruby'

'Markham's Pink'

C. alpina 'Grandiflora'

'Inshriach Form'

'Pauline'

'Elizabeth'

C. montana

'Mayleen'

'Tetrarose'

C. × vedrariensis

'Pink Perfection'

C. montana var. rubens

⅖ life size. Specimens from Eccleston Square and Kew, 19th May

Clematis montana near Lijiang, Yunnan

Clematis chrysocoma var. sericea in Sichuan

Clematis alpina

Clematis chrysocoma in Yunnan

**Clematis alpina** (L). Miller (*Ranunculaceae*) (syn. *Atragene alpina* L.) Native of the Alps and mountains of C. Europe from France to Romania and Bulgaria, at 1000–2400 m, on rocks, usually limestone, in subalpine woods, flowering in June–August. Deciduous climber to 2.5 m. Flowers bluish or rarely pure white. Sepals 2.5–4 cm long, the central staminodes up to half as long. Any well-drained soil; partial shade or shaded roots. Hardy to −25°C. Requires no pruning. Late spring.

**C. alpina 'Ruby'** A reddish form of *C. alpina* (see above) raised by Markham around 1937.

**C. alpina 'Grandiflora'** A large-flowered form of *C. alpina* (see above).

**C. alpina 'Inshriach Form'** Raised at Jack Drake's Nursery near Aviemore, Inverness-shire.

**C. alpina 'Pauline'** Introduced by Washfield Nurseries, Sussex in 1970. The long staminodes suggest that it may be a hybrid with *C. macropetala*.

**C. montana** (Buch.-Ham.) DC. (*Ranunculaceae*) Native of the Himalayas from Afghanistan to S.W. and C. China, east to Hubei, growing in forest and scrub at 1800–4000 m, and often very

common, flowering in April–June; very variable. Deciduous climber to 6 m or more. Leaves with 3 leaflets, to 7.5 cm long. Flowers white or pale pink, 2–8 cm across. Requires no pruning. Any soil, preferably with northern aspect. Hardy to −15°C. Late spring.

**C. montana 'Elizabeth'** A variety of *C. montana* (see above) raised by Jackman's of Woking in 1958. Flowers slightly scented.

**C. montana 'Mayleen'** A form of *C. montana* with pale pink flowers.

**C. montana 'Pink Perfection'** A selection of *C. montana* var. *rubens*. Flowers 6–8 cm across. No pruning required. Hardy to −15°C.

**C. montana 'Tetrarose'** A tetraploid of *C. montana*, raised by colchicine treatment at the Boskoop Research Station in 1960. Leaves bronzy; flowers thick textured and up to 8 cm across.

**C. montana var. rubens** Wilson Native of W. Hubei and W. Sichuan, in thickets and rocky places, at 1300–3000 m, flowering in May–June. Differs from var. *montana* in its purplish foliage and pink or white pink-backed petals.

**C. chrysocoma** Franch. (*Ranunculaceae*) Native of Yunnan, on the Dali range and Lijiang on

mountain slopes and in scrub at 2800–3000 m, flowering from May onwards. In the wild a low sparse shrub to 1 m, woody only at the base, not climbing. Flowers pinkish; leaflets obovate, cuneate, obtuse, rugose above with deeply impressed veins, silky hairy. Any well-drained soil; sun or part shade. Hardy to −10°C. Late spring–summer.

**C. chrysocoma var. sericea** (Franch.) C. K. Schneid. (syn. *C. spooneri* Rehd. & Wilson) Native of W. Sichuan, in scrub and forest and on cliffs at 1600–2600 m, flowering in May and June. A deciduous climber or scrambling shrub to 3–6 m. Leaflets ovate, with usually one tooth on each side, and silky, yellowish hairs. Sepals obovate or orbicular, 3–4 cm long. Hardy to −15°C. Late spring.

**C. macropetala Ledeb. 'Markham's Pink'** A variety of *C. macropetala* (see p. 199) which grows up to about 3.5 m high. The flowers are about 8 cm across. Will do well on any soil, and in any situation. Requires no pruning. Hardy to −25°C. Late spring.

**Clematis × vedrariensis** Vilm. A hybrid between *C. montana* var. *rubens* and *C. chrysocoma*, raised in France by Vilmorin in *c*.1914. Leaves hairy; flowers 5–6 cm across. Hardy to −15°C.

*Clematis tangutica var. obtusiuscula*

*Clematis 'Orange Peel'*

*Clematis potaninii at Brodick*

**C. tangutica** Korsh   Native of the Tien-shan and Pamir-Alai of C. Asia eastwards to N. China and Siberia, also commonly found on river shingle. Var. *obtusiuscula* Rehd. & Wilson shown here, is recorded from W. Sichuan near Kangding and W. Gansu at 2600–3300 m. *C. tangutica* differs from *C. orientalis* in its acuminate sepals to 4 cm long, glabrous inside, and coarser green leaves. In var. *obtusiuscula* the sepals are 2.5–3 cm long, obtuse, apiculate. A robust climber to 3 m. Hardy to −15°C.

**Clematis vernayi** Fischer (syn. C. *thibetana* var. *vernayi*) L.S. & E.13342. 'Orange Peel'   In this form, collected in S. Tibet, the leaves are delicate, soft and green; the sepals are stiff, thick, held horizontal, vivid yellow, deepening to orange (hence the English name) as they fade: This is usually considered a form of *C. orientalis*, but is more similar to *C. glauca* Willd., or *C. tangutica* var. *obtusiucula* q.v. Many of the plants now in cultivation are probably hybrids with *C. tangutica*.

**C. potaninii** Maxim. (syn. *C. fargesii* Franch. var. *souliei* Finet & Gagnep.)   Native of Yunnan, W. Sichuan, Gansu, and Shaanxi, in woods and forest glades at 1400–4000 m, flowering in June–July. Deciduous climber to 6 m. Moist leafy soil. Hardy to −20°C.

**C. alpina** subsp. **sibirica** (L.) O. Kuntze Native of Norway, and the mountains of C. Asia and Siberia on cliffs and in subalpine woods, flowering in May–June. Scrambling shrub to 2 m, differing from *C. alpina* (p. 190) in its pale yellowish flowers with narrower sepals. Any good soil. Hardy to −40°C. Spring.

**C. armandii** Franch.   Native of Yunnan, Guizhou, Gansu, W. Hubei and W. Sichuan, in scrub and on river banks at 60–2400 m, flowering in April–May. Evergreen climber to 5 m. Flowers 3–6 cm across, scented, white or pink (8 cm across in f. *farquhariana* in W. Hubei). Any soil; sun or part shade with shelter. Hardy to −10°C. Spring.

**Clematis orientalis** L. (*Ranunculaceae*)   Native of Tinos, Kos, Rodhos and N. Turkey eastwards to S. Russia and the Crimea, C. Asia and W. Pakistan in hot dry valleys, especially on rocks by rivers and in scrub at up to 3000 m, flowering in July–September. A climbing or scrambling deciduous shrub to 2 m. Leaves greyish. Sepals 10–14 mm long, acute, silky on both sides, spreading and reflexing. Hardy to −15°C. Late summer.

**C. barbellata** Edgew.   Native of the Himalayas from Pakistan to C. Nepal, in scrub and forest at 2100–4000 m, flowering in June–July. Deciduous climber to 2 m. Leaves with 3 leaflets, 4–10 cm long. Flowers to 2.5 cm long hairy inside and out, and with very hairy stamens. Moist, leafy soil. Hardy to −15°C.

**C. cirrhosa** L.   See p. 22 for flowers and full text.

**C. phlebantha** L. H. Williams   Native of W. and C. Nepal, especially northwest of the Dhaulagiri massif, at 2700–3700 m, in rocky places and hot, dry cliffs, flowering in May–June. Trailing shrub to 1.5 m or more in cultivation. Leaves white-silky beneath. Flowers 2.5–4.5 cm across. Well-drained soil; full sun. Hardy to −10°C. Early summer.

*Clematis armandii*

*Clematis alpina subsp. siberica* near Alma Ata, C. Asia

*Clematis orientalis* in N.W. Turkey

*Clematis barbellata* at Kew

*Clematis cirrhosa* near Ronda, Spain

*Clematis phlebantha* at Ventnor Botanic Garden

# CLEMATIS

'Sylvia Denny'

'Maureen'

'Prince Heinrich'

'Gipsy Queen'

'Lawsoniana'

'Nellie Moser'

'Barbara Jackman'

'Miss Crawshay'

'Mrs Cholmondely'

½ life size. Specimens from Treasures Nursery, 3rd July

194

*Clematis* 'Sylvia Denny'  The medium-sized flowers (up to 10 cm across) are borne during early summer. Does best in sun or semi-shade. Light pruning only required. Hardy to −20°C.

*C.* 'Maureen'  A hybrid of rather bushy habit, with large flowers freely produced from mid-summer onwards. Prefers sun or semi-shade. Light pruning only required. Hardy to −20°C.

*C.* 'Prince Heinrich' (syn. 'Prins Hendrik')  A rather tender hybrid, best grown in a greenhouse, or outside on a wall. Hard pruning required. The very large flowers are produced in mid-summer, with a second flush following in late summer. Hardy to −20°C.

*C.* 'Gypsy Queen'  A vigorous hybrid, to 5 m high eventually. Flowers to 13 cm across, freely produced in mid-summer–autumn; the colour of the sepals changes slightly as they age. Does best away from deep shade. Hard pruning required. Hardy to −20°C.

*C.* 'Lawsoniana'  A vigorous hybrid, with very large (up to 20 cm across) flowers in mid-summer and sometimes again in late summer. Does well in any situation. Requires only light pruning. Hardy to −20°C.

*C.* 'Nellie (or Nelly) Moser'  One of the best known and most popular of all the hybrids, this clematis grows to about 3.5 m. The large (up to 18 cm across) flowers are freely produced in early summer and again in late summer. It is best planted in a shady position to avoid bleaching of flower colour. Requires light pruning. Hardy to −20°C.

*C.* 'Barbara Jackman'  A fairly vigorous hybrid, with flowers to about 15 cm across produced in late summer–early autumn. Flower colour fades on opening, so best planted away from full sun. Light pruning only required. Hardy to −20°C.

*C.* 'Miss Crawshay'  An old, fairly vigorous hybrid, with flowers up to 14 cm across, produced mid–late spring. Does best in sun or semi-shade. Requires only light pruning. Hardy to −20°C.

*C.* 'Mrs Cholmondely'  An old, vigorous hybrid which is exceptionally free-flowering. The very large flowers (up to 20 cm across) are borne in late spring, fading as they age. Will do well in any situation. Light pruning only required. Hardy to −20°C.

*C.* 'Lord Nevill'  A vigorous cultivar, growing to *c.*6 m. Leaves bronzy when young; flowers to 18 cm across, mid-summer–early autumn. Requires only light pruning. Hardy to −20°C.

*C.* 'Mrs Spencer Castle'  A moderately vigorous (up to 5 m high) member of the *viticella* group. The large flowers appear in early summer and the single blooms are borne on young wood in the autumn. Requires only light pruning. Hardy to −20°C.

*C.* 'Beauty of Richmond'  A vigorous cultivar with flowers to 16 cm across, from mid-summer. Will do well in any situation. Light pruning only required. Hardy to −20°C.

*C.* 'Beauty of Worcester'  A less vigorous grower than some others, this cultivar produces double flowers, on old wood, from early–mid-summer, and single flowers on young wood, until early autumn. Prefers a sunny position. Light pruning only required. Hardy to −20°C.

'Lord Nevill'  'Mrs Spencer Castle'  'Jackmanii Rubra'  'Beauty of Richmond'  'The President'  'Belle of Woking'  'Beauty of Worcester'  'Vyvyan Pennell'  'Proteus'

¼ life size. Specimens from Treasures Nursery, 3rd July

*C.* 'Jackmanii Rubra'  A fairly vigorous form of *C.* × *jackmanii* (see page 199) with semi-double flowers during mid-summer, followed by single blooms until early autumn. Light pruning only required. Hardy to −20°C.

*C.* 'The President'  A vigorous grower (up to 3.5 m high) with bronzy foliage when young. The flowers, up to 18 cm across, are slightly cupped, showing the pale underside of the sepals; these are freely produced in mid-summer–early autumn. Light pruning only required. Hardy to −20°C.

*C.* 'Belle of Woking'  One of the old hydrids, this is not particularly vigorous, but produces large (to 15 cm across) flowers during late spring. Prefers a sunny position. Light pruning only required. Hardy to −20°C.

*C.* 'Proteus'  An old hybrid, first introduced under the name 'The Premier'. Moderately vigorous, with double flowers during early summer, and a second crop of single flowers towards the end of the summer. Does best away from full sun or deep shade . Light pruning only required. Hardy to −20°C.

*C.* 'Vyvyan Pennell'  A vigorous hybrid which grows to 3.5 m. Large double flowers, to 20 cm across, in late spring–early summer with single, paler flowers produced on young wood in the autumn. Not good in deep shade. Light pruning only required. Hardy to −20°C.

'Ernest Markham'

'Corona'

'Carnaby'

'Edouard Desfosse'

'Serenata'

'Royalty'

'Ville de Lyon'

'Kathleen Wheeler'

'Ascotiensis'

'Richard Pennell'

'Countess of Lovelace'

½ life size. Specimens from Treasures Nursery, 3rd July

*C.* × *jackmannii 'Superba'* trained on a tree at Eccleston Square

**Clematis 'Ernest Markham'**   A vigorous grower, up to 2.5 m high, with large flowers, to 15 cm across. When pruned lightly, flowering begins in about mid-summer, but, if pruned hard, it begins blooming in late summer continuing to early autumn. Hardy to −20°C.

**C. 'Carnaby'**   Medium-sized blooms are produced in early summer. Best planted away from full sun, and pruned hard. Hardy to −20°C.

**C. 'Corona'**   A moderately vigorous hybrid, with large flowers measuring up to 14 cm across, produced in early summer, and sometimes again in late summer. Prefers sun or semi-shade. Requires light pruning. Hardy to −20°C.

**C. 'Serenata'**   An unusual new hybrid, with a long flowering season, running from early summer to early autumn; one of the few purple clematis which flowers early in the summer. Does well in any situation. Requires light pruning. Hardy to −20°C.

**C. 'Edouard Desfosse'**   An old hybrid, of moderate vigour, with large flowers measuring up to 15 cm across, during early summer. Best planted in sun or semi-shade, although flowers fade slightly on opening. Light pruning required. Hardy to −20°C.

**C. 'Countess of Lovelace'**   An old, quite vigorous, hybrid, with large (up to 15 cm across) flowers, which fade slightly, from late spring to early summer. A second crop of single flowers is produced in the autumn. Needs only light pruning. Hardy to −20°C.

**C. 'Ville de Lyon'**   An old, vigorous (up to 5 m high) hybrid, with large flowers (up to 14 cm across) produced from mid-summer–early autumn. The lower leaves of this hybrid often go brown in the summer. Prefers sun or semi-shade, and hard pruning. Hardy to −20°C.

**C. 'Kathleen Wheeler'**   A hybrid with very large (up to 16 cm across) blooms produced from mid-summer–early autumn. Needs only light pruning. Hardy to −20°C.

**C. 'Ascotiensis'**   A vigorous grower, with large (up to 13 cm across) flowers produced in mid–late summer. Needs hard pruning. Hardy to −20°C.

**C. 'Richard Pennell'**   A recent introduction with large flowers produced in late spring–mid-summer. Needs pruning firmly, but not too hard. Hardy to −20°C.

**C. × jackmanii 'Superba'**   Similar to *C. jackmanii*, this well-known cultivar has flowers of a deeper colour (with wider sepals) produced during mid- and late summer. Requires hard pruning. Hardy to −25°C.

**C. 'Royalty'**   A double-flowered variety of unknown origin.

**C. 'Dr Ruppel'**   Introduced by Fisk in 1975. No pruning required. 2.5–4 m high. Summer and early autumn.

**C. 'Niobe'**   Introduced by Fisk in 1975. Prune hard. Late summer flowering.

*'Dr Ruppel'*

*'Niobe'*

C. × durandii

C. viticella seedling

'Gravetye Beauty'

C. florida 'Alba Plena'

C. heracleifolia
'Stans'

C. scottiae

'Etoile Violette'

C. × jackmannii

C. viticella
'Purpurea Plena Elegans'

C. florida
'Sieboldii'

C. integrifolia

'Venosa Violacea'

C. macropetala

²/₅ life size. Specimens from Treasures Nursery, 3rd July

Clematis 'Etoile Rose'

Clematis campaniflora

Clematis × durandii

Clematis viticella

**Clematis × durandii** A. Kuntze A hybrid between *C. × jackmannii* and *C. integrifolia* raised in about 1870. A scrambling shrub to 2.5 m, best grown through other plants for support. Leaves to 12 cm long; flowers about 11 cm across. Any soil; sun or part shade. Prune hard in spring. Hardy to −20°C. Late summer. 'Pallida' has paler, pinker flowers.

**C. viticella** L. (*Ranunculaceae*) Native of S.E. Europe from Italy and Yugoslavia east to Turkey, N.W. Iran and W. Syria, in scrub and hedges near the sea up to 900 m. Leaves pinnate with 3 often deeply lobed leaflets. Flowers 2.5–4.5 cm long, dark purple, nodding. Styles not silky in fruit. Well-drained soil; full sun. Hardy to −15°C.
**C. viticella** 'Purpurea Plena Elegans' See p. 201.

**C. 'Gravetye Beauty'** A vigorous sub-shrubby climber which is rather short-lived in Britain. The bell-like flowers open out to about 8 cm across. Best in a sunny or semi-shady position, and pruned hard. A hybrid of *C. texensis*. Summer.

**C. scottiae** Porter & Coult (syn. *C. douglasii* var. *scottiae*; *C. hirsutissima*) Native of dry grassland and sage bush, and open pine forests in British Columbia, and Washington east to Montana and Wyoming. Tufted herbaceous perennial, to 1 m, with many simple stems from a woody base. Full sun and dry soil. Hardy to −20°C. Summer.

**C. florida 'Alba Plena'** (syn. *C. florida* 'Plena') This old garden variety of *C. florida* is now rather rare; it is thought that it was originally

introduced from Japan in the 18th C. and was commonly cultivated during the 19th C. Best in a sunny situation; needs hard pruning. Hardy to −15°C.

**C. florida** Thunb. 'Sieboldii' (syn. *C. florida* var. *bicolor* Lendl.) Native of China in W. Hubei near Ichang, but long cultivated. Height to 2.5 m. Flowers to 8 cm across, with stamens modified into purple staminodes. Does best in a sunny, rather sheltered position. Needs old flowering wood removed. Hardy to −15°C. Mid–late summer.

**C. heracleifolia** DC. var. **stans** (Sieb & Zucc.) Kuntze Native of Honshu, and of Shikoku and Kyushu, in open places in the mountains, flowering in August–October. Stems herbaceous to 1 m, sometimes woody at the base. Flowers 15–20 mm long, male and female usually on different plants. Hardy to −20°C.

**C. 'Etoile Violette'** A vigorous hybrid of *C. viticella* raised by Morel; height to 3.5 m. The flowers, to 10 cm across, are freely produced in mid-late summer. Does well in any situation. Requires hard pruning. Hardy to −20°C.

**C. × jackmanii** T. Moore This famous hybrid of *C. lanuginosa × C. viticella* was raised at Messrs Jackman's nursery at Woking in 1860, and is the parent of many of the well-known large-flowered hybrids. A deciduous climber to about 3.5 m high. Leaves about 11 cm. Flowers up to 13 cm across. Does well in any situation. Hardy to −25°C. Summer to autumn. Requires hard pruning.

**C. integrifolia** L. (*Ranunculaceae*) Native of Austria south to Bulgaria, and eastwards to C. Asia, and the Caucasus, in grassland, flowering in June–August. Herbaceous perennial to 1 m, sometimes woody at the base. Any good soil; full sun. Hardy to −25°C. Summer.

**C. 'Venosa Violacea'** An old hybrid of uncertain origin known since 1860, probably between *C. viticella* and *C. patens*.

**C. macropetala** Ledeb. (*Ranunculaceae*) Native of Siberia and N. China in rocky places in the mountains, flowering in May–June. Deciduous climbing shrub to 3 m. Leaves biternate, to 15 cm long. Flowers to 5 cm long, bluish, with 4 large sepals and numerous narrow petals. Fruits with silky styles. Any soil; sun or part shade. Hardy to −25°C. Early summer. No pruning needed.

**C. 'Etoile Rose'** A fairly vigorous sub-shrubby climber, growing up to 3.5 m, raised in 1903 by Victor Lémoine et Fils of Nancy, France. A hybrid of *C. texensis*. The nodding flowers which are about 5 cm across and the same in length, are produced in late summer. Warm position in full sun. Any soil. Hardy to −20°C.

**C. campaniflora** Brot. (*Ranunculaceae*) Native of Portugal and S. and W. Spain, in scrub, hedges and rough places, flowering in May–July. Deciduous climber to 8 m. Leaves pinnate. Flowers to 3 cm across, pale violet, scented. Any soil; full sun or part shade. Hardy to −15°C. Summer. Prune hard in spring. A rampant climber for a tree or high wall.

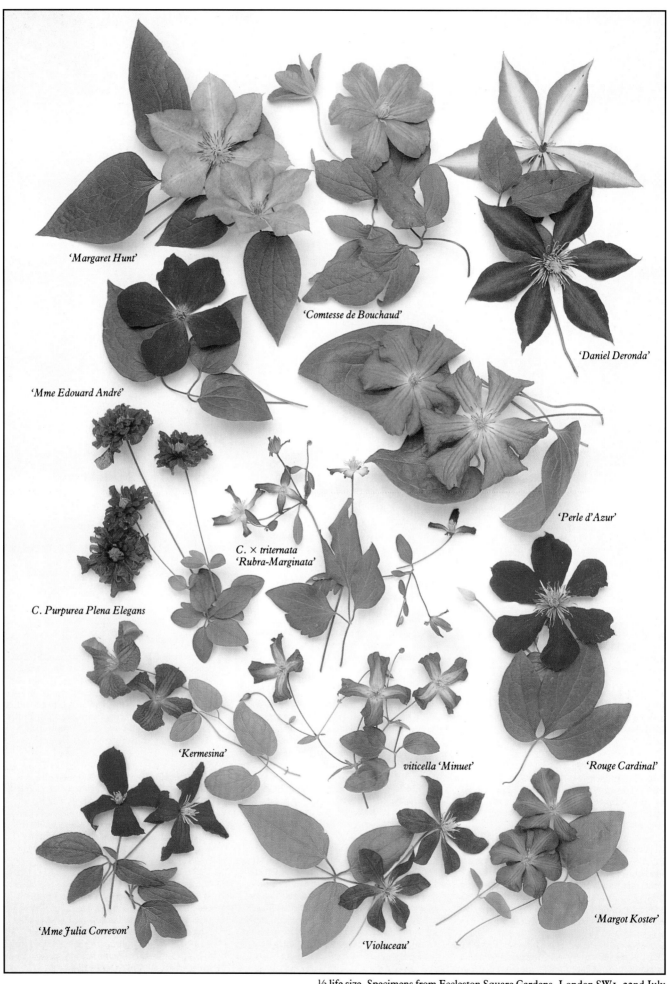

'Margaret Hunt'

'Comtesse de Bouchaud'

'Daniel Deronda'

'Mme Edouard André'

'Perle d'Azur'

C. × triternata
'Rubra-Marginata'

C. Purpurea Plena Elegans

'Kermesina'

viticella 'Minuet'

'Rouge Cardinal'

'Mme Julia Correvon'

'Violuceau'

'Margot Koster'

⅓ life size. Specimens from Eccleston Square Gardens, London SW1, 22nd July

*Clematis viticella 'Abundance'*

*Clematis viticella 'Alba Luxurians'*

*Clematis 'Huldine'*

**Clematis 'Margaret Hunt'** A vigorous hybrid, to 4.8 m. Flowering in summer. Hardy to −20°C.

**C. 'Comtesse de Bouchaud'** Raised by F. Morel early this century. A vigorous grower to 3.6 m, very free-flowering in summer. Requires hard pruning. Hardy to −20°C.

**C. 'Daniel Deronda'** A fairly vigorous hybrid, with flowers to 17 cm across in late spring–late summer. The early flowers are usually double or semi-double, the later ones are single. Requires only light pruning. Hardy to −20°C.

**C. 'Mme Edouard André'** Only about 2 m high. Flowers to 12 cm across in mid–late summer. Does well in sun or semi-shade. Requires hard pruning. Hardy to −20°C.

**C. 'Perle d'Azur'** A vigorous *jackmanii* hybrid, raised by Morel in 1885, which grows to 4.5 m high. The superb flowers, up to 15 cm across, are freely produced in mid–late summer. Does well in sun or semi-shade. Needs only light pruning. Hardy to −20°C.

**C. viticella 'Alba Luxurians'** A vigorous cultivar, with flowers up to 8 cm across, borne from mid-summer–early autumn. The first blooms to appear are often entirely green but later ones are white, sometimes with green tips to the sepals. Hardy to −15°C.

**C. viticella 'Abundance'** A cultivar named by Jackmans but possibly originally raised by Morel at the turn of the century. A vigorous grower, it bears flowers up to 5 cm across in mid-summer–early autumn. Hardy to −15°C.

**C. viticella 'Purpurea Plena Elegans'** (syn. *C.v.* 'Plena Elegans') An ancient variety, recorded by Parkinson in 1629, this was rediscovered, propagated and distributed by Graham Thomas *c.* 1945. A vigorous climber (up to 2.8 m) with flowers to 5 cm across in mid-summer–early autumn. Prune hard. Hardy to −20°C.

**C. viticella 'Mme Julia Correvon'** A vigorous variety, with flowers to 13 cm across produced freely in mid-summer–early autumn. Requires hard pruning. Hardy to −15°C.

**C. viticella 'Margot Koster"** A vigorous plant with flowers up to 10 cm wide, borne in late summer. Requires hard pruning. Hardy to −15°C.

**C. viticella 'Minuet'** A vigorous variety which will grow up to 8 m high; flowers up to 5 cm in mid–late summer. Requires hard pruning. Hardy to −15°C.

**C. × triternata** DC. **'Rubra-Marginata'** *C. × triternata* is a cross between *C. flammula* and *C. viticella*, and 'Rubra-Marginata' is a cultivar (sometimes, incidentally, listed under *C. flammula*) which has been known since 1880. It is vigorous (up to 4 m high), free-flowering, requires hard pruning. Hardy to −20°C.

**C. 'Kermesina'** (Syn. *C. viticella* 'Rubra') A vigorous viticella hybrid raised by Lémoine; very vigorous to 6 m, and free-flowering in mid–late summer. Prune hard. Hardy to −20°C.

**C. 'Violuceau'** (syn. *C.* 'Voluceau') A hybrid raised by Girault with flowers up to 10 cm wide, in mid–late summer. Requires hard pruning. Hardy to −20°C.

**C. 'Huldine'** A vigorous (up to 6 m high) but rather temperamental hybrid, which thrives in full sun. Flowers, up to 10 cm across, are freely

*Clematis rehderiana*

produced in mid-summer–autumn, but sometimes the plant will produce a lot of growth but no blooms at all; the reason for this is not known. Hard pruning is recommended. Hardy to −20°C.

**C. 'Rouge Cardinal'** A fairly vigorous hybrid, growing up to 3.6 m high, flowering in mid-summer and again in very early autumn. The flowers have a reddish tinge at first but become purple later. Prune hard. Hardy to −20°C.

**C. rehderiana** Craib (*Ranunculaceae*) Native of W. Sichuan, near Kangding in mountain scrub at 2300–3300 m, flowering in June–September. Deciduous climber to 8 m. Leaves pinnate, with 7–9 leaflets. Flowers pale yellow, scented, to 1.5 cm long. Fruits with long, silky styles. Any soil, full sun. Hardy to −15°C.

# LAVENDERS

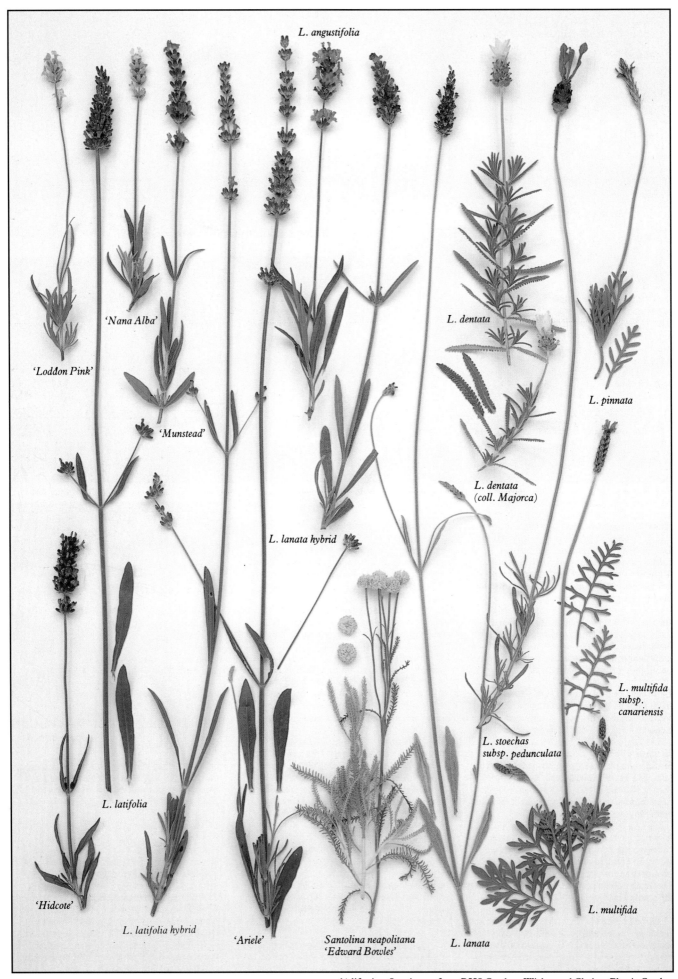

*L. angustifolia*

'Loddon Pink'

'Nana Alba'

'Munstead'

*L. dentata*

*L. pinnata*

*L. dentata (coll. Majorca)*

*L. lanata hybrid*

*L. multifida subsp. canariensis*

*L. stoechas subsp. pedunculata*

*L. latifolia*

'Hidcote'

*L. latifolia hybrid*

'Ariele'

*Santolina neapolitana 'Edward Bowles'*

*L. lanata*

*L. multifida*

½ life size. Specimens from RHS Garden, Wisley and Chelsea Physic Garden

202

**Lavandula angustifolia** Miller (*Labiatae*)
Lavender   Native of the Mediterranean region
from Yugoslavia west to Spain and N. Africa, on
dry hills, flowering in May–June. Much
branched evergreen shrub to 1 m. Flower spike
2–8 cm long, with lowest bracts 3–9 mm, broadly
obovate, acuminate. Flowers 10–12 mm long.
Well-drained soil; full sun. Hardy to −15°C.
Summer.
*L.* 'Loddon Pink'   Early-flowering; height 60–
75 cm.
*L.* 'Nana Alba'   Early-flowering; height to
30 cm.
*L.* 'Hidcote'   Early-flowering; height 60–
80 cm; flowers deep violet. Popular and common
in cultivation.
*L.* 'Munstead'   Early-flowering; height 60–
75 cm. Flowers bluish-violet.
*L.* 'Ariele'   Late-flowering; height to 1.2 m;
leaves broad; spike often branched. Probably a
hybrid between *L. angustifolia* and *L. latifolia*,
similar to 'Vera'.

**L. latifolia** Medicus   Native of the
Mediterranean region from Spain and N. Africa
to Yugoslavia, on dry, usually limestone hills,
flowering in May–June. Differs from *L.
angustifolia* in having greyer, hairier leaves,
linear-lanceolate bracts and flowers, 8–10 mm
long.

**L. lanata** Boiss.   Native of S. Spain, on rocky
limestone mountains at up to 1800 m, flowering
in May–June. Low, very white, woolly subshrub
to 50 cm. Leaves 35–50 mm long. Flowers
8–10 mm, in a long spike to 10 cm. Hardy to
−15°C. Summer.

**L. dentata** L.   Native of the Balearic Is., S. and
E. Spain, on dry hills, flowering in March–May.
Evergreen greyish shrub to 1 m, rather floppy in
cultivation. Leaves 15–35 mm, toothed or lobed.
Spike 2.5–5 cm. Flowers 8 mm long, purple,
rarely whitish. Full sun. Hardy to −10°C.

**L. stoechas** L. subsp. *stoechas*   French
Lavender   Native all round the Mediterranean,
in open pine woods, in scrub and on dry hills on
limestone and granite at up to 700 m, flowering
in March–June. Evergreen shrub to 50 cm.
Flowers small, very dark mauve, on a short-
stalked spike. Full sun; hardy to −10°C.
Subsp. *pedunculata* (Mill.) Samp. ex Roseira
Native of C. Spain and Portugal, in the
mountains. Flower spike long-stalked. Subsp.
*cariensis* from Turkey is similar.

**L. multifida** L.   Native of Italy, Sicily, N.
Africa, Spain and Portugal, on dry sandy and
rocky hills, flowering from March onwards.
Evergreen rounded shrub to 1 m; flowers
12 mm, deep purplish, in a slender spike 2–7 cm
long. Hardy to −10°C, perhaps.
Subsp. *canariensis* from the Canary Is., the
leaves are less lobed. Hardy to −5°C.

**L. pinnata** L.   Native of the Canary Is., on dry
hills. Leaves once pinnate. Hardy to −5°C.

**Santolina neapolitana** Jord. 'Edward Bowles'
(*Compositae*) Lavender Cotton   Native of C.
Italy on dry rocky slopes near the sea, flowering
in May–June. Evergreen greyish shrub to 50 cm.
Leaves with lobes more than 2.5 mm. Peduncles
thickened at the top. Flowers yellow. Hardy to
−15°C.

**Santolina pinnata** Viv.   Native of N.W. Italy,
on grassy limestone slopes at *c.* 1000 m, flowering
in July. Evergreen shrub to 25 cm. Leaves with
lobes 2.5–7 mm long.

*Lavandula stoechas subsp. stoechas* in S. Spain

*Lavandula lanata*

*Lavandula multifida*

*Lavandula* 'Lodden Pink'

*Santolina pinnata*

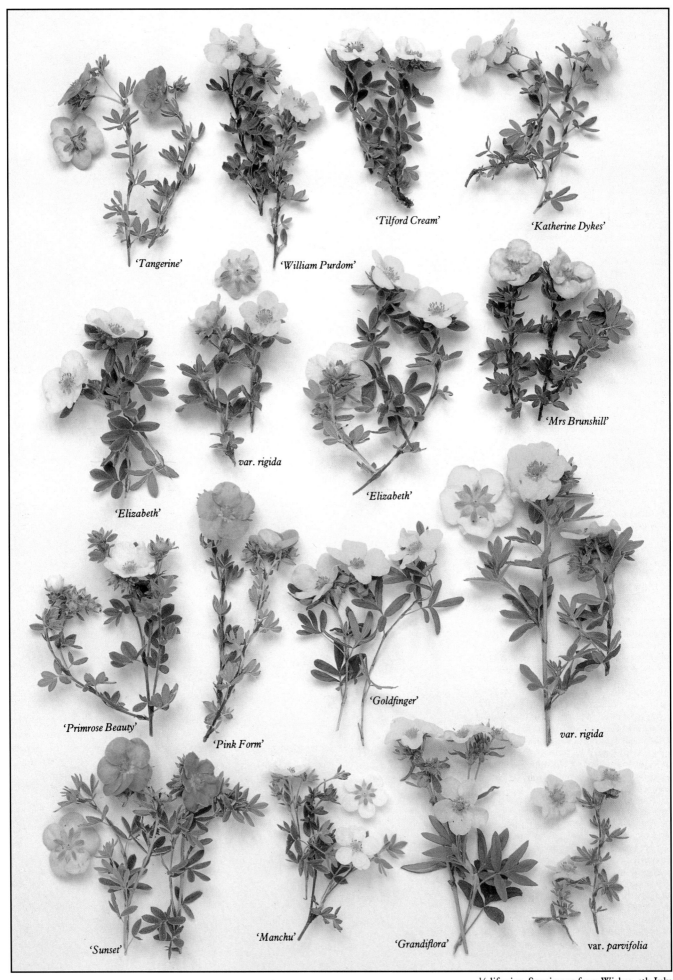

'Tilford Cream'

'Katherine Dykes'

'Tangerine'

'William Purdom'

'Elizabeth'

var. rigida

'Elizabeth'

'Mrs Brunshill'

'Primrose Beauty'

'Pink Form'

'Goldfinger'

var. rigida

'Sunset'

'Manchu'

'Grandiflora'

var. parvifolia

½ life size. Specimens from Wisley, 4th July

# POTENTILLAS

**Potentilla fruticosa** L. (*Rosaceae*)  Native of
the whole northern hemisphere; in Europe,
south to the Pyrénées, including England and
Ireland; in Turkey and Caucasus; in the
Himalayas from Pakistan west to Yunnan in
Japan; in N. America south to California and
New Mexico in the mountains, often in damp
places, flowering through mid-summer. Hardy
to −25°C, or lower, and prefers cool climates
and moist, well-drained soil.

**P. fruticosa** L. from Co. Clare  This is the
form native to Co. Clare, where it grows on
periodically flooded limestone pavement.

**P. fruticosa** var. **dahurica** Nestl. f. **rhodocalyx.**
A distinct form found by G. Forrest in Yunnan.

**P. fruticosa** var. **dahurica** 'Manchu'  A low-
growing dense shrub, up to about 1 m high.

**P. fruticosa** var. **rigida** (Wall. ex Lehm.) Wolf,
syn. *P. arbuscula* D. Don.)  Found commonly
in N. India, Nepal, Bhutan and W. China at
2700–4300 m.

**P. fruticosa** var. **parvifolia**  This variety, with
very small, silky hairy leaves, is typical of those
found in Nepal.

**P. 'Beesii'** (syn. *P. rigida* var. *albicans*, *P.*
'Nana Argentea')  A slow-growing dwarf to
60 cm, with exceptionally silvery leaves, raised
from seed collected by Kingdon Ward in S.
Xizang.

**P. 'Vilmoriniana'**  A vigorous shrub up to
about 1.8 m high, raised by Vilmorin from seeds
sent from Sichuan in 1905.

**P. 'Elizabeth'**  (syn. 'Sutter's Gold' in USA)
A dwarf, bushy shrub, up to about 1 m high,
raised at Hilliers Nurseries in about 1950. It is
probably a hybrid between var. *rigida* and
'Manchu'.

**P. fruticosa 'William Purdom'**  Collected in
Gansu in 1911.

**P. 'Pink Form'**  A pinkish-orange flowered
seedling.

**P. 'Tangerine'**  Raised at Slieve Donard
Nursery in *c.* 1955. Flowers 3 cm across.
Farrer, in 1920, collected seed of a 'red form' on
the border of Burma and Yunnan. This seed
produced 'Tangerine'. The red colour has
recently (*c.* 1975) reappeared in 'Red Ace'.
**P. 'Red Ace'**  A small weak bush to about
60 cm high, and rather wider; the flowers fade
in hot, dry weather.
**P. 'Tilford Cream'**  A hybrid, perhaps
between var. *dahurica* and a dwarf yellow
variety.
**P. 'Katherine Dykes'**  Found in Mr W. R.
Dykes's garden in about 1925.
**P. 'Mrs Brunshill'**  A variety of unknown
origin, with pale orange flowers, close to var.
*rigida*.
**P. 'Primrose Beauty'**  A dense, spreading
hybrid up to about 1 m high, raised in Holland.
**P. 'Grandiflora'**  (syn. 'Jackman's variety') A
vigorous shrub with flowers up to 5 cm across.
**P. 'Goldfinger'**  A form raised by Knol of
Holland.
**P. 'Sunset'**  A sport of 'Tangerine' (see above).
**P. 'Princess'**  A good pink clone.
**P. 'Abbotswood'**  A dwarf (up to 60 cm high
and 90 cm wide) shrub of spreading habit.

Potentilla fruticosa from Co. Clare, Ireland

Potentilla 'Beesii'

Potentilla 'Princess'

Potentilla 'Abbotswood'

P. fruticosa var. dahurica f. rhodocalyx

Potentilla 'Vilmoriniana'

Potentilla 'Red Ace'

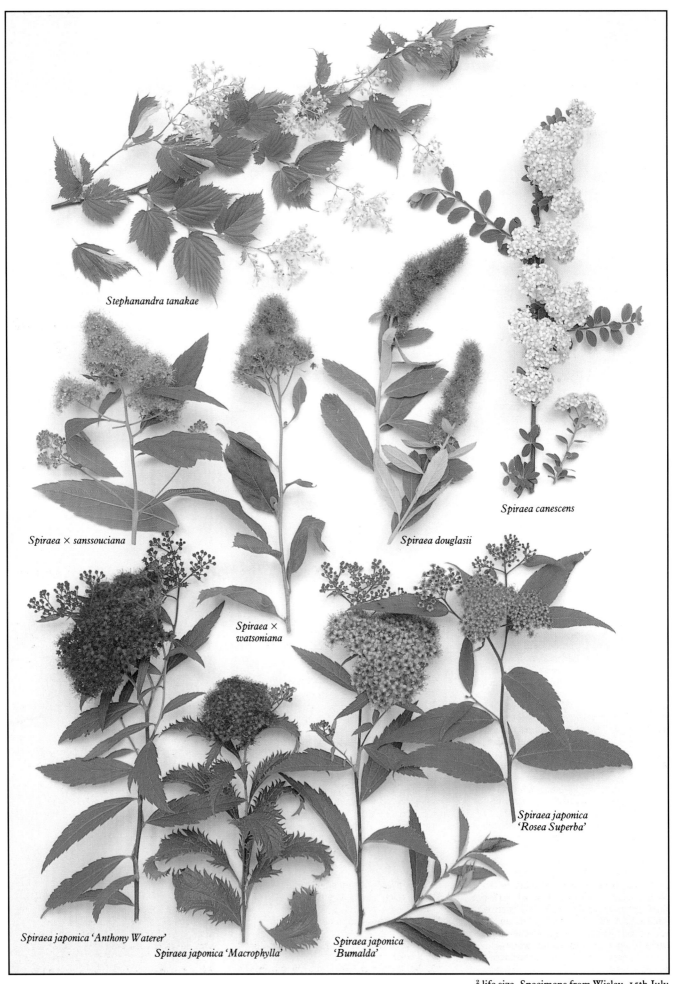

*Stephanandra tanakae*

*Spiraea canescens*

*Spiraea × sanssouciana*

*Spiraea douglasii*

*Spiraea ×
watsoniana*

*Spiraea japonica
'Rosea Superba'*

*Spiraea japonica 'Anthony Waterer'*

*Spiraea japonica 'Macrophylla'*

*Spiraea japonica
'Bumalda'*

$\frac{2}{3}$ life size. Specimens from Wisley, 15th July

Sorbaria arborea in Cambridge

Spiraea salicifolia

Spiraea japonica 'Little Princess'

Nevieusia alabamensis

Physocarpus monogynus

**Stephanandra tanakae** Fr. & Sav. (*Rosaceae*) Native of central Honshu, in scrub in the mountains, flowering in May and June. Elegant, graceful deciduous shrub to 2 m. Flowers with 15–20 stamens (10 in *S. incisa*). Autumn colour, scarlet to yellow. Hardy to −20°C.

**Spiraea × sanssouciana** K. Koch   A hybrid between *S. douglasii* and *S. japonica* known since 1857. Deciduous shrub to 1.5 m; flowers pale pink, on an inflorescence intermediate between those of the parents, in July and August.

**Spiraea × watsoniana** Zab.   A hybrid between *S. douglasii* and *S. densiflora*, another W. North American species with flat corymbs, known since 1890 in cultivation, but found wild in Oregon. Deciduous shrub to 1.2 m. Hardy to −25°C.

**Spiraea douglasii** Hook. (*Rosaceae*)   Native of N. California and British Columbia, in Redwood and coniferous forest below 1800 m, forming thickets in damp places, flowering from June to September. Naturalized also in Scotland and elsewhere in N. Europe. Deciduous suckering shrub to 2 m. Leaves white – tomentose beneath. Flowers *c*.4 mm across. Hardy to −25°C.

**S. salicifolia** L. is similar, but has leaves glabrous beneath. It is found from Austria and Poland, east to Japan and is often naturalized elsewhere.

**Spiraea canescens** D. Don   Native of the Himalayas from Pakistan east to Yunnan and S.W. Sichuan, in scrub and hedges at 1500–3000 m, flowering in May and June. Deciduous shrub to 5 m, but usually 2 m, with arching branches. Leaves 1–2 cm, greyish beneath. Flowers 4–6 mm across. Hardy to −25°C. Summer.

**Spiraea japonica** L. fil.   Native of Japan where it is common in the mountains, flowering from May to August, with varieties in China, west to Yunnan. Deciduous, upright shrub to 1.5 m. (Var. *fortunei* from China, is up to 2 m, with larger, compound flat corymbs.) Any good soil; sun or part shade. Hardy to −20°C. Summer.
**'Macrophylla'**   A mutant with characteristic leaves, which appeared in the nursery of Messrs Simon-Louis before 1866.
**'Rosea Superba'**   A pale pink form of unknown origin.
**'Little Princess'**   A cultivar of a dwarf form of *S. japonica*, to 1 m tall.
**'Anthony Waterer'**   This cultivar arose as a

sport on *S. japonica* 'Bumalda', which generally had white-edged or variegated leaves. 'Anthony Waterer' also often has variegated leaves, or often pink or white shoots, but has flowers of a better colour than the original 'Bumalda'.

**Nevieusia alabamensis** Gray (*Rosaceae*) Native of Alabama, growing on cliffs, notably above the Black Warrior River, near Tuscaloosa. Deciduous shrub to 2 m. Flowers without petals, but with 5 petaloid sepals, and long stamens, about 2.5 cm across. Fruit fleshy. Any soil; full sun. Hardy to −20°C. Summer.

**Physocarpus monogynus** (Torr.) Coult. (*Rosaceae*)   Native of South Dakota and Wyoming south to Texas and New Mexico, in open pine forest and rocky, sunny places at 1200–3200 m, flowering in May–July. Deciduous shrub to 2 m, usually less in the wild, with arching branches. Fruit with 2 inflated follicles. Hardy to −25°C.

**Sorbaria arborea** C. K. Schneid. (*Rosaceae*) Native of W. Hubei, and W. Sichuan, in scrub and forest at 1500–3100 m, flowering in July and August. Deciduous shrub to 6 m; leaves often pubescent beneath, with stellate hairs. Inflorescence with spreading branches (upright in *S. sorbifolia*). Hardy to −20°C. Summer.

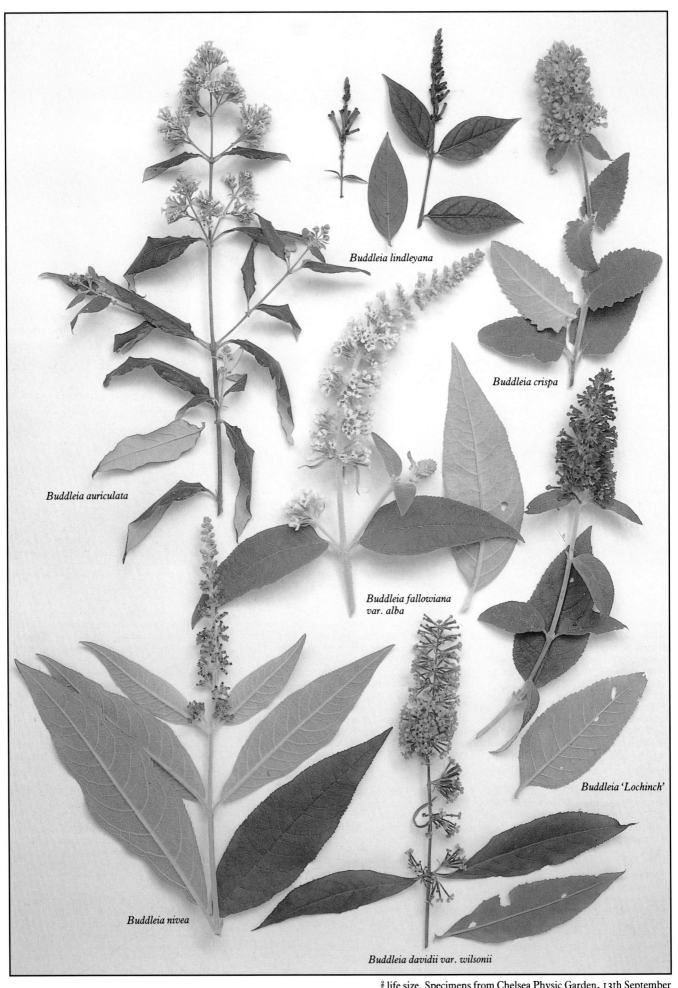

*Buddleia lindleyana*

*Buddleia crispa*

*Buddleia auriculata*

*Buddleia fallowiana var. alba*

*Buddleia 'Lochinch'*

*Buddleia nivea*

*Buddleia davidii var. wilsonii*

$\frac{2}{9}$ life size. Specimens from Chelsea Physic Garden, 13th September

*Buddleia globosa*

*Buddleia alternifolia* at Wisley

**Buddleia auriculata** Benth. (*Buddleiaceae*)
Native of South Africa, where it is widespread
from the Cape north and eastwards, among
rocks by streams and rivers, flowering in June–
August. Evergreen shrub to 6 m with support.
Leaves thin, to 10 cm long. Flowers 6–8 mm
long, sweetly scented. Hardy to −10°C.
Autumn and winter flowering. Grown primarily
for its sweet scent in winter.

**B. lindleyana** Fortune   Native of E. China
west to W. Sichuan, on river banks, roadsides
and in scrub at up to 1300 m, flowering in June–
July. Naturalized in S.E. North America.
Deciduous shrub to 2 m. Flowers in a long
spike, to 20 cm long, opening rather few at a
time; each 1.5 cm long, with a curved tube. Any
soil; full sun. Hardy to −15°C. Late summer.

**B. crispa** Benth.   Native of the Himalayas
from Afghanistan to Yunnan, at 1200–4000 m,
in scrub and open hillsides, flowering in April–
June, often before the leaves expand.
Deciduous shrub to 4 m or more. Flowers
fragrant, each *c*.8 mm long. Any well-drained
soil; full sun, in cool climates on a wall. Hardy
to −10°C. Flowers in spring if not pruned;
summer to autumn if pruned in spring. *B.
farreri* Balf. fil. & W. W. Sm. from Gansu and
*B. tibetica* W. W. Sm. are similar.

**B. fallowiana** Balf. fil & W. W. Sm. var. **alba**
Sabourin   Native of Yunnan in dry rocky
places, among scrub at 2400–3300 m, flowering
in August. Deciduous shrub to 3 m, but
reaching 1.5 m in one season from the ground.
Flowers lavender or white, each 1 cm long, the
stamens attached and near the middle of the
tube. Any soil; full sun. Hardy to −10°C. Late
summer.

**B. 'Lochinch'**   A hybrid between *B.
fallowiana* and, perhaps, *B. davidii*, raised at
Lochinch, Wigtown, S. W. Scotland and
introduced in 1959. Hairier than *B. davidii*,
with mauve-blue flowers; hardier than *B.
fallowiana*, to −15°C.

**B. nivea** Duthie   Native of W. Sichuan and
Yunnan in scrub at 1300–3600 m, flowering in
July–August. Deciduous shrub to 3 m. Underside
of leaves and stems white woolly. Leaves ovate-
lanceolate, 10–25 cm long. Flowers in a narrow
spike or panicle, to 15 cm long, each 6 mm long,
with stamens inserted just below the mouth. Var.
*yunnanensis* (Dop) Rehd. & Wils. has yellower,
thinner indumentum, and larger flowers, to
5 mm across the lobes. Hardy to −15°C.

**B. davidii** var. **wilsonii** Rehd. & Wils.   Native
of W. Hubei, at 1600–2000 m, flowering in
August. Distinguished from var. *davidii*
(p. 210), by its lax-flowered, delicate panicles,
narrow leaves, and large individual flowers with
reflexed margins to the lobes. Hardy to −15°C.

**B. globosa** Hope   Native of Chile, Argentina
and Peru, at up to 2000 m, and commonly
cultivated for medicine. Evergreen shrub to 5 m.
Leaves brownish woolly beneath. Flowers in
balls *c*.2 cm across, scented. Full sun. Hardy to
−15°C with shelter from cold dry wind, but good
near the sea. Early summer.

**B. alternifolia** Maxim.   Native of S. E. Gansu,
on dry slopes, and in hedges, flowering in May–
June. Deciduous shrub or small tree to 6 m, with
drooping branches and above also in 'Argentea'.
Flowers in tight clusters *c*.2.5 cm across, each
8 mm long, all along the previous year's shoots.
Any soil; good on chalk. Hardy to −20°C. Early
summer. Prune only *after* flowering, not in
spring like other Buddleias.

**B. officinalis** Maxim.   Native of W. Hubei,
Sichuan and Yunnan, in scrub and on cliffs and
rocky places at up to 1000 m, flowering in
February–March. Evergreen shrub to 2.5 m.
Leaves lanceolate, softly hairy, grey beneath to
15 cm long. Flowers in terminal panicles of
rounded clusters, scented, 8 cm long. Any soil;
full sun. Hardy to −10°C. Early spring. A very
pretty winter-flowering shrub for the
conservatory, flowering when a small plant in a
pot, but surviving outdoors in only the mildest
climates.

*Buddleia officinalis*

*Buddleia alata*

**B. alata** Rehd. & Wils.   Native of W. Sichuan,
in rocky valleys at *c*.1300 m, flowering in
August. Deciduous shrub to 2 m, with 4-angled
and winged stems. Leaves lanceolate, acuminate
14–28 cm long, greyish woolly beneath. Flowers
in a narrow panicle 10–20 cm long, each 5 mm
long, hairy outside. Hardy to −10°C.

'Variegata'

'Royal Red'

'Nanho Blue'

'Fortune'

'Black Knight'

Buddleia davidii

'Golden Glow'

'White Cloud'

'White Bouquet'

⅓ life size. Specimens from Kew, 12th September

**Buddleia davidii** Franchet (*Buddleiaceae*)
Native of E. and W. Sichuan and W. Hubei,
growing on shingle by rivers and streams, on
roadside cliffs, and in scrub, at 1300–2600 m,
flowering in June–August. Deciduous shrub to
2.5 m or more. Leaves lanceolate, opposite.
Flowers rose-purple to violet-purple or white,
fragrant. Variable in the wild. Commonly
cultivated and naturalized in W. Europe where
it colonizes chalk cliffs, and old bomb sites in
cities, in E. North America north to Maryland,
and in California. Many cultivars are named; all
do best in well-drained, chalky or limestone
soil, in full sun, pruned hard in spring,
flowering best on strong new shoots. The
fragrant flowers, especially the white ones,
attract butterflies, and are at their best in late
summer. Hardy to −15°C, but flowering in one
season if cut to the ground by frost.

**B. davidii** Franch. var. **nanhoensis**
(Chittenden) Rehd. **'Nanho Blue'**   Native of
Gansu. Smaller, to 1.5 m and more elegant than
var. *davidii*, with smaller leaves and shorter
spikes of flowers. Two clones are common:
'Nanho Purple' and 'Nanho Blue', and a rare
white-flowered form is also grown.

**B. davidii 'Black Knight'**   One of the best *B.
davidii* cultivars raised by Ruys in 1959.

**B. davidii** Fortune   A shrub up to 2 m high,
with a rather 'open' habit, introduced in 1936
by Schmidt. Panicles up to 40 cm long.

**B. davidii 'Royal Red'**   A popular cultivar
raised by Good and Reese and introduced in
1941. There are two variegated forms of this
cultivar: **'Variegata'** (illustrated) and
'Harlequin', a lower-growing sport.

**B. davidii 'White Cloud'**   A cultivar which will
grow up to 3 m high, and produces small, but
dense, panicles of flowers.

**B. davidii 'White Bouquet'**   A rare, rather
low-growing cultivar, raised by Tarnok in
1942.

**B. davidii 'Ile de France'**   A vigorous variety,
up to 3 m high, raised by Nonin in 1930.

**B. 'Dartmoor'**   A robust hybrid probably
between *B. davidii* and var. *nanhoensis*, with
branching spikes of purple flowers, and long
narrow leaves. Known since 1971.

**B. forrestii** Diels   Native of N.W. Yunnan
above Dali in scrub and on dry cliffs at 2000–
3000 m, flowering in June and July. Deciduous
shrub to 3 m, though usually *c*.2 m in
cultivation. Leaves 20–30 cm long. Flowers
8–10 mm long, with a wide tube 3.5 mm across,
in lax spikes, opening pale purple, fading yellow
and brownish. Well-drained soil; full sun and
warm position. Hardy to −10°C. Late summer.

**B. japonica** Hemsl.   Native of Honshu and
Shikoku, on sunny hills and scrub in the
mountains, flowering in July–October. Flowers
15–20 mm long, slightly curved, pale purple
with brown hairs on the outside. Well-drained
soil; full sun. Hardy to −20°C.

**B. × weyeriana 'Golden Glow'**   A hybrid
between *B. globosa* (p. 209) and *B. davidii* var.
*magnifica* raised by Mr Van de Weyer in Dorset
in 1914. Semi-evergreen shrub to 3 m high;
flowers in various shades of cream or yellow to
orange, often shaded with purple. Five other
named clones are in cultivation.

Buddleia 'Dartmoor'

Buddleia forrestii

Buddleia 'Dartmoor'

Buddleia 'Ile de France'

Buddleia japonica

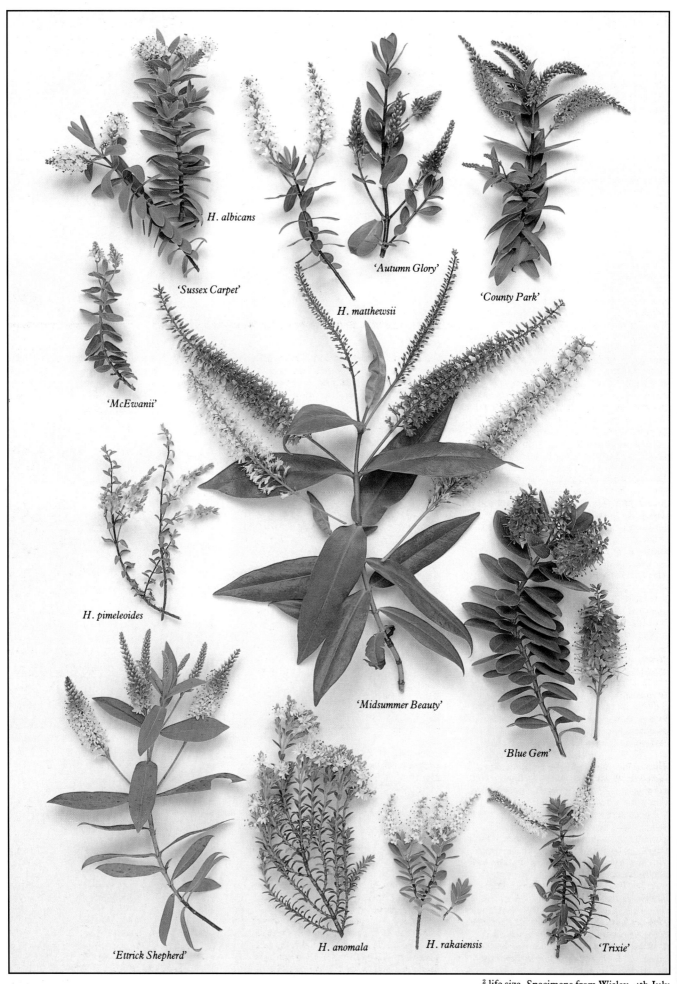

*H. albicans*

'Sussex Carpet'

'Autumn Glory'

*H. matthewsii*

'County Park'

'McEwanii'

*H. pimeleoides*

'Midsummer Beauty'

'Blue Gem'

'Ettrick Shepherd'

*H. anomala*

*H. rakaiensis*

'Trixie'

⅗ life size. Specimens from Wisley, 4th July

*Richea scoparia* at the Royal Botanic Gardens, Edinburgh

*Hebe cupressoides*

**Hebe albicans** (Petrie) Ckn. (*Scrophulariaceae*) Native of the mountains in the north of South Island, New Zealand. An evergreen bush 30–60 cm high, 1 m wide, with white flowers in racemes *c*.6 cm long. Hardy to −15°C. **'Sussex Carpet'** is a form with prostrate stems forming mats 15–30 cm high and 1 m or more wide, with very grey, stalkless leaves, named in around 1985.

**Hebe matthewsii** (Cheesem.) Ckn.    Native of the mountains of South Island, New Zealand. An evergreen shrub to 1.2 m high, with small dark green leaves and unusually long racemes (to 10 cm) of white or pale mauve flowers in summer. The oval seed capsule is slightly hairy. Hardy to −10°C.

**Hebe 'Autumn Glory'**    Raised in Northern Ireland about 1900 and believed to be *H.* × *franciscana* × *H. pimeleoides*, it is a small, rather open bush about 60 cm tall and wide, with broad, glossy purplish-green leaves and deep purple flowers in late summer. Hardy to −10°C.

**Hebe 'County Park'**    A hardy, low-growing and fairly compact plant forming a mat about 20 cm high and 45–60 cm wide. It was raised from a good form of *H. pimeleoides*, from which it differs mainly in being more compact. The greyish leaves have red edges and in early summer spikes of violet flowers appear. Introduced in 1974. Hardy to −15°C.

**Hebe 'McEwanii'**    A low-growing, grey-leaved shrub which is probably a hybrid of *H. pimeleoides*, known since 1941. The specimen illustrated is poor – usually the inflorescence is 3-branched. Hardy to −10°C.

**Hebe 'Midsummer Beauty'**    A handsome large bush up to 2 m tall and wide, raised sometime before 1950. Light violet flowers are produced for several months from early summer. It is one of the most hardy of the large-leaved hebes. Hardy to −10°C.

**Hebe anomala** (J. F. Armstr.) Ckn.    A curious plant sometimes considered to be a natural hybrid, originally introduced from Rakaia, South Island, New Zealand. A compact bush up to 1 m. Hardy to −15°C.

**Hebe pimeleoides** (Hook. fil.) Ckn. & Allan. Native to mountain areas in S. South Island, New Zealand. The combination of dark stems, small glaucous leaves, often red-edged, and light violet flowers is fairly constant and distinctive, but plants vary greatly in habit and leaf size (see also *H*. 'County Park'). Hardy to −15°C.

**Hebe × franciscana** (Eastwood) Souster **'Blue Gem'** see p. 19.

**Hebe rakaiensis** (J. F. Armstr.) Ckn.    Native to rocky places at low altitudes in South Island, New Zealand. A low, dome-shaped bush with rather pale green foliage, eventually 60–100 cm high and 1–1.5 m wide (sometimes taller in the wild). Hardy to −15°C.

**Hebe 'Trixie'**    A seedling from *Hebe albicans* introduced in 1970, 'Trixie' differs from its parent in having narrower, more pointed, and green rather than glaucous leaves. Hardy to −10°C.

**Hebe 'Ettrick Shepherd'**    Of uncertain origin, known since 1953. The flowers open purple or magenta but fade quickly to white, to produce a bicoloured raceme. Hardy to −10°C.

**Hebe cupressoides** (Hook. fil.) Ckn. & Allan Native to river valleys up to 1500 m in South Island, New Zealand, this is the most conifer-like of the whipcords and its foliage even has a resinous scent, noticeable in hot weather. It forms a bush about 2 m high and 1.5 m in width. Hardy to −15°C. The cultivar 'Boughton Dome' is only 30–45 cm tall.

**Hebe macrantha** (Hook. fil.) Ckn. & Allan Native to mountain areas in the northern part of South Island, New Zealand, easily recognized by its large, pure white flowers, produced 2–6 in a raceme in summer. Hardy to −5°C.

**Richea scoparia** Hook. fil. (*Epacridaceae*) Native to Tasmania, in mountains to over 4000 m. The dense spikes of flowers are produced in summer on evergreen bushes about 1 m in height but in the wild it may exceed 2 m. The flower colour is variable and in the wild plants with red, pink or white flowes may be found. Moist acid soil. Hardy to −15°C.

*Hebe 'Ettrick Shepherd'*

*Hebe macrantha*

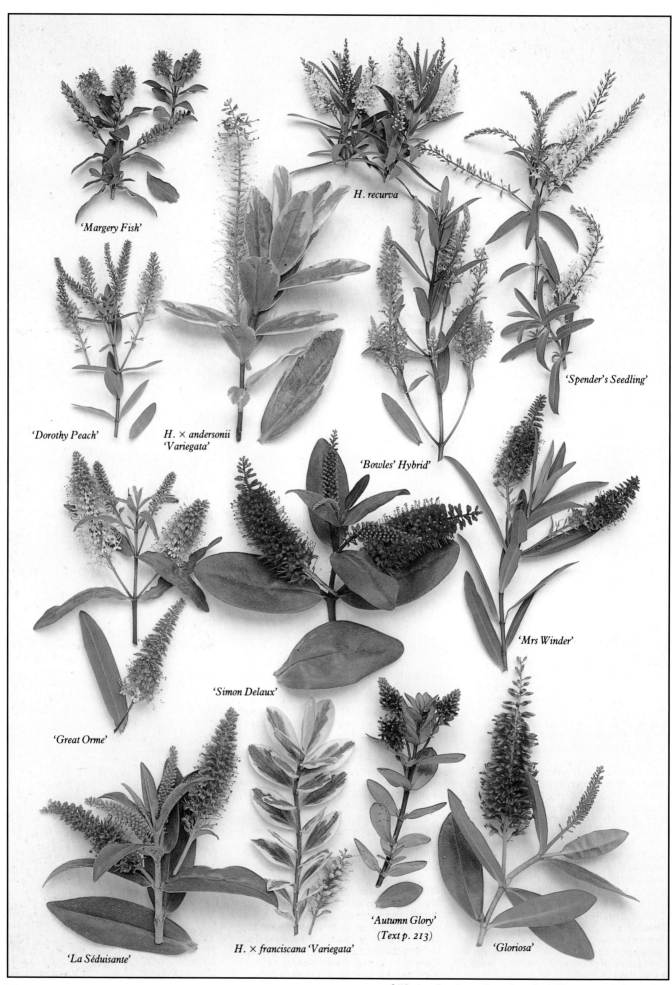

'Margery Fish'

*H. recurva*

'Spender's Seedling'

'Dorothy Peach'

*H. × andersonii*
*'Variegata'*

'Bowles' Hybrid'

'Mrs Winder'

'Great Orme'

'Simon Delaux'

'La Séduisante'

*H. × franciscana 'Variegata'*

'Autumn Glory'
(Text p. 213)

'Gloriosa'

$\frac{2}{3}$ life size. Specimens from Goatcher's Nursery, 11th September

**Hebe 'Margery Fish'** (syn. 'Primley Gem') (*Scrophulariaceae*)  Originated at Paignton Zoo in Devon before 1966, but was distributed by the late Margery Fish from her garden at Lambrook Manor, Somerset. A low bush about 60 cm high and up to 1 m in width. The flowers are violet-blue with white tubes, borne in racemes 5–8 cm long. Hardy to −10°C.

**Hebe recurva** Simpson & Thomson  A variable species native to rocky places in the north of South Island, New Zealand. The most common clone in gardens is 'Aoira', with strikingly glaucous and rather recurved leaves. Racemes of pink-budded, white flowers appear in the summer. Hardy to −5°C. or −10°C.

**Hebe 'Dorothy Peach'**  This plant appears to be identical to one previously known as 'Watson's Pink'. It may be a seedling from 'Great Orme' which is similar but altogether larger. The flowers of 'Dorothy Peach' are smaller, with infertile stamens. Hardy to −5°C.

**Hebe × andersonii** (Lindl. & Paxt.) Ckn. **'Variegata'**  The name *H. × andersonii* is used for hybrids between *H. speciosa* and *H. salicifolia*. 'Variegata' is the commonest variegated cultivar of this hybrid, and is a plant for coastal gardens; it is fairly tender, but in good conditions can grow to about 2 m in height and spread. Hardy to −5°C.

**Hebe 'Bowles' Hybrid'**  This attractive plant is one of a group of confusingly similar cultivars. It has rather pale leaves and light violet flowers in lax racemes in summer, and often again in autumn. Hardy to −10°C.

**Hebe 'Spender's Seedling'**  Two somewhat similar plants are found in gardens under this name but it seems that the one illustrated is the original one. The other differs in its narrower, more obtusely tipped leaves and tightly cylindrical leaf buds. The flowers of 'Spender's Seedling' are male-sterile, while the narrower-leaved plant, probably the cultivar 'C. P. Raffill', has fertile stamens. Hardy to −10°C.

**Hebe 'Great Orme'**  Flowers larger than those of 'Dorothy Peach', with fertile stamens, and of clear pink, an unusual colour in the smaller hebes. Hardy to −5°C.

**Hebe 'Simon Delaux'**  This is an old hybrid, derived *H. speciosa*.

**Hebe 'Mrs Winder'** (syns. 'Warley', 'Warleyensis')  Several different names are applied rather freely to numerous similar hybrids. Most are fairly hardy bushes about 60–80 cm high and spreading in habit. They have narrow, often purplish leaves and loose racemes of blue-violet flowers borne in the summer and autumn. Hardy to −10°C or lower.

**Hebe 'La Seduisante'**  Many hybrids were raised from *H. speciosa* in the 19th C. in France, and their showy flowers have ensured that several are still in cultivation. 'La Seduisante' has reddish-purple flowers and the young leaves are often reddish. Hardy to −5°C.

**Hebe × franciscana** (Eastwood) Souster **'Variegata'**  A good cultivar of this hybrid between *H. elliptica* and *H. speciosa*. It probably originated as a sport on a plant of 'Blue Gem'. 'Variegata' is a more compact plant and is slightly more tender. Hardy to −10°C.

*Hebe 'Great Orme'*

*Hebe carnulosa*

**Hebe 'Gloriosa'** (syn. 'Pink Pearl')  There is some doubt as to the correct name for the plant depicted. It has the typical large leaves and fine racemes of hybrids derived from *H. speciosa*. Hardy to −5°C.

**Hebe carnosula** (Hook. fil.) Ckn.  A somewhat 'doubtful' species, perhaps a natural hybrid, originally collected in the mountains in the north of South Island, New Zealand. It is allied to *H. pinguifolia*, which differs in having hairy seed capsules and smaller, less clearly stalked leaves. Hardy to −15°C.

**Hebe ochracea** M. B. Ashwin  A whipcord hebe, native to mountains in the northern part of South Island, New Zealand. In the past it has been much confused with *H. armstrongii*, and it is still often grown under this name. It differs however in the strikingly ochre-coloured foliage and more blunt leaves. It normally grows to about 60 cm tall, and rather more in spread, but 'James Stirling' is a more compact cultivar introduced about 1975. Hardy to −15°C.

*Hebe ochracea*

*Embothrium coccineum*, narrow-leaved form

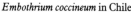

*Embothrium coccineum* in Chile

*Embothrium coccineum* at Logan

**Embothrium coccineum** Forst. (*Proteaceae*)
A very variable evergreen shrub or tree, native to Chile and southwest Argentina, where it grows in open woodland at low altitudes. In cultivation it forms a small tree up to 10 m, or occasionally more in the most sheltered sites. Scarlet flowers appear in spring and early summer. The leaf shape is particularly variable, from narrowly lanceolate to broadly oblong. In the wild, yellow-flowered forms occur occasionally. Introduced in 1846 and hardy in sheltered places, it grows well in light woodland. The narrow-leaved forms are the hardiest. Hardy to −10°C or −15°C with shelter.

**Philesia magellanica** Gmel. (syn. *P. buxifolia* Lam.) (*Philesiaceae*)   Native to southern Chile, growing in rain forests at low altitudes as a suckering shrub, or climbing tree trunks by means of adventitious roots. In cultivation it generally makes a dwarf, evergreen shrub less than 1 m high, but wide-spreading. Fleshy crimson flowers are borne in late summer, but a form with rose-coloured flowers is occasionally seen. Introduced in 1847 by William Lobb, it is best suited to conditions in gardens on the Atlantic or Pacific seaboard. Elsewhere it requires a humus-rich, moist soil in a cool shady situation. Hardy to −15°C.

**Azara serrata** Ruiz & Pavon (*Flacourtiaceae*)
Another Chilean evergreen shrub, this species grows to 5−6 m, occasionally becoming tree-like. The flowers are borne in mid-summer in clearly stalked umbels or short racemes and are almost scentless. It is fairly hardy but flowers more freely when grown against a warm wall. Hardy to −10°C.

**Azara lanceolata** Hook. fil. (*Flacourtiaceae*)
Native of S. Chile and Argentina, in moist rain forest. An evergreen shrub or small tree to 6 m. Leaves to 6 cm long, lanceolate to narrowly oval, hanging from the arching branches. Flowers scented. Moist acid soil; part shade and shelter or wall protection. Hardy to −5°C. Late spring. See p. 263.

**Grevillea rosmarinifolia** A. Cunn. (*Proteaceae*)
Native to New South Wales in eastern Australia, this shrub can grow to 2 m in good conditions but in gardens is often less than 1 m. The evergreen, needle-like leaves are greyish beneath. It was introduced in the 1820s and is only reliably hardy in sheltered western gardens; elsewhere it requires protection, for example at the foot of a west facing wall. It does not do well on chalk but is best suited by a peaty, acid soil. Hardy to −10°C.

**Fabiana imbricata** Ruiz & Pavon (*Solanaceae*)
Native to the Andes from Bolivia to Chile and flowering in early summer. This evergreen shrub with heath-like foliage can grow to 2 m in height, but most forms in cultivation are more compact, seldom exceeding 60 cm. Forms with pale mauve flowers are sometimes distinguished as var. *violacea*; one such clone, 'Prostrata', makes a low spreading shrub. Hardy to −10°C.

**Berberidopsis corallina** Hook. fil. (*Flacourtiaceae*)   Native to moist forests in C. Chile but now rare or even extinct there. It is a vigorous lax shrub growing to 4−5 m when trained against a wall and flowering in late summer. Introduced in 1862, it has turned out to be rather tender but good specimens are sometimes seen in cool gardens on moist acid or neutral soils, usually grown against a shady wall. Hardy to −10°C.

**Crinodendron patagua** Molina (*Elaeocarpaceae*)
Native of Chile, this evergreen flowers in late summer. It grows into a large shrub or occasionally a small tree to 10 m in height. It was introduced by H. J. Elwes in 1901. It appears to be slightly more tolerant of dry conditions than *C. hookerianum*, and is possibly a little more hardy. It is vigorous and grows well at Kew and the Chelsea Physic Garden with the protection of a wall. Hardy to −10°C.

**Crinodendron hookerianum** Gay (syn. *Tricuspidaria lanceolata* Miq.) (*Elaeocarpaceae*)
An evergreen shrub or small tree native to C. Chile. Large shrub 3−4 m tall, but rarely 10 m. The flower buds appear in late autumn but do not open until the following spring. Introduced by William Lobb in 1848, it requires a cool, sheltered site and a lime-freesoil. Hardy to −10°C.

**Desfontainia spinosa** Ruiz & Pavon (*Potaliaceae*)   Native to much of the Andes of South America, south to the Straits of Magellan, growing in cool moist habitats in coastal areas in the south, and on low mountains in the north of its range. Flowering in late summer, it forms a spreading evergreen shrub, in suitable conditions 3−4 m tall. Introduced by Lobb in 1843 and requiring similar conditions to *Philesia*. 'Harold Comber' ('Comber's Form') has reddish-orange flowers. Hardy to −10°C.

# CHILEAN SHRUBS

*Azara serrata*

*Grevillea rosmarinifolia*

*Fabiana imbricata*

²⁄₃ life size. Specimens from Cannington, Somerset, 10th June

*Crinodendron patagua*

*Crinodendron hookerianum*

*Azara lanceolata*

*Berberidopsis corallina*

*Desfontainia spinosa* at Nymans, Sussex

*Philesia magellanica*

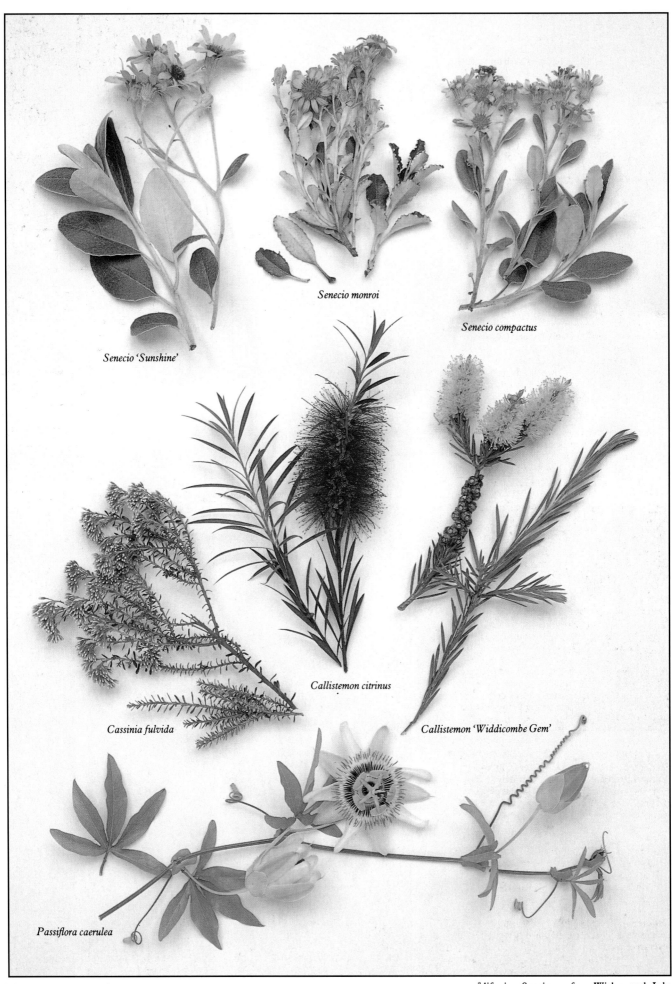

*Senecio monroi*

*Senecio compactus*

*Senecio 'Sunshine'*

*Callistemon citrinus*

*Cassinia fulvida*

*Callistemon 'Widdicombe Gem'*

*Passiflora caerulea*

⅔ life size. Specimens from Wisley, 15th July

**Senecio 'Sunshine'** (syn. *S. greyi* hort., *S. laxifolius* hort.) (*Compositae*)   A hybrid of garden origin and rather hardier than its parents *S. compactus* and *S. laxifolius*. In most areas it forms a somewhat lax evergreen bush up to 1 m, but it may reach 2 m. Hardy to −15°C.

**Senecio monroi** Hook. fil. (*Compositae*)   Native to the South Island of New Zealand where it grows in scrubland in low mountains up to about 1000 m. It makes a compact evergreen shrub up to about 1 m tall. Easily grown in a sunny position in mild areas. Hardy to −10°C.

**Senecio compactus** Kirk (*Compositae*) Confined in nature to a small area of coastal limestone cliffs in the North Island of New Zealand. It is a compact evergreen shrub up to 1 m in height. Only hardy to −5°C.

**Cassinia fulvida** Hook fil. (*Compositae*)   Native to lowland areas in much of New Zealand and flowering in mid-summer. It forms an erect evergreen bush to 2 m tall in the wild, but is usually less than 1 m in cultivation. The leaves have a honey-like scent. Hardy to −15°C.

**Callistemon citrinus** (Curt.) Skeels (*Myrtaceae*) Native to eastern Australia, occurring in damp situations, growing 1–3 m in height. The bright crimson 'bottle-brush' flower heads are produced in the summer. The leaves, lemon-scented when crushed, vary considerably in shape. Hardy to −10°C.

**Callistemon 'Widdicombe Gem'**   A garden selection, probably derived from *C. sieberi*, one of the hardier species, native to mountains in southeast Australia. In the wild, *C. sieberi* grows to 4 m in height, but is usually only 1–2 m in cultivation. 'Widdicombe Gem' has unusually deep yellow stamens. Hardy to −10°C.

**Passiflora caerulea** L. (*Passifloraceae*)   Native to southern Brazil, it is a vigorous evergreen climber, flowering from early summer often into early autumn. Requires the protection of a cool greenhouse or a warm wall. Hardy to −10°C.

**Euryops pectinatus** Cass. (*Compositae*)   Native to South Africa where it occurs in mountainous areas. It may survive outside in the mildest areas, given a sunny position in well-drained soil. Hardy to −5°C.

**Lippia citriodora** (Ortega) H.B.K. (syn. *Aloysia triphylla* (L'Herit.) Britt.) (*Verbenaceae*) Native to Chile, this is an erect bushy deciduous shrub 1.5–2 m in height. Spikes of tiny white or pale mauve flowers are produced in summer, but it is grown mainly for the powerfully scented ('lemon verbena') foliage. Hardy to −10°C.

**Drimys winteri** J. R. & G. Forster (*Winteraceae*) An evergreen shrub or small tree widely distributed in South America. Umbels of fragrant creamy-white flowers appear in spring. Hardy to about −10°C.

**Tepualia stipularis** (Hook. fil.) Griseb. (*Myrtaceae*)   Native to Chile and western Argentina, this shrub grows in open areas in *Nothofagus* forest often on the edge of moorland. It forms an erect shrub up to 3 m tall. Not in cultivation and hardiness unknown.

**Hibbertia scandens** (Willd.) Dryand. (*Dilleniaceae*)   A vigorous but very tender evergreen twining shrub native to eastern Australia, where it grows in forests at low altitudes. Summer-flowering. Hardy to −5°C.

*Euryops pectinatus*

*Drimys winteri* in Cornwall

*Lippia citriodora*

*Tepualia stipularis*

*Callistemon citrinus*

*Hibbertia scandens* in Palo Alto, California

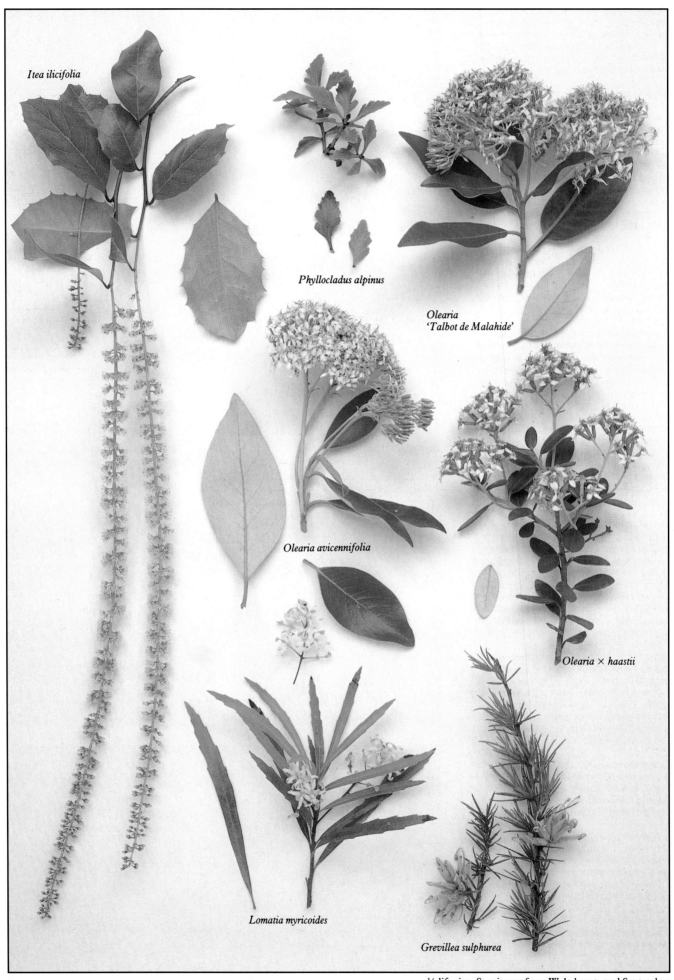

*Itea ilicifolia*

*Phyllocladus alpinus*

Olearia
'Talbot de Malahide'

*Olearia avicennifolia*

*Olearia × haastii*

*Lomatia myricoides*

*Grevillea sulphurea*

½ life size. Specimens from Wakehurst, 2nd September

**Itea ilicifolia** Oliver (*Iteaceae*)  An evergreen shrub, native to W. China and flowering in mid–late summer. In a sheltered position it may grow to 3 m, but in the wild it can exceed 5 m. The flowers have a honey-like scent. Requires the shelter of a wall in most gardens. Hardy to −15°C.

**Phyllocladus alpinus** L. C. & A. Rich. (*Podocarpaceae*)  Native to mountain forests in both the main islands of New Zealand, growing at up to 1600 m. Hardy to −10°C.

**Olearia 'Talbot de Malahide'** (syn. *O. albida* hort.) (*Compositae*)  A hybrid of *O. avicenniifolia*. It differs from that species in its flowers which have 3–6 ray florets. It forms an evergreen shrub up to 3 m tall. Hardy to −10°C.

**Olearia avicennifolia** (Raoul) Hook. fil. (*Compositae*)  An evergreen shrub or small tree native to subalpine scrub in South Island, New Zealand at up to 1000 m. Up to 6 m tall in the wild, in gardens it is more usually 2–3 m. Sweetly scented flowers are produced in early summer. Useful in seaside areas because of its tolerance of salt-laden winds. Hardy to −10°C.

**Olearia × haastii** Hook. fil. (*Compositae*)  A hybrid between *O. avicenniifolia* and *O. moschata*, occurring in the wild in New Zealand but common in gardens. It forms a compact bush 1–2 m tall. A good seaside hedging plant. Hardy to −15°C.

**Lomatia myricoides** (Gaertn.) Dorrien (*Proteaceae*)  An evergreen shrub native to S.E. Australia where it grows in thin forests and may form a small tree to 4 m tall. In cultivation it seldom exceeds 2 m. Hardy to −5°C.

**Grevillea sulphurea** A. Cunn. (*Proteaceae*)  Native to New South Wales in Australia where it grows in low mountains. Hardy to −5°C.

**Lomatia ferruginea** R. Br. (*Proteaceae*) Native to rain forests in Chile and growing there as a sparsely branched tree. Hardy to −10°C.

**Sollya heterophylla** Lindl. (syn. *S. fusiformis* (Labill.) Briq.) (*Pittosporaceae*)  An evergreen twining shrub native to western Australia. In cultivation it grows to 2 m and flowers in late summer. Hardy to −5°C.

**Abutilon × suntense** Brickell **'Jermyns'** (*Malvaceae*)  A hybrid between *A. ochsenii* and *A. vitifolium*, of which several clones are in cultivation. It is a vigorous deciduous shrub or small tree, growing to 5–6 m and producing abundant mauve flowers over a long period in the summer. It grows freely in a sunny position and a light soil. Hardy to −10°C.

**Abutilon ochsenii** (Phil.) Phil. (*Malvaceae*) Native of Chile. It is closely allied to *A. vitifolium* from which it differs mainly in its deeper violet flowers and less hairy leaves and shoots. Hardy to −10°C.

**Abutilon vitifolium** (Cav.) Presl. **'Veronica Tennant'** (*Malvaceae*)  A deciduous shrub native to Chile. It grows to 5 m or more in a sheltered site. It is less hardy than the other species of *Abutilon* shown here, but grows quickly to make a handsome large shrub in the mildest areas. Hardy to −5°C.

**Felicia petiolata** (Harv.) N.E. Br. (*Compositae*) An evergreen subshrub native to Lesotho and Cape province in South Africa, in rocky places, often trailing over cliffs. Hardy to −10°C.

*Felicia petiolata*

*Abutilon × suntense 'Jermyns'*

*Sollya heterophylla*

*Abutilon ochsenii*

*Abutilon 'Veronica Tennant'*

*Lomatia ferruginea* in Chile

'Apple Blossom'

'Donard Seedling'

'Slieve Donard'

'Crimson Spire'

'Donard Radiance'

'Donard Beauty'

'Langleyensis'

E. rubra

'William Watson'

E. rosea

E. × exoniensis

½ life size. Specimens from Goatcher's Nursery, 15th July

Escallonia tucumanensis

Escallonia 'Iveyi'

Escallonia virgata

**Escallonia 'Slieve Donard'** (*Escalloniaceae*)
This is one of a number of hybrids raised in the
Slieve Donard nursery at Newry, County
Down, Northern Ireland, by crossing and re-
crossing *E. rubra*, *E. rubra* var. *macrantha* and
*E. virgata*. A vigorous evergreen shrub up to
2 m tall, with somewhat arching branches and
flowers with outcurved petals. Hardy to −15°C.
**E. 'Donard Seedling'** A large evergreen shrub
of 2–3 m in height, this cultivar is hardier in
inland gardens than many hybrid escallonias.
The petals are rounded but with a narrow base
(the 'claw') and are somewhat outcurved
towards the tip. Hardy to −15°C.
**E. 'Apple Blossom'** A very popular cultivar
that forms a compact evergreen shrub growing
to about 1.5 m tall. The broad-clawed petals are
incurved to produce a flower shape often
likened to that of a chalice. Hardy to −15°C.
**'Donard Radiance'** is similar.
**E. 'Langleyensis'** One of the earliest hybrids
raised at Veitch's nursery at Langley,
Buckinghamshire, in 1893. It is a hybrid
between a form of *E. rubra* and *E. virgata* and is
a robust and free-flowering shrub 2–3 m tall,
flowering in mid-summer. Hardy to −10°C.
**E. 'Donard Beauty'** This is a small-leaved
plant of robust growth and rather arching habit.
It may grow to 2 m tall and flowers in early
summer. Hardy to −10°C.
**E. 'Crimson Spire'** A fast-growing shrub
growing to 2 m or more in height and much
used for seaside hedges. It arose as a chance
seedling in Treseder's nursery in Cornwall. The
petals have long narrow claws held close
together to give a tubular shape to the flowers.
Hardy to −10°C.
**E. 'William Watson'** A hybrid between *E.*

*rubra* and *E. virgata*, this forms a compact
evergreen shrub 1–1.5 m in height. It has deep
rosy-red flowers from mid-summer, often well
into the autumn. Hardy to −15°C.

**Escallonia rubra** (Ruiz & Pavon) Pers.
(including *E. punctata* DC.)  Native to Chile
and Argentina, this species is very variable in
the wild state. It is a very robust and vigorous
species with somewhat aromatic and heavily
gland-dotted glossy leaves and a glandular
calyx-tube and flower stalks. Invaluable for
hedging in maritime areas. Hardy to −10°C.

**Escallonia rosea** Griseb.  Native to S. Chile.
In spite of the specific epithet, the slightly
scented flowers, produced in mid-summer, are
white. It forms an evergreen bush 2–3 m tall
with angled shoots. Requires a sheltered site in
inland gardens. Hardy to −10°C.

**Escallonia × exoniensis** Veitch  A hybrid
between *E. rosea* and *E. rubra* that originated in
the Exeter nurseries of Veitch & Sons in the
1880s. It is a robust evergreen shrub growing
4–6 m tall in mild areas, 2–3 m elsewhere. Late
summer. Hardy to −10°C.

**Escallonia 'Iveyi'** Originated as a chance
seedling in the garden at Caerhays in Cornwall
in the 1920s. It is thought to be a hybrid
between *E. bifida* and *E. × exoniensis*. It forms a
robust shrub with large, rounded dark green
leaves that show up well the abundant white
flowers in summer. Hardy to −15°C.

**Escallonia tucumanensis** Hosseus  A
deciduous species native to northwestern

Vallea stipularis

Argentina where it grows at 800–2000 m. It
forms a large bush to 6 m, with white flowers in
summer. Hardy to −10°C.

**Escallonia virgata** (Ruiz & Pavon) Pers.
Native to southern Chile and Argentina,
growing in scrub at altitudes up to the tree-line.
A deciduous shrub to 3 m, and one of the
hardiest species and grows well in inland
gardens, except on chalky soils. Hardy to −15°C.

**Vallea stipularis** L. fil. (*Elaeocarpaceae*)
Native to the Andes from Bolivia to Venezuela
where it grows in scrubland in the mountains at
2000–4000 m. It forms an evergreen shrub
3–5 m tall with deep rose or crimson flowers in
mid–late summer. Hardy to −5°C.

Eucryphia milliganii

Eucryphia × intermedia 'Rostrevor'

Eucryphia × intermedia 'Rostrevor'

Eucryphia 'Nymansay'

Eucryphia glutinosa

Eucryphia cordifolia

Eucryphia glutinosa double form

⅔ life size. Specimens from Wakehurst Place, Sussex, 24th August

*Eucryphia moorei* at Nymans, Sussex

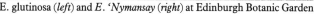

E. glutinosa (*left*) and E. '*Nymansay* (*right*) at Edinburgh Botanic Garden

*Eucryphia milliganii* at the Hillier Arboretum

**Eucryphia × intermedia** Bausch **'Rostrevor'**
A vigorous hybrid between *E. glutinosa* and *E. lucida* that originated in the garden at Rostrevor, County Down, Northern Ireland as a chance seedling, some time in the 1930s. It forms a narrow evergreen tree to 10 m tall, flowering in late summer. The leaves may be simple or trifoliate and are only slightly toothed. *E. × intermedia* is tolerant of light shade and is probably better with a cool root run. However, it requires sun to induce free-flowering and is best suited by a soil that is rich in humus. Hardy to −10°C in a sheltered position.

**Eucryphia milliganii** Hook. fil.    Native to mountainous areas in Tasmania, this species forms a compact shrub up to 3–4 m, but often smaller in cultivation. The small, simple leaves are evergreen and the white flowers are about 1.5 cm wide – smaller than the otherwise similar *E. lucida*. Introduced in 1929, it requires an open but sheltered site in lime-free and moist soil. Hardy to −10°C or −15°C.

**Eucryphia × nymansensis** Bausch **'Nymansay'**
A spontaneous hybrid between *E. cordifolia* and *E. glutinosa* that first appeared about 1914 at Nymans in West Sussex. A seedling of similar parentage subsequently arose at Mount Usher in County Wicklow, Eire. 'Nymansay' is a vigorous evergreen shrub or slender tree, growing to 12–15 m in height. The large, pure white flowers appear in late summer and the serrated leaves vary from simple to trifoliate on the same plant. It grows well on moisture retentive soils but requires a sunny aspect with some shelter from cold winds, which scorch the leaves. Hardy to −15°C.

**Eucryphia glutinosa** (Poepp. & Endl.) Baill. (*Eucryphiaceae*)    This species is native to Chile where it is now rare. Flowering in mid–late summer it grows into a large bush 4–8 m tall. It is usually deciduous, the leaves colouring well in muted shades of orange and red before falling. The flowers are scentless but attractive to bees. It was introduced in 1859 by one of the Veitch Nursery's collectors and has proved to be reliable and hardy in much of W. Europe though slow growing. A moist, lime-free soil suits it and, in sunny climates, slight shade. Hardy to −15°C.
**Eucryphia glutinosa**, double forms    When raised from seeds, plants with double or semi-double flowers sometimes appear. Although of some curiosity value, these are less attractive than the single-flowered plants.

**Eucryphia cordifolia** Cav.    Native of central Chile where it grows in cool rain forests at low altitudes, growing into a substantial evergreen tree up to 20 m tall. In cultivation the largest trees approach this size but it is more often seen as a large shrub or small tree of 8–10 m. The leaves are invariably simple and entire, except on young plants. Introduced in 1851, it has proved to be quite tolerant of chalky soils but it only really thrives in cool moist maritime climates. Hardy to −10°C.

**Eucryphia moorei** F. von Muell.    Native of New South Wales, Australia, where it occurs in forests at low altitudes, growing to 20 m. In cultivation it is more often a large evergreen shrub or small tree of about 10 m, flowering in mid-summer. The flowers are smaller than those of the more commonly cultivated species

*Eucryphia lucida* at the Hillier Arboretum

and the pinnate leaves are very distinctive with their numerous (11–13) leaflets. Introduced in 1915 and hardy only in sheltered maritime gardens . Hardy to −5°C.

**Eucryphia lucida** (Labill.) Baill.    An evergreen tree native to Tasmania where it grows in forests, often along river banks at low altitudes. In the wild it may reach 30 m, but in cultivation it is more usually a large columnar shrub or small tree of 8–12 m. It requires a sheltered but open position and a moist but light, lime-free soil. Hardy to −10°C. A pink-flowered form with a crimson centre has recently been discovered in N.W. Tasmania, and named 'Pink Cloud'. 'Leatherwood Cream' has pale-yellow edged leaves.

Olearia × oleifolia

Ozothamnus hookeri

Escallonia virgata

Olearia moschata

Hoheria lyallii

Leptospermum lanigerum

Lomatia silaifolia

½ life size. Specimens from Wakehurst Place, Sussex, 26th July

***Olearia* × *oleifolia*** Kirk (*Compositae*)   Hybrid between *O. avicenniifolia* and *O. odorata*. A compact evergreen bush 1–2 m high. Summer. Hardy to −10°C.

***Ozothamnus hookeri*** Sond. (syn. *Helichrysum hookeri* (Sond.) Druce) (*Compositae*)   Endemic to Tasmania, where it grows on mountains at 1000–1300 m, forming compact, aromatic evergreen bushes 1–2 m tall, flowering in summer. Hardy to −5°C.

***Escallonia virgata*** (Ruiz & Pavon) Pers. (*Escalloniaceae*) see p. 223.

***Olearia moschata*** Hook. fil. (*Compositae*)   Native to mountain scrubland in South Island, New Zealand where it grows to 4 m tall. In cultivation it seldom exceeds 2 m. The leaves have a distinctive musky scent. Hardy to −5°C.

***Hoheria lyallii*** Hook. fil. see p. 229.

***Leptospermum lanigerum*** (Ait.) Sm. (*Myrtaceae*)   An evergreen shrub or small tree, native to Tasmania and S.E. Australia, from coastal areas to low mountains. In the wild it may reach 6–7 m, but in cultivation only 1–2 m. Plant in light soil. Hardy to −15°C.

***Lomatia silaifolia*** (Sm.) R. Br. (*Proteaceae*) An evergreen shrub native to coastal regions of S.E. Australia and growing in suckering thickets to about 1 m. Flowers scented; in mid-summer the leaves are often more divided than shown here. Well-drained soil; full sun. Hardy to −10°C.

***Olearia macrodonta*** Baker (*Compositae*)   Native to both the main islands of New Zealand, where it forms an evergreen shrub or small tree to 6 m tall, in forests up to 1300 m. In cultivation usually a shrub to 3 m. Hardy to −15°C.

***Olearia* × *scilloniensis*** Dorrien-Smith (*Compositae*)   A chance hybrid between *O. lyrata* and probably *O. phlogopappa*, that arose at Tresco, Isles of Scilly, in 1910. A compact shrub 1–2 m tall; late spring. Hardy to −10°C.

***Feijoa sellowiana*** (Berg) Berg (syn. *Acca sellowiana* Berg) Burret (*Myrtaceae*)   A small evergreen tree native to southern Brazil and Uruguay, but in cultivation a shrub about 2–3 m. The fruits are edible. Requires a sunny sheltered site and well-drained soil, ideally with the protection of a wall. Hardy to −15°C.

***Gevuina avellana*** Molina (*Proteaceae*)   Native of Chile; a large evergreen shrub or small tree up to 12 m. The leaves may be pinnate or bipinnate, the leaflets varying in size and in number from 3 to about 30. The cherry-like fruits are red at first, ripening to black. Hardy to −10°C.

***Ozothamnus ledifolius*** (DC.) Hook. fil. (syn. *Helichrysum ledifolium* (DC.) Benth.) (*Compositae*)   A compact evergreen shrub native to mountains in Tasmania at about 1000 m. The flowers are produced in summer. It grows to about 1 m tall, with a slightly sticky and aromatic exudate covering the stems and undersides of the leaves. Introduced by Harold Comber and quite hardy in a sunny site and well-drained soil. Hardy to −10°C.

***Metrosideros excelsa*** Sol. ex Gaertn. (*Myrtaceae*)   An evergreen tree native to North Island, New Zealand at low altitudes, where it forms a tree up to 20 m tall, flowering in mid-summer. Hardy to −5°C.

*Olearia macrodonta*

*Olearia* × *scilloniensis*

*Feijoa sellowiana*

*Gevuina avellana*

*Ozothamnus ledifolius*

*Metrosideros excelsa*

*Hoheria sexstylosa*

*Clethea alnifolia*

*Clethra monostachya*

*Clethra delavayi*

½ life size. Specimens from Wakehurst Place, Sussex, 28th August

Hoheria lyallii at Wakehurst Place

Clethra fargesii

Hoheria glabrata at the Hillier Arboretum

Hoheria 'Glory of Amlwch'

Clethra barbinervis

**Clethra alnifolia** L. Sweet Pepperbush, White Alder   Native of S. Maine, south to Florida along the seaboard and inland to E. Texas, in swamps, and damp woods flowering in July–September. Deciduous shrub to 3 m suckering to form a thicket. Leaves 3.5–7 cm long. Flowers white or pink in f. *rosea* Rehd., scented, in upright racemes. Moist, sandy soil; full sun. Hardy to −30°C. Late summer.

**Clethra monostachya** Rehd. & Wils.   Native of W. Sichuan, Yunnan and S.E. Xizang, in woods at 1600–2800 m, flowering in July–August. Deciduous shrub or small tree to 6 m. Leaves 8–14 cm long. Sepals acute. Flowers in unbranched, usually solitary (or 3) racemes 10–20 cm long. Petals equalling the stamens. Moist acid or lime-free soil; part shade. Hardy to −15°C. Late summer.

**Clethra fargesii** Franch.   Native of W. Hubei and E. Sichuan, in scrub at 1300–2500 m, flowering in July–August. Deciduous rounded shrub to 3 m. Leaves 8–14 cm long. Flowers scented, in panicles 10–25 cm long. Petals shorter than the stamens. Moist acid or lime-free soil; part shade. Hardy to −20°C. Late summer.

**Clethra delavayi** Franch. (*Clethraceae*)   Native of N.W. Yunnan near Dali, in fir forests on limestone crags at *c*.3000 m, flowering in June–July. Deciduous upright shrub or small tree to 15 m. Leaves 5–15 cm long, pale and pubescent beneath. Petals longer than the stamens, to 1 cm, ciliate. Racemes 10–15 cm long. Moist acid (?) soil; part shade. Hardy to −10°C. Late summer.

**Clethra barbinervis** Sieb & Zucc.   Native of Hokkaido, Honshu, Shikoku and Kyushu and Quelpaet Is. (Korea), in woods in the mountains, flowering in July–September. Deciduous tree to 10 m with peeling orange bark, or shrub in cultivation. Leaves 6–12 cm long. Petals 5–6 mm, shorter than the stamens. Flowers scented, in panicles 10–15 cm long. Moist acid or lime-free soil; part shade. Hardy to −20°C. Late summer.

**Hoheria sexstylosa** Col. Lacebark   Native of both islands of New Zealand, in lowland forests, flowering in March–April. Evergreen spreading tree or large shrub to 6 m. Leaves 6–7.5 cm long. Flowers *c*.2 cm across in 2–5 flowered cymes. Full sun. Hardy to −15°C. Late summer. The closely-related *H. populnea* A. Cunn. differs in its taller habit, broader leaves, and larger (to 2.5 cm) flowers in 5–10 flowered cymes. Said to be more tender. Var. *osbornei* with purple stamens and leaves purple beneath is found on Great Barrier Island.

**Hoheria lyallii** Hook. fil. (*Malvaceae*) Ribbonwood   See also p. 226. Native of the South Island of New Zealand, along forest edges and by streams in subalpine forests on the E. side of the southern Alps; in the southern part often forming scrub-like groves on the upper margins of the forest; flowering in November–February. Leaves downy on both sides, 5–11 cm long. Flowers to 3.5 cm across. Any well-drained soil; full sun. Hardy to −15°C. Late summer. Easily grown but subject to die-back in winter if the new growths are too soft.

**Hoheria glabrata** Sprague & Summerhays Native of the South Island of New Zealand, on forest edges and by streams on the W. (rainy) side of the Southern Alps, flowering in November–February. Deciduous shrub or small tree to 6 m. Leaves 5–10 cm long. Flowers to 2.5 cm across. Well-drained soil; full sun. Hardy to −15°C. Late summer.

**Hoheria 'Glory of Amlwch'**   A hybrid, perhaps between *H. glabrata* and *H. sexstylosa*, raised by Dr Jones of Amlwch, Anglesey before 1948. A small tree, with semi-evergreen leaves and flowers about 4 cm across, with purplish styles.

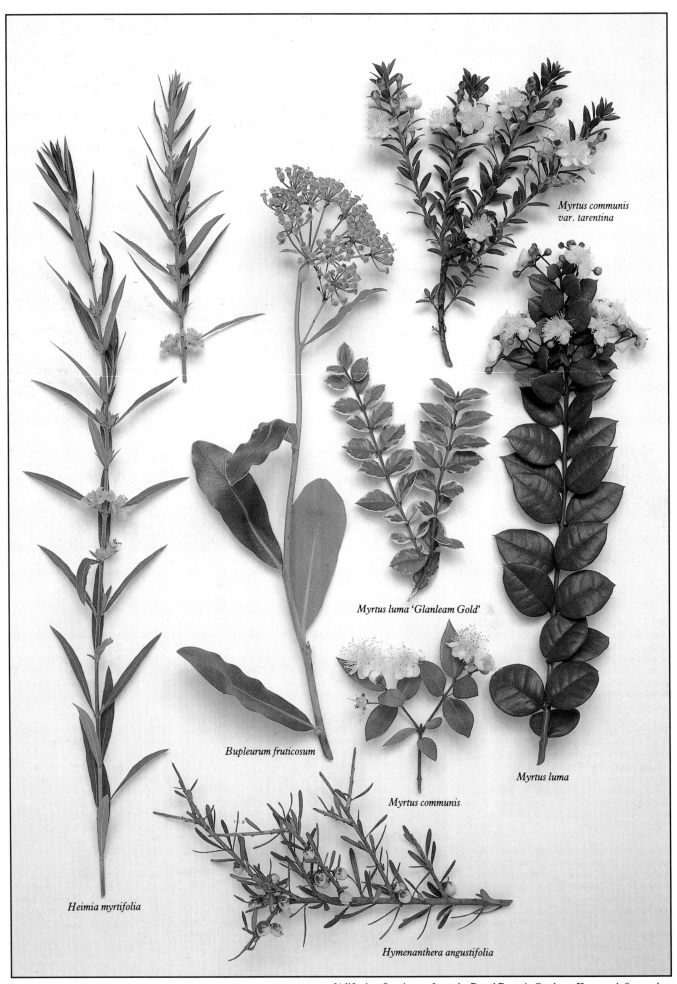

Myrtus communis
var. tarentina

Myrtus luma 'Glanleam Gold'

Bupleurum fruticosum

Myrtus luma

Myrtus communis

Heimia myrtifolia

Hymenanthera angustifolia

¾ life size. Specimens from the Royal Botanic Gardens, Kew, 12th September

**Heimia myrtifolia** Cham. & Schlecht. (syn. *H. salicifolia* hort.) (*Lythraceae*)   Native to Brazil and Uruguay where it forms a deciduous shrub about 2 m tall. Flowers 8–12 mm across. In cultivation it is often nearly herbaceous, forming a mass of erect stems. Requiring a sheltered position in full sun and with a well-drained soil. Hardy to −15°C. Late summer.

**Bupleurum fruticosum** L. (*Umbelliferae*)   An evergreen shrub 1–2 m high. Native to S. Europe in scrub and on cliffs. Hardy to −15°C.

**Myrtus luma** Molino (syn. *M. apiculata* (DC.) Niedenzu) (*Myrtaceae*)   Native of Chile where it may grow into a tree up to 20 m tall. In cultivation it forms a medium-sized to large shrub, only in the most favoured gardens becoming tree-like and exceeding 15 m. It flowers in late summer but is equally notable for the beautiful cinnamon coloured bark which peels to reveal a cream or grey underbark. The best specimens in the British Isles are in the mild and moist west. Hardy to −10°C.
**Myrtus luma** 'Glanleam Gold' (syn. *M. apiculata* 'Glanleam Gold') (*Myrtaceae*)   A cultivar introduced in 1975 by Treseder's Nurseries. Probably hardy to −10°C.

**Myrtus communis** L. (*Myrtaceae*)   Native to the Mediterranean region and western Asia. It forms an evergreen bush up to 4 m, flowering in summer. The white flowers are followed by deep purple berries. Like all the myrtles, the leaves are strongly aromatic when crushed. Hardy to −10°C or −15°C, with shelter.
**Myrtus communis** L. var. **tarentina** L. (*Myrtaceae*)   Differs from the typical form of the species in its much smaller leaves and more compact growth and in having white berries. Hardy to −15°C.

**Myrtus ugni** Molina (*Myrtaceae*)   Native to Chile where it grows in scrub and on the margins of forests, forming an evergreen shrub 1–2 m tall. The white flowers are borne in the late spring and are followed by purplish-brown fruits that are edible and delicious. Hardy to −10°C, with shelter.

**Hymenanthera angustifolia** DC. (*Violaceae*)   Native to Tasmania, as a mountain plant, and to lower altitudes in New Zealand, where it grows as an erect shrub 1–2 m tall. The evergreen leaves are very thick and rigid; the small yellow flowers appear in the summer, and are followed by creamy-white berries which are sometimes heavily blotched with purple. The plant illustrated may be *H. alpina*, differing mainly in its more compact habit and rigid branches. Hardy to −10°C.

**Aralia elata** (Miq.) Seem. (*Araliaceae*)   Native of Japan and adjacent parts of north-east Asia, growing in thin woodland and thickets at low altitudes. Forming a large deciduous shrub or small tree up to 10 m, it is notably sparsely branched with stout shoots that are conspicuous in the winter. In cultivation, the leaves seldom colour as well in the autumn as those of the wild plant illustrated. The cultivar **'Variegata'** has leaflets with broad creamy-white margins. Acid soil; part shade. Hardy to −15°C.

**Jasminum fruticans** L. (*Oleaceae*)   Native to the Mediterranean region where it grows in open scrub in low hills. The unscented flowers are produced from mid- to late summer. It forms a more or less evergreen plant 1–2 m. Hardy to −15°C.

*Aralia elata* in northern Hokkaido in October

*Myrtus luma* in Cornwall

*Myrtus ugni* in Chile

*Jasminum fruticans*

*Aralia elata* 'Variegata'

*Clerodendrum trichotomum var. fargesii*

*Abelia × grandiflora*

*Abelia chinensis*

*Abelia schumannii*

*Pileostegia viburnoides*

*Clerodendrum bungei*

½ life size. Specimens from the Royal Botanic Gardens, Kew, 12th September

**Abelia chinensis** R. Br. (*Caprifoliaceae*)   Native of China from W. Hubei eastwards, flowering in July and August. Deciduous shrub to 1.5 m. Branches finely pubescent. Flowers scented. Full sun. Hardy to −10°C. Early summer.

**Abelia × grandiflora** (André) Rehder A hybrid between *A. chinensis* and *A. uniflora* (from E. China), raised by Rovelli in Italy before 1880. Semi-evergreen shrub to 2.5 m. Branches pubescent. Sepals 2–5; corolla 2 cm long. Any soil. Hardy to −15°C. Summer–autumn. There is also a prostrate form, used for ground cover in N. America.

**Abelia schumannii** (Graeb.) Rehder   Native of W. Sichuan, in dry valleys and by rivers, at 1200–3600 m, flowering in May–August. Deciduous shrub to 1.5 m. Young twigs purple and pubescent. Flowers with 2 sepals, 6–10 mm long; and corolla 2.5–3 cm. Hardy to −15°C.

**Trachelospermum asiaticum** (Sieb. & Zucc.) Nakai (*Apocynaceae*)   Native of Korea, Honshu, Shikoku and Kyushu, in woods and scrub in the hills, flowering in May–June. Evergreen climber to 6 m. Leaves 3–6 cm long. Flowers with anthers slightly exserted, and the narrow part of the tube twice as long as the broad part. Sun or part shade. Hardy to −15°C with wall protection. Early summer.

**Jasminum grandiflorum** L. (*Oleaceae*)   Native of Arabia, but long-cultivated and found naturalized from China to Spain. Similar to *J. officinale*, but with a looser inflorescence and larger flowers, to 4 cm across, pink in bud. Sun or part shade. Hardy to −5°C. Early summer.

**Jasminum × stephanense** Lémoine   A hybrid between *J. beesianum* (see p. 100) and *J. officinale*, raised in c.1918 by T. Javitt, but also known wild. Deciduous climber to 3 m. Flowers c.1.5 cm across. Leaves often yellowish. Sun. Hardy to −15°C. Summer.

**Jasminum officinale** L. Jasmine   Native of the Caucasus and Iran eastwards to China, in scrub and forest, flowering in May–July. Woody climber to 4 m. Leaflets 5–7. Flowers scented, 2.5 cm across. Hardy to −15°C. Late summer.

**Jasminum humile** L.   Native of the Himalayas from Afghanistan to Sichuan, in scrub and dry valleys, at 1500–3000 m, flowering in April–July. Deciduous shrub to 2 m. Flowers c.14 mm across. Sun. Hardy to −10°C. Summer.

**Clerodendrum trichotomum** Thunb. (*Verbenaceae*)   Native of Japan, south to the Philippines, of Korea, and E. China, with var. *fargesii* (Dode) Rehder in W. China to Yunnan, in woods, on roadside cliffs and in scrub at up to 2300 m, flowering in July–October. Deciduous, rounded shrub to 6 m. Leaves foetid. Flowers scented. Full sun. Hardy to −15°C. Var. *fargesii*, from higher altitudes, to −20°C?.

**Clerodendrum bungei** Sted.   Native of W. Hubei, Sichuan(?) and Yunnan, in woods and scrub to 2300 m, flowering in June–September. Deciduous, upright shrub to 2 m. Leaves foetid. Full sun. Hardy to −10°C.

**Pileostegia viburnoides** Hook. fil. & Thoms. (*Saxifragaceae*)   Native of China from W. Sichuan, east to Taiwan, and of the Khasia Hills, on cliffs and trees at up to 1000 m, flowering in August. Evergreen shrub, climbing by short roots to 10 m. Leaves leathery to 18 cm long. Moist soil. Hardy to −15°C.

*Clerodendrum trichotomum* in Yakushima

*Jasminum humile*

*Jasminum grandiflorum*

*Trachelospermum asiaticum*

*Jasminum × stephanense*

*Jasminum officinale* at the Chelsea Physic Garden, London

H. aspera subsp. aspera

H. 'Rosthornii'

H. aspera subsp.
strigosa var. macrophylla

H. quercifolia

H. paniculata 'Floribunda'

'Tardiva'

H. paniculata 'Grandiflora'

H. paniculata

H. heteromalla

¼ life size. Specimens from Wakehurst Place, Sussex, 2nd September

***Hydrangea aspera*** Buch–Ham. ex D. Don.
subsp. ***aspera*** (syn. *H. villosa* Rehd.)
(*Saxifragaceae*)    Native of the Himalayas from
N.W. India east to Taiwan, and south to Java
and Sumatra, in scrub and forest in the
mountains at 1200–2700 m. Deciduous shrub or
small tree to 7 m; leaves to 30 cm long. Flowers
usually purplish, sometimes white, in flat heads
to 25 cm across. Good soil, including chalk.
Hardy to −15°C.
Subsp. ***strigosa*** (incl. *H. strigosa* var.
*macrophylla* Rehder)    Native of W. Hubei, and
W. Sichuan in scrub and woods at 900–1800 m.
Deciduous shrub to 3 m. Leaves to 28 cm long in
var. **macrophylla** (shown here), with rough
appressed hairs beneath. Hardy to −20°C.
**'Rosthornii'**    A large-leaved form of *H. aspera*.
The true *H. rosthornii*, now considered part of *H.
aspera* subsp. *robusta*, has leaf-stalks which may
be up to 20 cm long.
Subsp. ***sargentiana*** (Rehd.) McClintock
Native of W. Hubei, in scrub at 1500–1800 m.
Deciduous shrub to 2 m or more, often gaunt in
cultivation. Leaves to 30 cm long. Sterile flowers
whitish, or pinkish, in a head to 20 cm across.
Shade or part shade, with shelter. Hardy to
−15°C. Late summer.

***H. quercifolia*** Bartram Oakleaf Hydrangea
Native of Alabama, Florida and Georgia, on the
banks of streams and on bluffs, flowering in
June. Deciduous shrub to 2 m in the wild,
usually *c.* 1 m in Europe. Sterile flowers 3–4 cm
across, white becoming purplish. Acid soil.
Hardy to −20°C, but requiring heat in summer
to do well. Summer.

***H. paniculata*** Sieb.    Native of S.E. China
(rare), Sakhalin and Japan; in bamboo scrub,
open forest and by streams, flowering from July
(in Hokkaido) to October (in Yakushima). Erect
shrub to 6 m. Leaves to 12 cm long. Moist, rich
soil. Hardy to −25°C.
**'Floribunda'**    In this clone the sterile flowers
are more numerous and exceptionally large and
rounded, on an elongated inflorescence.
**'Tardiva'**    A late-flowering clone, shown here
in bud, usually flowering in early autumn.
The earliest-flowering clone in cultivation
**'Praecox'**, which flowers about 6 weeks earlier
than 'Grandiflora', originated in Hokkaido. The
plant, shown here, growing in Hokkaido near
Shari, was well past flowering at the end of
September. The rather flat, loose head of flowers
is typical of 'Praecox'.
**'Grandiflora'**    In this clone most of the flowers
are sterile, giving a dense, rather rounded head.

***H. heteromalla*** D. Don. (syn. *H. xanthoneura*
Diels, *H. bretschneideri* Dipp.)    Native of the
Himalayas from N. India, at up to 3300 m, east
to Beijing (from whence the form called *H.
bretschneideri* was collected). Deciduous shrub or
small tree to 6 m. Leaves 15–25 cm long. Flowers
white or pinkish. Moist, good soil; sun or part
shade. Hardy to −20°C. Summer. Shown here
B. L. & M., 222 from Nepal.

***H. angustipetala*** Hayata (syn. *H. grosseserrata*
Engl.)    Native of Yakushima, the Ryukyu
islands, Taiwan and Jiangxi, in scrub and open
places in the forest, and by streams at *c.* 1200 m,
flowering in July–September. Hardy to −10°C?

***H. anomala*** subsp. ***petiolaris*** (Sieb. & Zucc.)
McClintock    Native of Sakhalin, Japan,
Quelpart Is (S. Korea) and Taiwan, in forest in
the mountains, on old, dying or dead trees.
Deciduous shrub to 25 m, climbing with aerial
roots. Leaves 4–10 cm long. Flower heads 15–
25 cm across. Good soil; part shade. Good on
shaded walls. Hardy to −20°C. Summer.

*Hydrangea angustipetala* in Yakusima, Japan, in October

*Hydrangea aspera subsp. sargentiana*

*Hydrangea anomala subsp. petiolaris*

*Hydrangea paniculata* in Hokkaido

*Hydrangea heteromalla* B.L. & M.222

*H. serrata* 'Preziosa'

'Blue Bird'

*H. serrata*
(Wilson 7820)

*H. serrata* 'Rosalba'

'Ayesha'

'Blue Wave'

'Grant's Choice'

'Lilacina'

*H. macrophylla f. normalis*

'Lanarth White'

¼ life size. Specimens from Wakehurst Place, Sussex, 2nd September

Hydrangea aspera at Wallington Park

Decumaria barbara

Schizophragma hydrangeoides 'Roseum' at the High Beeches

Hydrangea 'Veitchii'

**Hydrangea serrata** (Thunb.) Sér. (syn. *H. macrophylla* var. *acuminata* (Sieb. & Zucc.) Makino) (*Saxifragaceae*) Native of Honshu, Shikoku and Kyushu, where it is common in woods in the mountains at up to 1500 m, flowering in June–August. Deciduous shrub to 1.5 m, with slender, often blackish, stems. Leaves lanceolate to elliptic, 5–15 cm long. Flower heads about 14 cm across. Acid or neutral soil; sun or part shade. Hardy to −20°C. Late summer. Shown here: Wilson 7820, an attractive dwarf variety, blue on acid soil, and **'Rosalba'** with white flowers, becoming heavily blotched with red, only 5–7 on each head, the sepals toothed.

**H. serrata 'Bluebird'** A strong-growing, hardy cultivar, up to 1.6 m high. Foliage turns red in autumn. Hardy to −15°C. Late summer. Var. *thunbergii* is similar, with dark stems and very rounded sterile flowers. The dried leaves are sweet, and used to make tea in Japan.

**H. 'Preziosa'** A cross between *H. macrophylla* and *H. serrata* raised by Ahrends of W. Germany in 1961. The flowers are pink at first, later turning deep red.

**H. 'Ayesha'** (syn. 'Silver Slipper') A shrub up to 1 m high, usually described as a hortensia but with distinctive, rather fleshy, fragrant

flowers. Does well in sun or semi-shade.

**H. macrophylla 'Blue Wave'** A very popular lacecap raised by Lémoine of Nancy from seed in about 1900. It forms a large bush up to 2 m high and wide and is exceptionally hardy. The flowers are a good blue on very acid soils, pink or lilac on others.

**H. macrophylla 'Grant's Choice'** J. M. Grant was head gardener at Grayswood, Haslemere during the 1930s. He sowed seeds of 'Blue Wave' and 'Grayswood' – so this is perhaps a selection of one of these seedlings of 'Blue Wave'.

**H. macrophylla 'Lilacina'** A strong growing hybrid raised by Lémoine of Nancy early this century, this lacecap makes a bush up to about 1.6 m high.

**H. macrophylla 'Lanarth White'** A compact shrub, up to about 1 m high and the same across, first observed in the garden of Lanarth, Cornwall.

**H. macrophylla** (Thunb.) DC f. **normalis** (Wilson) Hara Native of Honshu, in the Sagami and Izu districts, on the Chiba peninsula (near Tokyo), and on the offshore islands, growing in sunny places near the shores forming thickets up to 3 m, flowering in June–July. This is the wild

form of *H. macrophylla* and is like a small lacecap. Hardy to −10°C.

**H. 'Veitchii'** A lacecap of rather lax habit, up to 1.6 m high, introduced in 1903 by Veitch of Exeter, who imported it from Japan. Very hardy (to −15°C) and lime tolerant, but prefers light shade.

**H. aspera** Buch-Ham. ex. D. Don A fine specimen growing at Wallington Park, Northumberland. For text see p. 235.

**Schizophragma hydrangeoides** Sieb. & Zucc. **'Roseum'** (*Saxifragaceae*) Native of Hokkaido, Honshu, Shikoku and Kyushu, in damp forests, growing like ivy, both on the forest floor, with very small leaves, and climbing on trees and flowering at up to 10 m or more, in June–July. A climbing shrub, clinging by aerial roots. Moist leafy soil. Part shade especially at the roots. Hardy to −20°C. Summer.

**Decumaria barbara** L. (*Saxifragaceae*) Native of Virginia south to Louisiana and Florida, growing on trees, flowering in May–June. Climbing semi-deciduous shrub to 10 m. Leaves ovate to elliptic, 5–10 cm long, usually smooth. Flower heads 5–10 cm across, without sterile florets. Petals 9–10. Hardy to −15°C.

237

'Parsifal'

H. arborescens 'Grandiflora'

'Hamburgh'

'Niedersachsen'

'Mousseline'

'Generale Vicomtesse de Vibraye'

'Kluis Superba'

'Mme E. Moullère'

'Amethyst'

¼ life size. Specimens from Wakehurst Place, Sussex, 2nd September

*Hydrangea arborescens 'Grandiflora'* in New Jersey

*Hydrangea serrata*

*Hydrangea arborescens 'Annabelle'*

*Hydrangea 'Kluis Superba'*

*Hydrangea 'Nikko Blue'*

**Hydrangeas** There are many garden varieties, descended from *H. macrophylla* or *H. serrata*, and they are divided into groups, the 'Hortensias' and the 'Lacecaps'. The Hortensias are mop-headed, and most are hardy grown outside in Britain, W. Europe, and coastal North America. Most reach about 1.8 m high, and flower from mid-summer onwards. They do especially well near the sea, on neutral or acid, moist soil. On soils with pH below 5.5, most cultivars are blue; above pH7 pink; hydrangea colourant can be applied if blue flowers are required. Prune after flowering, or in spring, and thin the young shoots. Lacecaps tend to be hardier than Hortensias, and have large, flat, slightly scented flower heads. In continental Europe *H. macrophylla* hybrids are considered hardy to −20°C. to −25°C, in N. America to −15°C. Cold winds at −15°C will kill poorly ripened wood to the ground.

**H. 'Parsifal'** A Hortensia, up to 1 m high, with flowers deep pink, deep blue, or a mixture, depending on the soil type.

**H. 'Hamburgh'** A vigorous Hortensia, with large flowers which last into autumn. On acid soil they are deep blue, on neutral they are bright pink, turning deep red in autumn. Prefers a sheltered, shady position.

**H. 'Niedersachsen'** A rather tender Hortensia, up to 1.3 m high. Pale pink or pale blue flowers produced in late summer–autumn.

**H. 'Mousseline'** A good, vigorous Hortensia which is very hardy, with flowers over a long season. Good autumn colour. Easy to make blue.

**H. 'Generale Vicomtesse de Vibraye'** (syn. 'Vibraye') A hardy Hortensia variety up to 1.6 m high, with long, rather weak stems. Does well on any acid soil, when the flowers will be a pure vivid blue. Will flower from side-shoots if terminal bud is killed by frost.

**H. 'Kluis Superba'** A compact Hortensia, up to 1 m high; very free-flowering, with dark blue flowers, which unfortunately fade in hot sun. Very sensitive to soil pH, so flowers are often pink.

**H. 'Mme E. Mouillère'** An old Hortensia, whose flowers are borne over a long season, until the first frosts, and turn pink if grown in the sun. A suitable variety for limy soil.

**H. 'Amethyst'** A vigorous grower, with strong stems up to 1 m high. Late flowering, with the best blooms produced in the early autumn, so

needs sheltered position and protection from frost.

**H. 'Nikko Blue'** A free-flowering form of *H. macrophylla* of unknown, perhaps Japanese, origin.

**H. serrata** (Thunb.) Sér. A graceful species with small lace-cap heads of flowers. See p. 237.

**H. arborescens** L. **'Annabelle'** A selected form of *H. arborescens* 'Grandiflora' with large flower heads to 20 cm across. The wild *H. arborescens* is native from New York to Iowa, south to Florida and Louisiana, growing in woods and on shady rocks, flowering in May–July. A deciduous straggly shrub to 1 m, rarely more. Flower heads 5–15 cm across, with few sterile flowers. Any good soil; part shade. Hardy to −25°C.

**H. arborescens 'Grandiflora'** A form of *H. arborescens* introduced to Britain in 1907, and descended from a plant found in the wild in Ohio. A deciduous shrub to about 1.2 m high, although unfortunately it has weak stems. Any acid or neutral soil; light shade. Hardy to −15°C. Late summer.

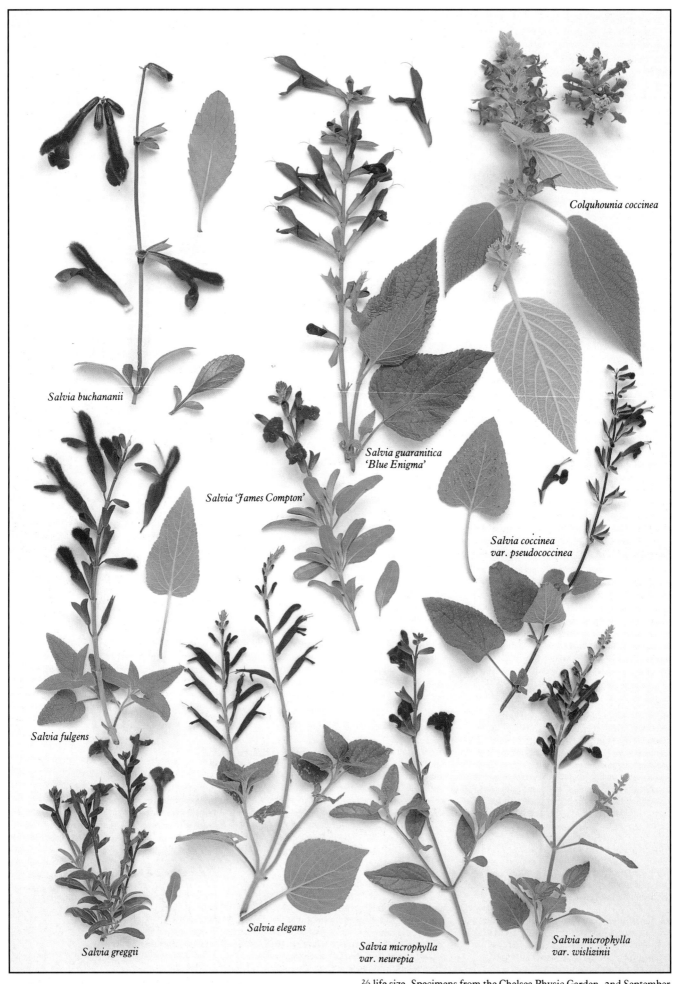

Colquhounia coccinea

Salvia buchananii

Salvia guaranitica
'Blue Enigma'

Salvia 'James Compton'

Salvia coccinea
var. pseudococcinea

Salvia fulgens

Salvia greggii

Salvia elegans

Salvia microphylla
var. neurepia

Salvia microphylla
var. wislizinii

⅔ life size. Specimens from the Chelsea Physic Garden, 2nd September

***Salvia buchananii*** Hedge (*Labiatae*) Probably native of Mexico. Found in a garden in Mexico City and introduced to England by Sir Charles Buchanan. Evergreen subshrub, producing suckers. Flowers 4.5–5 cm long. Moist soil; full sun. Hardy to −5°C. Summer.

***Salvia guaranitica*** St. Hil. ex Benth. **'Blue Enigma'** Native of Brazil, Paraguay, Uruguay and Argentina, growing in scrub by streams and in woods. Subshrub to 2 m or more. Leaves hairy, 4–15 cm long. Flowers with tube 20–33 mm; the upper lip 11–19 mm. Any soil; full sun. Hardy to −5°C, perhaps. Summer.

***Colquhounia coccinea*** Wall. (*Labiatae*) Semi-deciduous shrub to 3 m. Flowers 1.5–5 cm long, reddish or orange. Well-drained soil; full sun. Hardy to −10°C. with protection from cold wind. Autumn. See also p. 254.

***Salvia fulgens*** Cav. Native of Mexico, in coniferous and oak woods in the mountains at 2650–3400 m. Evergreen or semi-deciduous shrub to 4 m. Leaves 3–6 cm long. Flowers in whorls of 6–12. Corolla tube 25–28 mm; upper lip 13–15 mm. Hardy to −5°C, perhaps.

***Salvia* 'James Compton'** A hybrid between *S. greggii* and *S. microphylla*, raised by James Compton at the Chelsea Physic Garden in 1985. Evergreen shrub to 2 m. Hardy to −5°C.

***Salvia coccinea*** Juss. var. ***pseudococcinea*** Gray Probably native of Brazil, but now widely naturalized in the subtropics and in the USA as far north as South Carolina. Subshrub or annual to 1 m. Leaves with lamina 3–6 cm long. Flowers with tube 13–17 mm; upper lip 3–5 mm long. Hardy to −5°C, perhaps.

***Salvia greggii*** Gray Native of Mexico and Texas, in oak and pine forests from 1500–2600 m. Subshrub to 1 m or more in cultivation. Leaves 1–2 cm long, rarely to 2.5 cm. Flowers with tube 18–22 mm; upper lip 8–10 mm long. Any soil; full sun. Hardy to −5°C, perhaps.

***Salvia elegans*** Vahl Native of Mexico, in scrub, *Abies*, *Pinus* and *Quercus* forest at 2550–3100 m. Subshrub to 2 m. Leaves to 6 cm long. Corolla 2.2–3 cm long. Full sun. Hardy to −5°C, perhaps.

***Salvia microphylla*** H. B. K. var. ***neurepia*** and var. **wislizinii** Native of Mexico, in scrub, oak and conifer woods at 1600–2800 m. Subshrub to 1.2 m. Hardy to −10°C.

***Salvia leucantha*** Cav. Native of Mexico at around 2500 m, in scrub near Villa N. Romero, but commonly cultivated. Subshrub to 1.5 m. Leaves 8–15 cm long. Calyx densely purplish-woolly, rarely white. Corolla white, 16–20 mm long. Hardy to −5°C, perhaps.

***Salvia officinalis*** L. **'Purpurascens'** A purple-leaved form of the common garden sage, known since the early 19th C. *S. officinalis* L. is native of S. Europe, on dry hills. Low spreading evergreen shrub to 50 cm. Flowers to 35 mm long, violet, pink or white. Any well-drained soil, dry in summer. Full sun. Hardy to −15°C.

***Trichostema lanatum*** Benth. (*Labiatae*) Woolly Blue-curls Native of California from Monterey Co., south to San Diego Co., on dry wooded hills and chaparral near the coast at up to 1000 m. Evergreen shrub to 1.5 m. Leaves linear, to 7.5 cm long, aromatic. Flowers to 2.6 cm long, with style and stamens to 3 cm. Hardy to −10°C. Summer.

*Salvia microphylla* and *Opuntia* naturalized in S. Spain

*Salvia leucantha*          *Salvia officinalis* 'Purpurascens'

*Trichostema lanatum* near San Luis Obispo, California

¹⁄₃ life size. Specimens from Wakehurst Place, 2nd September

**Hypericum pseudohenryi** N. Robson Lancaster 1029 (*Guttiferae*)  Native of Yunnan, Sichuan and Xizang, in open grassy places in forest at *c*. 3000 m, flowering in May–July. Deciduous shrub to 1.5 m. Leaves, with short (0.5–1 mm) petiole, to 6.6 cm long, narrowly ovate to lanceolate. Sepals more or less erect in bud. Close to *M. acmosepalum* which has narrower spreading sepals. Flowers to 5.5 cm across, stamens about ¾ as long as petals. Any soil. Hardy to −10°C. Early–late summer.

**H. androsaemum** L. Tutsan  Native of England, southward to N. Africa, and east to the Black Sea and Caspian forests, in woods or hedges, flowering from May to September. Deciduous shrub to 1 m. Leaves sessile, ovate, to 10 cm long, cordate at base. Flowers small, to 2 cm across, in a flat head. Fruits rounded, fleshy, turning red, then black and often as decorative as the flowers. Hardy to −20°C, but often cut down and will regrow from the base.

**H. monogynum** L. (syn. *H. chinense* L.) Native of W. Hubei, E. Sichuan, Jiangxi and Taiwan, in scrub in gorges at *c*. 500 m, flowering in May–September. Evergreen shrub to 70 cm. Leaves sessile, narrowly oblong to 9 cm long, acute at apex, net-veined beneath. Sepals erect in bud. Flowers to 6 cm across. Stamens almost as long as the petals. Styles much longer than ovary, united almost to apex. Any soil; warm situation. Hardy to −5°C? Summer to autumn.

**H. henryi** Leveillé & Vanniot subsp. **henryi** Lancaster 653  Native of Yunnan, in open pine forest and scrub on dry hillsides at 2000–2400, flowering from April onwards. Deciduous or semi-evergreen shrub to 1.5 m.

**H. subsessile** N. Robson SBEC 551  Native of W. Yunnan, above Dali, and of C. Sichuan on open hillsides at 3200 m, flowering from June onwards.

**H. bellum** Li  Native of N.E. India, S.E. Tibet, N. Burma and Yunnan, in scrub on open hillsides, flowering May to July. Deciduous shrub to 70 cm. Leaves shortly stalked, to 3.5 cm long, 1.1–1.7 times longer than broad, rounded or retuse at apex, wavy-edged. Sepals elliptic to obovate, erect in bud. Flowers to 4 cm across. Stamens about ⅓ m as long as petals. Any soil; sun. Hardy to −10°C. Summer.

**H. hircinum** L. subsp. **albimontanum** (Greuter) N. Robson  Native of the Peloponnese, Crete and Cyprus, in moist places by streams at up to 600 m, flowering in June–August. Deciduous or semi-evergreen shrub to 1 m. Leaves broad, with wavy margins. Flowers 3–5 cm across. Hardy to −15°C.

**H. forrestii** (Chitt.) N. Robson  Lancaster 1048 Native of N.E. India, N. Burma, Yunnan and W. Sichuan, flowering in May–July. Deciduous shrub to 2 m. Leaves shortly stalked, to 4.5 cm long, 1.8–2.5 times longer than broad. Sepals rounded, erect in bud. Flowers to 6 cm across. Stamens about half as long as the petals. Close to *pseudohenryi* and *bearii*. Any soil; sun or part shade. Hardy to −10°C. Early–late summer.

**H. acmosepalum** N. Robson  Lancaster 683 Native of Yunnan and Guizhou, on hillsides and open places in forest at 1850–3000 m, flowering in June onwards. Semi-evergreen shrub to 1 m. Leaves short-stalked, elliptic or oblong to oblanceolate, glaucous beneath, 2–6 cm long. Sepals tapering to a long point, spreading. Flowers 3.5–5.5 cm across. Stamens ¾–⅞ as long as petals. Hardy to −15°C.

*Hypericum balearicum*

*Hypericum* × *inodorum* 'Elstead'

**H. balearicum** L.   Native of the Balearic Islands, growing in dwarf scrub on rocky hills flowering in May and June. A small shrub to 50 cm high. Twigs warty. Leaves wavy-edged, to 1.5 cm long. Flowers c.3–5 cm across. Well-drained soil, dry in summer; full sun. Hardy to −5°C. Early–late summer.

**H. × inodorum** Miller **'Elstead'** (syn. *H. elatum*) Aiton   A hybrid between *H. androsaemum* and *H. hircinum*, known in the wild, but the cv. 'Elstead' shown here raised by W. Ladhams of Elstead. A semi-evergreen shrub to 1 m, usually less. Leaves sessile to 7.5 cm long. Flowers small, c.2.5 cm across. Fruit more elongated than in Tutsan, orange-pink to red and more showy than the flowers, at best in August and September. Susceptible to rust, but recently *H. calycinum* has been infected instead.

**H. beanii** N. Robson. (syn. *H. patulum* var. *henryi* Bean) Lancaster 752.   Native of Yunnan and Guizhou. Semi-evergreen shrub to 1.5 m. Leaves ovate, short-stalked, to 7 cm long. Sepals closed in bud, ovate to elliptic pointed. Flowers cup-shaped to 6 cm across. Stamens ½–¾ as long as petals. Any soil. Sun or part shade. Hardy to −10°C. Summer.

**H. hookerianum** Wight & Arn. B. L. & M. 253, Kingdon Ward 21484   Native of the Himalayas from Nepal to N. Burma and Thailand, and in the hills of S. India, growing in grassy places and open scrub, flowering in May–July. Evergreen shrub to 1.5 m. Leaves short-stalked, lanceolate or narrowly ovate to 6 cm long. Flowers cup-shaped to 5 cm across, smaller in the N.E. part of the range; sepals obovate, spathulate, to circular. Styles very short, ⅕ to ½ as long as ovary. Stamens ¼ to ⅓ as long as petals. Any good soil; sun or part shade. Hardy to −5° or −10°C. Summer.

**H. 'Hidcote'**   Most probably a hybrid between *H. × cyathiflorum* 'Gold Cup' and *H. calycinum*, distributed in cultivation from Hidcote Manor gaden, but possibly originating elsewhere. Deciduous shrub to 1.5 m, more across. Leaves triangular-lanceolate, pale and densely net-veined below. Sepals erect in bud. Flowers to 7.5 cm across, in June–October, almost flat. Stamens ⅓ as long as the petals with orange anthers. Styles equalling ovary. Any soil; sun or part shade. Hardy to −10°C, but usually sprouting again from the ground.

**H. 'Rowallane'**   A hybrid between *H. hookeranium* 'Charles Rogers' and *H. leschenaultii* found at Rowallane, Co. Down. Flowers large, to 7.5 cm across, flattish. Sepals oblanceolate, sometimes pointed. A large shrub to 2 m in mild western gardens. Any good soil; sun or part shade. Hardy to −5°C.

**H. kouytchense** Léveillé (syn. *H. patulum* 'Sungold' and *H. patulum* var. *grandiflorum*) Native of Yunnan and Guizhou. Semi-evergreen shrub to 1.5 m, with dropping branches. Leaves with short stalks, ovate to narrowly ovate, to 5.5 cm long. Sepals erect or ascending, lanceolate, acuminate. Flowers c.6 cm across; stamens c.⅔ as long as petals. Any good soil; sun or part shade. Hardy to −10°C.

**H. calycinum** L.   Native of S. Bulgaria and N. Turkey, growing in grassy places and open woods at up to 1800 m, flowering in July to September. Usually evergreen suckering shrub, covering large areas. Stems to 50 cm tall, ending

H. beanii R.L. 752

H. hookerianum B.L.M. 253

H. hookerianum K.W. 21484

H. beanei

H. 'Hidcote'

H. 'Rowallane'

H. kouytchense

H. calycinum

H. × moserianum

H. patulum

⅓ life size. Specimens from Wakehurst Place, 2nd September

in one large solitary flower 10 cm across. Stamens with reddish anthers. Styles longer than the ovary. Useful for ground cover and tolerant of drought, shade and poor soil. Hardy to −25°C.

**H. × moseranium** André   A hybrid between *H. patulum* and *H. calycinum*, raised at Moser's nurseries at Versailles in around 1887. Evergreen shrub to 50 cm, but usually dying back to ground level in winter. Leaves to 5 cm long; flowers to 6 cm across, in July to October. Styles equal or 1.3 times as long as ovary. Anthers reddish. Any soil; full sun or part shade. Hardy to −10°C. There is also a form

with white variegated, pink-edged leaves, Tricolor, which we have not seen.

**H. patulum** Thunb. ex Murrray   Native of Yunnan and Xizang, east to Kiangsu and Chekiang, and long-cultivated in Japan. Evergreen shrub to 1 m; branches 2–4 lined, or 4-angled. Young leaves short-stalked to 6 cm long, ovate, obtuse, apiculate. Flowers cup-shaped, 5 cm across. Sepals ovate to circular, finely toothed, usually mucronate. Styles ⅔ to almost as long as ovary. Anthers yellow. Any soil; sun or part shade. Hardy to −5°C, but sprouting again if cut to the ground. Summer–autumn.

243

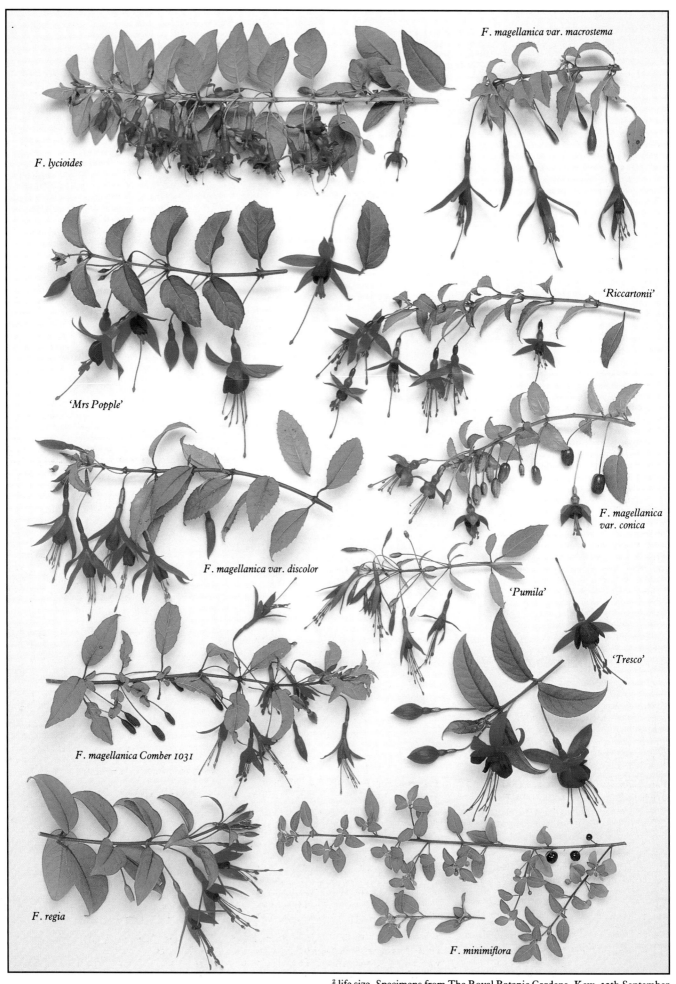

F. magellanica var. macrostema

F. lycioides

'Riccartonii'

'Mrs Popple'

F. magellanica var. conica

F. magellanica var. discolor

'Pumila'

'Tresco'

F. magellanica Comber 1031

F. regia

F. minimiflora

$\frac{2}{5}$ life size. Specimens from The Royal Botanic Gardens, Kew, 12th September

*Fuchsia 'Riccartonii'* at Trebah, Cornwall

**Fuchsia lycioides** Andr. (*Onagraceae*) Native of Chile, between Coquimbo and Valparaiso where it is frequent on sandy hills near the sea, flowering throughout the year. Deciduous or semi-evergreen shrub to 3 m. Flowers, including the tube, *c*.2 cm long. Any soil; sun or part shade. Hardy to −10°C, perhaps. Summer.

**F. magellanica** Lam. Hardy Fuchsia Native of Chile from Valparaiso *c*.31°S., and S. Argentina from 40°S., south to Tierra del Fuego, especially on west-facing mountains, along streams and marshes in *Nothofagus* forest, and in coastal *Drimys-Nothofagus* forest, flowering in April; pollinated by humming birds. Deciduous shrub to 5 m, but usually *c*.2 m or less in cold climates. Leaves opposite, to 5 cm long. Flowers with tube 5–12 mm long. Any moist soil, preferably peaty; sun or part shade with protection from dry wind. Hardy to −10°C, or lower where the rootstalk is protected from frost and the plant can behave as an herbaceous perennial. Late summer–autumn.

**F. magellanica** var. **macrostema** (Ruiz & Pavon) Munz Found in the northern part of the range of *F. magellanica*. Notable for its long sepals and long flower stalks, 4–6 cm long, and larger leaves.

**F. magellanica** var. **conica** (Lindl.) Bailey Native of Chile. Distinguished from var. *magellanica* by its broader leaves and very short expanded calyx tube. One of the parents of 'Riccartonii', through the hybrid 'Globosa', which this may be, although the numerous fruits suggest it is a species, not a hybrid.

**F. magellanica** '**Pumila**' Several clones are said to be in cultivation under the name 'Pumila'; that shown here is a dwarf, but free-

flowering variety of *F. magellanica*. Another is close to 'Tom Thumb' (p. 247), a hybrid with a short-tubed flower.

**F. magellanica** Lam. (H. Comber 1031) This form of *F. magellanica* was collected by Harold Comber near Lake Calafquen, Valdivia, Chile, at 300 m.

**F. magellanica** '**Riccartonii**' Raised in the garden at Riccarton, near Edinburgh, Scotland, *c*. 1830. Now considered a variant of *F. magellanica*. 'Riccartonii' is the common fuchsia planted for hedges in W. Ireland and Scotland; it may be recognized by its short tube *c*.8 mm long, and stiff spreading sepals 18–22 mm long. Moist, humus-rich soil; sun or part shade. Hardy to −15°C when established.

**F. magellanica** var. **discolor** (Lindl.) Bailey A dwarf variety, introduced from near the Straits of Magellan by Capt. King's Survey in 1826–30. Said to be exceptionally hardy.

**F. excorticata** (J. R. & B. Forst.) L. fil. Kotukutuku Native of both islands of New Zealand, where it is common in lowland and subalpine forest, along forest edges, streams and shady gullies, flowering in August–December. Deciduous shrub or small tree to 12 m, with reddish, papery, peeling bark, revealing a smooth green inner layer. Leaves alternate, to 10 cm long. Flowers 20–30 mm long, with blue pollen. Moist, leafy soil and cool, humid conditions. Hardy to −10°C. Spring. Grows well on the W. coasts of Scotland and Ireland.

**F. regia** (Vand.) Munz Native of Brazil, in the Organ Mts. near Rio de Janeiro at *c*.900 m, where it is a scrambler to 6 m. Deciduous shrub with climbing or arching branches. Leaves

*Fuchsia excorticata* at Logan

usually narrower than those shown here. Sepals not reflexed. Good, humus-rich soil; part shade. Late summer. Hardy if planted deep, so that the roots and rootstalk are protected from frost.

**F. minimiflora** Hemsl. Native of S.C. Mexico. Deciduous shrub to 4 m, but usually less in cultivation. Leaves 1–2 cm long. Flowers with petals less than 2.5 mm long; sepals 1.5–2.5 mm long. Moist soil; part shade. Hardy to −5°C perhaps, but lower with protection.

**F. 'Mrs Popple'** An old variety, known since before 1934. Probably a hybrid of 'Corallina'. See also p. 249. Hardy to −10°C, or lower if the rootstalk is protected.

**F. 'Tresco'** Vigorous, bushy, spreading and free-flowering, probably a hybrid of *F. magellanica* and a large-flowered hybrid, raised at Tresco in the Scilly Isles. Hardy to −10°C.

245

'Cliff's Hardy'

'Ruth'

'Sleepy'

'Pee Wee Rose'

'Sealand Prince'

'Susan Travis'

'Thornley's Hardy'

'Pixie'

½ life size. Specimens from Wisley, 26th September

**'Mme Cornellissen'**
**'Rufus'**
**'Variegata'**
**'Versicolor'**
**'Tom Thumb'**
**'Corallina'**
*F. magellanica* var. *molinae*

⅖ life size. Specimens from Wisley, 26th September

**Fuchsia 'Cliff's Hardy'** A cross between 'Athela' and 'Bon Accorde' raised in Britain in 1966. Bushy, upright growth, to 1 m. Hardy to −10°C.

**F. 'Ruth'** A bushy, upright-growing fuchsia, raised in Britain in 1949. Free-flowering. Hardy to −10°C or lower with protection for the rootstock. Late summer to autumn.

**F. 'Sleepy'** A dwarf fuchsia, up to only about 36 cm, but with bushy, upright habit. Raised in the Scilly Isles in 1954; hardy to −10°C.

**F. 'Sealand Prince'** Upright, bushy plant, raised in Britain in 1967. Free-flowering. Hardy to −10°C.

**F. 'Pee Wee Rose'** Perhaps a seedling of *F. magellanica* var. *molinae*, raised in the USA in 1939. Rather open habit which can be trained against a wall; vigorous when grown under glass. Small flowers freely produced. Hardy to −10°C.

**F. 'Susan Travis'** A vigorous, spreading bush eventually up to 75 cm high and wide. Raised in Britain in 1958. Free-flowering. Hardy to −10°C.

**F. 'Thornley's Hardy'** A chance seedling which occurred in Britain in 1970; lax, trailing habit of growth. Small flowers, freely produced. Hardy to −10°C.

**F. 'Pixie'** An upright, bushy sport of 'Graf Witte', which occurred in Britain in 1960. Vigorous grower, up to 1 m; can be used as a hedge plant. Free-flowering. Hardy to −10°C.

**F. 'Mme Cornellissen'** A vigorous, bushy plant, up to 1 m, suitable for hedging. Raised in Belgium in 1860. Very free-flowering. Hardy to −10°C.

**F. 'Rufus'** A vigorous, bushy, upright-growing cultivar, raised in the USA in 1952. Easy to grow; free-flowering over a long season. Hardy to −10°C.

**F. magellanica** var. **gracilis** (Lindl.) Bailey **'Variegata'** Leaves with a wide, whitish margin; otherwise similar to 'Versicolor'. Sometimes reverts to normal green var. *gracilis*. Hardy to −10°C. Late summer to the first frost.

**F. magellanica** var. **gracilis** (Lindl.) Bailey **'Versicolor'** (syn. var. *gracilis* 'Tricolor') Leaves greyish, pinkish when young, sometimes edged with white, often in threes. Flowers slender. The unusual leaf colour is developed best in full light. Hardy to −10°C.

**F. 'Tom Thumb'** A dwarf, bushy cultivar, thought to have been raised in France in the 1850s. Very free-flowering. Hardy to −10°C.

**F. magellanica** var. **molinae** Espinosa (syn. **F. m.** var. **alba** Native of the island of Chiloe. Flowers very pale pink. A graceful but shy-flowering variety, said to be the hardiest of all fuchsias, perhaps to −15°C.

**F. 'Corallina'** An old hybrid raised in Exeter, Devon in 1844. A lax, spreading bush up to 1 m; leaves often in threes. Hardy to −10°C.

**Mitraria coccinea** Cav. (*Gesneriaceae*) Native of S. Chile and S. Argentina, from around 35°S southwards, and in the mist forest south of Coquimbo, growing on moss-covered tree trunks and rocks in deep shade. Evergreen climber or scrambling shrub to 3 m or more. Leaves 2–3 cm long, hairy on the midrib and stalk. Flowers 2.5–3.5 cm long. Fruit fleshy, 10 cm across. Moist leafy or peaty soil in shade, growing best on the cool Atlantic and Pacific coasts. Hardy to −10°C.

*Mitraria coccinea* at Brodick, Arran

*F. magellanica var. molinae 'Sharpitor'*

*'Howlett's Hardy'*

*'Alice Hoffman'*

*'Chillerton Beauty'*

*'Genii'*

*'Goldsworth Beauty'*

*'Lady Thumb'*

*'C. J. Howlett'*

*'Purple Splendour'*

*'Eva Boerg'*

*'Pink Lace'*

½ life size. Specimens from Wisley, 9th September

**Fuchsia 'Howletts Hardy'**   Makes bushy growth up to about 80 cm high. Fairly free-flowering. Hardy to −10°C.

**F. magellanica** var. **molinae 'Sharpitor'**   An unusual cultivar originating in the garden of the same name and introduced by the National Trust during the 1970s. Hardy to −15°C, perhaps.

**F. 'Chillerton Beauty'**   A bushy cultivar, up to 1 m, suitable for hedging. ? Raised at Chillerton on the Isle of Wight during the 1840s. Very free-flowering. Hardy to −10°C.

**F. 'Goldsworth Beauty'**   A bushy cultivar with upright habit, raised in Britain in 1952. Free-flowering. Hardy to −10°C.

**F. 'Alice Hoffman'**   A compact, bushy plant, up to 60 cm high, raised in Germany in 1911. Free-flowering. Hardy to −10°C?.

**F. 'C. J. Howlett'**   A bushy, upright cultivar, raised in Britain in 1911. Flowers single, sometimes semi-double, freely produced. Hardy to −10°C.

**F. 'Lady Thumb'**   A sport of 'Tom Thumb' introduced in Britain in 1966. Dwarf, but upright, growth. Very free-flowering. Hardy to −10°C.

**F. 'Genii'**   Introduced in America in 1951, where it was known as 'Jeane'. Bushy, upright growth. Free-flowering. Leaves yellowish; stems red.

**F. 'Pink Lace'**   A vigorous, upright, bushy cultivar to 80 cm, raised in the Scilly Isles in the 1970s. Free-flowering. Hardy to −5°C.

**F. 'Eva Boerg'**   A low-growing cultivar, with a rather 'open' habit, raised in Britain in the 1940s. Free-flowering. Hardy to −10°C.

**F. 'Purple Splendour'**   A vigorous plant with spreading habit, up to 60 cm high. Hardy to −10°C.

**F. 'Mrs Popple'**   One of the most popular fuchsias, 'Mrs Popple' makes upright, bushy growth and is very vigorous, up to 1 m. Free-flowering. Hardy to −10°C suitable for hedging in mild areas.

**Mutisia decurrens** Car. (*Compositae*)   Native of the Andes in Chile and Argentina, growing in dry rocky places. Evergreen climbing and scrambling shrub to 3 m. Leaves narrow, untoothed, 7.5–12.5 cm long, ending in a tendril. Flowers 10–12.5 cm across. Well-drained dry rocky soil, full sun. Hardy to −10°C. With this and other mutisias it is recommended to place a large stone over the root, to protect the suckers.

**Mutisia oligodon** Poepp. & Endl.   Native of the Andes in Chile and Argentina, at 1000–1500 m, in rocky places and hot dry slopes. Evergreen climbing shrub to 3 m or more in cultivation. Leaves to 3 cm long with toothed edges, whitish woolly beneath, ending in a slender tendril. Flowers about 7 cm across, produced only in warm summers in cultivation. Well-drained stony soil; full sun. Hardy to −15°C. Summer.

*Fuchsia 'Mrs Popple'* at Castle Howard, Yorkshire

Bedded out fuchsias at Nymans

An old conservatory fuchsia at Wallington

*Mutisia oligodon*

*Mutisia decurrens*

*Hibiscus syriacus*
'Woodbridge'

*H. sinosyriacus*
'Ruby Glow'

'Comte de Flandres'

'Redheart'

'Pink Giant'

'Diana'

'Mauve Queen'

⅜ life size. Specimens from Wisley, 25th September

*Hibiscus sinosyriacus 'Lilac Queen' at the Hillier Arboretum*

*Hibiscus syriacus 'Blue Bird'*

*Alyogyne huegellii*

**Hibiscus sinosyriacus** L. H. Bailey (*Malvaceae*)   Native of S. Yunnan, Guizhou, Hunan, Gansu and Shaanxi, where it is commonly cultivated. Deciduous shrub to 3 m, stronger-growing than *H. syriacus*, with broader, more finely-toothed leaves, and slightly larger flowers in early autumn. Introduced from China by H. G. Hillier in 1936, who named two cultivars 'Ruby Glow' and 'Lilac Queen'. Any soil; warm position; full sun. Hardy to −15°C.

**H. syriacus** L.   Native of China, but long cultivated there and in Japan, so that its native range is obscured, and it is not known for certain wild. It has been known and grown in Europe since the late 16th C., when it was thought to have originated in the Middle East, hence the name *syriacus*. Many varieties have been raised and named. All are hardy throughout most of Britain and S. Europe, tolerating cold to −20°C. In cool climates wall protection or a very warm site will help them to flower freely. They are valuable, late-flowering shrubs, to 3 m. Leaves 3-lobed, to 10 cm long. Flowers to 6 cm across (to 12 cm in recent cultivars), originally purplish-pink, from mid–late summer in gardens. Well-drained soil; full sun. No regular pruning needed.

**H. syriacus 'Woodbridge'**   A popular variety raised by Notcutts at Woodbridge, Suffolk, in 1928, and still probably the best single red.

**H. syriacus 'Comte de Flandres'** (syn. 'Boule de Feu')   An old hybrid, known prior to 1856. Flowers to 7 cm across. It doesn't bloom well in cold weather.

**H. syriacus 'Redheart'**   Flowers very large. Origin not recorded.

**H. syriacus 'Pink Giant'**   A hybrid of 'Woodbridge' (q.v.) and 'Red Heart', which bears large flowers.

**H. syriacus 'Dianau'**   A shrub up to 2 m high, raised by Egolf, and introduced by the USA National Arboretum in 1963. The flowers, measuring up to 12 cm across, are freely borne.

**H. syriacus 'Mauve Queen'**   Raised by Notcutts.

**H. syriacus 'Blue Bird'** (syn. 'Oiseau Bleu')   A vigorous shrub, up to 2.5 m high, raised by Croux Fils of France before 1958. The large (up to 8 cm across) flowers are borne from mid–late summer; they close in wet weather.

**H. syriacus 'Hamabo'**   A vigorous shrub, up to 2 m high, with large flowers. (Not to be confused with the Japanese species *H. hamabo*, which has pale yellow flowers with a dark red centre.)

**Alyogyne huegellii** (Endl.) Fryx (syn. *Hibiscus huegellii* Endl.) (*Malvaceae*) Lilac Hibiscus Native of S. and W. Australia, on rocky hillsides and in gorges, especially in the S. Flinders Ranges, flowering in June–January. Upright shrub to 2 m. Leaves deeply 3–5 lobed, suborbicular in outline, to 3 cm long. Flowers 4.5–7 cm long, voilet or purple. Any well-drained soil; full sun. Hardy to −5°C. Good for a Mediterranean climate. 'Moora' is a selected form.

*H. syriacus 'Hamabo'*

*Ceanothus thyrsiflorus var. repens*

*Ceanothus 'Gloire de Versailles'*

*Ceanothus 'Burkwoodii'*

*Ceanothus thyrsiflorus*

*Cestrum parqui*

*Fremontodendron 'California Glory'*

*Calceolaria integrifolia*

*Ceanothus 'Autumnal Blue'*

*Ceanothus 'A. T. Johnson'*

$\frac{2}{5}$ life size. Specimens from Goatcher's Nursery, Sussex, 17th October

*Cestrum aurantiacum*

*Cestrum elegans*

*Fremontodendron decumbens*

*Solanum jasminoides 'Album'*

*Caryopteris × clandonensis*

*Dendromecon harfordii*

**Ceanothus thyrsiflorus** Esch.    Native of California and S. Oregon, near the coast in woods and canyons. A tall shrub, to 6 m. Hardy to −10°C.

**Ceanothus thyrsiflorus** Esch. var. **repens** McMinn. (Rhamnaceae)    Native of C. California from Marin to Monterey Co., growing in scrub and on cliff tops near the sea. A prostrate or hummock-forming evergreen shrub to 2 m or more across, to 1 m high. Leaves to 5 cm long. Flowers in early summer and often again in early autumn in gardens. Full sun; tolerant of summer drought. One of the hardiest species, to −15°C.

**Ceanothus 'Gloire de Versailles'**    A hybrid raised before 1891. Semi-deciduous shrub to 4 m or more. Leaves to 8 cm long. Flowers from late summer to the first hard frost. Full sun. Hardy to −15°C.

**Ceanothus 'Burkwoodii'**    A hybrid raised in England. Evergreen shrub to 2 m. Leaves 3 cm long, grey beneath. Flowers to 6 cm long. Full sun. Hardy to −10°C, with shelter from cold winds. Summer to autumn.

**Ceanothus 'A. T. Johnson'**    A hybrid with a long flowering season, but best in spring and autumn. Well-drained soil; full sun and shelter. Hardy to −10°C.

**Ceanothus 'Autumnal Blue'**    A hybrid of *C. thyrsiflorus*; evergreen shrub to 1.5 m. Leaves to 4 cm long. Flowers in lax panicles. Full sun.

Hardy to −15°C. Summer to autumn.

**Cestrum parqui** L'Herit (*Solanaceae*)    Native of Chile. Deciduous shrub to 2 m. Leaves to 14 cm long. Flowers *c*.2 cm long, in July–September in gardens. Full sun. Hardy to −10°C, but often cut down by frost.

**Cestrum elegans** Schlecht.    Native of Mexico. Deciduous shrub to 3 m. Leaves to 10 cm long. Flowers to 20 mm long. Fruits purplish-red, fleshy. Hardy to −10°C. Early summer.

**Cestrum aurantiacum** Lindl.    Native of Guatemala. Deciduous shrub to 2 m. Leaves 8–9 cm long. Flowers *c*.1.5 cm long in late summer to autumn. Full sun. Hardy to −5°C perhaps.

**Fremontodendron decumbens** Lloyd (syn. *F. californicum* subsp. *decumbens* (Lloyd) Munz) (*Sterculiaceae*)    Native of Eldorado Co., California, in chaparral and scrub. Evergreen prostrate shrub to 4 m across, 1 m high. Flowers 3.6 cm in diameter, in late spring. Hardy to −10°C.

**Fremontodendron 'California Glory'**    A hybrid raised at the Santa Ana Botanic Garden, California. Flowers to 10 cm across, spring–late summer. A fast-growing, showy shrub, but short-lived. Well-drained soil; full sun with wall protection. Hardy to −10°C.

**Dendromecon harfordii** Kell. (*Papaveraceae*) Tree Poppy    Native of California, in scrub on dry slopes flowering mainly in April–July, but intermittently later. Evergreen shrub or small tree to 6 m. Flowers to 6.5 cm across. *D. rigida* Benth. is similar, but has narrower leaves and longer-stalked flowers. Both need well-drained soil; full sun. Hardy to −5°C. Summer.

**Calceolaria integrifolia** (*Scrophulariaceae*) Native of Chile. Evergreen shrub to 1.5 m. Leaves to 10 cm long. Flowers *c*.13 mm across. Well-drained soil; full sun and shelter from cold wind. Hardy to −10°C. Summer.

**Solanum jasminoides** Paxt. **'Album'** (*Solanaceae*) Potato Vine    Native of S. Brazil and Paraquay, on the edges of forest and in scrub. Evergreen or deciduous climber to 5 m. Leaves to 5.5 cm long. Flowers 10–20 in a flat-topped corymb, 1.5–2.5 cm across. Hardy to −10°C.

**Caryopteris × clandonensis** Simmonds (*Verbenaceae*)    A hybrid between *C. incana* (Thunb.) Miq. and *C. mongolica* Bunge known since 1933. *Caryopteris* species are native of Mongolia and W. & N. China to Japan, growing in dry scrub on steep slopes. Deciduous shrub to 1 m, dying back to a woody base in winter. Flowers in August–September. *C. incana* has broader, toothed leaves. Full sun. Hardy to −15°C.

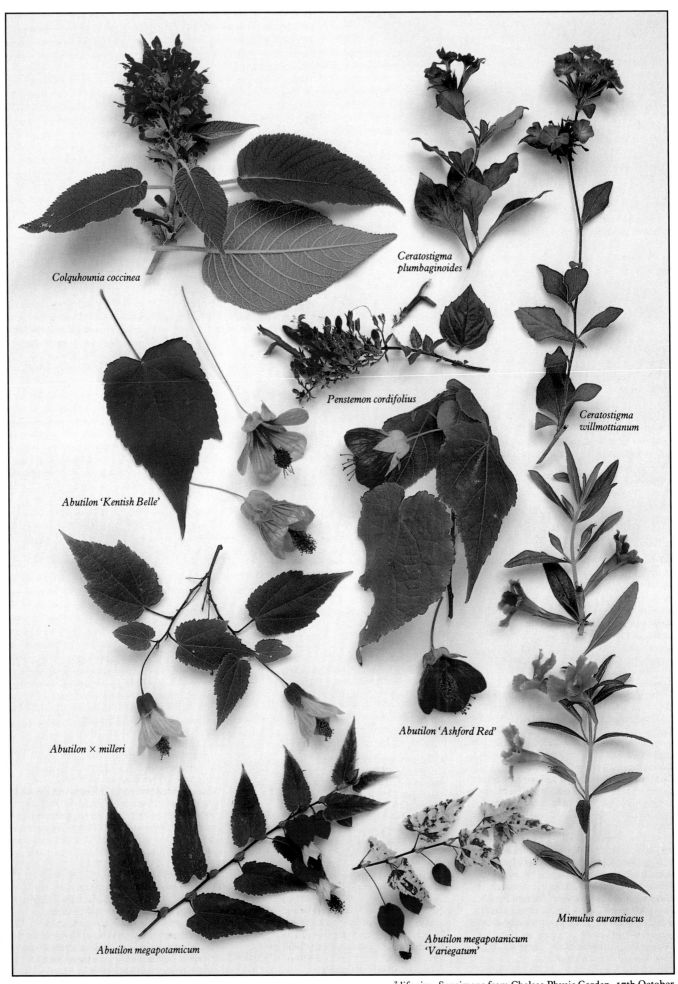

Colquhounia coccinea

Ceratostigma
plumbaginoides

Penstemon cordifolius

Ceratostigma
willmottianum

Abutilon 'Kentish Belle'

Abutilon × milleri

Abutilon 'Ashford Red'

Abutilon megapotamicum

Abutilon megapotanicum
'Variegatum'

Mimulus aurantiacus

$\frac{2}{5}$ life size. Specimens from Chelsea Physic Garden, 17th October

Isoplexis canariensis in Tenerife

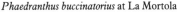
Phaedranthus buccinatorius at La Mortola

Campsis radicans

**Ceratostigma willmottianum** Stapf
(*Plumbaginaceae*) Native of W. Sichuan, on
dry slopes in the Min river valley at 1000–
2000 m, flowering in May–July. Deciduous
shrub to 1 m, usually dying to near the ground
in winter. Full sun. Hardy to −15°C, with
protection for the rootstock. Late summer.

**Ceratostigma plumbaginoides** Bunge Native
of N. China, subshrubby perennial with a
creeping rootstock, forming large patches.
Stems to 35 cm. Hardy to −20°C.

**Colquhounia coccinea** Wall. (*Labiatae*)
Native of the Himalaya, from N. India to
Burma, N. Thailand and Yunnan, in scrub at
1200–3000 m, flowering in September–October.
Upright semi-deciduous shrub to 3 m. See also
p. 241. Hardy to −10°C.

**Abutilon megapotamicum** St. Hil. & Naud.
(*Malvaceae*) Native of Brazil, possibly near
the Rio Grande. Evergreen shrub to 2 m. In the
form with white blotched leaves, **'Variegatum'**,
the variegation is probably caused by virus
infection. Hardy to −10°C, on a warm wall.

**Abutilon 'Kentish Belle'** A hybrid between
*A. megapotamicum* and *A.* 'Golden Fleece', with
slightly hairy leaves. Evergreen shrub to 2 m.
Hardy to −5°C, perhaps hardier. Summer. *A.*
'Golden Fleece' is a sister to 'Ashford Red'.
**A. 'Ashford Red'** Possibly a hybrid between
*A. darwinii* and *A. striatum*, with softly hairy
leaves. Evergreen shrub to 2 m, usually *c.*1 m.
Hardy to −5°C, perhaps. Summer. May be
planted outside in summer.

**Abutilon × milleri** hort. A group of hybrids
between *A. megapotamicum* and *A. pictum*,
flowering more or less throughout the year.
Evergreen shrubs to 1.5 m, with arching
branches. Hardy to −5°C.

**Penstemon cordifolius** Benth.
(*Scrophulariaceae*) Native of California from
San Luis Obispo southwards in scrub in
canyons and rocky slopes, below 1000 m,
flowering in May–July. Twiggy, sprawling
shrub to 3 m. Flowers sometimes yellow. Well-
drained soil, dry in summer. Hardy to −5°C.

**Mimulus aurantiacus** Curt. (syn. *M. glutinosus*
Wendl) (*Scrophulariaceae*) Native of California
in the coast ranges and the N.W. foothills of the
Sierra Nevada, and W. Oregon, on rocks,
roadside banks and dry slopes below 600 m,
flowering in March–August. Sprawling
evergreen shrub to 1.2 m. Leaves 2.5–5 cm,
sticky. Hardy to −10°C. Summer.

**Phaedranthus buccinatorius** (syn. *Distictis
buccinatoria* (*Bignoniaceae*) Native of Mexico.
Evergreen climber, to 5 m or more. Leaves with
2 leaflets and a 3-fid tendril. Flowers to 12 cm
long. Good soil; full sun and warmth. Hardy to
−5°C, perhaps. Midsummer.

**Isoplexis canariensis** (L.) Steud.
(*Scrophulariaceae*) Native of the Canary
Islands, in open places in laurel forest, and tree
heather forest at up to 1000 m, flowering from
November to June. Evergreen shrub to 2 m.
Leaves lanceolate to 10 cm long. Flowers to
5 cm long. Any soil; sun or part shade. Hardy to
−5°C. Mainly early summer.

Campsis grandiflora

**Campsis radicans** (L.) Seem. (syn. *Bignonia
radicans* L.) (*Bignoniaceae*) Native of New
Jersey east to Iowa, south to Texas and Florida,
and naturalized further north, in woods and
scrub, climbing on trees by aerial roots,
flowering in April–June. Woody climber to
20 m. Flowers 6–8 cm long, rarely yellow. Any
good soil; full sun and added heat from a wall
for optimum flowering. Hardy to −20°C.

**Campsis grandiflora** (Thunb.) K. Schum.
Native of C. China, in Hubei and Jiangxi, at
*c.*100 m, flowering in August. Deciduous
climber to 6 m or more. Leaves with 7–9
leaflets, rugose above, glabrous. Flowers about
7.5 cm across, in a panicle. Calyx more deeply
lobed than in *C. radicans*. Hardy to −10°C,
requiring hot summers to flower well.

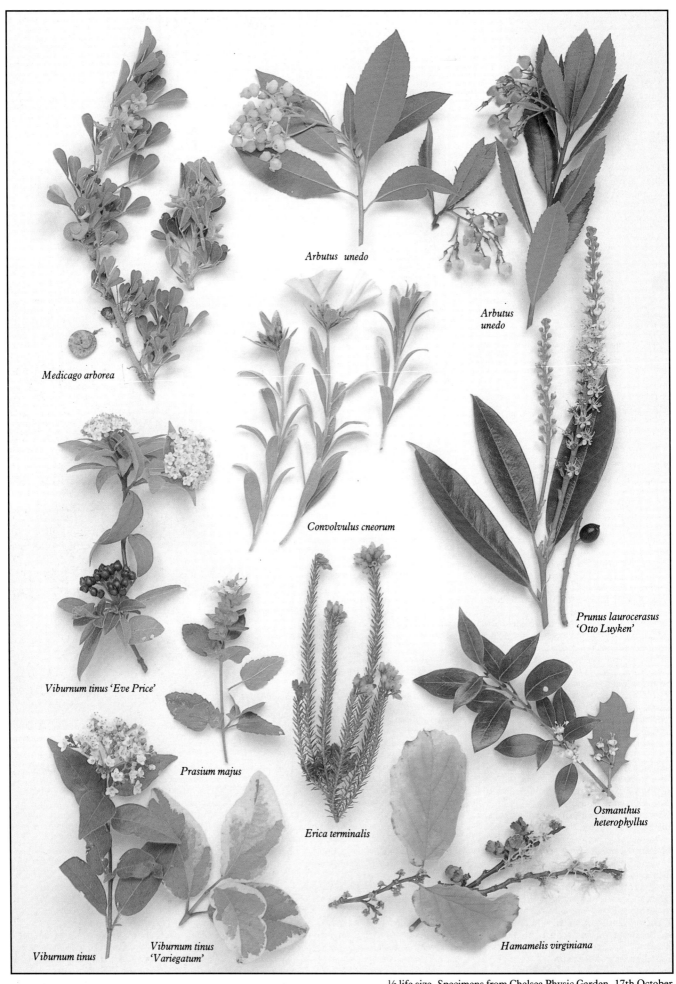

Arbutus unedo

Arbutus
unedo

Medicago arborea

Convolvulus cneorum

Prunus laurocerasus
'Otto Luyken'

Viburnum tinus 'Eve Price'

Prasium majus

Erica terminalis

Osmanthus
heterophyllus

Viburnum tinus

Viburnum tinus
'Variegatum'

Hamamelis virginiana

½ life size. Specimens from Chelsea Physic Garden, 17th October

# LATE-FLOWERING SHRUBS

**Medicago arborea** L. (*Leguminosae*) Native of the Mediterranean in scrub and on rocky hillsides. Evergreen shrub to 4 m. Flowers 12–15 mm long. Full sun. Hardy to −10°C.

**Arbutus unedo** L. (*Ericaceae*) Native of W. Ireland, Brittany, and the Mediterranean, in scrub and woods often on limestone. Evergreen shrub to 12 m. Leaves to 12 cm. Flowers to 9 mm long, pink in f. **rubra**. Fruits red. Well-drained soil; full sun. Hardy to −15°C with shelter from dry cold wind. Autumn.

**Convolvulus cneorum** L. (*Convolvulaceae*) Native of the Mediterranean on limestone by the sea. Evergreen shrub to 50 cm. Leaves to 4 cm. Flowers 15–25 mm. Well-drained, poor soil; full sun. Hardy to −10°C with shelter.

**Prunus laurocerasus** L. **'Otto Luyken'** (*Rosaceae*) A low-growing, evergreen, narrow-leaved clone of *P. laurocerasus*. Leaves to 11 cm. Flowers in spring–autumn. Hardy to −15°C.

**Viburnum tinus** L. (*Caprifoliaceae*) Laurestinus Native of the Mediterranean, in woods, scrub and garrigue, by the sea. Evergreen shrub to 7 m. Leaves 3–10 cm long. Flowers 5–9 mm across. Full sun and shelter. Hardy to −10°C. Autumn–spring. Shown here are clones: **'Eve Price'** with pink buds; **'Variegatum'** rather tender.

**Prasium majus** L. (*Labiatae*) Native of Portugal and the Mediterranean on dry hills by the sea. An evergreen shrub to 1 m. Flowers 17–20 mm long, white or mauve. Hardy to −10°C.

**Erica terminalis** Salisb. (*Ericaceae*) Native of the Mediterranean in damp places. Evergreen shrub to 2.5 m. Leaves 3–5.5 mm. Flowers 5–7 mm long. Acid soil; full sun. Hardy to −10°C. Summer to autumn.

**Osmanthus heterophyllus** See p. 79.

**Hamamelis virginiana** L. See also p. 269.

**Nerium oleander** L. (*Apocynaceae*) Oleander Native of the Mediterranean and S. Portugal, by water. Evergreen shrub to 4 m. Leaves 6–12 cm. Flowers 3–4 cm across, usually pink in the wild, but also red, white and yellowish in cultivation. Full sun. Hardy to −10°C. Summer.

**Lagerstroemeria indica** L. (*Lythraceae*) Crape Myrtle Native of China and Korea, in grass and on cliffs at 30–800 m. Deciduous shrub to 8 m. Leaves 3–5 cm long. Flowers to 4 cm across, reddish in the wild, but also white and pink in cultivation. Any soil; full sun. Hardy to −10°C, if the wood is well ripened. Summer. Requires a very hot summer to flower in S. England. Good autumn colour.

**Solanum crispum** Ruiz. & Pav. **'Glasnevin'** (*Solanaceae*) Native of S. America. Semi-evergreen climber to c. 10 m. Leaves to 12.5 cm; flowers to 3 cm across. Good on chalk. Sun or part shade. Hardy to −10°C. Summer–autumn.

**Phyllerea angustifolia** L. (*Oleaceae*) Native of the Mediterranean on dry hills. Evergreen to 2.5 m. Leaves to 80 mm long. Full sun. Hardy to −20°C. Spring.

**Teucrium fruticans** L. (*Labiatae*) Native of the Mediterranean on dry hills. Evergreen shrub to 2.5 m. Leaves to 4 cm long. Flowers pale blue, pinkish or almost white, 15–25 mm long. Well-drained soil; full sun. Hardy to −10°C.

*Nerium oleander*

*Nerium oleander*

*Lagerstroemeria indica*

*Solanum crispum 'Glasnevin'*

*Phyllerea angustifolia*

*Teucrium fruticans* in S. Spain

Leycesteria formosa

Viburnum betulifolium

Viburnum plicatum 'Pink Beauty'

Lonicera maackii

Viburnum henryi

Viburnum setigerum

Viburnum sargentii

Viburnum opulus
'Compactum'

Viburnum opulus 'Xanthocarpum'

½ life size. Specimens from the Savill Garden, Windsor, 30th October

**Leycesteria formosa** Wall. (*Caprifoliaceae*)
Native of the Himalayas from N. Pakistan to
Yunnan and W. Sichuan (var. *stenosepala*
Rehd.), in scrub and forest by streams, at 2000–
3000 m, flowering in May–July. Deciduous
shrub to 2 m, with green, hollow upright
shoots. Moist soil; sun or part shade. Hardy to
−15°C. Late summer–autumn.

**Viburnum betulifolium** Batal. (*Caprifoliaceae*)
Native of W. Hubei and W. Sichuan, in scrub
and open forest at 1350–2400 m, flowering in
June–July, fruiting in September–October.
Deciduous , many-stemmed shrub to 4 m.
Moist soil; sun or part shade. Hardy to −25°C.

**Viburnum plicatum 'Pink Beauty'** See p. 177
for flowers.    Free-fruiting.

**Viburnum henryi** Hemsl.    Native of W. Hubei
and W. Sichuan, in scrub at 1500–2700 m,
flowering in June–August. Evergreen or semi-
evergreen shrub to 3 m. Leaves thick, fleshy,
5–12 cm long. Hardy to −10°C.

**Viburnum setigerum** Hance    Native of W.
Hubei, W. Sichuan and Jiangxi, in scrub at
1200–2100 m, flowering in May–July.
Deciduous shrub to 4 m. Leaves 7–12 cm long,
with silky hairs on the veins beneath. Flowers
6 m across, all fertile, with a purple calyx. Fruit
8 mm long. Hardy to −20°C.

**Viburnum sargentii** Koehne    For flowers and
text see p. 177. The fruits are slightly larger
than those of *V. opulus*.

**Viburnum opulus 'Compactum'**    A dwarf
form of *V. opulus* (see p. 177) up to 1.5 m free
fruiting. **'Xanthocarpum'**    A low-growing
form, to 1.5 m, with orange-yellow fruit in
hanging bunches. Any moist soil; full sun or
part shade. Hardy to −25°C. White flowers in
summer.

**Viburnum furcatum** Bl.    See p. 175 for flowers
and text. In this photograph, taken in E.
Hokkaido, can be seen *Euonymus macropterus*,
*Acer japonicum*, *Quercus mongolica* and *Aralia
elata*.

**Viburnum acerifolium** L. Maple-leaf
Viburnum    Native of Quebec south to Florida
and west to Tennessee and Minnesota, in
deciduous woods in mountains, and hills,
flowering in May–August. Deciduous shrub to
2 m. Flowers all fertile, 6 mm across.

**Lonicera maackii** Maxim. (*Caprifoliaceae*) See
p. 99 for flowers and text.

**Symphoricarpus albus** (L.) S. F. Blake
(*Caprifoliaceae*) Snowberry    Native of Quebec
south to W. Virginia, west to Minnesota and
Colorado, flowering in May–July. Suckering
shrub with upright shoots to 2 m. Leaves
2.5–8 cm long, ovate-orbicular to ovate,
pubescent or glabrous beneath, scented.
Flowers pink, 6 mm long, campanulate. Berries
spongy, 1.3 cm across. Any moist soil; sun or
part shade. Hardy to −25°C.

**Sambucus sieboldiana** Blume ex Graebn.
(*Caprifoliaceae*)    Native of Japan, from
Honshu southwards, Korea and N. & W.
China, in scrub and woods in the hills, flowering
in April–June. Deciduous shrub to 4 m.
Leaflets 5–7, rather distant.4–12 cm long.
Flowers greenish-white, 3–4 mm across. Fruit
red or yellow-orange, about 4 mm across.

Mixed shrubs in E. Hokkaido in early October

*Viburnum furcatum*

*Symphoricarpus albus*

*Sambucus sieboldiana*

*Viburnum acerifolium*

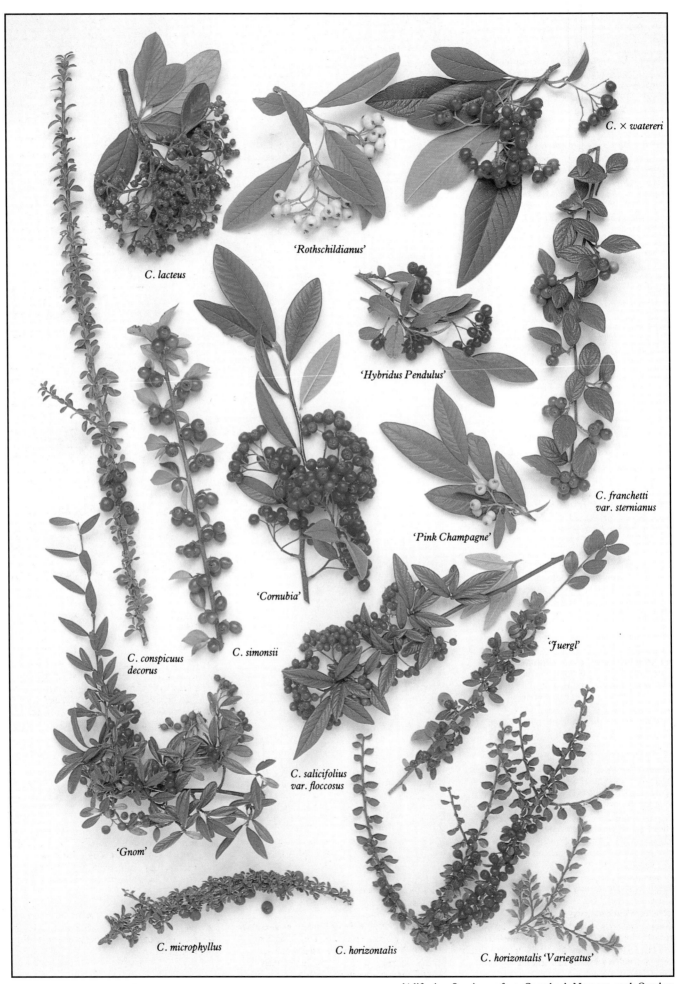

*C. × watereri*

*'Rothschildianus'*

*C. lacteus*

*'Hybridus Pendulus'*

*'Cornubia'*

*C. franchetti
var. sternianus*

*'Pink Champagne'*

*C. conspicuus
decorus*

*C. simonsii*

*'Juergl'*

*C. salicifolius
var. floccosus*

*'Gnom'*

*C. microphyllus*

*C. horizontalis*

*C. horizontalis 'Variegatus'*

½ life size. Specimens from Goatcher's Nursery, 30th October

*Berberis vulgaris* near Erzurum, in N.E. Turkey

*Berberis georgii*

*Osmanthus decorus* (p. 79)

*Cotoneaster bullatus*

*Cotoneaster 'Cornubia'*

**Cotoneaster lacteus** W. W. Sm. (*Rosaceae*) Native of N.W. Yunnan, in scrub. Evergreen shrub to 5 m. Hardy to −15°C. Summer.

**C. 'Rothschildianus'** A hybrid between *C. salicifolius* and *C. frigidus* 'Fructo-luteo' raised at Exbury in 1930. A graceful shrub, to 5 m.

**C. × watereri** Exell. A group of hybrids between *C. frigidus* and *C. henryanus*. Evergreen or semi-evergreen shrubs to 5 m. Hardy to −15°C.

**C. franchetii** Boiss. var. **sternianus** Turrill Native of Xizang, N. Burma (var. *sternianus*), Yunnan and W. Sichuan, in scrub at 2000–3000 m, flowering in June, fruiting in September–October. Evergreen or semi-deciduous shrub to 3 m. Flowers small, pinkish. Hardy to −15°C. Shown here: Farrar 1325.

**C. 'Hybridus Pendulus'** (syn. 'Pendulus') Origin unknown, Stems prostrate, or pendulous when grafted as a standard. Leaves deciduous.

**C. conspicuus** Marquand Native of S. E. Xizang, growing over rocks by the Tsangpo, so they 'looked as if they were simmering like red-hot lava' (Kingdon Ward). Evergreen shrub to 2 m in cultivation, or prostrate. Hardy to −15°C.

**C. simonsii** Baker Native of the Khasia hills in Assam. Erect, semi-evergreen shrub to 4 m, with long shoots. Hardy to −20°C.

**C. 'Cornubia'** A seedling of unknown parentage, raised at Exbury around 1930. A spreading shrub to 7 m, and as much across, with arching branches.

**C. 'Pink Champagne'** A hybrid close to *C. salicifolius*, with yellow berries becoming pinkish.

**C. salicifolius** Franch. var. **floccosus** Rehd. & Wils. Native of W. Sichuan in scrub at 2600–3000 m, flowering in July, fruiting in November. Evergreen or semi-evergreen shrub to 4 m, with arching branches. Hardy to −20°C.

**C. 'Juergl'** A hybrid between *C. dammeri* and probably *C. rotundifolius*. Evergreen shrub to 50 cm.

**C. 'Gnom'** A seedling of *C. salicifolius*, forming an evergreen carpet. Leaves *c*.2 cm.

**C. microphyllus** Wall. ex Lindl. Native of the Himalayas, from Afghanistan to W. Sichuan (var. *cochleatus* Franch.), on rocks, and on alpine slopes at 2000–5400 m, flowering in May–June, fruiting in September–December.

Prostrate or low evergreen to 60 cm. Hardy to −25°C.

**C. horizontalis** Dcne. Native of W. Hubei and W. Sichuan, growing prostrate over rocks, flowering in June, fruiting in November. Deciduous sprawling shrub to 2 m across. Flowers pinkish, visited by wasps. Hardy to −25°C. **'Variegatus'** is a slow-growing form with white-edged leaves.

**C. bullatus** Boiss. Native of S.E. Xizang and W. Sichuan, in scrub and forest at 1900–2800 m, flowering in May–June, fruiting in September–October. Deciduous shrub or small tree to 8 m, usually to 3 m. Flowers small, pink. Hardy to −20°C.

**Berberis vulgaris** L. (*Berberidaceae*) Native of Europe from France to central Russia and N.E. Turkey, in hedges, scrub and rocky slopes, flowering in May–June, fruiting in September–October. Deciduous shrub to 3 m. Hardy to −35°C.

**Berberis georgii** Ahrendt. A hybrid of unknown origin, probably of *B. vulgaris*. Shrub to 1.5 m, with arching branches; exceptionally free-fruiting.

Stranvaesia davidiana

S. d. 'Fructuluteo'

S. d. 'Prostrata'

Pyracantha 'Orange Glow'

Pyracantha atalantoides

S. davidiana var. undulata

Pyracantha 'Lalandei'

Pyracantha rogersiana 'Flava'

Pyracantha rogersiana

× Gaulnettya wisleyensis

Pyracantha 'Mohave'

Pernettya 'Snow White'

'White Pearl'

'Cherry Ripe'

flowering branch

P. 'Mulberry Wine'

'Mother of Pearl'

'Pink Pearl'

'Crimsonia'

'Lilian'

'Lilacina'

½ life size. Specimens from the Savill Garden, Windsor, 30th October

**Stranvaesia davidiana** Dcne. (*Rosaceae*)   Native of W. Sichuan (on Omei Shan) and W. Hubei (var. *undulata* Rehd. & Wils.), south to Vietnam, on cliffs and in scrub flowering in June, fruiting in October. Evergreen shrub or small tree to 10 m. Leaves 6–11 cm long. Flowers white, 8 mm across. Fruit 7–8 mm across, in nodding, loose bunches. Any soil; sun or part shade. Hardy to −15°C. Similar to a large *Cotoneaster*, but differing in its soft-, not hard-shelled seeds.

**S. davidiana 'Fructuluteo'** Dcne.   Raised by the Slieve Donard Nursery, Co. Down, before 1920.

**S. davidiana 'Prostrata'** Dcne.   A prostrate form raised at Hidcote Manor, probably from seed sent by G. Forrest from Yunnan. Forming a wide-spreading carpet, with occasional upright branches.

**S. davidiana** Dcne. var. **undulata** (Dcne.) Rehd. & Wilson   Introduced from Hubei, where it was reported by Wilson to be 'exceedingly common'; it has smaller leaves and nearly glabrous flowers, on a more spreading shrub.

**Pyracantha atalantoides** (Hance) Stapf (syn. *P. gibbsii* A. B. Jacks) (*Rosaceae*)   Native of Guizhou, S.E. Sichuan, W. Hunan and W. Hubei, in hedges and by streams at 300–1300 m, flowering in May–July, fruiting in November–December. Evergreen shrub to 6 m. Leaves glabrous and glaucescent beneath, usually entire, widest at the middle, oblong or oval, 3–7 cm long. Flowers white, 8–9 mm across. Fruits 6–7 mm across. Any good soil; full sun. Hardy to −15°C. Fruiting through the winter.

**P. 'Orange Glow'**   A chance seedling found in a garden at Wageningen, Holland around 1930. Leaves 2–4 cm long. Fruits 9 × 7 mm.

**P. rogersiana** (A. B. Jacks) Chittenden   Native of N.W. Yunnan, in hedges and scrub, at *c*.2500 m, flowering in May. Evergreen shrub to 4 m. Leaves oblanceolate or narrowly obovate, smaller than other species, 15–35 mm long, 5–10 mm wide, tapering gradually into the stalk. Flowers 7 mm across. Fruits 6 mm across, orange-red to yellow. Any soil; full sun or part shade on a wall. Hardy to −15°C. Autumn–winter fruiting. 'Flava' is a yellow-berried form.

**P. 'Mohave'**   A hybrid between *P. koidzumii* and *P. coccinea* 'Wyatt' raised by D. E. Egolf at the US National Arboretum, Washington DC in 1963. Robust shrub to 4 m, more across. Leaves obovate. Hardy to −20°C, perhaps.

**P. coccinea 'Lalandei'** Roem.   Raised in France by Lalande of Nantes in around 1874. Erect evergreen shrub to 6 m. Leaves ovate-oblong, 2–4 cm long, acute, slightly crenate. Fruits 10 × 8 mm, orange, in rather dense clusters.

× **Gaulnettya wisleyenis** (*Ericaceae*) (for flowers see p. 167)   A hybrid between *Pernettya mucronata* and *Gaultheria shallon* which appeared in the Wild Garden at Wisley. Hardy to −15°C.

**Pernettya mucronata** (L. fil.) Gaud. (*Ericaceae*)   Native of S. Chile and S. Argentina to about 40°S, forming extensive heathland. Evergreen shrub to 1.5 m, suckering to form thickets. Leaves spine-tipped, to 1.8 cm long. Flowers white, 6 mm long. Fruits spongy, to 15 mm across, varying from white to purple. Many clones have been named, and a selection is shown here. The plants are said to be partly unisexual, partly hermaphrodite, and to ensure good fruit production, it is advisable to plant a good male close to the female fruiting clones. Acid, moist soil; sun or part shade. Hardy to −15°C. Winter–spring fruiting.

**Crataegus orientalis** Pallas ex M. Bieb. (*Rosaceae*)   Native of S. Europe, Crimea, the Caucasus and Turkey, on rocky hillsides and in open woods at up to 2240 m, flowering in May–July. Deciduous shrub or small tree to 5 m. Leave rhombic or obovate-oblong, 3–7 lobed, with greyish hairs. Flowers 1.5–2 cm across.

Fruit reddish-orange, to 2 cm across. Any well-drained soil; full sun. Hardy to −20°C.

**Prunus padus** L. (*Rosaceae*) Bird Cherry   For flowers see p. 77.   The black, juicy berries are not edible, being very acid.

**Azara lanceolata** Hooker fil. (*Flacourtiaceae*)   For flowers see p. 216. Native of S. Chile, and neighbouring Argentina, on the edges of evergreen *Nothofagus* forest, and by lakes, flowering in November–December, fruiting in February. Moist soil, with humidity. Very sensitive to drying winds which cause the leaves to blacken and drop. Seen here fruiting at Brodick on the Isle of Arran, S.W. Scotland.

*Crateagus orientalis* near Ankara in C. Turkey

*Pyracantha* on a cottage wall in Dorset

*Prunus padus*

*Azara lanceolata* at Brodick

*Euonymus hamiltonianus*
'Coral Chief'

*Euonymus planipes*

*Euonymus europaeus*

*Euonymus grandiflorus*

*Euonymus alatus var. apterus*

⅖ life size. Specimens from Wisley, 9th September

*Euonymus alatus*

*Euonymus oxyphyllus*

*Euonymus macropterus*

**Euonymus hamiltonianus** Wall. **'Coral Chief'**
Native of Afghanistan to S.E. Xizang, Burma,
and Yunnan (with var. *sieboldianus* (Bl.) in N.E.
Asia and Japan) in forest and scrub at 700–
2700 m, flowering in April–July, fruiting in
September–November. Deciduous large
spreading shrub or small tree to 5 m or more.
Leaves oblong, elliptic, or ovate-oblong,
5–12 cm long, minutely serrulate. Flowers pale
green, 4-petalled. Fruits pinkish, lobed. Any
good soil; sun or part shade. Hardy to −15°C. or
lower. Cultivars with good fruiting and autumn
leaf colour have been selected, including 'Coral
Charm', 'Coral Chief' and 'Fiesta'.

**Euonymus planipes** (Koehne) Koehne (syn. *E.
sachalinensis* hort.) Native of Hokkaido, N.
Honshu, N.E. China, Korea, and E. Siberia, in
woods and scrub in the mountains, flowering in
May–June, fruiting in September–October.

Deciduous shrub to 4 m. Leaves variable in
shape, 7–13 cm long. Flowers green, in hanging
bunches of 10 or more (brown, in fewer-
flowered bunches in the true *E. sachalinensis*,
endemic to Sakhalin). Fruits 5-angled, with
narrow wings, 18 mm across. Sun or part shade.
Hardy to −25°C. Early autumn fruiting.

**Euonymus europaeus** L. (*Celastraceae*)
Spindleberry Native of Europe, except the far
north and the Mediterranean coast, in scrub and
hedges, especially on chalk and limestone,
flowering in May–June, fruiting in September–
November. Deciduous shrub or small tree to
6 m. Leaves 3–8 cm long, ovate-lanceolate to
elliptic crenate-serrulate. Flowers with 4 petals;
fruits pink, 10–15 mm wide, angled. Any well-
drained soil; sun or part shade. Hardy to
−25°C. Numerous good forms have been
selected, e.g. 'Red Cascade'.

**Euonymus grandiflorus** Wall. Native of the
Himalayas from Nepal to Yunnan, and Shanxi,
in forests and by streams at 1000–3400 m. Large
shrub or small tree to 7.5 m, rarely to 15 m.
Leaves obovate or obovate-oblong, to 12 cm
long (including petiole). Flowers 2 cm across.
Fruit 4-lobed and ribbed, yellowish to pale
pink. Hardy to −15°C. Autumn flowering.

**Euonymus alatus** (Thunb.) Sieb. Native of
Japan, where it is common in all islands, Korea,
E. Siberia and N.E. China, in scrub and woods
in lowlands and mountains, flowering in May–
June. Deciduous twiggy shrub to 2 m, with
horizontal fan-shaped branches. Leaves
1.5–7 cm long. Flowers solitary, or few
together, 4-petalled, pale green, 6 mm across.
Fruit deeply lobed, each lobe with one seed.
Any soil, sun or part shade. Hardy to −25°C.
The form shown here, with unwinged branches

*Euonymus planipes*

*Camellia sasanqua 'Cotton Candy'* in Oregon

in var. *apterus* Loes; normal *E. alatus* has twigs variably winged with 2 or 4 corky outgrowths.

**Euonymus oxyphyllus** Miq.    Native of all Japan, Korea and C. China, in woods and scrub on low mountains, flowering in May–June, fruiting in September–October. Deciduous shrub to 4 m; in the wild to 7.5 m. Leaves to 5–10 cm long. Flowers greenish or pinkish, more than 10 in a branch, 7 mm across. Fruit globose, 10–12 mm across, with 4 or 5 ribs, on long slender stalks. Hardy to −25°C.

**Euonymus macropterus** Rupr.    Native of Hokkaido, N. Honshu and Shikoku, N.E. China, E. Siberia, Sakhalin and Korea, in mixed and coniferous forest, and scrub, flowering in June–July. Deciduous shrub to 4 m. Leaves obovate, shortly acuminate, 6–12 cm long. Flowers in bunches of around 10, 4-petalled, pale green, 6 mm across. Fruit to 2–5 cm wide, with 4 broad wings. Any moist soil; sun or part shade. Hardy to −25°C.

**Euonymus latifolius** (L.) Mill.    Native of S. France and C. Italy east to N. Turkey, the Caucasus and the Crimea, on hillsides in scrub, among bracken and on wooded cliffs, flowering in May–June, fruiting in September–October. Deciduous shrub to 6 m, with arching branches. Leaves 8–16 cm long, oblong-elliptical to obovate. Flowers green, usually 5-petalled. Fruits 15–20 mm across, winged on the angles. Any soil; sun or part shade. Hardy to −20°C.

**Camellia sasanqua** Thunb. (*Theaceae*)    Native of Kyushu, Yakushima and the Ryukyu islands, in scrub, on grassy slopes and in open *Cryptomeria* forest, flowering in October–December. Evergreen, rather upright shrub to 4 m. Leaves glossy, 3–7 cm long, broadly oblanceolate to narrowly obovate, serrulate. Flowers white in the wild, 4–7 cm across; petals obovate or oblong, retuse. Acid soil; sun or part shade. Hardy to −10°C, with shelter. Autumn. Numerous cultivars of *C. sasanqua*, mostly with single pink or red flowers, have been raised in Japan. Shown here are an Anemone-flowered Japanese cultivar, possibly 'Choji Guruma', and a semi-double from America, possibly 'Cotton Candy'.

**Schizandra grandiflora** (Wall.) Hooker fil. var. **rubriflora** (Franch.) Schneid. (*Schizandraceae*) The flowers of this dioecious species are shown on p. 87. It is normally necessary to have male and female plants growing nearby to ensure a good set of fruit; the fleshy arils are attached to the elongated receptacle of the female flowers.

*Camellia sasanqua* in Yakushima

*Camellia sasanqua 'Choji Guruma'*

*Euonymus latifolius* near Trabzon

*Schizandra grandiflora var. rubriflora*

*Vitis coignetiae* climbing into *Tilia mongolica* in N. Hokkaido, near Shari, in October

**Vitis coignetiae** Pulliat ex Planch. (*Vitaceae*)
Native of Japan, in Hokkaido, Honshu,
Shikoku, of Korea and Sakhalin, climbing high
into forest trees. Deciduous vine to 25 m or
more. Leaves rugose, 8–30 cm long and across,
purplish or red in autumn. Fruits small black,
in long narrow bunches. Any good soil; sun or
part shade. Hardy to −25°C. One of the finest
foliage climbers for large gardens.

**Vitis vinifera** L.   Native of S.E. Europe from
Germany, France and Corsica east to Turkey,
Iran, the Caucasus and C. Asia, on river banks
and in damp woods. The wild grape, subsp.
*sylvestris* (Gmel.) Hegi has male and female
flowers on different plants, small black grapes
and more deeply lobed leaves on the male
plants. The cultivated grape, subsp. *vinifera* was
probably derived from this, and first grown in
Asia Minor. It has hermaphrodite flowers and
variably coloured grapes. The decorative
varieties are grown primarily for foliage and
especially autumn colour. Any soil; full sun or
part shade. Hardy to −20°C.
'Incana'   has leaves covered in white, fine
hairs, especially when young, and black grapes.
Autumn colour pale reds.
'Purpurea'   has leaves rich reddish purple with
a bloom when young, later dark purplish, and
small black grapes.

**Vitis 'Brant'**   A hybrid between *V. vinifera*
'Black St Peters' and an American grape,
'Clinton', a cultivar of *V. riparia*, raised by
Charles Arnold in Paris, Ontario in *c.* 1860.
Fruits sweet, black but small. Leaves turning
red, with contrasting green veins, in late
summer.

**Parthenocissus quinquefolia** (L.) Planchon
(*Vitaceae*)   Native of Quebec east to Minnesota
and to Mexico and Florida, in woods and on
rocks. Rampant climber to 20 m or more,
climbing by discs on the curling tendrils.
Leaves 3–7 foliolate, red in autumn. Any soil;
sun or shade. Hardy to −25°C. Colouring in
early autumn, but leaves soon falling.

**Parthenocissus tricuspidata** Planch. (*Vitaceae*)
Native of Japan, where it is common, Korea and
W. Hubei and Jiangxi, on rocks and in forests,
at up to 1200 m. A rampant climber to 20 m
clinging by round pad-like suckers on the
tendrils. Leaves shining, thick, to 12 cm long;
on creeping shoots, the leaves 3-foliolate; on
climbing, the smaller leaves cordate, crenate,
the larger 3-lobed, colouring well in autumn.
Any soil; sun or shade. Hardy to −15°C.

**Smilax lasioneura** Hooker (*Liliaceae*)   Native
of S. Ontario to Montana, south to Colorado
and Georgia in scrub by rivers, or on the edges
of woods, flowering in May–June. Twining
herbaceous climber to 3 m. Leaves glaucous.
Berries black. Flowers greenish, smelling of bad
meat, attracting flies. Any soil, full sun. Hardy
to −25°C.

**Smilax aspera** L. (*Liliaceae*)   Native of the
Azores, Portugal and the Mediterranean region,
in scrub and among rocks, flowering in August–
October, fruiting in September onwards.
Evergreen climber with hooked spines on the
stems to 15 m. Leaves to 11 cm long, tough.
Flowers greenish, very small, male and female
on separate plants. Any soil; full sun. Hardy to
−10°C. Late summer.

*Vitis coignetiae*

*Vitis vinifera 'Incana'*

# VINES

*Parthenocissus tricuspidata*

*Vitis vinifera 'Purpurea' on the Long Pergola at West Dean, Sussex*

*Parthenocissus quinquefolia*

*Smilax lasioneura*

*Vitis 'Brant'*

*Smilax aspera*

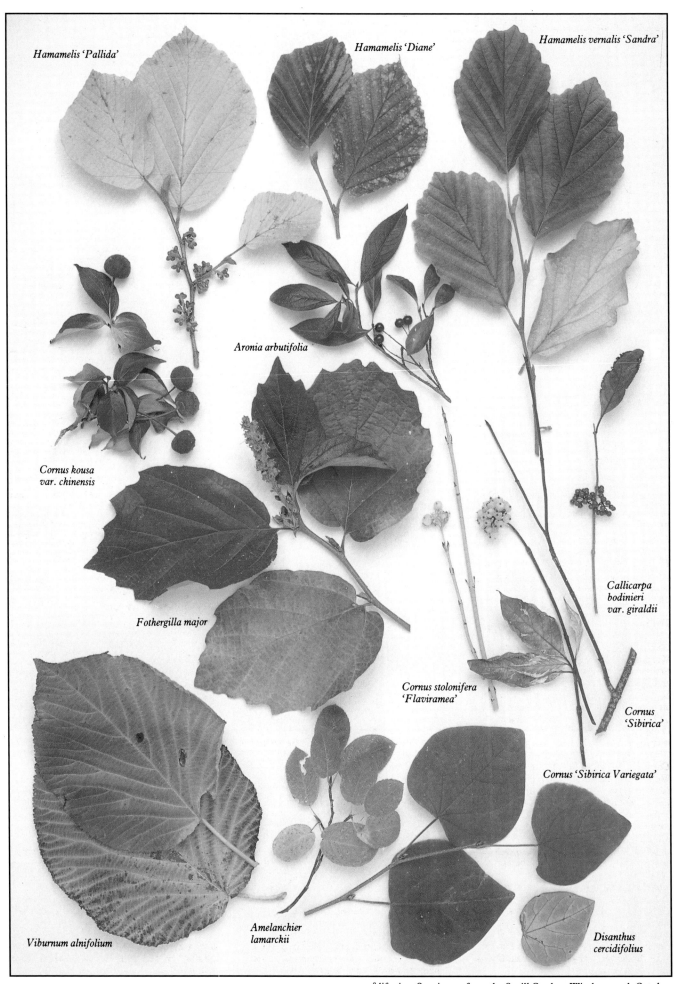

Hamamelis 'Pallida'

Hamamelis 'Diane'

Hamamelis vernalis 'Sandra'

Aronia arbutifolia

Cornus kousa
var. chinensis

Fothergilla major

Callicarpa
bodinieri
var. giraldii

Cornus stolonifera
'Flaviramea'

Cornus
'Sibirica'

Cornus 'Sibirica Variegata'

Viburnum alnifolium

Amelanchier
lamarckii

Disanthus
cercidifolius

⅔ life size. Specimens from the Savill Garden, Windsor, 30th October

*Hamamelis virginiana* in New York State

Fall colour in Westchester Co., New York

*Cornus alba 'Sibirica'* at the Savill Gardens, Windsor

**Hamamelis mollis 'Pallida'** For flowers see p. 15.
Autumn colour yellow.

**Hamamelis × intermedia 'Diane'** (for flowers
see p. 15) Leaves 6–12 cm long. Autumn
colour red. Most clones of *H. japonica* have
orange-yellow autumn leaves.

**Hamamelis vernalis** Sarg. **'Sandra'** See also p. 15.

**Hamamelis virginiana** L. (*Hamamelidaceae*)
Witch Hazel Native from Nova Scotia
eastward to Wisconsin, south to Texas (rarely)
and N. Florida, in deciduous woods, flowering in
September–October either with the leaves or
after the leaves have fallen. Deciduous shrub to
9 m, usually in the understory of tall forest.
Petals uncurling in warmth, curling up again
when cold. Acid soil. Hardy to −35°C.

**Cornus alba** L. **'Sibirica'** (*Cornaceae*)
Westonbirt Dogwood Native of Siberia
eastwards to N.E. China and Korea, by lakes and
along rivers and streams in mixed forest. Twigs
deep red. Deciduous shrub to 3 m. Flowers
creamy white, in heads 3.5–5 cm across Fruit
white or very pale blue. Hardy to −35°C. This
clone is less robust than the others in cultivation,
growing to 1.5 m, and is probably best pruned
hard every 2 or 3 years.
**'Sibirica Variegata'** (syn. 'Elegantissima',
'Argenteo-marginata') Pale green leaves, with
a broad white edge and slightly deeper red twigs
than 'Sibirica'.

**Cornus kousa** Hance var. *chinensis* Osborn See
p. 180 for flower. Compare the fruits *C. florida*
and *C. nuttallii* on p. 271.

**Cornus stolonifera** Michx. **'Flaviramea'**
(*Cornaceae*) A yellow-twigged form of *C.
stolonifera*, which is native from Newfoundland
east to Yukon, and south to Virginia, New
Mexico and California, in wet scrub, by lakes
and rivers, flowering in May–August, fruiting
July–October. Suckering, thicket-forming
shrub to 2.5 m. Flowers dirty white, in a head
3–5 cm across. Hardy to −35°C. and below.
Grown for its winter twigs.

**Aronia arbutifolia** (L.) Elliott (*Rosaceae*) Red
Chokeberry Native of Massachusetts west to
Minnesota, and south to Florida and Texas, in
woods, and scrub, flowering in April–May,
fruiting in September–October. Deciduous
shrub to 3 m, of upright, rather sparse growth.
Flowers 9–20 in a rather dense cluster, each
1 cm across, white or pinkish. Fruit 5–7 mm
across. Hardy to −25°C.

**Disanthus cercidifolius** Maxim
(*Hamamelidaceae*) Native of S.E. China (?)
and Japan, in moist woods in C. Honshu and
Shikoku, flowering in October–November, as
soon as or before the leaves have fallen.
Deciduous multi-stemmed shrub with arching
branches to 3 m. Leaves smooth, 5–12 cm long
and wide, glaucous beneath. Flowers 12 mm
across. Moist acid soil, with humidity and
warmth to grow well; partial shade or high
overhead cover of deciduous trees, with shelter,
or in the open in very moist soil. Hardy to
−15°C.

**Fothergilla major** (Sims) Lodd. See p.151 for
flower. All *Fothergilla* species are noted for
their excellent autumn colour.

*Disanthus cercidifolius* in flower

**Callicarpa bodinieri** Lev. var. **giraldii** (Rehd.)
Rehder (*Verbenaceae*) Native of C. & W.
China, in woods and scrub, flowering in June–
August, fruiting in October onwards.
Deciduous shrub to 2 m. Leaves elliptic, to
ovate-elliptic, acuminate, 5–12 cm long,
glabrous above. Flowers purplish *c.*7 mm long.
Fruits mauve or purple 3–4 mm across, in dense
clusters at each node along the stem. Hardy to
−20°C.

**Viburnum lantanoides** Michx. (*Caprifoliaceae*)
See p. 175 for flower and text.

**Amelanchier lamarckii** See p. 76. Most
*Amelanchier* species are exceptionally reliable for
autumn colour.

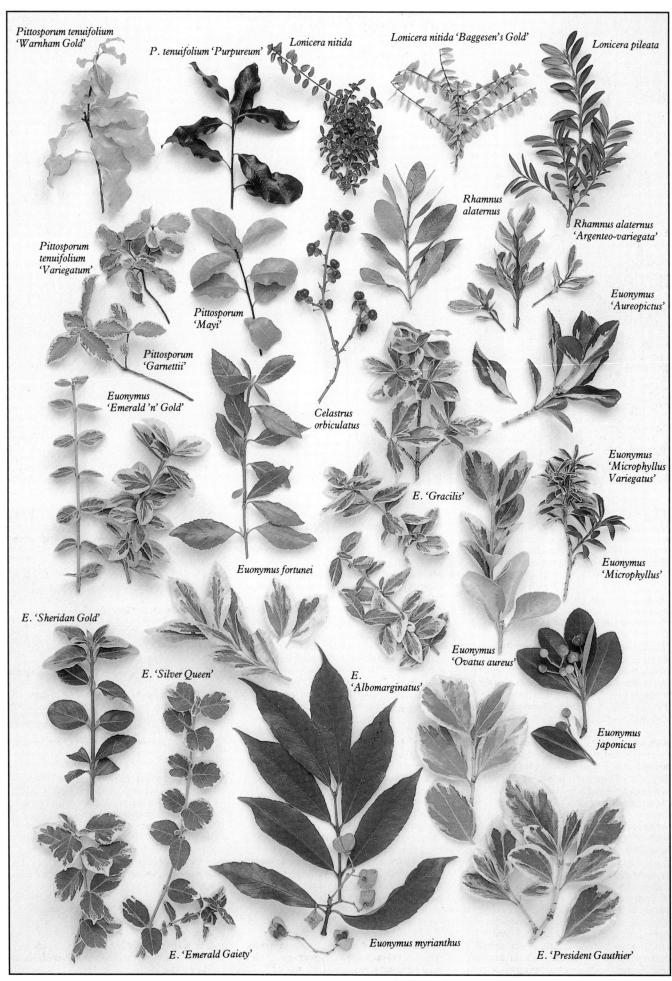

Pittosporum tenuifolium 'Warnham Gold'

P. tenuifolium 'Purpureum'

Lonicera nitida

Lonicera nitida 'Baggesen's Gold'

Lonicera pileata

Rhamnus alaternus

Rhamnus alaternus 'Argenteo-variegata'

Pittosporum tenuifolium 'Variegatum'

Pittosporum 'Mayi'

Euonymus 'Aureopictus'

Pittosporum 'Garnettii'

Celastrus orbiculatus

Euonymus 'Emerald 'n' Gold'

Euonymus 'Microphyllus Variegatus'

E. 'Gracilis'

Euonymus fortunei

Euonymus 'Microphyllus'

E. 'Sheridan Gold'

Euonymus 'Ovatus aureus'

E. 'Silver Queen'

E. 'Albomarginatus'

Euonymus japonicus

E. 'Emerald Gaiety'

Euonymus myrianthus

E. 'President Gauthier'

⅓ life size. Specimens from Goatcher's Nursery, 5th December

270

*Cornus florida*

*Paliurus spina-christi*

*Pistacia lentiscus*

*Cornus nuttallii*

*Hippophäe rhamnoides*

*Cornus sanguinea*

**Pittosporum tenuifolium** Gaertn.
(*Pittosporaceae*)   Native of New Zealand,
except Westland, common in coastal and
lowland forest up to 1000 m, flowering in
October–November. Evergreen graceful tree to
8 m. Hardy to −10°C, but killed by freezing
wind. Several varieties are cultivated:
**'Mayi'**   does best near the sea on the west
coasts of Europe; it is a form of *P. tenuifolium*.
**'Warnham Gold'**   was selected at Warnham
Court, Sussex, in 1959.
**'Purpureum'**   has mature leaves purple, young
leaves green. A tender variety.
**'Variegatum'**   has leaves edged with white.
**'Garnettii'**   has leaves pink-flushed in winter,
longer than *P. tenuifolium*, hairy beneath.
Possibly a hybrid with *P. ralphii*, raised in New
Zealand.

**Lonicera nitida** Wilson (*Caprifoliaceae*)   Native
of Yunnan and West Sichuan, in scrub and
along streams at 1200–3000 m flowering in
June. Evergreen shrub to 2 m. Fruits purple,
rarely seen in gardens. Hardy to −15°C.
**'Baggesen's Gold'** has yellowish leaves.

**Lonicera pileata** Oliver (*Caprifoliaceae*)   Native
of W. Hubei and W. Sichuan, in scrub and by
streams at 300–1800 m, flowering in June.
Evergreen shrub to 1 m, more across with
spreading branches. Hardy to −15°C.

**Euonymus japonicus** Thunb. (*Celastraceae*)
Native of Japan, Korea and China, in scrub and
woods, especially near the sea, flowering in
June–July, fruiting in December–January.
Evergreen shrub or small tree to 5 m, upright
and dense. Any soil; sun or shade. Hardy to
−10°C., with shelter from freezing wind.

Commonly planted in Victorian shrubberies,
especially near the sea.
**'Microphyllus'**   Dwarf, upright to 1 m.
**'Microphyllus Variegatus'** (syn. 'Microphyllus
Albomarginatus') Has a narrow white margin.
**'Ovatus aureus'** (syn. 'Aureovariegatus')
Leaves variable in colour on the same plant.
**'Aureopictus'** (syn. 'Aureus')   Rather tender
cultivar.
**'Albomarginatus'**   With creamy-white edge.
**'President Gauthier'**   Close to 'Latifolius
Albomarginatus' but leaves darker in the centre,
tapering into the stalk .

**Euonymus fortunei** (Turcz.) Hand-Mazz. (syn.
*E. radicans* Sieb ex Miq.) (*Celastraceae*)   Native
of Japan, Korea and China, in woods and scrub,
flowering in June–July. An ivy-like climber or
trailing shrub to 5 m, with aerial roots. Hardy to
−25°C. Good for evergreen ground-cover.
**'Silver Queen'**   A shrub to 1 m, or more.
**'Emerald Gaiety'**   An erect shrub to 1.5 m.
**'Sheridan Gold'**   Shrubby, rounded growth to
50 cm. A hardy, Canadian variety.
**'Gracilis'** (syn. 'Variegatus', 'Silver Gem',
'Argenteomarginatus')   Upright to 40 cm or
creeping and climbing.
**'Emerald 'n' Gold'**   Erect stems to 50 cm.

**Euonymus myrianthus** Hemsl. (*Celastraceae*)
Native of W. China, in Hubei and Sichuan,
Guizhou, etc., in wet scrub and on cliffs at 1000–
2100 m. Evergreen to 4.5 m. Hardy to −10°C.

**Celastrus orbiculatus** Thunb. (*Celastraceae*)
Native of Japan, China, Korea, E. Siberia,
Sakhalin and the S. Kurile islands, in scrub,
woods and grassy slopes. Flowering May–June.
Climbing shrub to 12 m. Hardy to −25°C.

**Rhamnus alaternus** L. (*Rhamnaceae*)   Native
of Portugal and the Mediterranean region from
Spain to Israel, in scrub and maquis, especially
on limestone, flowering in March–April.
Evergreen shrub to 5 m. Hardy to −15°C.
'Argenteo-variegata' has smaller, rather twisted
leaves with a white margin.

**Cornus sanguinea** L. (syn. *Thelycrania
sanguinea* (L.) Fourr) (*Cornaceae*) Dogwood
Native of England and Ireland east to Russia
and W. Asia, in scrub and hedges often on
chalk, flowering in May–June. Upright shrub to
4 m. Hardy to −25°C. Flowers on p. 180.

**Cornus nuttallii** Audub.   Fruits with many
seeds, 1 cm across. See p. 181.

**Cornus florida** L.   Fruits with rather few
almost separate berries, 1 cm long. For flowers
and text see p. 181.

**Paliurus spina-christi** L.   Fruits flat, disc-
like, 2–3 cm across. See p. 161.

**Hippophäe rhamnoides** L. (*Elaeagnaceae*)
Native of England and N.W. France eastwards
to C. Asia and N.W. China, on coastal dunes, or
on river gravels or bare sandy areas left by
glaciers, flowering in April–June, fruiting in
September–November. Deciduous rounded
shrub to 11 m. Hardy to −25°C. Plants of both
sexes must be grown side by side for good
fruiting.

**Pistacia lentiscus** L. (*Anacardiaceae*)   Native
of Portugal and the Mediterranean region, in
scrub on dry hillsides, flowering in April–June,
fruiting in September–October.

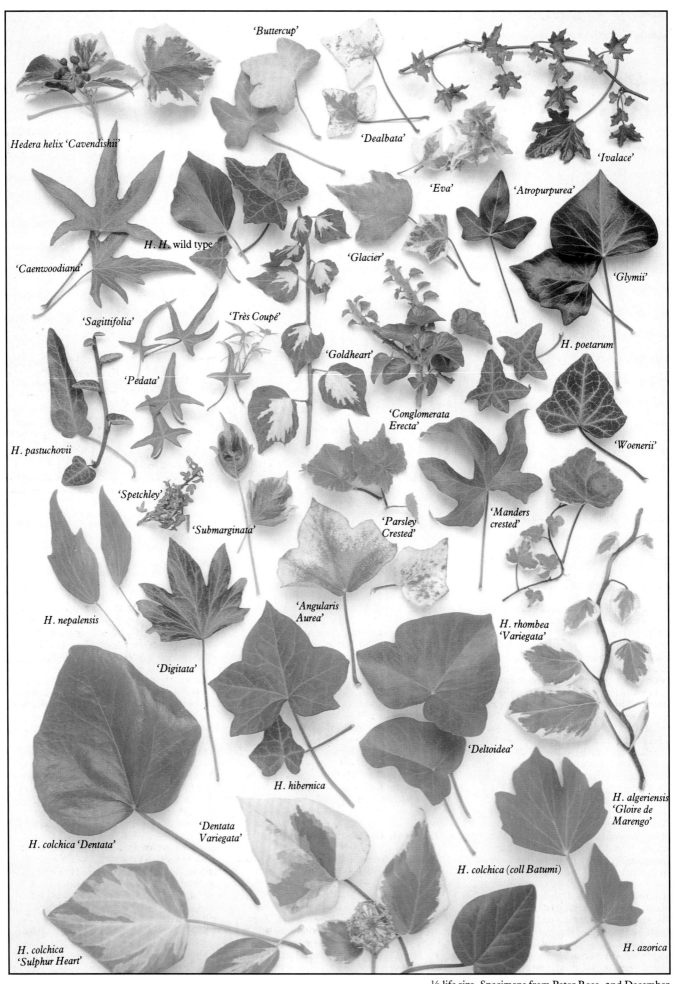

'Buttercup'

Hedera helix 'Cavendishii'

'Dealbata'

'Ivalace'

'Eva'

'Atropurpurea'

H. H. wild type

'Glacier'

'Caenwoodiana'

'Glymii'

'Sagittifolia'

'Très Coupé'

H. poetarum

'Goldheart'

'Pedata'

'Conglomerata Erecta'

H. pastuchovii

'Woenerii'

'Spetchley'

'Submarginata'

'Parsley Crested'

'Manders crested'

'Angularis Aurea'

H. nepalensis

H. rhombea 'Variegata'

'Digitata'

'Deltoidea'

H. hibernica

H. algeriensis 'Gloire de Marengo'

H. colchica 'Dentata'

'Dentata Variegata'

H. colchica (coll Batumi)

H. colchica 'Sulphur Heart'

H. azorica

⅓ life size. Specimens from Peter Rose, 2nd December

*Fatsia japonica* in a London garden

*Dicksonia antarctica* in Trewidden, Cornwall

*Hedera helix* 'Cavendishii'

**Hedera helix** L. (*Araliaceae*) Common Ivy
Native of most of Europe except the far north,
east to Turkey and the Caucasus, climbing on
trees, rocks and walls, flowering in September–
October. In the juvenile stage a creeper or
climber, to 30 m, in the adult stage, shrubby,
with less-lobed leaves and flowers. Leaves
evergreen, usually less than 15 cm long, variably
lobed. Flowers in umbels, greenish, much
visited by flies, bees and butterflies for late
nectar. Fruit ripening in spring, usually black.
Any good moist soil; shade or sun. Hardy to
−25°C. Autumn. A selection of the many
cultivars is shown opposite.

**H. helix** subsp. **poetarum** Nyman Distinguished
from subsp. *helix*, by its larger orange-yellow
fruit, to 12 mm across, and paler, less deeply
lobed leaves. Found wild in Greece, Crete,
Turkey, the Caucasus, Sicily and N. Africa,
though in some of these it may have been
introduced by the Romans as it was associated
with the cult of Bacchus. Close to *H. nepalensis*.

**H. pastuchovii** G. Woron.   Native of the
Caspian forests of Iran and of S.E. Caucasus in
Soviet Georgia, especially in the Lagodekhi
valley, on shaded limestone cliffs and on trees.

**H. nepalensis** K. Koch   Native of the
Himalayas from Afganistan east to Burma and

Sichuan and E. China (var. *sinensis*) in forest at
300–3000 m, flowering in September–October.
Climbing evergreen to 30 m; leaves entire or 3–5
lobed, 5–15 cm long. Fruit often yellow, less
than 10 mm across. Any soil; part shade. Hardy
to −15°C. Autumn.

**H. rhombea** (Miq.) Bean **'Variegata'**   A
variegated form of *H. rhombea*, a native of S.
and C. Japan and S. Korea. Fruit always black.
Hardy to −10°C, perhaps.

**H. hibernica** (Kirch.) Bean   Native of S.W.
Scotland, W. Wales, W. England, Ireland, W.
France, Spain and Portugal, in sheltered places
usually near the coast. Differs from *H. helix*, in
chromosome number, and flat starfish-like
hairs.

**H. algeriensis** Hibberd **'Gloire de Marengo'**
(syn. 'Variegata')   A form of *H. algeriensis*
discovered at the Villa Marengo in Algeria.
Often listed under *H. canariensis*, but with
different chromosome number. Hibberd's old
name is now recognized again.

**H. colchica** C. Koch   Native of N.E. Turkey,
N. Iran and the S. Caucasus, in woods and on
cliffs. Fruit black. The clone shown here
collected by Roy Lancaster in Batumi (R. L.
313). Hardy to −15°C.

**H. colchica** **'Dentata'**   A vigorous, climbing
form, with stiff branches. Large leaves with
small, distant teeth. Said to be good for acid
soils. **'Sulphur Heart'** (syn. 'Paddy's Pride')
and **'Dentata Variegata'** are also shown.

**H. azorica** Carrière   Native of the Azores.
Leaves large, soft, matt green, variably lobed.
Tips of young shoots whitish with long hairs.

**Dicksonia antarctica** Labill. (*Cyatheaceae*)
Native of Tasmania, New South Wales,
Victoria, S. Australia and Queensland, in moist
forests and along streams. Evergreen tree-fern
to 6 m, rarely to 15 m. Leafy moist soil; shade,
humidity and shelter from wind are important.
Hardy to −5°C, perhaps more if sheltered.
Grows well, even seeding itself, in shady
Cornish, Scottish and Irish coastal gardens.

**Fatsia japonica** (Thunb.) Decne & Planchon
(*Araliaceae*)   Native of E. Honshu, Shikoku,
Kyushu, the Ryuku Islands and S. Korea,
growing in woods near the sea, flowering in
October–November. Evergreen shrub to 4 m.
Flowers white in broad panicles 20–40 cm
across. Fruits black. Any soil; shelter and
shade. Hardy to −10°C. Autumn.

'Crassifolia'

'Flavescens'

'Amber'

'Ferox'

'Ferox Argentea'

'Crispa Aureopicta'

Ilex aquifolium

'Crispa'

'Ovata'

'Aurifodina'

'J. C. van Tol'

'Baciflava'

'Argentea Marginata'

'Golden King'

'Nellie R. Stevens'

'Golden Milkboy'

'Handsworth New Silver'

I. dipyrena

I. × koehneana 'Chestnut Leaf'

'Camelliifolia'

I. kingiana

'Silver Queen'

I. altaclerensis 'Hodginsii'

I. latifolia

I. altaclerensis 'Purple Shaft'

'Lawsoniana'

'Balearica'

'Howick'

'Wilsonii'

⅓ life size. Specimens from Valley Gardens, Windsor, 19th November

*Ilex canariensis* in W. Tenerife in March

**Ilex aquifolium** L. (*Aquifoliaceae*)   Native of
W. and S. Europe from Scotland to N. Africa
eastwards to Austria, S. Turkey and N. Iran, in
woods, hedges and on cliffs, usually on acid soils.
Evergreen shrub or tree to 16 m. Leaves stiff,
wavy-edged, usually with spines at least on lower
branches, shining dark green above. Fruits
8–10 mm across. Hardy to −15°C, for short
periods. The following varieties are shown:
**'Crassifolia'**   An unusual, slow-growing form,
with leaves to 6 cm long. Young shoots purple.
**'Flavescens'**   Known as 'Moonlight Holly' the
leaves are suffused with yellow, particularly
when young. Female.
**'Amber'** A clone which originated in Hillier's
nursery prior to 1955. Evergreen.
**'Ferox'**   The Hedgehog Holly is one of the
oldest cultivars still in existence, having been
grown since the 17th century. Male.
**'Ferox Argentea'**   A silver form of 'Ferox',
similar but slower-growing.
**'Crispa'**   A sport of 'Scotica'. Male.
**'Crispa Aureopicta'**   Similar to 'Crispa' but
with a blotch of yellow on the leaves. Male.
**'Ovata'**   A slow-growing form up to about 2 m
high with purple stems. Male.
**'J.C. van Tol'**   (syn. *I. a.* 'Polycarpa
Laevigata')   Raised in Holland *c.* 1895, this is
one of the most freely-fruiting hollies.
**'Bacciflava'** (syn. *I. a.* 'Fructoluteo')   A yellow-
fruited form, sometimes found in the wild.
**'Argentea Marginata'**   Probably the most
commonly grown variegated holly. Leaves to
8 cm long. Hermaphrodite.
**'Golden Milkboy'**   (syn. *I. a.* 'Aurea Picta
Latifolia') A striking form, similar to 'Golden
Milkmaid' but with larger leaves. Male.
**'Handsworth New Silver'**   A purple-stemmed
form, with leaves to 10 cm long. Female.
**'Silver Queen'**   A rather slow-growing form
with a pyramidal habit. Purple stems. Male.
**'Aurifodina'** (syn. 'Goldmine') A purple-
stemmed, free-fruiting form.

**I. canariensis** Poir.   Native of Madeira and the
Canary islands, where it is quite common in the
remnants of the laurel and heather forests in
Tenerife and Gomera, at around 700 m,
flowering in May. A shrub or tree to 15 m.
Leaves usually without spines. Fruit 1 cm in
diameter. Hardy to −5°C perhaps.

**I. perado** Ait. var. **platyphylla** (Webb & Berth.)
Loes   Native of Tenerife and Gomera, in laurel
and heather woods, at *c.* 1000 m. Shrub or tree to
12 m. Hardy to −10°C, with shelter.

**I. colchica** Pojak   Native of the S. Caucasus
and N. Turkey, in beech and mixed woods up to
*c.* 1000 m. Low spreading evergren shrub to
1.5 m. Leaves rather soft. Hardy to −15°C.

**I. dipyrena** Wall.   Native of the Himalayas,
from Pakistan to Yunnan at 1500–3000 m, in
forest and damp gorges. Evergreen tree or large
shrub to 14 m. Leaves 5–10 cm long. Fruit red,
8 mm long, with 2 seeds. Hardy to −20°C.

**I. kingiana** Cockerell   Native of the Himalayas,
1800–2500 m. Small evergreen tree. Leaves 15–
20 cm long. Fruit 5 mm long, red. Hardy to
−10°C, with shelter.

**I. latifolia** Thunb.   Native of S. Honshu,
Shikoku and Kyushu, in woods. Leaves 12–
17 cm long, with many small teeth. Berries 8 mm
across. Hardy to −15°C.

**I. × altaclerensis** (Loud.) Dallimore   Hybrid
between *I. aquifolium* and *I. perado* var.
*platyphylla* raised originally at Highclere, near

*Ilex colchica* above Trabzon

*Ilex aquifolium* 'Aurifodina'

*Ilex* 'Nellie R. Stevens'

*Ilex perado* var. *platyphylla*

Newbury, Berks. Numerous cultivars have
been named. Hardy to −15°C. with shelter.
**'Golden King'**   A sport from *I. × a.*
'Hendersonii', which occurred at Lawson's
nursery near Edinburgh during the late 19th
century. Female.
**'Camelliifolia'**   A large tree, with a pyramidal
habit. Young stems purple. Berries very freely
produced.
**'Purple Shaft'**   A strong, fast-growing sport of
*I. × a.* 'Balearica'. Young shoots purple. Free-
fruiting.
**'Hodginsii'**   Raised by T. Hodgins in Ireland
during the early 19th C. Makes a good
pyramidal tree up to 15 m high. Purple stems;
leaves to 11 cm long. Male.
**'Lawsoniana'**   A variegated sport from
'Hendersonii', liable to revert to plain green.

Raised by Lawson's nursery, Edinburgh.
**'Howick'**   A sport of 'Hendersonii'; a tall tree
with recurved whitish leaf-margins.
**'Balearica'**   A strong-growing form, whose
origins are obscure. Makes a medium-sized,
pyramidal shrub. Free-fruiting.
**'Wilsonii'**   A strong-growing form up to 10 m
high. Leaves to 12 cm long.

**'Nellie R. Stevens'**   A hybrid, raised in the
USA, of *I. aquifolium* × *I. cornuta*. Free-
fruiting. Female. Evergreen.

**I. × koehneana** Loes. **'Chestnut Leaf'**   A
strong-growing clone of *I. × koehneana*, a
hybrid of *I. aquifolium* × *I. latifolia*. Leaves to
16 cm long. Hardy to −15°C. Evergreen.

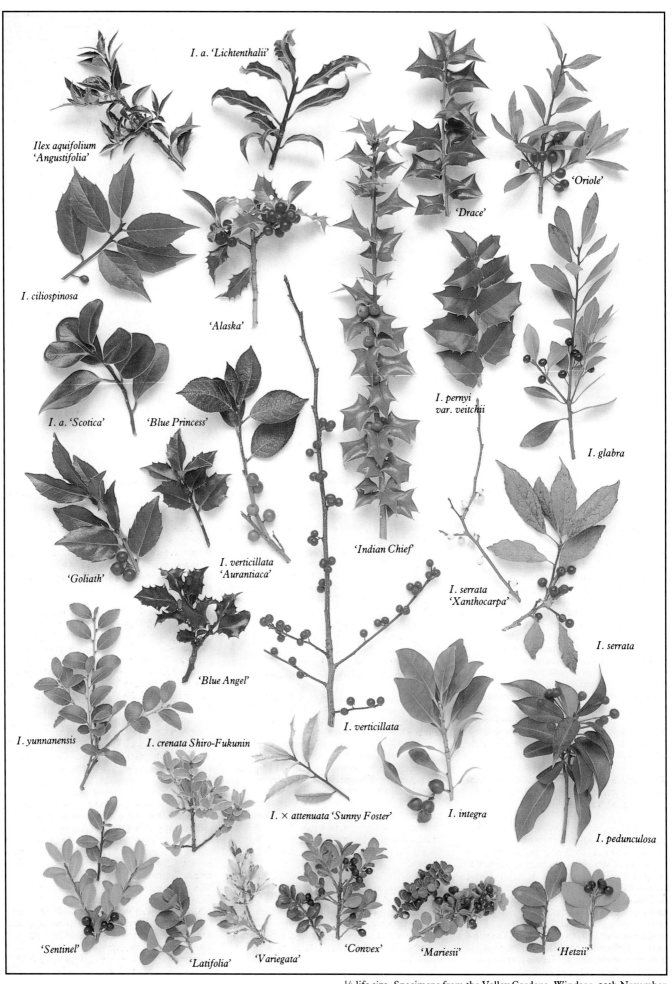

I. a. 'Lichtenthalii'

Ilex aquifolium
'Angustifolia'

'Drace'

'Oriole'

I. ciliospinosa

'Alaska'

I. pernyi
var. veitchii

I. glabra

I. a. 'Scotica'    'Blue Princess'

'Goliath'

I. verticillata
'Aurantiaca'

'Indian Chief'

I. serrata
'Xanthocarpa'

I. serrata

'Blue Angel'

I. yunnanensis

I. crenata Shiro-Fukunin

I. verticillata

I. × attenuata 'Sunny Foster'

I. integra

I. pedunculosa

'Sentinel'

'Latifolia'    'Variegata'    'Convex'    'Mariesii'    'Hetzii'

⅓ life size. Specimens from the Valley Gardens, Windsor, 19th November

Daphniphyllym macropodum in Yakushima

Ilex opaca in New York State

Rhamnus crocea subsp. ilicifolia

Ilex cornuta

Ilex serrata

*Ilex aquifolium* 'Angustifolia'  A narrowly upright, compact form with leaves to about 6 cm long. Male. Known since 1838.
*I. aquifolium* 'Lichtenthalii'  A form with purple shoots and long, narrow leaves.
*I. aquifolium* 'Alaska'  A very hardy form, with leaves to 6 cm long. Female.
*I. aquifolium* 'Scotica'  A form with spineless leaves up to 7 cm long, purple stems. Female.

*I.* 'Drace'  A hybrid between *I. cornuta* and *I. pernyi* raised in America. Female.

*I.* 'Oriole'  A second generation hybrid between *I. myrtifolia* and *I. opaca*. Female.

*I. glabra* (L.) A. Gray Inkberry  Native of Nova Scotia to Florida west to Montana in wet, acid soil, flowering in June. Evergreen shrub to 3 m, usually *c*.1 m. Hardy to −20°C.

*I. ciliospinosa* Loes.  Native of W. Sichuan, in woods at 1500 m, flowering in May. Evergreen shrub to 4 m. Hardy to −20°C.

*I. pernyi* Franch. var. *veitchii* hort. ex Bean Native of Yunnan, W. Sichuan and W. Hubei, east to Taiwan, at 1200–2100 m, in scrub, flowering in May. Evergreen shrub or small tree to 10 m. Flowers pale yellow. Hardy to −15°C..

*I.* 'Indian Chief'  A hybrid between *I. cornuta* and *I. pernyi*. Female.

*I. yunnanensis* Franch.  Native of Yunnan and W. Sichuan, in scrub at 1200–2000 m. Evergreen shrub to 4 m. Fruit 6 mm across, red. Hardy to −15°C.

*I. verticillata* (L.) Gray Black Alder  Native of Newfoundland east to Minnesota, south to Georgia and Tennessee, in swamps and by ponds, fruiting from October onwards. Deciduous spreading shrub to 3 m. Fruit 6 mm across, red, or orange in 'Aurantiaca'. Moist, acid soil. Hardy to −35°C.

*I.* × *meservae*  Hybrids between *I. aquifolium* and *I. rugosa*, a very hardy species native of N. Japan. 'Blue Princess', 'Blue Angel' and 'Goliath' are selected clones, hardier than *I. aquifolium* and good in a continental climate.

*I.* × *attenuata* 'Sunny Foster'  A form of *I.* × *attenuata*, which is a naturally occurring hybrid of *I. cassine* and *I. opaca*, making a tall, rather narrow shrub. Evergreen.

*I. cornuta* Lindl.  Native of of E. China, westwards to W. Hubei, in ravines and on hills at 150–600 m. Evergreen, rounded shrub to 3 m. Leaves 3.5–10 cm long. Hardy to −15°C.

*I. opaca* Ait.  Native of Massachusetts south to Florida west to Texas, in woods, hedges and fields, flowering in June. Evergreen shrub or small tree to 15 m. Leaves matt-green. Hardy to −25°C.

*Daphniphyllum macropodum* Miq. (*Euphorbiaceae*)  Native of Japan and Korea, in forests by streams, flowering in May–June. Evergreen shrub or small tree; leaves 15–20 cm long. Flowers numerous, small yellowish-green. Fruit dark-bluish, *c*.1 cm long. Hardy to −20°C.

*I. pedunculosa* Miq.  Native of S. Honshu, Shikoku and Kyushu, in woods in the mountains, flowering in June. Evergreen shrub or small tree. Flowers white, 4 mm across, 1–5 together on long, slender stalks. Fruits 7 mm across. Hardy to −10°C.

*I. serrata* Thunb.  Native of Honshu, Shikoku and Kyushu, in wet places in the mountains, flowering in June. Deciduous shrub to 3 m. Flowers pale purple to white, 3.5 mm across, male and female on separate plants. Fruit about 5 mm across, red or yellow in 'Xanthocarpa', white in 'Leucocarpa'. Moist, acid soil; full sun. Hardy to −20°C. Fruiting in autumn, the berries remaining on the bare twigs.

*I. integra* Thunb.  Native of Honshu, Shikoku, Kyushu, Taiwan, and E. China in woods in hills, often near the sea, flowering in April. Shrub or small tree. Hardy to −10°C.

*I. crenata* Thunb.  Native of Hokkaido, Honshu, Shikoku and Kyushu, in scrub, by streams in forests, and in wet places, flowering in June–July. Evergreen, usually compact shrub, or small tree. Leaves 1.5–3 cm long, with small teeth. Flowers white, 5 mm across. Hardy to −20°C. Good in E. North America, and often planted in the same positions as box (*Buxus*). A selection of varieties is shown opposite.

*Rhamnus crocea* Nutt. subsp. *ilicifolia* (Kell) C. B. Wolf (*Rhamnaceae*)  Native of California and Arizona, in scrub and open forest below 1500 m, fruiting in August–November. Evergreen shrub to 4 m, with fruit 8 mm long. Hardy to −15°C, perhaps.

# Nurseries

## United Kingdom

Axletree Nursery, Starvecrow Lane, Peasmarsh, Rye, East Sussex TN31 6XL

Bamboo Nursery, Kingsgate Cottage, Wittersham, Tenterden, Kent TN30 7NS

Bodnant Garden Nursery, Tal-y-Cafn, Colwyn Bay, Clwyd LL28 5RE

J. Bradshaw & Son, Busheyfield Nursery, Herne, Herne Bay, Kent CT6 7LJ

Bulwood Nursery, 54 Woodlands Road, Hockley, Essex SS5 4PY

Burncoose & South Down Nurseries, Gwennap, Redruth, Cornwall TR16 6BJ

Clapton Court Gardens, Crewkerne, Somerset TA18 8PT

Mrs Susan Cooper, Churchfields House, Cradley, Malvern, Worcs WR13 5LJ

County Park Nursery, Essex Gardens, Hornchurch, Essex RM11 3BU

Crown Estates Commissioners, Savill Gardens, The Great Park, Windsor, Berks SL4 2HT

Daisy Hill Nurseries, Hospital Road, Newry, Co. Down, N. Ireland BT35 8PN

Drysdale Nurseries, 96 Drysdale Avenue, Chingford, London E4 7PE

Exbury Gardens, Exbury, Nr. Southampton, Hants SO4 1AZ

Fairlight Camellia Nursery, Three Oaks Village, Guestling, Nr. Hastings, E. Sussex

Fibrex Nurseries Ltd, Honeybourne Road, Pebworth, Stratford-on-Avon, Warwick CV37 8XT

Fisk's Clematis Nursery, Westleton, Saxmundham, Suffolk IP17 3AJ

The Fortescue Garden Trust, The Garden House, Buckland Monachorum, Yelverton, Devon PL20 7LQ

Fuchsiavale Nurseries, Stanklyn Lane, Summerfield, Kidderminster, Worcs DY10 4HS

Glendoick Gardens Ltd, Glencarse, Perth, Scotland PN2 7NS

Great Dixter Nurseries, Northiam, Rye, E. Sussex TN31 6PH

Green Farm Plants, Bentley, Farnham, Surrey GU10 5JX

Hatfield House Garden Shop, Hatfield House, Herts AL9 5NQ

The Heather Garden, 139 Swinston Hill Road, Dinnington, Sheffield, S. Yorks S31 7RY

Hillier Nurseries (Winchester) Ltd, Ampfield House, Ampfield, Nr. Romsey, Hants SO51 9PA

Hollington Nurseries, Woolton Hill, Newbury, Berks RG15 9XT

Hydon Nurseries Ltd, Clock Barn Lane, Hydon Heath, Godalming, Surrey GU8 4AZ

King & Paton, Barnhourie Mill, By Dalbeattie, Scotland DG5 4PU

Knaphill & Slocock Nurseries, Barrs Lane, Woking, Surrey GU21 2JW

Knightshayes Garden Trust, The Garden Office, Knightshayes, Tiverton, Devon EX16 7RG

The Knoll Gardens, Stapehill Road, Stapehill, Wimborne, Dorset BH21 7ND

Langthorns Plantery, High Cross Lane West, Little Canfield, Dunmow, Essex CM6 1TD

Lechlade Garden & Fuchsia Centre, Fairford Road, Lechlade, Glos GL7 3DP

Leonardslee Gardens, Lower Beeding, Nr. Horsham, W Sussex RH13 6PP

Longstock Park Nursery, Stockbridge, Hants SO20 6EH

Mallet Court Nursery, Curry Mallet, Taunton, Somerset TA3 6SY

Marwood Hill Gardens, Barnstaple, N. Devon EX31 4EB

Millais Nurseries, Crosswater Farm, Churt, Farnham, Surrey GU10 2JN

Norfolk Lavender, Caley Hill, Heacham, King's Lynn, Norfolk PE31 7JE

Notcutts Nurseries Ltd, Woodbridge, Suffolk IP12 4AF

The Old Manor Nursery, Twyning, Glos GL20 6DB

Pennells Nurseries, Brant Road, Lincoln, Lincs LN5 9AF

Perryhill Nurseries, Hartfield, Sussex TN7 4JP

Peverill Clematis Nursery, Christow, Exeter, Devon EX6 7NG

Ramparts Nurseries, Bakers Lane, Colchester, Essex CO4 5BB

Raveningham Gardens, Norwich, Norfolk NR14 6NS

G. Reuthe Ltd, Foxhill Nursery, Jackass Lane, Keston, Nr. Bromley, Kent BR2 6AW

Rosemoor Garden Trust, Torrington, Devon EX2 7JY

K. D. Rushforth, 176 Rownhams Lane, North Baddesley, Hants SO52 9LQ

L. R. Russell Ltd, Richmond Nurseries, Windlesham, Surrey GU20 6LL

Scotts Nurseries (Merriott) Ltd, Merriott, Somerset TA16 5PL

Sealand Nurseries Ltd, Sealand, Chester, Cheshire CH1 6BA

Spinners, Boldre, Lymington, Hants SO41 5QE

Starborough Nursery, Starborough Road, Marsh Green, Keston, Kent BR2 6DG

Stone House Cottage Nurseries, Stone, Nr. Kidderminster, Worcs

Stonehurst Nurseries, Ardingly, Haywards Heath, Sussex RH17 6TN

Stone Lane Gardens, Stone Farm, Chagford, Devon TQ13 8JU

Sunningdale Nurseries Ltd, London Road, Windlesham, Surrey GU20 6LN

Treasures of Tenbury Ltd, Burford House Gardens, Tenbury Wells, Worcs WR15 8HQ

Trehane Camellia Nursery, Stapehill Road, Hampreston, Wimbourne, Dorset BH21 7NE

Trewithen Nurseries, Grampound Road, Truro, Cornwall TR2 4DD

Wall Cottage Nursery, Lockengate, Bugle, St Austell, Cornwall PL28 8RU

Westfield Plants, Great Chalfield, Melksham, Wilts SN12 8NN

Whitehouse Ivies, Hylands Farm, Rectory Road, Tolleshunt Knights, Essex CM9 8EZ

Geoffrey Yates, Stagshaw, Ambleside, Cumbria LA22 0HE

## Australia

Allan's Garden Suppliers, 285 Bass Highway, Launceston, Tasmania 7250

Bond's Nursery, 277 Mona Vale Road, Terrey Hills, NSW 2004

Darwin Plant Wholesalers, PO Box 39196, Winnille, NT 5789

Garden World, Springvale Road, Keysborough, Victoria 3173

Hawkin's Nursery Garden Centre, 623 Albany Creek Road, Albany Creek, Queensland 4035

Hillier's Nursery Garden Centre, 1666 Old Cleveland Road, Chandler, Queensland 4155

Ironstone Lagoon Nursery, Lagoon Road, Berrimah, NT 5794

Lasscock's Garden Centers, 334 Henley Beach Road, Lockleys, SA 5032

Linton's Nurseries, Cnr. Nepean Hwy and Canadian Bay Road, Mt Eliza, Victoria 3930

Swane's Nursery, Swane Bros Pty Ltd Inc., Galston Road, Dural, NSW 2158

Waldeck Garden Centres, Wanneroo Road, Kingsley, WA 6005

Westland Nurseries, 143 Pottery Road, Lenah Valley, Tasmania 7008

## United States of America

W. Atlee Burpee Co., 300 Park Ave, Warminster PA 18974

Eastern Plant Specialties, PO Box 40, Colonia, NJ 07067

Girard Nurseries, Box 428, OH 44041

Gossler Farms Nursery, 1200 Weaver Road, Springfield, OR 97477

Greer Gardens, 1290 Goodpasture Island Road, Eugene, OR 97401

Klehm Nursery, Rte. 5, 197 Fenny Road, South Barrington, IL 60010

Louisiana Nursery, Rte. 7, Box 43, Opelousas, LA 70570

Oliver Nurseries Inc., 1159 Bronson Road, Fairfield, CT 06430

Roslyn Nursery, PO Box 69, Roslyn, NY 11576

Siskiyou Rare Plant Nursery, 2825 Cummings Road, Medford, OR 97501

The Cummins Garden, 22 Robertsville Road, Marlboro, NJ 07746
Transplant Nursery, Parkertown Road, Lavonia, GA 30553
Wayside Gardens, Hodges, SC 29695
Weston Nurseries, E. Main Street (Rte. 135), Box 186,
   Hopkinton, MA 01748
White Flower Farm, Rte. 63, Litchfield, CT 06759
Woodlanders, 1128 Colleton Ave, Aiken, SC 29801
Sonomona Horticultural Nursery, 3970 Azalea Ave, Sebastopol,
   CA 95472
Trillium Lane Nursery, 18855 Trillium Lane, Fort Bragg,
   CA 95437 (Rhododendrons) (707) 964 3282
Maple Leaf Nursery, 4236 Greenstone Road, Placerville,
   CA 95667
Brown's Kalmia and Azalea Nursery, 8527 Semi-ah-moo Drive,
   Blaine, WA 98230 (206) 371 2489
North Coast Rhododendron Nursery, PO Box 308, Bodega,
   CA 94922
Holly Mills Inc., 1216 Hillsdale Road, Evansville, IN 47711
Ericaceae, PO Box 293, Deep River, CT 06417 (Rhododendrons)
Berkeley Horticultural Nursery, 1310 McGee Ave, Berkeley,
   CA 94703 (California natives)
California Flora Nursery, Somers & D. Street, Fulton, CA 95439
   (707) 528 8813

# Shrub Gardens to Visit

Most of these gardens are open to the public at some time during
the summer, but many are not open all the time, so it is essential
to check opening hours before planning a visit.

### England
The Savill Gardens, Windsor, Berks
The Valley Gardens, Windsor, Berks
The University Botanic Garden, Cambridge
The Liverpool University Botanic Gardens, Ness, Cheshire
Trewithen House and Gardens, Probus, Nr Truro, Cornwall
Glendurgan Garden, Helford River, Cornwall
Trengwainton Garden, Penzance, Cornwall
Trelissick Garden, Truro, Cornwall
Caerhays Castle, Cornwall
The Garden House, Buckland Monachorum, Yelverton, Devon
Rosemoor Garden, Great Torrington, Devon
Marwood Hill, Barnstaple, Devon
Overbecks Museum and Garden, Sharpitor, Salcombe, Devon
Knightshayes Court, Tiverton, Devon
Abbotsbury-Swannery and Sub-Tropical Gardens, Abbotsbury,
   Weymouth, Dorset
Blakenham Woodland Garden, Essex
Hidcote Manor Garden, Hidcote Bartrim, Nr Chipping Camden,
   Gloucestershire
Stancombe Park, Dursley, Gloucestershire
Lydney Park, Lydney, Gloucestershire
Exbury Gardens, Southampton, Hampshire
The Hillier Gardens and Arboretum, Ampfield, Romsey,
   Hampshire
Hergest Croft Gardens, Kington, Herefordshire
Ventnor Botanic Gardens, Ventnor, Isle of Wight
Tresco Abbey Gardens, Isles-of-Scilly
Sandling Park, Hythe, Kent
Blaydon, Nr Newcastle upon Tyne
Oxford University Botanic Garden, Oxford
East Bergholt Place, Suffolk
The Royal Horticultural Society's Gardens, Wisley, Surrey
The Royal Botanic Gardens, Kew, Richmond, Surrey
Wakehurst Place Gardens, Nr Ardingly, Sussex
Nymans Garden, Handcross, Sussex
The High Beeches Gardens, Handcross, Sussex
Borde Hill Garden, Haywards Heath, Sussex
Highdown, Worthing, Sussex
Great Dixter, Northiam, Sussex
Broadleas Gardens, Devizes, Wiltshire
Castle Howard, Malton, Yorkshire

### Ireland
Annes Grove Gardens, Castletownroche, Co. Cork
Ilnacullan, Glengariff, Co. Cork
Mount Stewart, Co. Down
Rowallane Garden, Saintfield, Co. Down
National Botanic Gardens, Glasnevin, Dublin
Malahide Castle, Malahide, Co. Dublin
Rossdohan, Co. Kerry
Birr Castle Demesne, Co. Offaly
Barons Castle, Co. Tyrone
Glanleam, Valencia Island
Mount Usher, Ashford, Co. Wicklow

### Scotland
Dawyck Garden, Stobo, Peebleshire
Logan Botanic Garden, Port Logan, Dumfries and Galloway
Glendoick Garden, by Perth
The Royal Botanic Garden, Edinburgh
Crathes Castle and Garden, Banchory, Grampian Region
The Younger Botanic Garden, Benmore, Dunoon, Strathclyde Region
Brodick Castle Garden, Isle of Arran, Strathclyde Region
Crarae Glen Garden, Inverary, Strathclyde Region
Branklyn Garden, Perth, Tayside Region
Inverewe, Poolewe, Wester Ross

### Wales
Dyffryn Gardens, St Nicholas, Nr Cardiff, South Glamorgan
Bodnant Garden, Tal-y-Cafn, Gwynedd
Portmeirion Gardens, Gwynedd

### Belgium
Arboretum Kalmthout, M and Mme de Belder, Heural 2, 2180
   Kalmthout

### Denmark
Arboretum Horsholm

### France
Bambuseraie de Prafrance, Anduze
Jardin Thuret, Chemin G. Raymond, Antibes
Jardin de la Chevre d'Or, Biot
Kerdale, en Tredarzec, c. 5km N. of Treguier, Bretagne
Jardin de la Roche Fauconnière, Cherbourg
Jardin de la Villa Noailles, avenue Guy-de-Maupassant, Grasse
Parc Saint-Bernard, Montée de Noailles, Hyères
Jardin Botanique Exotique de Menton-Gavarre, Villa 'Val
   Rahmeh', avenue Saint-Jaques, Menton-Gavarre
Arboretum de la Fosse, Montoire-sur-Loire
Jardin des Plantes de Montpellier, 163 rue Auguste-Broussonnet,
   Montpellier
Arboretum des Barres, Nogent-sur-Vernisson
Jardin et Arboretum de L'École du Breuill, Route de la Pyramide,
   Bois de Vincennes, Paris
Parc Floral des Moutiers, Varengeville-sur-Mer
Jardin du Vasterival, Varengeville-sur-Mer
Parc Vilmorin, Verrières-le-Buisson
Jardin Botanique de Montet, 100 rue du Jardin Botanique,
   Villers-les-Nancy

### Germany
Insel Mainau, Bodensee, W. Germany

### Holland
Westbroekpark and Zuiderpark, The Hague
Trompenburg Arboretum, near Rotterdam
Gimborne Arboretum, University of Utrecht
Agricultural University, Wageningen

### Australia
Mount Lofty Botanical garden, near Adelaide

### New Zealand
Pukeite Rhododendron Trust, North Island

**United States of America**
Birmingham Botanical Garden, 2612 Lane Park Road,
   Birmingham, AL 35223
Bellingrath Gardens and Home, Route 1, Box 60, Theodore,
   AL 36582
Boyce Thompson Southwest Arboretum, Box AB, Superior,
   AZ 85273
Los Angeles State and County Arboretum, 301 North Baldwin
   Avenue, Arcadia, CA 91006
University of California Botanical Garden, Centennial Drive,
   Berkeley, CA 94720
Rancho Santa Ana Botanic Garden, 1500 North College Avenue,
   Claremont, CA 91711
University of California Arboretum – Davis, Dept of Botany,
   University of California, Davis, CA 95616
San Diego Zoo, PO Box 551, San Diego, CA 92112
Strybing Arboretum and Botanical Gardens, Ninth Ave. at
   Lincoln Way, San Francisco, CA 94122
Santa Barbara Botanic Garden, 1212 Mission Canyon Road, Santa
   Barbara, CA 93105
Denver Botanic Gardens, 909 York Street, Denver, CO 80206
Winterthur Museum and Gardens, Winterthur, DE 19735
United States National Arboretum, US Department of
   Agriculture, 3501 New York Ave. N.E., Washington,
   DC 20002
Fairchild Tropical Garden, 10901 Old Cutler Road, Miami,
   FL 33156
The State Botanical Garden of Georgia, 2450 South Milledge Ave,
   Athens, GA 30605
Callaway Gardens, Pine Mountain, GA 31822
Waimea Arboretum and Botanical Garden, Waimea Falls Park,
   59–964 Kamehameha Hwy, Haleiwa, HI 96712
Chicago Botanic Garden, Lake Cook Road, P.O. Box 400,
   Glencoe, IL 60022
The Bartlett Arboretum, Box 39, Belle Plaine, KS 67013
Brookside Gardens, 1500 Glenallen Ave, Wheaton, MD 20902
The Arnold Arboretum, Jamaica Plain, MA 02130
Minnesota Landscape Arboretum and Horticultural Research
   Center, University of Minnesota, 3675 Arboretum Drive,
   PO Box 39, Chanhassen, MN 55317
Missouri Botanical Garden, 4344 Shaw Blvd., St Louis,
   MO 63110
Willowwood Arboretum, PO Box 129R, Morristown, NJ 07960
Skylands, Ringwood State Park, PO Box 302, Ringwood,
   NJ 07456
Wave Hill, 675 W. 252nd Street, Bronx, NY 10471
Brooklyn Botanic Garden, 1000 Washington Ave, Brooklyn,
   NY 11225
Old Westbury Gardens, PO Box 430, Old Westbury, NY 11568
Planting Fields Arboretum, Planting Fields Road, Oyster Bay,
   NY 11771
North Carolina State University Arboretum, Dept of
   Horticultural Science, North Carolina State University,
   Raleigh, NC 27695
Holden Arboretum, 9500 Sperry Road, Mentor, OH 44060
Longwood Gardens, PO Box 501, Kennett Square, PA 19348
Morris Arboretum of the University of Pennsylvania, 9414
   Meadowbrook Ave., Chestnut Hill, Philadelphia, PA 19118
The Scott Arboretum of Swarthmore College, Swarthmore
   College, Swarthmore, PA 19081
Memphis Botanic Garden, 750 Cherry Road, Memphis,
   TN 38117
San Antonio Botanical Center, 555 Funston Pl., San Antonio,
   TX 78209
State Arboretum of Utah, University of Utah, Building 436, Salt
   Lake City, UT 84112
Washington Park Arboretum, University of Washington, (xD-10)
   Seattle, WA 98195
The University of Wisconsin Arboretum – Madison, 1205
   Seminole Hwy, Madison, WI 53711
Morton Aboretum, Route 53, Lisle, IL 60532

# Bibliography

**General**
Bean, W. J. (revised by D. L. Clarke), *Trees and Shrubs Hardy in
   the British Isles*, 8th ed. revised John Murray (1976, 1980).
Beckett, Kenneth A., *Climbing Plants*, Croom Helm/Timber
   Press (1983).
*Curtis's Botanical Magazine* since 1984; *The Kew Magazine*
   London (1787–).
Dirr, M. A. & Henser, Charles R. (Jnr.), *The Reference Manual of
   Woody Plant Propagation: from seed to tissue culture*, Varsity
   Press Inc., Georgia (1987).
*Hillier's Manual of Trees and Shrubs*, ed. 4 (1974)
Haworth-Booth, Michael, *Effective Flowering Shrubs*, Collins
   (1970).
Ingram, Collingwood, *A Garden of Memories*, Witherby (1970).
*International Dendrology Society Yearbook*, London (1976–).
*Journal of the Royal Horticultural Society* since June 1975, 'The
   Garden', R.H.S., London
Krussman, G., *Manual of Cultivated Broad-Leaved Trees and
   Shrubs* (in English), Batsford/Timber Press (1986).
*Plantsman, The*, (1979–), R.H.S., London
Rehder, Alfred, *Manual of Cultivated Trees and Shrubs Hardy in
   North America*, Macmillan, New York ed. 2 (reprinted 1977).
*Royal Horticultural Society Dictionary of Gardening*, 2nd ed.
   revised, Oxford University Press (1977).
Wyman, Donald, *Shrubs and Vines for American Gardens*, New
   York (1949).

**Europe**
Heywood et al., *Flora Europaea*, Cambridge University Press
   (1964–80).
Polunin, Oleg, *Flowers of Greece and the Balkans*, Oxford
   University Press (1980).
Polunin, Oleg and Smithies, B. E., *Flowers of Southwest Europe*,
   Oxford University Press (1973).

**Australia and New Zealand**
Salmon, J. T., *New Zealand Flowers and Plants in Colour*, Reed
   (1963).

**Asia**
Cowan, J. M. (ed.) George Forrest, *Journeys and Plant
   Introductions*, R. H. S. and Oxford University Press (1952).
Davies, P. H. (ed.), *Flora of Turkey*, Edinburgh University Press
   (1965–87).
Fang, Wei-pei, *Flora Sichuanica* vol. I (1981–?).
Grierson, A. J. C. and Long, D. G., *Flora of Bhutan*, Edinburgh
   University Press (1983, 1984–).
Kingdon-Ward, F., *Pilgrimage for Plants*, Harrap (1960).
Ohwi, J., *Flora of Japan* (in English), Smithsonian, Washington
   (1965).
Polunin, Oleg and Stainton, Adam, *Flowers of the Himalaya*,
   Oxford University Press (1984).
Rechinger, K. H., *Flora Iranica*, Graz (1963–).
Sakhokia, M. F. (ed.), *Botanical Excursions over Georgia*, Georgia
   S. S. R. Acad. of Sci. Tblisi (1961).
Sargent, C. S. (ed.), *Plantae Wilsonianae*, Harvard (3 vols) (1913–
   1917).
Wang, Chi-Wu, *The Forests of China*, Harvard (1961).
*Woody Plants of Japan*, Yama-Kei (1985).

**United States of America**
Fernald, M. L., *Gray's Manual of Botany*, ed. 8 (1950).
Little, E. L., *The Audubon Society Field Guide to North American
   Trees (eastern region)*, Knopf (1980).
Munz, P. A., *A Californian Flora and Supplement*, University of
   California Press (1968).
Vines, Robert A., *Trees, Shrubs and Woody Plants of the Southwest*
   (1960).

**South America**

Moore, David M., *Flora of Tierra del Fuego*, Nelson and Missouri Botanical Garden (1983).

**Selected Genera**

Ahrendt, L. W., '*Berberis* and *Mahonia, A Taxonomic Revision*', Journ. Linn . Soc. London 57: 1–410 (1961).

Andrews, Susyn, 'Notes on some Ilex × altaclerensis clones', *The Plantsman* 5 (2): 65–81 (1983). *The Blue Hollies: The Garden* 113 (1): 43–45 (1988).

Brickell, C. D. & Mathew B., *Daphne. The genus in the wild and in cultivation*, Alpine Garden Society (1976).

Brown, P. D., 'The Genus Skimmia, as found in cultivation,' *The Plantsman* 1 (4) 224–249 (1980).

Chamberlain, D. F., *A revision of Rhododendron II*, Notes, R. B. G. Edinb. 39 (2): 209–486 (1982).

Cox, Peter, *The Larger Species of Rhododendron*, Batsford (1977).

Cullen, I., *A revision of Rhododendron I*, Notes, R. B. G. Edinb. 39 (1): 1–207 (1980).

Fang, Wei-pei et al., *Rhododendrons of China* (in English), Binford and Mort 1980, with a Chinese-English glossary of botanical terms and place names.

Galle, Fred C., *Azaleas*, Timber Press (1987).

Haworth Booth, M., *The Hydrangeas* (1959).

Hu, Shin-Ying, *A monograph of the genus Philadelphus*, Journ. Arnold Arbor (1954, 1955, 1956).

Lloyd, Christopher, *Clematis*, Collins 1977

Macaboy, S., *The Colour Dictionary of Camellias*, Landsdowne Press (1981).

McAlister, H., *New Work on Ivies*, I. D. S. Yearbook 1981: 106–109 (1982).

McClintock, D., 'Bamboos' in Walters et al., *European Garden Flora* vol. 2, C. U. P. (1985–?).

Munz, P. A., *A revision of the Genus Fuchsia*, Proc. Cal. Acad. Sci. 25: 1–138 (1943).

*Rhododendron Yearbook*, now *Rhododendrons, with Camellias and Magnolias*, R. H. S., London (1939–).

Robson, N. K. B., Shrubby Asiatic Hypericum Species, *Jour. Roy. Hort. Soc.* 95: 482–497 (1970).

Rose, P. Q., *Ivies*, Blandford Press (1980)

Salley, H. E. & Greer, H. E., *Rhododendron Hybrids: A Guide to their Origins*, Batsford (1986).

Saunders, E., *Wagtail's Book of Fuchsias* vols I–IV, Wagtails Fuchsia Publications (1971–87).

Treseder, Neil and Hyams, Edward, *Growing Camellias*, Nelson (1975).

Vertrees, J. D., *Japanese Maples*, Timber Press (1978).

Zaikonnikora, T. I., *Monograph of the genus Deutzia*, Leningrad (1966) (in Russian).

# Glossary

ACUMINATE: gradually tapering to an elongated point
APICULATE: ending in a sharp point
APPRESSED: lying along the surface
ARIL: a fleshy appendage or coating of a seed
AXIL: angle between leaf stalk and stem
BRACT: a modified leaf below a flower
BRACTEOLES: small bracts
CAMPANULATE: shaped like a bell
CARPEL: the part of a flower which produces the seeds
CILIATE: with a fringe of hairs on the margin
CORDATE: heart-shaped at the base
COROLLA: usually the coloured part of a flower; the petals, especially when joined to make a tube
CORYMB: broad flat-topped inflorescence with stems of different lengths
CRENATE: with shallow, rounded teeth
CUNEATE: tapering into the stalk (of a leaf base)
CUSPIDATE: ending in a sharp point
CYME: inflorescence in which the terminal flower opens first
DIOECIOUS: with male and female flowers on separate petals

EGLANDULAR: without glands
EMARGINATE: with a small indentation at the apex
EPIPHYTE: growing on the surface of a tree
EXSERTED: sticking out; usually of style or stamens from a tubular flower
GLABROUS: without hairs or glands
HOSE-IN-HOSE: with one corolla inside another
HYPANTHIUM: the base of a flower to which the stamens, sepals and petals are attached
INDUMENTUM: hairs, glands or fine prickles
INFLORESCENCE: the flowers and flower stalks, etc.
LAMELLATE: with thin plates
LANCEOLATE: shaped like a spearhead, widest below the middle
LOBULATE: with irregular, rounded lobes
MUCRONATE: with a short sharp point
OBLANCEOLATE: shaped like a spearhead, but widest above the middle
OBOVATE: shaped like an egg but broadest above the middle
OBTUSE: blunt with an angle of more than 90°
ORBICULAR: almost round
OVATE: shaped like an egg but broadest below the middle, shaped like a spearhead
PANICLE: a branched raceme
PEDICEL: stalk of a flower
PETIOLE: stalk of a leaf
PEDUNCLE: stalk of an inflorescence
PHYLLODES: leaf-like stalks
PILOSE: with long, scattered hairs
PINNAE: leaflets of a pinnate leaf
PINNATE: with leaflets on either side of a stalk
PINNATISECT: deeply cut
PRUINOSE: with a greyish coating
PROCUMBENT: creeping or sprawling on the ground
PUBESCENT: with a fine but not particularly dense coating of short hairs
RACEME: an elongated inflorescence in which the stalked flowers open first at the base
RUGOSE: rough with impressed veins
SEMI-ROTATE: saucer-shaped, almost flat (of a flower)
SERRULATE: with small, sharp teeth
SESSILE: without a stalk
SPATHULATE: widening to a rounded apex
SPIKE: inflorescence with unstalked flowers on an elongated axis
STAMINOIDES: stamens which do not contain pollen
STELLATE: star-shaped
STIPULES: leafy or scale-like outgrowth at the base of a leaf stalk
STOLONIFEROUS: producing underground shoots
SUBSHRUB: a small shrub, woody only at the base
SUBULATE: needle-like
TETRAPLOID: with four times the basic number of chromosomes
TOMENTOSE: with numerous fine short hairs

# Index

# INDEX

# INDEX

# INDEX